THE JEWISH CONTRIBUTION TO CIVILIZATION

THE LITTMAN LIBRARY OF JEWISH CIVILIZATION

Dedicated to the memory of
LOUIS THOMAS SIDNEY LITTMAN
who founded the Littman Library for the love of God
and as an act of charity in memory of his father
JOSEPH AARON LITTMAN
and to the memory of
ROBERT JOSEPH LITTMAN
who continued what his father Louis had begun
יהא זכרם ברוך

Get wisdom, get understanding:
Forsake her not and she shall preserve thee
PROV. 4: 5

THE JEWISH CONTRIBUTION TO CIVILIZATION

◆

Reassessing an Idea

◆

Edited by

JEREMY COHEN

and

RICHARD I. COHEN

London

The Littman Library of Jewish Civilization

in association with Liverpool University Press

The Littman Library of Jewish Civilization
Registered office: 4th floor, 7–10 Chandos Street, London W1G 9DQ

in association with Liverpool University Press
4 Cambridge Street, Liverpool L69 7ZU, UK
www.liverpooluniversitypress.co.uk/littman

Managing Editor: Connie Webber

Distributed in North America by
Oxford University Press Inc., 198 Madison Avenue,
New York, NY 10016, USA

First published 2008
First published in paperback 2012

Catalogue records for this book are available from the
British Library and the Library of Congress
ISBN 978–1–906764–43–2

Publishing co-ordinator: Janet Moth
Copy-editing: Laurien Berkeley
Proof-reading: Philippa Claiden
Index: Sharon Sweeney
Designed by Pete Russell, Faringdon, Oxon.
Typeset by Hope Services (Abingdon) Ltd., Abingdon, Oxon.

Printed and bound in Great Britain by
CPI Group (UK) Ltd., Croydon, CR0 4YY

In memory of

AVRAHAM GOLDSTEIN-GOREN

Acknowledgements

THIS book represents the first in a new series of conferences and publications entitled New Perspectives on European Jewry, a series recently launched by the Goldstein-Goren Diaspora Research Center at Tel Aviv University. The conference convened in Tel Aviv early in June 2004, and this thematically designed collection of essays, though not the proceedings of our meetings, has taken shape in their aftermath.

As the field of Jewish history positions itself at the beginning of a new century and a new millennium, 'New Perspectives' will grapple afresh with theoretical, topical, and methodological issues that nourish the relationship between the Jewish present and the Jewish past. We hope that *The Jewish Contribution to Civilization* signals an auspicious beginning for this venture; that, in questioning old assumptions, it will engage a broad range of readers in a new, imaginative, and fruitful discussion.

The editors express their profound thanks to Tel Aviv University's Goldstein-Goren Diaspora Research Center and its dedicated staff—above all, to Ora Azta, Aviva Rosental, Haim Cohen, and Daphna Schnabel—and to the editors and officers of the Littman Library of Jewish Civilization for their good-natured, unflinching commitment in moving this project forward from beginning to end. We thank Elliott Horowitz for his help in planning the 2004 conference. And we gratefully acknowledge the generous support of the Goldstein-Goren family foundation in facilitating our conference and volume, as well as the others to follow in their wake. Appropriately, we dedicate our book to the memory of Avraham Goldstein-Goren (1905–2005), who, throughout one of the most tumultuous centuries in all of human history, never wavered in his belief that the Jews—and Jewish Studies—have an invaluable contribution to offer the world at large.

Tel Aviv and Jerusalem — *J.C.*
Erev Shavuot 5766/2006 — *R.I.C.*

Contents

Note on Transliteration

THE transliteration of Hebrew in this book reflects consideration of the type of book it is, in terms of its content, purpose, and readership. The system adopted therefore reflects a broad approach to transcription, rather than the narrower approaches found in the *Encyclopaedia Judaica* or other systems developed for text-based or linguistic studies. The aim has been to reflect the pronunciation prescribed for modern Hebrew, rather than the spelling or Hebrew word structure, and to do so using conventions that are generally familiar to the English-speaking reader.

In accordance with this approach, no attempt is made to indicate the distinctions between *alef* and *ayin*, *tet* and *taf*, *kaf* and *kuf*, *sin* and *samekh*, since these are not relevant to pronunciation; likewise, the *dagesh* is not indicated except where it affects pronunciation. Following the principle of using conventions familiar to the majority of readers, however, transcriptions that are well established have been retained even when they are not fully consistent with the transliteration system adopted. On similar grounds, the *tsadi* is rendered by 'tz' in such familiar words as bar mitzvah, mitzvot, and so on. Likewise, the distinction between *ḥet* and *khaf* has been retained, using *ḥ* for the former and *kh* for the latter; the associated forms are generally familiar to readers, even if the distinction is not actually borne out in pronunciation, and for the same reason the final *heh* is indicated too. As in Hebrew, no capital letters are used, except that an initial capital has been retained in transliterating titles of published works (for example, *Shulḥan arukh*).

Since no distinction is made between *alef* and *ayin*, they are indicated by an apostrophe only in intervocalic positions where a failure to do so could lead an English-speaking reader to pronounce the vowel-cluster as a diphthong—as, for example, in *ha'ir*—or otherwise mispronounce the word.

The *sheva na* is indicated by an *e*—*perikat ol*, *reshut*—except, again, when established convention dictates otherwise.

The *yod* is represented by *i* when it occurs as a vowel (*bereshit*), by *y* when it occurs as a consonant (*yesodot*), and by *yi* when it occurs as both (*yisra'el*).

Names have generally been left in their familiar forms, even when this is inconsistent with the overall system.

Introduction

JEREMY COHEN

Without the Jews, we would see the world with different feelings. And not only would our sensorium, the screen through which we receive the world, be different: we would think with a different mind, interpret all our experience differently, draw different conclusions from the things that befall us. And we would set a different course for our lives.[1]

A JEW did not pen these words. They appeared in print at the end of the twentieth century in a highly respectable, widely read book entitled *The Gifts of the Jews*. They demonstrate that the idea of a distinct 'Jewish contribution to civilization' traverses religious, social, and cultural boundaries, just as it has survived and evolved over the course of much of human history. In the Bible's foundational story of God's revelation to the children of Israel at Mount Sinai, God instructs Moses to tell his people, 'You shall be to me a kingdom of priests and a holy nation' (Exod. 19: 6). Forty years thereafter, when Moses addresses the Israelites on the eve of his death and their entry into the promised land, he declares that the Torah 'will be proof of your wisdom and discernment to other peoples, who on hearing these laws will say, "Surely, this is a great nation of wise and discerning people"' (Deut. 4: 6). Centuries after that, the prophet Isaiah explained that non-Jews would not only come to recognize the greatness of the Jews but would also appropriate it for themselves.

The many peoples shall go and say, 'Come, let us go up to the mount of the Lord, to the house of the God of Jacob; that he may instruct us in his ways and that we may walk in his paths.' For instruction (*Torah*) shall come forth from Zion, the word of the Lord from Jerusalem. (Isa. 2: 3)

Preaching consolation and salvation to the Jews of the Babylonian exile, Second Isaiah proclaims in God's name that Israel's rosy future would entail more than the restoration of the people to their land: 'I will also make you a light of nations, that my salvation may reach the ends of the earth' (Isa. 49: 6).

This notion that the Jews have a particular contribution to offer human civilization—an idea bound up with the Bible's particularistic concept of the

[1] Thomas Cahill, *The Gifts of the Jews: How a Tribe of Desert Nomads Changed the Way Everyone Thinks and Feels* (New York, 1998), 3.

chosen people on one hand, and its universalistic prophecies of salvation for all nations on the other hand—made its way into Christianity as well. To be sure, Christian doctrine offered new definitions of Israel, divine election, and the covenant that would bring redemption to all, but it retained a specific, indispensable role for the Jews in the drama that would lead human history to its fulfilment. In his Epistle to the Romans, Paul explained that God had revealed his law to the Jews in order to show that men and women could not merit salvation on the basis of their own works; God then displaced the Jews in order to allow for the salvation of the non-Jews; but the salvation of the world will not be complete until the Jews return to God and take part in the redemptive process. Paul therefore admonishes non-Jewish Christians:

> Now if their trespass means riches for the world, and if their failure means riches for the Gentiles, how much more will their full inclusion mean . . . ! If their rejection means the reconciliation of the world, what will their acceptance mean but life from the dead? If the dough offered as first fruits is holy, so is the whole lump; and if the root is holy, so are the branches. . . . If you have been cut from what is by nature a wild olive tree, and grafted, contrary to nature, into a cultivated olive tree, how much more will these natural branches be grafted back into their own olive tree. . . . I want you to understand this mystery, brethren: a hardening has come upon part of Israel, until the full number of the Gentiles come in, and so all Israel will be saved. (Rom. 11: 12–26)

And as ancient times gave way to the Middle Ages, the great Church Father St Augustine of Hippo ventured further still, arguing that Jews contribute to Christian civilization even in the present age, and not only at the end of time. Augustine instructed that the Church requires a Jewish presence wherever Christianity spreads, for the Jews bear witness—both in their sacred texts and in their lifestyles and very persons—to the precepts of the Old Testament that bespeak the truth of the New. Understanding the divine injunction in Psalm 59: 12 as bearing upon the Jews, Augustine elaborated:

> The Jews who slew him and chose not to believe in him . . . having been vanquished rather pathetically by the Romans, completely deprived of their kingdom . . . and scattered throughout the world so that they are not lacking anywhere, are testimony for us through their own scriptures that we have not contrived the prophecies concerning Christ. . . . There is a prophecy given previously in the Psalms . . . 'Slay them not, lest at any time they forget your law . . .' Therefore he [God] did not kill them . . . lest . . . they not be able to provide testimony on our behalf.[2]

Yet it is truly during the last three or four hundred years that the issue of 'the Jewish contribution' has assumed a place at the top of the Jewish

[2] Augustine, *On the City of God*, 18.46.

cultural agenda. Augustine's admonitions notwithstanding, late medieval western Europe did come to expel most of its Jews—for reasons that fall well beyond the purview of this volume. In the seventeenth century, when Jews began to make their way back to the western lands that had banished them, the issue of their worthiness as residents triggered extensive debate. Jews touted the manifold benefits that they conferred upon their non-Jewish hosts. Non-Jews had mixed reactions. Political and economic factors blended with considerations of theology and culture in the forging of various positions. Enlightenment, its Jewish counterpart the Haskalah, and possibilities for the political emancipation of Jews added new dimensions to the discourse of Jewish contribution, which touched both Jew and non-Jew in their perceptions of self and other.

Even after Jews achieved emancipation throughout most of Europe and the Americas, the discussion did not abate. On the contrary, the generation between the two world wars saw the publication of Joseph Jacobs's *Jewish Contributions to Civilization: An Estimate* (1919), Chaim Newman and Israel Zangwill's collection *The Real Jew: Some Aspects of the Jewish Contribution to Civilization* (1925), the Oxford compendium of *The Legacy of Israel* (1927) planned by Israel Abrahams, and Cecil Roth's *The Jewish Contribution to Civilization* (1938)—among others. According to Roth, the Hebraic and Jewish impact on modern civilization extended from monotheism, religious ethics, and social justice, to politics, economics, medicine, mathematics and science, literature, philosophy, and the arts. The president of the Board of Deputies of British Jews adumbrated Roth's thesis in an address to a distinguished Welsh gentlemen's club in 1937, an address that bore nearly the same title as Roth's book and reviewed many of the same achievements. The Jews' greatest contribution of all, argued Neville Laski, was their commitment to ascertaining the truth.

During the last two thousand years, the Jews have devoted themselves wholeheartedly, in the midst of a hostile world, to the spirit of study, to scientific enquiry, to the search for Truth. In every land to which they penetrated, their first step was to set up academies for higher study. Everywhere, long before the days of compulsory education, they had their own educational system of a comprehensiveness and universality almost undreamed of until our own generation. . . . Truth, according to Jewish legend—is the seal of the Holy One, Blessed be He. If we have pursued it, humbly and untiringly during our long history, we have perhaps fulfilled the Divine purpose, and we have, I think, thereby deserved a better acknowledgment than we have received from our fellow-men.[3]

[3] Neville J. Laski, 'The Jewish Contribution to Western Civilisation: An Address', Cardiff Business Club, 25 Nov. 1937, 19.

Somehow, the discussion of 'the Jewish contribution to civilization' invariably returns, in one guise or another, to the prophetic notion of 'a light to the nations'. Some Jewish intellectuals of the last generations—from the American theologian Richard Rubenstein to the Israeli author A. B. Yehoshua—have condemned the Jews' notion of their own distinctiveness as the root of antisemitism, ancient, medieval, and modern. Yet in addressing their fellow Jews, most Jewish rabbis, intellectuals, and reformers over the centuries have proposed various ways in which to make their Judaism live up to their prophetic mission. Addressing non-Jews, they have enthusiastically found and created opportunities to explain just how the Jews have enriched civilization, how the world ought therefore to accept them, treating them well with respect and toleration. Some non-Jews, as we have seen, have concurred. Others have disagreed, often vehemently, sometimes even violently.

Curiously, the issue continues to engage us, and one can only wonder why. Surely the biblical heritage that Jews, Christians, and, to a lesser extent, Muslims share spotlights 'the people of the book' and the impact of biblical monotheism on the history of religions. No doubt the survival of the Jews as both a distinct ethnic group and a multinational religious community over thousands of years, despite a long history of persecution and misfortune, induces Jews and non-Jews alike to wrestle with the phenomenon, seeking to understand the reasons for their survival. The small size of world Jewry makes the puzzle only more fascinating. The tragedy of the Nazi Holocaust and the re-establishment of a Jewish state in its wake—over 2,000 years after the Jews last enjoyed political independence in their homeland—has undoubtedly piqued the curiosity of the world even further. The world may not agree with the words of Thomas Cahill that opened this Introduction, but it certainly retains its obsession with the question.

In this book we seek neither to document nor to discredit the 'Jewish contribution to civilization'—nor, for that matter, to understand the enigma of Jewish survival. Rather, we shall investigate *the idea* of 'the Jewish contribution' as it has borne on Jews, non-Jews, and the interaction between them in modern times, from the seventeenth century to our own. What role has the concept played in Jewish self-definition? How has it influenced the political, social, and cultural history of the Jews—and of others? Does discussion of the Jewish contribution still have relevance in the world today? Should it still exercise Jewish historians, even as they continue to draw heavily on the scholarship of writers like Israel Abrahams, Joseph Jacobs, and Cecil Roth concerning numerous other subjects?

The chapters that follow divide rather neatly into three groups. Part I addresses various aspects of the question, its formulation, and its ramifications. Reviewing landmarks of Jewish historiography from Simone Luzzatto to Jacob Katz, Richard I. Cohen affords special attention to the nexus between notions of 'Jewish contribution' and those of 'Jewish superiority'. Although discussion of the former frequently appeared to acquiesce to the value system of others, aiming to prove the worthiness of Jews according to the criteria of a non-Jewish (that is, Christian) world-view, Cohen asserts that many Jewish apologists still asserted their cultural superiority—whether in their title to the Bible, their prophetic mission, or the virtuosity and pristine singularity of their Judaism.

In the next chapter David N. Myers shifts his focus from *contribution* to *civilization*, arguing that this term, especially when counterpoised against the German Romantic notion of a distinct national culture (*Kultur*), often served the interests of Jewish intellectuals far better. Myers probes the significance of 'civilization' at three key 'rhetorical moments' during the last two hundred years: early in the nineteenth century, when German Jews endeavoured to reach a high standard of civilization through 'concerted self-cultivation' and social integration; later in the nineteenth century, when European Jews applied their own standards of civilization to other, 'oriental' Jews; and the years between the Great Depression and the outbreak of the Second World War, when Mordecai Kaplan equated Jewish peoplehood and civilization, an impulse Myers deems 'at once unsurprising in an age alive with Jewish national sentiments and yet surprising in an age rife with talk of "the decline of civilization" '.

Moshe Rosman closes Part I with a survey of the Jewish 'contribution discourse' that extends to the twenty-first century. Academic disparagement of the study of 'the Jewish contribution' notwithstanding, the regnant values of multiculturalism have offered the idea new life and possibilities. Some now construct the Jews, 'whose identity is always in flux', as 'an allegory, metaphor, or trope representing all of the people sinned against by modern Western civilization'. Reacting against this denial of any distinctive and intrinsically valuable substance to Jewish identity, others have seen the Jews not as trope but as model; they, their texts, and their experiences have something special and worthwhile to offer our postmodern society and culture.

In Part II we turn to the relationship between Judaism and other monotheistic cultures—Christian and Muslim—and to instructive instances where the issue of 'Jewish contribution' has arisen in modern historiography. Testifying to Christianity's transmission of that contribution to the world at large, the biblical sabbath figured prominently in the apologetic works of Newman, Kaplan, Roth, Cahill, and many others; Roth, for one, reasoned that it 'raises man above the beasts and asserts man's moral dignity as a human being'.[4] In Elliott Horowitz's chapter, 'Day of Gladness or Day of Madness?', the sabbath serves us as an illuminating test case for the dynamic

[4] Cecil Roth, *The Jewish Contribution to Civilisation*, 2nd edn (Oxford, 1943), 159.

and complexity of the 'contribution' debate: in the works of Jewish apologists and religious reformers; in critical, yet ideologically grounded investigations of this biblical precept, its origins, and its evolution; and in initiatives for ecumenical dialogue and cooperation between Christians and Jews. As such a test case, the sabbath helps us to identify more general, theoretical issues surrounding the 'contribution debate'.

David Berger expands some of these in his chapter, which recounts how discussion of Christianity's Jewish legacy—on either side of the interreligious divide—developed in the late nineteenth and twentieth centuries. Jewish apologetic and Christian antisemitism confronted one another against the background of the new biblical criticism, which suggested that the universalist prophetic ethic immortalized in Christianity (especially in its liberal Protestant denominations) preceded and therefore outweighed the Mosaic law at the bedrock of traditional Judaism. As Berger rightly concludes, such questions of Jewish versus Christian, legalistic versus ethical, and particularist versus universalist bore no less on Judaism's efforts 'to define its own contours and to penetrate the depths of its soul' than on its encounter with the dominant Western faith.

In Susannah Heschel's chapter, 'Judaism, Islam, and Hellenism', we see how this Jewish–Christian encounter spilled over into the study of other non-Western 'others' in Germany. As late nineteenth-century German intellectuals looked to classical Hellenism as the cultural (and racial) foundation of the Aryan ideal in their own day, German Jewish scholars could find themselves hard-pressed to explain how the biblical religion of Israel was indeed the progenitor of contemporary German *Kultur*. Alternatively, many of them looked to classical Islamic civilization as the cultural context in which Judaism had truly flowered in earlier times, especially along rationalist, philosophical, and aesthetic lines. Islam more than Christianity, they argued, preserved the genuine legacy of the Greeks. And rational Judaism, which had once spawned both the teachings of Jesus and those of Muhammad, continued (especially in its nineteenth-century liberal German guises) to carry the torch forward into modernity.

Yet in so far as the 'contribution discourse' bore on the civilization of Islam and the 'oriental' Jews living in its midst, Daniel Schroeter's chapter reveals that the 'orientalism' of European Jewish scholars was hardly one-dimensional. To be sure, Western Jewish historians from Graetz to Goitein typically cast Islam as more tolerant and more enlightened than Christianity, facilitating the unique Judaeo-Arabic cultural symbiosis that nourished the 'golden age' of Spanish Jewry. Nevertheless, in the wake of the Spanish Jewish expulsion in 1492, oriental Jewry embarked upon a cultural decline—or so it appears in Western historiography—a decline from which only a regenerated European Jewry can rescue them. Schroeter investigates this 'rise and decline' model of Sephardi and Middle Eastern Jewry, raising revealing questions about the altogether Eurocentric character of the 'contribution discourse'.

Finally, Part III introduces us to various applications and consequences of debate over 'the Jewish contribution to civilization', in both those lands of the Western Diaspora where modern Jewish civilization has developed most creatively in modern times: Germany and the United States. Returning us to notions of Jewish superiority on the one hand and the idealized *Kultur* of modern Europe (especially that of Germany) on the other, Yaacov Shavit probes the delicate balance forged by nineteenth-century German Jewish intellectuals between an array of desiderata: Jewish acculturation, Jewish participation and partnership in the culture of the enlightened Christian majority, and yet the retention of an essential Judaic character that they deemed superior and unique. The heroes of Shavit's story, alas, envisioned neither Nazism nor the Final Solution, and Shavit wonders if their endeavour proved 'a vain waste of the Jews' cultural vitality and productivity' and 'a disastrous self-delusion'. All the more interesting, if not perplexing, then, are the renewal of German Jewish culture and the birth of German Jewish Studies as an academic discipline in post-war Germany.

In 'German-Jewish Literature and Culture and the Field of German-Jewish Studies', Mark H. Gelber delineates the parameters of these developments and their relationship to the 'contribution discourse'. Paradoxically, Gelber notes, the very marginality of Jewish culture in present-day Germany, coupled with its 'global' character, has enabled the field to emerge as 'the quintessential post-modern field of cultural studies' in Germany today—popular, in vogue, and the basis for diverse criticism.

Bringing this volume to its conclusion, David Biale's chapter transports us across the Atlantic to the shores of North America, where he compares three twentieth- and twenty-first-century overviews of Jewish culture and civilization: Mordecai Kaplan's *Judaism as Civilization* (1934), Louis Finkelstein's edition of *The Jews: Their History, Culture, and Religion* (1949)—whose second and third volumes were subtitled *The Role of Judaism in Civilization*—and Biale's own compendium *Cultures of the Jews: A New History*. Biale explains how this last collection subjects 'some of the treasured dichotomies of what might be called "Judaism" to new criticism: exile versus sovereignty, Jewish versus non-Jewish culture, elite versus popular culture', and, one might add, Jewish distinctiveness versus cultural hybridity and pluralism. Yet, albeit in different fashion, the question of 'Jewish contribution' weighs upon Biale no less than it exercised his predecessors. As he writes, now that the impetus for defending the singularity of the Jewish contribution has all but vanished among Jewish scholars, the puzzle of Jewish alterity persists. How ought we to understand the 'otherness' of the Jew?

We seek to advance no single perspective on 'the Jewish contribution to civilization' in this volume. Instead, we have attempted to offer readers a broad spectrum of academic opinion: from tempered advocacy to reasoned disavowal, with many alternative variations on the theme in between. If anything, we hope to illustrate the centrality of the question in modern Jewish culture in general, and its importance for modern Jewish Studies in particular. As Jewish historiography moves ahead into the twenty-first century, the career of the 'contribution discourse' still ensues and engages. It demands our attention and sensitivity, and we hope that this book will offer its own contribution in focusing the former and enhancing the latter. At the end of the day, the question remains. As we have seen, it just will not go away.

PART I

FORMULATING THE QUESTION

ONE

'Jewish Contribution to Civilization' and its Implications for Notions of 'Jewish Superiority' in the Modern Period

RICHARD I. COHEN

JOSEPH JACOBS, CECIL ROTH, and others, have often been derided for their studies on 'Jewish contribution to civilization'. They are seen as apologetic, naive works that respond to antisemitic claims about Jews in a caricaturistic manner. Clearly these established scholars believed that by acclaiming the many distinguished figures of Jewish origin, a more accurate representation of the Jews would emerge. They, like their predecessors in the last quarter of the nineteenth century, praised the diversity of the Jewish contribution to society and argued that Christian civilization was heavily indebted to it. Jacobs and Roth were indefatigable in this agenda, and their individual efforts in editing Jewish encyclopedias (the American version of 1901–6, and the Jerusalem edition of 1971) can be considered part of this overall effort.

Yet their work, and others like theirs, can be cast in a different mould and viewed as an integral and recurrent discourse in modern Jewish history dating from the seventeenth century; specifically, how notions of 'Jewish contribution' figured in the self-representation of Jews and in the minds of non-Jews when they reflected on Jewish participation in modern society. Pre-Enlightenment and post-Enlightenment discussions in Europe often returned to the question whether Jews could be integrated into European society and whether their contribution in the past and present warranted it. The contours of the discussions changed over the centuries. At times occupations maintained by Jews, at times their creativity and sensitivity, at times patriotism and their physical ability to serve their country functioned prominently in this discourse, but themes relating to religion permeated positive and negative attitudes throughout. Not always defined within the context of 'Jewish contribution', these persistent deliberations touched, nevertheless, on the worthiness of the Jews and whether they could suitably be part of European society. The question was repeatedly posed whether their collective characteristics, religion, race, professional bias, habits, and customs prevented their integration into and contribution to society.

It appears that this recurrent discourse significantly penetrated the sense of self of many Jews, and sensitized others, consciously and subconsciously, to confront the question, time and again, of their sense of belonging to a particular society. It often occasioned efforts to demonstrate, in literature and visually, their individual and collective achievements. At some junctures, as I will show, this discourse went even further and prompted certain figures to highlight, openly or circumspectly, the unique and/or superior nature of the Jews or Judaism. Jacobs, Roth, and various other writers discussed in this chapter and in those of others embarked on their efforts in response to growing antisemitism, but they were very much within a wider discourse of the modern period. As Jacobs put it in his *Jewish Contributions to Civilization: An Estimate* (1920), published posthumously:

> The claim of the Jews to a 'place in the sun,' in modern life, must, in the last resort, be based on their capacity for contributing valuable elements to that life. This can only be determined by the history of the past, remote and recent. Unless they have shown themselves in the past capable of contributing to the higher aspects of European culture, it would be improbable that they would be able to join fully in it now with their fellow-citizens.

And he continued,

> In short, to appraise the contributions of Jews to the world's advancement is little less than to write the history of civilization for the past two thousand years.[1]

That notion—to prove the right of Jews to a 'place in the sun'—was already a prominent feature in apologetic tracts, by Jews and non-Jews, in their attempt to bring about a new approach towards Jews in Europe from the seventeenth century.

Simone (Simhah) Luzzatto, in his *Discorso circa il stato de gl'hebrei* (Discourse on the Condition of the Jews) of 1638, was the first of a series of Jewish apologists to equate 'Jewish contribution' with the right of Jews to a 'place in the sun'. He argued, in the spirit of the day, that the Venetian state had benefited economically and politically from the presence of Jews on their territory. Luzzatto turned the historical, extra-territorial nature of the Jews and the restrictions on their residence to a source of strength, making them into remarkable businesspeople with a special acumen. Restricted from owning land, Jews had succeeded in certain localities in amassing substantial sums of money, attesting to their unique qualities as merchants. In accumu-

[1] Joseph Jacobs, *Jewish Contributions to Civilization: An Estimate* (Philadelphia, 1920), 44–5, 48; see a similar argument by Cecil Roth, *The Jewish Contribution to Civilization* (New York, 1940), 367–8.

lating great wealth, they proved their usefulness to the state, increasing its economic strength considerably. It was thus against the advancement of Venetian society to succumb to the call to expel the Jews from the state, and against its economic welfare, as all Jews, and not only a minority of them, brought commercial utility to the Venetian state. Advocating this mercantilist theme, Luzzatto further argued that it was incomprehensible that states such as France, Spain, and England, and cities in Germany, banned Jews from their midst.

In advancing the mercantilist notion of utility, Luzzatto launched the modern discourse on Jewish contribution to society. Toleration of Jews was viewed from the perspective of *raison d'état*, as Luzzatto boldly claimed their unique ability to raise the economic status of the countries they inhabited. Indeed, those who would follow Luzzatto's argument, as did Manasseh b. Israel in his attempts to persuade the English to allow Jewish re-entry into England, made 'Jewish contribution' a linchpin in their attempt to change attitudes to Jews.[2]

A different angle was taken by Isaac Cardoso in his *Las excelencias de los hebreos* (1679), when he praised beyond bounds the distinctive nature of Judaism, its highest moral and spiritual teachings, its singular value for the society in which they lived. Cardoso reassessed the nature of the Jewish exile. He viewed it as God's design to have the nations of the world encounter the Jews and thereby learn of monotheism and gradually dispense with idolatry, repeating a canard of Spanish Jewish exiles that, after coming into contact with Jews, Aristotle converted to Judaism. Jews embodied the superior nature of Judaism and were thus esteemed by distinguished non-Jewish scholars and were a most desired element in every society they inhabited. The Hebrew Bible remained pure and uncontaminated, serving Christians better than the Vulgate and other less pure translations. In so stressing the unique and ancient nature of Jews and Judaism, Cardoso, as Yosef Kaplan has pointed out, added his voice on Jewish superiority ('The Hebrews are of the most noble blood . . . the most noble nation on the face of the earth') and to the integral arsenal of the Marrano apologetics in the seventeenth century, adapting the discourse of Spanish writers on the Spanish monarchy and its traditions.[3] Thus, by the seventeenth century,

[2] See Benjamin Ravid, '"How Profitable the Nation of the Jewes Are": The *Humble Addresses* of Menasseh ben Israel and the *Discorso* of Simone Luzzatto', in Jehuda Reinharz and Daniel Swetchinski (eds), *Mystics, Philosophers, and Politicians: Essays in Jewish Intellectual History in Honor of Alexander Altmann* (Durham, NC, 1982), 159–80.

[3] Yosef Kaplan, 'Political Concepts in the World of the Portuguese Jews of Amsterdam during the Seventeenth Century: The Problem of Exclusion and the Boundaries of Self-Identity', in Yosef Kaplan, Henry Méchoulan, and Richard Popkin (eds), *Menasseh ben Israel and his World* (Leiden, 1989), 53. I have used Kaplan's Hebrew translation of sections of the work; see Isaac Cardoso, *Ma'alot ha'ivrim: perakim*, trans. Yosef Kaplan (Jerusalem, 1971). On Cardoso,

Jewish contribution theory had already joined hands with notions of Jewish superiority, a combination that moved more and more to the forefront of Jewish apologetics from the nineteenth century.

But it was Luzzatto's argument, and for that matter Manasseh b. Israel's as well, that was picked up by non-Jewish writers when they turned their attention to utilizing the contribution theory to advance Jewish status. Such was the case with John Toland (1670–1722) in his expressions of support for the naturalization of the Jews in England.

A controversial figure, who provoked the ire of many as he spoke and wrote openly and acerbically against the Scriptures and upheld the murder of Charles I, the Irish-born Toland published in 1714 his *Reasons for Naturalizing the Jews in Great Britain and Ireland*, directed towards their archbishops and bishops. In this pamphlet Toland considered and dismissed many of the common prejudices against Jews and called for their being placed 'on the same foot with all other nations'. Central to our concern, however, are his reflections on the Jews and the state. Toland, like Luzzatto, Manasseh b. Israel, and Cardoso before him, rejected the claims that Jews could not be loyal residents of the country they inhabited and would not bring value to the country. Following a theme that John Locke subscribed to in his *Letter on Toleration* (1689), Toland argued that, since Jews had no country of their own, and no foreign loyalties (unlike Catholics, for example, who were bound to the Vatican), they would become completely devoted residents and refrain from any political activity detrimental to the country's security. They would, he wrote, 'be ours for ever' if the English would put them on a par with other members of society. Jews, he claimed, were dedicated to those countries that granted them the privilege to remain in their midst, and in turn contributed significantly to the country's welfare. Moreover, they excelled in business, being the 'Factors, some the Carriers, some the Miners, others the Manufactorers, and others yet the Store-keepers of the world. Thus the *Jews* may properly be said to be the Brokers of it, who, whithersoever they come, create business as well as manage it.'

But Toland made no essentialist argument; Jews were not by nature inclined to these professions, but gravitated towards them according to circumstances, and if they were to change they would become equally competent seamen, soldiers, farmers, etc. The reasoning was clear: Jews could be perfect allies of the state as they would bring capable workmen and wealth and would be, in turn, forever grateful for the opportunities offered them.[4]

see Yosef Hayim Yerushalmi, *From Spanish Court to Italian Ghetto. Isaac Cardoso: A Study in Seventeenth-Century Marranism and Jewish Apologetics* (New York, 1971).

[4] [John Toland], *Reasons for Naturalizing the Jews in Great Britain and Ireland: On the Same Foot with All Other Nations* (London, 1714), 14; Richard I. Cohen, 'Jews and the State: The Historical Context', in Ezra Mendelsohn (ed.), *Jews and the State: Dangerous Alliances and the Perils of Privilege*, Studies in Contemporary Jewry, 19 (New York, 2003), 3–16.

In post-Reformation Europe, where the clash within the Christian Church was bitter and volatile and touched on all aspects of religion and state, 'Jewish proclivity' to being loyal citizens (*à la* Toland) and economically vibrant (*à la* Colbert and Toland) often worked in their favour. Such claims were reiterated in Jewish apologetic works in France in the eighteenth century, which now added the example of England to the list of prooftexts presented by Manasseh b. Israel to Oliver Cromwell; namely, that since the English had admitted the Jews, their trade had increased considerably, as had that of the Dutch and of certain cities, such as Hamburg and Livorno, that allowed Jews to flourish within their midst.

The economic ability of the Jews to jump-start the French economy and their deep loyalty to the state were two prominent arguments in these 'contrapuntal readings' (following the interpretation of Ronald Schechter) by Jews such as Isaac de Pinto, Isaac Bernard de Valabrègue, and Zalkind Hourwitz and their supporters in pre-emancipation debate, and were to merge with the orientation of Enlightenment thought and absolutist politics.[5] Those who supported their integration valued utility and believed that Jews could become useful to society and contribute to its growth, welfare, and development. Those who opposed their integration and denied their improved status often cited their ineffective nature, inability to serve in the military, and lack of productivity. Here was a clear call to Jews to defend themselves against their failure to contribute to society.

Enlightenment figures (*maskilim*), although scattered across different countries of the Jewish Diaspora in the modern period, showed themselves to be extremely sensitive to this claim. They responded in kind to the measures of enlightened absolute rulers to increase the level of Jewish utility to society. Seeking to promote Jewish involvement and productivity in society and to counteract the claims of Jewish insularity, *maskilim* called upon Jews to respond to what they considered benevolent acts of absolute rulers. Naphtali Herz Wessely's archetypical response to Joseph II's Toleration Act of 1781 is indicative of their attitude: 'And you brothers of Israel who live under this great ruler, how will you reciprocate for all of the great good he has done for you, or what will you be able to give him?'[6]

Representative of the maskilic viewpoint, Wessely's argument was launched from a totally different vantage point from that of Luzzatto, Manasseh b. Israel, de Pinto, and others. Wessely did not wave the flag of Jewish contribution to society, but apologized for and rationalized Jewish

[5] Ronald Schechter, *Obstinate Hebrews: Representations of Jews in France, 1715–1815* (Berkeley, 2003), 110–31.

[6] Naphtali Herz Wessely, *Words of Peace and Truth* (Berlin, 1782). For a selection from his work in English, see Paul R. Mendes-Flohr and Jehuda Reinharz (eds), *The Jew in the Modern World: A Documentary History* (New York, 1980), 62–7.

reluctance to move beyond the four cubits of their lives, and for denying 'human knowledge' its rightful place in education. Wessely bemoaned this disregard for science and worldly affairs, and strongly advocated acceptance of the absolutist agenda. *Maskilim* like him viewed rabbinic authority, and the ideal of talmudic study, as incommensurate with the changing nature of society. The rabbis were held responsible for Jewish 'decadence', indicating the need to wrench Jewish education from their hands. The more radical maskilic elements, in the West and the East, were unrelenting in this regard, often going beyond the non-Jewish critics, claiming that the Jews themselves were to blame for building a wall around themselves and allowing a flagrant level of illiteracy to prevail in Jewish society. So a public announcement of *maskilim* in Vilna in 1840 stated unequivocally, 'Harabanim umorei ha'am hasibah harishonah ba'avurah yaradnu pela'im' ('The rabbis and teachers are the primary reason why we have declined so terribly'). In other words, *maskilim*, in western and later in eastern European society, accepted the terms of reference defined by the Enlightenment and absolutist rulers, and argued that Jewish involvement and potential contribution to non-Jewish society were a necessity to revamp the nature of Jewish society. (This would also reflect various voices in Islamic countries in the nineteenth and twentieth centuries.) Such a transformation of Jewish society would enable a different setting for the coexistence of Jews and non-Jews. In a sense, one could claim that the vision of the *maskilim* materialized in the content of Cecil Roth's *Jewish Contribution*. Productivity in letters, arts, medicine, science, journalism, etc. was part of their utopian vision for true social integration with non-Jewish society; similarly, Roth's belief was that such productivity showed the significant contribution of Jews to Western civilization, that 'The world could not afford to dispense with it any more than with that of England, of France, or of Germany.'[7]

Yet this profoundly negative self-image of Jewish society that the *maskilim* projected had a contradictory but significant side to it. The *maskilim* could not simply debase the Jews and show them to be empty of all value and distinction, for then they would be regarded as beyond the pale and unworthy of citizenship or emancipation. Indeed Jews may have declined, some maintained, but they stemmed from superior stock, their roots were biblical, a point that echoed the theme of nobility that Cardoso and other Spanish and Portuguese authors had raised in the seventeenth century. As Isaiah Berr Bing observed on the eve of the revolution in France, Jewish values were ancient, sacred, and of divine origin. Jewish republicanism was biblical, marked by a pristine nature, and a perfect guide for how to live, inasmuch as God was the author of this way of life. Berr Bing argued that Jews had a right

[7] Roth, *The Jewish Contribution to Civilization*, 363.

to equality, not because their religion merely conformed to the moral requirements of citizenship but because their religion was the source of citizenship. Similarly, his contemporary Zalkind Hourwitz, while very critical of the rabbis and the Talmud, held Moses in the highest esteem, viewing him as 'the most tolerant and the most charitable of all legislators', whose openness in belief and charity to strangers was symptomatic of that revolutionary doctrine.[8] Hourwitz also praised Jews for their superior character in a wide variety of areas, making them a model for other nations to emulate. By driving a wedge between the Bible, the foundation of Judaism and the Jewish contribution to civilization, and the Talmud, the Bible asserted the superiority of Jewish genealogy and granted Jews in a period of conflict and confrontation a modern claim to having been chosen by God. This claim was to reassert itself time and again by Berr Bing's successors in France and elsewhere. Let us recall for a moment the writings of the Jewish Saint-Simonian Joseph Salvador (1796–1873), following the revolution.

Salvador directly challenged Christian claims on the nature of the state and the role of Judaism in the progress of humankind. Going beyond his pre-emancipation predecessors, he praised the Bible and the Mosaic system, hailing the Decalogue as the foremost contribution to humankind and, moreover, the foundation of the revolution's triad of liberty, equality, and fraternity. The Hebrew republic was the most advanced system of public order, the wisest and simplest, and none had superseded it. But Salvador went further. While taking the Roman Catholic Church to task for appropriating the mission of the Bible, he envisioned a time when its rule would be overturned.[9] To the claim that the Bible and Judaism had been inherited by Christianity, Salvador responded in an unprecedented manner:

> Your argument is erroneous. You have power on your side for the present, but we have time. Your world is ephemeral, you are not the last stage of salvation. The Day will come when nations will rise up and reject the yoke of the Roman Church, which will lay claim to a new world of justice, or, in the words of the Bible, a new Jerusalem.[10]

Salvador thus upheld Judaism's mission to the world by positioning the Bible as the Jewish contribution to civilization.

Salvador's lead was followed by other Jewish Saint-Simonians who adopted his radical view, which gave the political origins of Judaism a new

[8] Schechter, *Obstinate Hebrews*, 128–9.

[9] Richard I. Cohen, 'Urban Visibility and Biblical Visions: Jewish Culture in Western and Central Europe in the Modern Age', in David Biale (ed.), *Cultures of the Jews: A New History* (New York, 2002), 778–9.

[10] Ibid. 779, as quoted in Michael Graetz, *The Jews in Nineteenth-Century France: From the French Revolution to the Alliance Israélite Universelle*, trans. Jane Marie Todd (Stanford, Calif, 1996), 228–9.

significance for the evolution of society. Judaism, the 'mother of religions', could take pride in its conceptualization of God as the God of reason and universality, impacting on its role in societal transformation. Alexandre Weill's exegesis *The Five Books of Moses* at the end of the nineteenth century signified the merger of 'Jewish contribution' and 'Jewish superiority'. Reiterating notions that had already appeared in Cardoso's apologia of 1679 and in a wide variety of English texts that related to the Bible, Weill recognized Hebrew as the 'mother of all languages, ancient and modern'.[11] He also designated Moses 'the single and unprecedented legislator of all times and periods', and chastised Christianity for being unable to come to terms with the glaring fact that all things good, such as liberty and progress, extended from Moses and the Jews.[12] The overwhelming superiority of Mosaic law, profusely reiterated by Weill, caused the other religions to view Judaism with discomfort and to feel eclipsed by it.

This strong affirmation of identity with the Bible and recognition of its centrality to civilization grew steadily from the time of the *maskilim* to the end of the nineteenth century among Jews of different persuasions, lay and clerical. It enabled them to situate themselves in relation to non-Jewish society with a proud internal sense of their genealogy at moments when questions of Jewish continuity proliferated.

Heinrich Graetz, the distinguished Jewish historian of the nineteenth century, epitomized this orientation. Although he did not develop his notions on Jewish contribution from the Bible alone, Graetz's many years of inquiry, translation, and research of its text, language, and historical context convinced him of its unique place in human civilization. His judgements of the Bible were often full of superlatives; the religious notions of monotheism emerged there; its poetry, in the case of Psalms or Ecclesiastes, reached unmatched levels; and its ethical teachings left their mark on generations.[13] Graetz argued at times indirectly and at times directly that 'the only defenders of true monotheism . . . of rationalism in religion, are still the adherents of Judaism'. Having raised the world from the 'slough of moral corruption', Judaism continued to play a significant function in society and to have a mission to 'overcome erroneous belief' and bring rationalism to the world. According to Graetz, 'The visionary images which becloud thousands of minds and produce the maddest enthusiasms can only be dispersed by that

[11] David S. Katz, *Philo-Semitism and the Readmission of the Jews to England, 1603–1655* (Oxford, 1982).

[12] Cohen, 'Urban Visibility and Biblical Visions', 777–9.

[13] These notions permeated his writings on the Bible in various contexts, especially in his essays in *Monatsschrift für Geschichte und Wissenschaft des Judentums* from 1850. See Heinrich Graetz, *Essays, Memoirs, Letters* (Heb.), ed. Shmuel Ettinger (Jerusalem, 1969); id., *The Structure of Jewish History and Other Essays*, ed. and trans. Ismar Schorsch (New York, 1975); Reuven Michael, *Heinrich Graetz: The Historian of the Jewish People* (Heb.) (Jerusalem, 2003).

pure idea of God formulated by Judaism.' The Jews represent 'Judaism and its mission' and continue to carry an ethical goal, to establish morality as the basis for all governments.[14] Foreshadowing the position of Jacobs and Roth, Graetz cherished Judaism's contribution to the moral principles of state institutions that penetrated the 'consciousness of all civilized humanity'. These scholars bemoaned the fact that this seminal Jewish contribution was often overlooked by society. Like Roth four decades later, Graetz valued the Jewish contribution as the source of humanity and religious monotheism: 'If it vanished from the world, if its adherents one and all deserted it, a mighty factor for the progress of ethical and religious civilization would be wanting; it would be wanting now, just as much as it would have been wanting of old, if Judaism had disappeared before the rise of Christianity.'[15] In his attempt to utilize the writing of history to rebuild Jewish consciousness, Graetz offered a historiosophical interpretation that emphasized Judaism's superiority and contribution to the foundations of society, and harshly criticized Christianity, and often Jesus himself. These perspectives, which permeated Graetz's monumental historical writing, were inevitably to clash with those of German nationalist thinkers like Heinrich von Treitschke, but Graetz did not completely back down from them even after the famous polemic of 1879–80. Yet he was not alone among Jewish writers and thinkers of the nineteenth century who, faced with the growing theological, cultural, and social proximity between Judaism and Christianity, dismissed the latter's originality and superiority.

A significant road led from Eduard Gans's assertion in 1822 that Jerusalem must take up its rightful position in civilization beside Rome and Greece to Abraham Geiger's stinging critique of Jesus as a religious teacher who derived all his teachings from Hillel. Geiger's dramatic minimization of Jesus's teachings and significance coincided with his critical appraisal of Christianity in general. According to Geiger, Christianity was repeatedly at loggerheads with society, enlightenment, and science, thus preventing it from contributing to the development of humanity. Christianity, he claimed, opted for subjection to its doctrines, and, as it became a world power shorn of the influence of the Jewish religion, a purer and vital religion, it tried to extinguish all expressions of the humane. Christianity was criticized for its opposition to cultural development and religious toleration and its failure to reach the level of the more refined Judaism on which it was based. Geiger was relentless in this regard. As Susannah Heschel has convincingly argued,

[14] Quotations from Graetz, *The Structure of Jewish History*, 285–6; first pub. in Graetz, 'The Significance of Judaism for the Present and the Future', *Jewish Quarterly Review*, 1 (1889), 4–13; 2 (1890), 257–69.

[15] Ibid. 287. Compare to Roth's quotation above on the indispensability of the Jews to the world.

he was totally obsessed in the 1860s and 1870s with denying Christianity its relevance and upholding Judaism's superior nature.[16]

Although Joseph Jacob did not subscribe to Geiger's approach to Christianity, he was fully in tune with the trend that saw Judaism as seminal to the development of civilization. In the first chapter of his *Jewish Contributions to Civilization*, 'The People of the Book', he created a genealogical connection between contemporary Jews and the Bible, asserting that 'the book [the Bible] that has thus made the Jews what they are has also, in large measure, laid the foundation of European civilization'.[17] Without discounting Babylonian influence on the Bible, Jacob went on to claim that 'European civilization derived its fundamental faith from the Jews . . . and Europe has learnt from the Jewish Bible the fundamentals of social justice and righteousness as part of its religion.'[18]

Considering the recurrent emphasis in the nineteenth century on Judaism's overarching significance to society, as opposed to the seventeenth- and eighteenth-century mercantilist position of Luzzatto, Manasseh b. Israel, and others, we are struck by a similar strategy but a dramatically different presentation. The earlier writers, who were concerned with marshalling evidence to prove that Jews would be not only loyal citizens but productive ones, believed that emphasizing the ability of Jews to improve commerce and business would speak in their favour to countries interested in improving their economic standing. Jewish virtuosity in the world of economics was also belaboured to gloss over the religious divide that continued to be a source of contention for wider elements in European society, as is borne out by the debate over the Jew Bill in Britain in 1753.

In these works, some were careful to avoid direct criticism of the dominant religion while making reference to Judaism's unique spiritual nature, but among certain Marrano apologists in seventeenth-century Amsterdam we encounter both overt criticism of the dominant religion and a paean to Judaism's pristine, unique nature—even to its superior qualities. In attempting to consolidate the sense of belonging of conversos to Judaism, a wide range of manuscripts and books held up the way of life of Jews as an ideal for others. What transpired in the late eighteenth and nineteenth centuries, even where emancipation was yet to be achieved, goes against the common perception of a passive Jewish response to modernity. In the age in which nations were redefining themselves in terms of their historical traditions and often questioning the viability of integrating 'foreign' elements like the Jews, Jewish traditions and contributions to society were being negatively assessed and cast aside. The national processes that challenged the Jewish contribution were

[16] Susannah Heschel, *Abraham Geiger and the Jewish Jesus* (Chicago, 1998).

[17] Jacobs, *Jewish Contributions to Civilization*, 64.

[18] Ibid. 79, 83.

buttressed by a constant, vigorous diminution of the hallmarks of Jewish civilization, principally the Bible. Faced with the challenge, many Jews acquiesced in this negative assessment. But others, in all European countries, turned the public discussions on their head, and reviewed their relationship with Christianity in a forthright, even aggressive, manner, asserting their ownership of the Bible, and demanding recognition of the fundamental Jewish contribution to civilization, both in classical and in contemporary terms.

'Mission theory', most often associated with Reform Jewry, was one manifestation that gave pride of place to an internal sense of Jewish superiority. Significantly, this mission of contribution and sense of superiority developed during a period of growing ideological, cultural, and social proximity to the surrounding culture. This was the case for converso Jews in the seventeenth century and for west European Jews in the nineteenth century. Clearly, proximity to Christian society and the breakdown of social and cultural barriers exacerbated, rather than weakened, the differences, accentuating Freud's notion of the 'narcissism of minor differences', which he described as 'a convenient and relatively harmless satisfaction of the inclination to aggression, by means of which cohesion between the members of the community is made easier'. Aggression towards those who are close by contributes to cohesiveness within the group. For Freud, Christian aggression against Jews in the Middle Ages is a prime example of humankind's inability to forgo its 'satisfaction of the inclination to aggression'.[19] That inclination to aggression in the service of creating cohesiveness among themselves was also not foreign to Jews.

The positions I have addressed above emerged from individuals writing in the vernacular, acculturated to the surrounding society. They certainly did not reflect the world of traditional Judaism, in its variegated forms. By way of contrast, we can merely highlight here two responses from within the Jewish world, which thrived on its desire to remain untouched by the process of modernization and acculturation: those of Rabbi Hayim of Volozhin (1749–1821) and Rabbi Akiva Joseph Schlesinger (1837–1922). Both of these rabbinic scholars were intensely concerned with preserving the traditional uniqueness of the Jews and their eternal mission. They saw their worlds as challenged by competing forces and sought ways to build a form of Jewish exclusivity that could impede the decline they feared. For R. Hayim, as Immanuel Etkes has pointed out, Torah study was to be a response both to the negative impact of hasidism, but also to its theological challenge to the study of Torah. Torah study in R. Hayim's construction was to unite the more traditional way of studying with a certain mystical

[19] Sigmund Freud, *Civilization and its Discontents*, ed. and trans. James Strachey (New York, 1962); based on first edn (Vienna, 1930), 61–2.

consciousness. It became the pillar of the cosmic system, and, if it were momentarily stopped, the universal consequences would be catastrophic. In R. Hayim's words:

And in truth without any doubt at all, if the entire world from one end to another of it were, perish the thought, truly vacant for a moment of our dealing with and contemplation of the Torah, at that moment all the upper and lower worlds would be destroyed and become nothing and chaos (*tohu vavohu* [Gen. 1: 2]), perish the thought.[20]

This statement reminds us, *mutatis mutandis*, of Graetz's notion of the constant need for Jewish presence in the universe, but with R. Hayim the implications are in a more mystical sense than in the here and now. For R. Hayim and the Lithuanian yeshivas in the nineteenth and twentieth centuries that followed his inspiration and teachings, the struggle was a wholly internal one—to preserve a way of life and learning, one that did not seek legitimization from the outside world, and had no concern with what Jews were bringing to it, save their unique way of life.

This perspective was a hallmark of Schlesinger's approach. Faced with the changing contours of the traditional life of Hungarian Jewry, forced by external pressure to adopt secular education and acculturate to a Magyar identity, and the serious erosion of traditional Jewish customs and way of life, Hungarian Orthodoxy moved further and further to the right. Schlesinger embodied this spirit more than his predecessors, as can be seen in his doctrinal work *Lev ha'ivri* (The Hebrew Heart). Schlesinger, as Michael Silber has shown, railed against secular studies for Jews, and constructed a 'division of labour' in which Jews devote their lives to the study of Torah while non-Jews explore and develop the sciences and technology. By maintaining their 'wholeness' (the Hebrew word for being 'whole' or 'perfect', *shalem*, is understood here as deriving from the initial letters of the three essential attributes of a Jewish identity: *shem*, one's name; *lashon*, one's language; and *malbush*, one's clothing) Jews would remain authentic. Although Schlesinger obviously viewed the Orthodox way of life as superior to all others, he apparently 'did not imply a value judgment as to whether Jew or gentile was superior'.[21] What non-Jews did was clearly worthwhile for society and culture, and Jews could also take advantage of their creativity and technology but should not be part of the process. The boundaries needed to be clear—Jews did not answer to non-Jewish expectations of

[20] Hayim of Volozhin, *The Soul of Life* (Heb.) (Vilna, 1874), as quoted in Immanuel Etkes, *The Gaon of Vilna: The Man and his Image*, trans. Jeffrey M. Green (Berkeley, 2002), 177.

[21] Michael K. Silber, 'The Emergence of Ultra-Orthodoxy: The Invention of a Tradition', in Jack Wertheimer (ed.), *The Uses of Tradition: Jewish Continuity in the Modern Era* (New York, 1992), 64.

them, but affirmed their eternal role in God's world. Thus, rabbis and writers of the Orthodox and Ultra-Orthodox world were certainly convinced of the superior nature of Torah Judaism and its eternal significance but had no need for it to be legitimized, accepted, and valued by 'civilization'. Not surprisingly, the worlds they represented did not find a place in the works of Roth or Jacobs as they remained confined to an insular view of the world.

The arguments that have been highlighted here call into question the conclusion of Jacob Katz's classic and pioneering work *Exclusiveness and Tolerance*.[22] Katz saw the Sanhedrin during the Napoleonic period as representing the height of the transformation of Jewish thinking. This forum was established in order to determine whether the Jews of France were willing and able to become citizens of the country. The twelve questions directed at the Jewish leadership originated in the negative image of Jews that predominated in many European circles of the period and were at the heart of the contemporary discussions on Jewish emancipation. Katz argued that the Sanhedrin's responses, upholding tolerance above exclusivity, accorded with the overriding positions on Christianity that emerged in Jewish society during the seventeenth and eighteenth centuries, as exemplified by Moses Mendelssohn's well-known letter to Rabbi Jacob Emden. According to Katz, this tolerant approach to Christianity signified a turn towards more universal positions, and can be recognized as a significant development in modern Jewish society. That is, with the gradual departure of the Jews from the 'ghetto', the long-standing rabbinic position that regarded Judaism as a superior religion gave way to a more universal one that dismissed the ambiguous attitudes towards Christianity. Katz argued that the notion of superiority emerged in periods of conflict and competition with Christian beliefs and pagan society. Rabbis were forced to address anew the significance of the Chosen People and their mission.

Yet it appears that it was not only at such times that conceptions of superiority emerged, but also at junctures when notions of Jewish continuity were challenged and at apparent moments of acceptance and coexistence. Proximity, as Freud pointed out, did not necessarily lend itself to a decline in such forms of self-representation. The Sanhedrin did not bring an end to exclusivism, and a moratorium on notions of superiority; these ideas continued among Jews (and Christians) and were an important strategy in formulating a response to processes of integration and accommodation to European society. 'Jewish contribution to civilization' was one such perspective, and it was fuelled from the late nineteenth century by a desire to redress the claims against the Jews.

[22] Jacob Katz, *Exclusiveness and Tolerance: Jewish–Gentile Relations in Medieval and Modern Times* (Oxford, 1961), ch. XV. See also Jay M. Harris (ed.), *The Pride of Jacob: Essays on Jacob Katz and his Work* (Cambridge, Mass., 2002).

TWO

Discourses of Civilization: The Shifting Course of a Modern Jewish Motif

DAVID N. MYERS

THE task of this chapter is not to shed light on the genre of 'Jewish contributions to civilization'. Others in this volume will probe the contexts in which the genre crops up, and trace the contours of a *shalshelet hakabalah* ('chain of tradition') that links figures such as Joseph Jacobs, Cecil Roth, Louis Finkelstein, and Thomas Cahill. Rather, the goal is to revisit the very idea of 'civilization' itself—particularly the way it has figured in modern Jewish collective self-perception, as well as in more recent debates over cultural values far beyond the Jewish context. In the first instance, we must ask: Does the term 'civilization' fit the diverse forms of Jewish culture? Or, in related fashion, when and why did modern Jews start to apply this standard to themselves? The answers to these questions may serve as a historical backdrop to a query of more immediate concern: Does the current discourse of civilization serve a useful function? Does it clarify or obscure, unite or divide?

A tentative response to these questions will come at the end of this chapter. However, to frame our discussion, some brief preliminary remarks are in order about the idea of 'civilization' in its present and past forms. Subsequently, the chapter will seek to analyse a number of distinct moments over the past two centuries in which we notice the criterion of 'civilization' informing and defining Jewish self-perception. Each of these moments reflects a different Jewish *mise en scène*, a different status and set of aspirations for Jews relative to their surroundings.

The first of these moments occurs in the early nineteenth century, when Jews in western Europe aimed to reach, through concerted self-cultivation and as an instrument of social integration, a high standard of civilization. The second moment, occurring later in the nineteenth century, is marked by the attempt of west European Jews to introduce the standard of civilization to other Jews (namely, the Jews of the 'Orient') rather than seek to attain this standard themselves (for they already believed themselves to possess it). The third moment, symbolized by Mordecai Kaplan's well-known book *Judaism as a Civilization* (1934), witnesses the equation of Jewish peoplehood and civilization, an impulse at once unsurprising in an age alive with Jewish national sentiments and yet surprising in an age rife with talk of 'the decline of civilization'.

These three moments hardly constitute an exhaustive list. But, by tracing them, we can gain a more nuanced sense of the importance and varied uses of the term 'civilization' in modern Jewish history. In the process, we might also be able to gain a new angle on the uneasy and yet often successful accommodation of the Jews to the modern West.

ON 'CIVILIZATION'

A new discourse of 'civilization' is upon us, stimulated in great measure by Samuel Huntington's best-selling book *The Clash of Civilizations* (1996).[1] The premiss of such a clash received extraordinary validation on 11 September 2001, in the wake of which the two major irreconcilable rivals, the West and Islam, were revealed. Since then, it often seems that the more we speak of this chasm, the more it exists—as rhetoric and deed become locked in a dangerously self-fulfilling relationship.

But if we look more carefully, the fixity of the two main civilizational foils becomes suspect. Is it possible, for example, to speak meaningfully of a single Western civilization, one that unites Germany and America a mere sixty years after the Holocaust? Conversely, can we reduce the entire Muslim world—from Morocco to Malaysia, Sunni to Shia—to a single voice?

Samuel Huntington was himself aware of the dangers of such an overstated and unnuanced 'cultural bifurcation', and thus proposed seven or eight world civilizations—rather than two main competitors—as the axes around which international relations and crises would revolve in a post-cold war era. He mentions incidentally the idea of a Jewish civilization in a footnote, but clearly doesn't regard it as a factor of any significance in the domain of greatest concern to him, international affairs. That said, for all of his analysis of a 'multicivilizational' world, Huntington invariably succumbs to the tendency to divide the world into two large camps, 'the West and the rest'.[2]

This tendency reinforces another point that Huntington elsewhere tries to challenge: the notion that civilizations are defined by rigid cultural borders.[3] On one hand, he states unequivocally that 'civilizations have no clear-cut boundaries and no precise beginnings and endings'—in short,

[1] Samuel Huntington, *The Clash of Civilizations and the Remaking of World Order* (New York, 1996).

[2] Ibid. 33.

[3] Ibid. 43.

no identifiably fixed properties. On the other hand, he describes Islam as 'a different civilization whose people are convinced of their culture and are obsessed with the inferiority of their power'.[4]

The point of this digression is to offer a rather obvious cautionary note. The term 'civilization', in contemporary discourse, often connotes a degree of fixity that belies the fluidity of political and cultural identities in our globalized, interdependent world. Moreover, the term, in its present-day usage, has moved a good distance from its original meaning. We do not need to undertake a full *Begriffsgeschichte* here. Others, including Lucien Febvre, Emile Benveniste, Philippe Bénéton, and Adam Kuper, have performed the task well.[5] Drawing on both Febvre and Benveniste, Bénéton notes that the term *civilisation* first surfaced in France in 1757 to indicate a 'more refined and civilized' state of individual and societal existence. Soon after, the term was employed to connote the antithesis of barbarism, or, in Bénéton's words, 'the collective movement that allowed humanity to leave behind barbarism for a state of civilized society'.[6]

In the nineteenth century two important developments occurred that altered the term's meaning. First, 'the immense empire of "La Civilisation"', as Adam Kuper calls it, 'was divided into autonomous provinces'.[7] Hence, the notion of a singular state of civilization—the opposite of barbarism—gave way to the idea of multiple civilizations. And secondly, a distinction began to emerge—later to develop into a well-known enmity—between French *civilisation* and German *Kultur*. The former implied an external, abstract or mechanical entity, and the latter an inner, intuitive, and spiritual entity—a juxtaposition that calls to mind Ferdinand Tönnies's renowned distinction between *Gesellschaft* and *Gemeinschaft*. This rift between *Kultur* and *civilisation* would linger throughout the nineteenth and early twentieth centuries, deepening in response to the oscillating political hostilities between Germany and France.[8]

And yet, there were those who thought the opposition entirely overdrawn. Fernand Braudel insisted that 'it is delusory to wish in the German

[4] Huntington, *The Clash of Civilizations and the Remaking of World Order*, 217. This point, particularly focused on the loss of Islam's military and cultural superiority over the West, informs two recent books by Bernard Lewis, *What Went Wrong? Western Impact and Middle Eastern Response* (New York, 2002) and *The Crisis of Islam: Holy War and Unholy Terror* (New York, 2003).

[5] See, *inter alia*, Lucien Febvre, *Civilisation: Le Mot et l'idée* (Paris, 1930); Émile Benveniste, *Problèmes de linguistique générale* (Paris, 1966); Philippe Bénéton, *Histoire de mots: Culture et civilisation* (Paris, 1975); and most recently, Adam Kuper, *Culture: The Anthropologists' Account* (Cambridge, Mass., 1999). Mention should also be made of Norbert Elias's study *The Civilizing Process*, trans. Edward Jephcott (New York, 1978).

[6] Bénéton, *Histoire de mots*, 32. See also Kuper, *Culture*, 25.

[7] Kuper, *Culture*, 25.

[8] Bénéton, *Histoire de mots*, 55–9, 73–6, 87–91.

way to separate *culture* from its foundation *civilization*'.[9] Notwithstanding his somewhat undermining jab at 'the German way', Braudel saw more points of commonality than difference between the two terms. Likewise, Freud averred in *The Future of an Illusion* (1927) that 'I scorn to distinguish between culture and civilisation'—a point perhaps unwittingly absorbed by his English translator, who rendered the title of his *Das Unbehagen in der Kultur* (1930) as *Civilization and its Discontents*.[10] This apparent conflation of culture and civilization is important for our purposes because Jews in modern Europe have frequently navigated between the poles marked off by these two terms—between the particularistic and bounded matter of culture and the universalistic aims and thrust of civilization. Indeed, we notice this conflation in the first of our key moments, a period marked by the constant mediation of Enlightenment and Romanticist sensibilities in the early nineteenth century.

THE INWARD GAZE

The story of German Jewry's romance with the ideal of *Bildung* is well known. One of its great narrators, George Mosse, delivered an encomium in *German Jews beyond Judaism* (1985) in which he demonstrated that the ideal of *Bildung* was a powerful force in shaping the aspirations of German Jews as they sought admission to a new Enlightened society.[11] And yet, those aspirations rarely bore the name of 'civilization' in this period. Ironically, they more often operated under the banner of *Kultur*. But what was signalled when German Jews used the term *Kultur*—and surely *Bildung*—was the kind of rational and progressive sensibility, steadfastly opposed to barbarism, that signified 'civilization' in its earlier French setting.

The point is that the imperative of civilization was deeply felt, if not always articulated, by German Jewish intellectuals in the late Aufklärung period. After all, it was in this era that Jews began to internalize the claims of non-Jews, including their friends (like Christian Wilhelm Dohm and Henri Grégoire), that they were in need of self-improvement. Moses Mendelssohn resisted this impulse, but his disciples were less reluctant. For example, Wessely's *Divrei shalom ve'emet* (Words of Peace and Truth, 1782) is a clarion call for Jewish cultural and intellectual edification, especially

[9] Fernand Braudel, *On History* (*Écrits sur l'histoire*), trans. Sarah Matthews (London: Weidenfeld & Nicolson, 1980), 205, quoted in Huntington, *The Clash of Civilizations and the Remaking of World Order*, 41.

[10] Sigmund Freud, *The Future of an Illusion* (New York, 1928), 5–6; id., *Civilization and its Discontents*, ed. and trans. James Strachey (New York, 1962; based on 1st edn, Vienna, 1930).

[11] George L. Mosse, *German Jews beyond Judaism* (Bloomington, Ind., 1985). For critical perspectives on this work and view, see Klaus L. Berghahn, *The German–Jewish Dialogue Reconsidered: A Symposium in Honor of George L. Mosse* (New York, 1996).

through acquisition of *torat ha'adam* (human-derived knowledge). The need was urgent since, Wessely noted, 'there is one people in the world alone who are not sufficiently concerned with "human knowledge" '—the Jews'.[12]

The sense of Jewish deficiency, both collective and individual, was hardly restricted to Wessely or his fellow *maskilim*. It continued into the early nineteenth century, as the more universal and optimistic aspects of the Aufklärung project yielded to darker and more exclusivist notions of a German *Volk*. Those who presided over the transition, figures like Herder and Fichte, saw the lifeblood of the nation in *Kultur*. Curiously, German Jews, though often deemed foreign to the German nation, held dearly to—and in the process, transvalued—the idea of *Kultur*. Thus, the first organized circle of university-trained Jewish scholars called itself Verein für Kultur und Wissenschaft der Juden. For this circle, *Kultur* was not simply or even primarily the repository of the national soul; it was a means of collective elevation beyond a state of depravity. In addressing his colleagues, Eduard Gans, the Verein's first president, declared:

> It is well enough known and not strange to the members gathered here or to any of those absent that about fifty years ago the light of better culture (*Kultur*) went out from Berlin to the German Jews . . . The bad mixture of a half oriental, half medieval life was dissolved; the dawn of a better education dispelled a completely alien culture; the previous assertion of a harsh total isolation gave way to inclination in a more universal direction.[13]

Gans's use of the term *Kultur* had less in common with the nationalistic inflections present in his day than with the ideal of 'civilization', both as antidote to barbarism and as standard of proper comportment. Nonetheless, his use of *Kultur*-cum-civilization represented at once an internal demand for Jewish self-improvement and an external panegyric on behalf of Jewish social integration. As such, it helps trace the distinctive and liminal status of Jews in Germany, who absorbed a key organizing principle of German national identity without gaining the full political benefits (e.g. citizenship) that usually accompanied it.

This first generation of university-trained Jewish scholars in Germany exemplified well the desire of Jews to attain the high water mark of civilization. The Jews, Immanuel Wolf wrote in the first issue of the *Zeitschrift für die Wissenschaft des Judentums* (1822), 'must raise themselves . . . to the level of a science (*Wissenschaft*), for this is the attitude of the European world'.[14]

[12] Cited in Paul Mendes-Flohr and Jehuda Reinharz (eds), *The Jew in the Modern World: A Documentary History* (New York, 1995), 71.

[13] Cited in Michael A. Meyer, *The Origins of the Modern Jew: Jewish Identity and European Culture in Germany* (Detroit, 1967), 167.

[14] Cited in Mendes-Flohr and Reinharz (eds), *The Jew in the Modern World*, 220.

Here *Wissenschaft*, like the more universal variant of *Kultur* we have discussed, evokes the sweep and teleology of civilization, but of 'civilization' *avant la lettre*. So when does the actual language of civilization first emerge in this German Jewish moment?

The fact of the matter is that I am not altogether certain. We might turn to Leopold Zunz, who perhaps best embodies the mediation of Enlightenment and Romanticist sensibilities among German Jewish scholars of this era. In 1818 (at the ripe age of 24), Zunz wrote a sweeping programmatic article, 'Etwas über die rabbinische Literatur', in which he took stock of the decline of Israel, the loss of her creative capacities, and the accompanying 'shades of barbarism'. In his own day, those 'shades' had begun to recede, replaced by the bright light of *Bildung*.[15]

Although he describes qualities often attributed to it, Zunz does not, as far as I can tell, employ the term 'civilization' in 1818. He does use it, though, in an 1830 review of Abbé Luigi Chiarini's *Théorie du judaïsme*. The Italian Polish cleric's attack on the Talmud as a repository of anti-Christian blasphemy demonstrated to Zunz that the question of the Jew's place in society was far from resolved. Indeed, Chiarini served as a reminder of 'the not fully ripened fruit of a developing *civilization*' in Europe.[16]

We run the risk of making too much of the appearance of our favoured word in Zunz's review. But its eventual arrival on the scene does allow us to set in relief those key terms—*Bildung*, *Wissenschaft*, and especially the putative rival of 'civilization', *Kultur*—frequently employed by German Jews in the early nineteenth century to convey a state of enlightened social comportment, intellectual attainment, and rational progress. These terms were used for a pair of purposes: intracommunally, to prompt Jews to rise above their own lack of civilization and extracommunally, to highlight the civic and cultural virtues of the Jews as they sought integration into European society. These tasks point, in turn, to a unique blend of collective insecurity and enduring group pride among west European Jews in the nineteenth century. In fact, it was this mix that compelled European Jews to make repeated appeals to the bar of civilization, while simultaneously proclaiming their attainment of it.

THE OUTWARD GAZE

These countervailing impulses played a significant role, I suspect, in the literary genre that stands at the centre of this volume. Presumably, they also

[15] Leopold Zunz, 'Etwas über die rabbinische Literatur', in Zunz, *Gesammelte Schriften* (Berlin, 1919), 1.

[16] Leopold Zunz, 'Beleuchtung der *Théorie du judaïsme* des Abbé Chiarini', in Zunz, *Gesammelte Schriften* (Berlin, 1919), 271.

figured in the mid-nineteenth-century efforts of German Jews, especially Reformers, to proclaim the unique religious 'mission of Israel' to the non-Jews.[17] The claim of a unique Jewish mission or contribution to civilization reflected, in part, the internalization of negative non-Jewish perceptions of Jews, followed by the projection outward of a newly idealized standard of civilization. Such a psychological process is different from the more self-assertive 'reversing of the gaze' that Susannah Heschel observes in Abraham Geiger, whereby Geiger projects the non-Jew's negative stereotype of the Jew back onto the non-Jew.[18] And it is different from (though clearly related to) the phenomenon that stands at the heart of the second moment that I would like to discuss—namely, that moment in which one Jewish group projected an ideal of civilization, not onto itself nor out to the broader world, but rather onto another, more distant Jewish group. In the first moment, we noticed that early nineteenth-century German Jews sought to assume the standard of civilization for themselves as a way of earning full admission to European society. In the second moment, Jews in western and central Europe profess their civilization but simultaneously express concern about the lack of civiilzation of other Jews—predictably, those in the 'East' (understood as both the Middle East and eastern Europe). I am thinking here of groups like the Alliance Israélite Universelle (founded in 1860) and the early twentieth-century Hilfsverein der deutschen Juden. While clearly manifesting a sense of fraternal compassion, they were also acting to affirm and validate their own status at home.

The distinction that such groups drew between themselves and other Jews was by no means new. Aron Rodrigue has identified precursors to the 'full-fledged Europeanising "civilising mission," aimed at transforming Sephardi and Eastern Jewries' that took root in the later half of the twentieth century. He notes, for examples, a Central Consistory report from 1842 that called for 'a mission to improve through moralisation' the debilitated state of the Jews of Algeria. And he traces the extent to which the European Jewish press, in the second quarter of the nineteenth century, turned its attention to the Jews of the East with a mix of 'Western superiority and a deeply internalized perception of Jewish unity'.[19]

Of course, the sense of superiority harboured by one Jewish group towards another is not a nineteenth-century invention. On the contrary, it

[17] For a discussion of this phenomenon, see Michael A. Meyer, *Response of Modernity: A History of the Reform Movement in Judaism* (New York, 1988), 137–8.

[18] Susannah Heschel, *Abraham Geiger and the Jewish Jesus* (Chicago, 1998), 1–22.

[19] See Rodrigue's comment to Eli Bar-Chen, 'Two Communities with a Sense of Mission: The Alliance Israélite Universelle and the Hilfsverein der deutschen Juden', in Michael Brenner, Vicki Caron, and Uri R. Kaufmann (eds), *Jewish Emancipation Reconsidered: The French and German Models* (Tübingen, 2003), 121, 123, 127.

has been a recurrent theme in the relationship between Sephardim and Ashkenazim, among other Jewish groups. We are reminded of this sensibility by the eighteenth-century Isaac de Pinto, who proclaimed in his *Apologie pour la nation juive* (1762) that a 'Portuguese Jew of Bordeaux and a German Jew of Metz appear two beings of a different nature!' To push the point further, he clarified his view that the latter was beset with a 'human nature debased and degraded'.[20]

De Pinto's cutting distinction between Portuguese (i.e. Sephardi) and German (i.e. Ashkenazi) Jews was recognized by the French National Assembly, which granted rights of citizenship *first* to Sephardim on January 1790 and nine months later to the entirety of French Jewry. Over the course of the nineteenth century, this distinction lost much of its force within the French Jewish community. But it was replaced by a newly drawn boundary between Jews of the West (Europe) and Jews of the East (Middle East). A clear articulation of this distinction comes in the opening charge of the Alliance Israélite Universelle from 1860:

> If you believe that a great number of your coreligionists, overcome by twenty centuries of misery, of insults and prohibitions, can find again their dignity as men, win the dignity of citizens;
>
> If you believe that one should moralize those who have been corrupted, and not condemn them, enlighten those who have been blinded, and not abandon them, raise those who have been exhausted, and not rest with pitying them . . .
>
> If you believe in all these things, Jews of all the world, come hear our appeal . . .[21]

This charge was squarely in line with the larger French project of a *mission civilisatrice* to the less civilized world—an enterprise marked by that familiar colonial mix of altruism and condescension. Thus, we read in an Alliance document from 1863 that 'the children of Israel will pursue, in the distant corners of Africa and Asia, the civilizing mission that divine Providence has entrusted to them'.[22] At the same time, the Alliance's sense of mission was a reflection of French Jewry's desire to export to Jews of the 'Orient' what it had itself internalized in the era of emancipation—most significantly, 'regeneration', as the Abbé Grégoire famously prescribed in 1789. Now projecting regeneration onto others, the French Jews of the Alliance fixed their attention on the realm of education as the most effective and appropriate vehicle of change.

[20] Quoted in Mendes-Flohr and Reinharz (eds), *The Jew in the Modern World*, 306–7. We should recall that de Pinto's distinction was made in response to Voltaire's assertion that 'the Jewish nation is the most singular that the world has ever seen . . . and the most contemptible of all' (ibid. 304). See the discussion now in Ronald Schechter, *Obstinate Hebrews: Representations of Jews in France, 1715–1815* (Berkeley, 2003), 112–15.

[21] Cited in Rodrigue, 'Two Communities with a Sense of Mission', p. xi.

[22] Ibid. 23.

As Rodrigue has shown in his seminal work on the Alliance, the language of 'regeneration', of a 'civilizing mission', indeed of 'civilization' itself, abounds in the organization's manifestos and memoranda. And, as he further shows, this language is picked up by local Jewish allies of the Alliance on the ground in the Middle East. Thus, the wealthy Jewish banker from Istanbul, Abraham de Camondo, insisted in 1864 that 'only instruction [could] open the path of progress' to those Jews of the East 'so backward in civilization'.[23] Even those who had not yet become part of the Alliance orbit made recourse to the resonant language of the day. For example, in 1867 the advocates of a new-style Jewish school in Adrianople in Turkey called on the Alliance to provide the school with teachers, declaring that they were 'convinced of the necessity of giving a good French education to our students in order to introduce them to European civilization'.[24]

More examples of this language and sense of mission could be adduced, but the point should be clear enough. There is in this second historical moment, marked most saliently by the Alliance Israélite Universelle, a projection (or perhaps deflection) of the civilizing imperative. Whereas once this imperative was directed at German or French Jews themselves, it was now directed at Eastern Jews situated at a remove from the cradle of European civilization (though of course more proximate to the cradle of ancient civilization).

THE KAPLANIAN SENSE OF 'CIVILIZATION'

The third and final moment that I would like to explore offers yet another twist on the relationship between Jews and the concept of civilization. It does not proclaim the explicit acknowledgement of the Jewish contribution to civilization, though it is closer in time to the well-known endeavours in this vein of Cecil Roth (*The Jewish Contribution to Civilization*, 1940) and Louis Finkelstein (*The Jews: Their History, Culture, and Religion*, 1949). Rather, in this moment Judaism, or Jewishness, is *equated* with civilization.

Of course, this moment immediately recalls the life project of Mordecai Kaplan, who published in 1934 *Judaism as a Civilization*, a text that became the intellectual foundation of the emerging Reconstructionist movement (as its subtitle already anticipates—*Toward a Reconstruction of American-Jewish Life*). There was in Kaplan's manifesto a degree of daring that derived from his American upbringing (might we call it a sort of Jewish 'manifest destiny' in his pushing of boundaries?). Hence, he aggressively advances the claim that the Jewish people constitute a holistic, or what he later called an 'organ-

[23] 'Two Communities with a Sense of Mission', 48. [24] Ibid. 51.

ismic', civilization.[25] Much less pronounced here are the insecurity and apologia that marked the previous two moments discussed. And with good reason, for the cultural landscape of Kaplan's America was much less marred with antisemitism than that of Europe.

Indeed, Kaplan's new system was manifestly American. He was well aware that the term 'civilization' had lost the lustre of high cultural attainment it possessed in the nineteenth century. Rather, it had come to symbolize decline and cast a dark pall over European intellectual culture, at least from the end of the First World War. The chief prophet of doom was Oswald Spengler, who asserted in *The Decline of the West* (1918–22) that civilization followed culture sequentially, 'like death following life, rigidity following expansion . . . [and] petrifying world-city following mother-earth'.[26] Kaplan utterly rejected this Spenglerian understanding of civilization, and instead infused the term with new meaning for his developing project of Jewish renewal.

At the same time, Kaplan, unlike his European Jewish predecessors, did not present civilization as either the means to or the embodiment of enlightened cultural comportment. On the firmer ground of America, he was aggressive in advancing a strong form of groupness that would have appeared unseemly or detrimental to Jewish interests in nineteenth-century western Europe. As he avers in the introduction to *Judaism as a Civilization*, 'The rediscovery of Judaism as a civilization I owe to the convergence of various social and cultural influences, many of which I, no doubt, would have missed, had I not been brought up in an American environment.'[27] And the contours of this revivified concept were sweeping. It was nothing less than 'that nexus of a history, literature, language, social organization, folk sanctions, standards of conduct, social and spiritual ideals, esthetic values, which in their totality form a civilization'.[28]

It is essential to add that Kaplan was writing in a post-emancipatory age when national conceptions of Jewish identity abounded. He himself admitted that 'Ahad Ha-am with his neo-rationalist and cultural approach to Jewish values', as well as 'Zionism with its realistic attitude toward the relation of the Jewish people to Palestine furnished the initial impulse to my thinking.'[29] Indeed, America and Zionism, combining audacity and innovation, prompted Kaplan to rethink the definition of Jewish group identity.

[25] See Kaplan's preface to *Judaism as a Civilization: Toward a Reconstruction of American-Jewish Life* (Philadelphia, 1967; repr. 1981), p. xi.

[26] Oswald Spengler, *The Decline of the West*, trans. Charles Francis Atkinson (New York, 1926), 24.

[27] Kaplan, *Judaism as a Civilization*, p. xvi.

[28] Ibid. 178.

[29] Ibid., p. xvi.

The relative security of his legal and social status allowed him to direct his attention inward to the Jewish collective. In *Judaism as a Civilization* there is little appeal to the non-Jewish world for validation. Neither is there a claim to Judaism's unique world mission.[30] Kaplan is rather intent on redressing a state of spiritual and cultural crisis within the Jewish world. In his diagnosis, the root cause of this crisis lay not in the Jew's otherness, but ironically in the absence of otherness in an open and free society like the United States.

This decidedly American dilemma—so distinct from the challenges facing Jews in Europe or Palestine in 1934—could not be resolved by the decidedly American (and American Jewish) idiom, religion. As Kaplan observed, 'the Jew's religion is but one element in his life that is challenged by the present environment'.[31] To invigorate a Jewish existence that had become moribund meant far more than adhering to one or another religious denomination; it meant retrieving the 'differentia' of Jewish life (land, language, social norms, folk ways, and above all, culture) that had been discarded as part of the social compact of Enlightenment. In this way, and only in this way, could Judaism fulfil itself as a civilization.

CONCLUSION

In light of this aim, it is understandable why Mordecai Kaplan would have had little interest in proclaiming Jewish contributions to world civilization.[32] Unlike those whom we examined earlier, he did not see civilization as either a pure and unblemished state or a high water mark to be attained. Rather, he was concerned to stitch together the tattered fabric of an extant civilization. In this regard, his anxiety was quite different from that of the early nineteenth-century German Jewish adepts of *Wissenschaft* or of the late nineteenth-century purveyors of a Jewish *mission civilisatrice*. He did not seek the approbation of the non-Jewish world. Nor did he attempt to mend the ways of distant co-religionists. He sought reform of his own Jewish world for its own sake.

But Kaplan, for all of his American-bred confidence, did have his own deep anxieties about the Jewish future—indeed, about the ability of Jews to endure the challenges of modernity. 'Civilization' was part of the solution to the problem for Kaplan; it signified the holistic entity that must be revived in order for a vibrant Jewish collective to survive and flourish. While distinct from others examined before, Kaplan's use of the term nonetheless allows us to follow its snaking course among various cohorts of modern Jews, noting

[30] 'Judaism is but one of a number of unique national civilizations guiding humanity toward its spiritual destiny' (p. 180).

[31] *Judaism as a Civilization*, 177.

[32] Ibid. 181.

when, where, and how it served as a balm to soothe anxiety and insecurity over the Jewish condition.

Tracing this current gives us new insight into the tenuous balance between collective insecurity and group pride that deeply informs the modern Jewish condition in Europe. At the same time, it returns us to the question of the term's present-day utility. Our post-cold war world is marked by vast political, economic, and social reconfigurations—globalization, European unification, American superpower, mass terror, revived antisemitism. Does the term 'civilization' make any sense in this context, either for the Jews or for any other group?

The impetus to rely on 'civilization' in the Jewish case is, at first glance, understandable. How better to grasp the vast temporal and spatial reaches of the Jewish historical experience? As Mordecai Kaplan intuited, 'civilization' might offer an attractive alternative to the age-old definitional question of whether the Jews are a religion, nation, people, or ethnicity. And yet, for all its allures, the term does induce serious reservations. For example, in a post-Enlightenment and post-Holocaust world, do Jews still need to prove that they represent the antithesis of barbarism and savagery, as invocation of the term 'civilization' invariably entailed in the nineteenth century? In fact, is it possible at all, to rephrase Adorno's famous aphorism about poetry, to write about civilization after Auschwitz? Even if it is, we must be mindful of the fact that the term 'civilization', with its rather grandiose pretensions, can privilege and canonize a thin stratum of high cultural activity and production. By contrast, civilization's perennial foil, culture (with which it earlier overlapped), may well be a more supple and versatile terminological tool—bespeaking a wider range of practices, products, and social strata.

This point relates to a final reservation about 'civilization' that is particularly germane today (and of which both Mordecai Kaplan and Samuel Huntington were aware). Namely, the term implies a singular, great, but rigid entity, when in fact enduring world cultures survive precisely because of their permeable and dynamic borders, ever changing in interaction with others, as in the case of the culture of the Jews. Similarly, it is important to note, as has a recent scholarly collection, that there are and have always been multiple cultures operating within the apparently singular Jewish collective.[33] This may be discomfiting to those in search of a monolithic Jewish civilization. But the presence of diversity within the Jewish collective can serve as a valuable lesson to all of those who believe that the world is perched on the brink of an unavoidable clash between seemingly essential civilizations.

[33] See David Biale (ed.), *Cultures of the Jews: A New History* (New York, 2002).

THREE

From Counterculture to Subculture to Multiculture: The 'Jewish Contribution' Then and Now

MOSHE ROSMAN

As a perennial minority the Jews seem always to need to fit in. One way to do this is to contribute, and to be seen to contribute, to the larger society, culture, and civilization in a meaningful way. The subject of 'the Jewish contribution to civilization', however, is usually thought of as referring to a certain variety of Jewish apologetic rejoinder to modern antisemitism's denial of the possibility or reality of full integration of Jews into European and American societies, from the late nineteenth to the mid-twentieth centuries and particularly after the rise of the Nazis to power in Germany.[1] This kind of apologetic concentrated on describing how Jews contributed to or benefited the societies in which they lived, or humankind in general. The genre was common enough for the Library of Congress to coin the subject headings 'Jews: Contribution to Civilization' and 'Civilization: Jewish Influences'.

It is noteworthy that this 'contribution discourse' appeared after the formal success of the Jewish political emancipation project and the incubation of a high degree of Jewish acculturation to general European values and lifestyle. It was a sign of Jewish unease, frustration, and fear in the face of indicators that, despite Jews' good faith efforts to conform to the legal, social, and cultural demands of the emancipating societies, and notwithstanding legal guarantees of civil and political equality, their integration was in reality but partial, contingent, tenuous, and even revocable. The persistence of active antisemitism and unofficial or informal barriers to complete Jewish

[1] One can find Jewish authors touting Jewish contributions to the benefit of the world in the ancient and medieval periods as well; but as a genre, literature of this type appears to be a modern phenomenon (see below). In fact there are still popular books appearing in this genre, such as Thomas Cahill, *The Gifts of the Jews: How a Tribe of Desert Nomads Changed the Way Everyone Thinks and Feels* (New York, 1998).

participation in social, cultural, and economic endeavours prompted Jews to attempt to demonstrate their worthiness to qualify as full-fledged members of society. Analysis of their contributions would serve this cause. At least it could bolster Jewish self-confidence and stiffen Jews' resolve in continuing their struggle for acceptance. It was paramount that Jews themselves have a sense of their own value and importance if they were to morally convince or legally coerce others to recognize finally that they really belonged.

CLASSIC CONTRIBUTION DISCOURSE

The best-known examples of the genre are Joseph Jacobs's *Jewish Contributions to Civilization: An Estimate* (1919) and Cecil Roth's *The Jewish Contribution to Civilization* (1938).[2] Neither was reticent about announcing his book's objective. Writing during the First World War, Jacobs subtitled his introduction 'The Higher Anti-Semitism' and spent most of it reviewing the history of antisemitism, especially in its modern racist guise. Jacobs explained his book's purpose thus:

> such an estimate of contemporary contributions to the world's progress is an essential part of the Jewish defence. Against the vague anti-Semitic denunciations of Jewish characteristics, which are mainly the results of prejudice and, in any case, cannot be checked or measured, we can here set down the definite results of Jewish achievement. We can even go further and, by the aid of modern statistical science . . . arrive at some measurable comparison between the output of Jewish ability and that of others.[3]

Roth also made the anti-antisemitism objective of his book clear:

> This work is intended as a contribution towards the settlement of a discussion of long standing, which is now once again to the fore. It is alleged by modern anti-Semites . . . that the Jew is essentially a middleman, who has produced nothing; that he is an alien excrescence on European life: and that the influence which he has had on western culture, during the past two thousand years, has been entirely negative, if not deleterious. Such a criticism demands an analysis based not on theory but on fact. . . . I am making no attempt to evaluate the Jewish genius, or

[2] There were many books and booklets of widely varying natures published with similar titles; e.g. Charles Archibald Stonehill (ed.), *The Jewish Contribution to Civilization* (Birmingham, 1940); Neville Laski, *The Jewish Contribution to Civilization* (Cardiff, 1937); Abraham J. Feldman, *Contributions of Judaism to Modern Society* (Cincinnati, 1930); Edwin R. Bevan and Charles J. Singer (eds), *The Legacy of Israel* (Oxford, 1927); Arthur J. Kirschstein, *The Jew: His Contribution to Modern Civilization* (Denver, 1930); Abraham A. Roback, *Jewish Influence in Modern Thought* (Cambridge, Mass., 1929); Dagobert D. Runes, *The Hebrew Impact on Western Civilization* (New York, 1951); Ignaz Maybaum, *Synagogue and Society: Jewish Christian Collaboration in Defence of Western Civilisation* (London, 1944).

[3] Joseph Jacobs, *Jewish Contributions to Civilization: An Estimate* (Philadelphia, 1919), 50.

even to decide whether such a thing exists. . . . I have tried to assemble and set down in this volume a representative selection (at least) of the contributions made to the civilization, the culture and the amenities of the western world by persons of Jewish lineage.[4]

While Jacobs and Roth approached the subject with at least a nod to critical sophistication, other works were more crass; for example, counting Jewish combat soldiers and casualties or Jewish Nobel prizewinners as methods of 'proving' how valuable Jews were to their countries and to the world.[5]

Ironically, this advertising of Jewish achievements can readily be interpreted as implicit acceptance of racial theory. It virtually grants the validity of antisemites' fundamental assertion, that the Jews were a race, differing only by insisting that the Jewish race was in possession of positive traits. Jacobs apparently did believe in a moderate version of racism, 'the notion of Chosen Races, each with its own special characteristics . . . by innate or acquired ability'.[6] Roth, faced with the Nuremberg Laws and early Nazi anti-Jewish depredations, was more sensitive to the ramifications of legitimizing racial theory and performed rhetorical contortions attempting to distance himself from it; claiming, for example, 'however distinct the Jews may have been from their neighbors ethnologically at the beginning of their settlement in Europe, this distinction has been progressively modified'.[7] The inconsonance was, however, obvious, and after the Second World War, as racial theory was progressively discredited and abandoned, most Jewish contribution boosters took pains to ascribe Jews' achievements to nurture and not nature.

While contribution literature was apologetically motivated, it still included several works of lasting scholarly value. Especially noteworthy among these are *The Jewish Encyclopedia*, Kaplan's *Judaism as a Civilization*, Baron's 'The Jewish Factor in Medieval Civilization', Finkelstein's *The Jews*, and Roth's *The Jews in the Renaissance*.[8]

[4] Cecil Roth, *The Jewish Contribution to Civilization* (London, 1938), p. vii.

[5] e.g. Michael Adler (ed.), *British Jewry Book of Honour* (London, 1922); Jacob De Haas (ed.), *The Encyclopedia of Jewish Knowledge* (New York, 1934), s.v. 'Jewish Nobel Prize Winners'. This practice continues today; see *Encyclopaedia Judaica* (Jerusalem, 1972; CD-ROM, 1997).

[6] Jacobs, *Jewish Contributions to Civilization*, 52.

[7] Roth, *The Jewish Contribution to Civilization*, p. viii.

[8] Cyrus Adler, Isidore Singer, et al. (eds), *The Jewish Encyclopedia: A Descriptive Record of the History, Religion, Literature, and Customs of the Jewish People from the Earliest Times to the Present Day*, 12 vols (New York, 1901–6); cf. Shuly Rubin Shwartz, *The Emergence of Jewish Scholarship in America: The Publication of the Jewish Encyclopedia* (Cincinnati, 1991); Mordecai Kaplan, *Judaism as a Civilization: Toward a Reconstruction of American-Jewish Life* (New York, 1934); cf. David Myers's chapter in this volume; Salo W. Baron, 'The Jewish Factor in Medieval Civilization', *Proceedings of the American Academy for Jewish Research*, 12 (1942), 1–48; cf. Robert Liberles, *Salo Wittmayer Baron: Architect of Jewish History* (New York, 1995); Louis Finkelstein (ed.), *The Jews: Their History, Culture and Religion* (New York, 1949); cf. David Biale's chapter in this volume; Cecil Roth, *The Jews in the Renaissance* (Philadelphia, 1959); cf. David B. Ruderman, 'Cecil Roth,

CONTRIBUTION DISCOURSE AS EXPRESSIVE HOSTILITY

Although specifically Jewish in its content, in its intent this 'contribution discourse' is related to a more general phenomenon typical of minority groups whose place in society is unstable. Sociologically speaking,[9] ethnic, racial, or other minority groups can be classified as subcultures; that is, groups within society differing from the larger society in such matters as language, values, religion, and lifestyle, and perpetuating their own normative systems. Simultaneously, however, the minority usually shares many of the values of the larger society, and strives to achieve them. The minority wants to be a *sub*culture, not a separate one. It aims for inclusion as a component of the total society and culture.

For its part, the majority disapproves of the subculture's separate norms, regarding them as inferior, divisive, and threatening. In such situations, historically, majorities have tended to resort to a mix of two strategies: encouraging the minority to shed its separateness and to assimilate; but also frustrating its attempts to share in the values and culture of the larger society by discriminating against it and making it the victim of various exclusionary

Historian of Italian Jewry: A Reassessment', in David N. Myers and David B. Ruderman (eds), *The Jewish Past Revisited: Reflections on Modern Jewish Historians* (New Haven, 1998); and Robert Bonfil, 'The Historian's Perception of the Jews in the Italian Renaissance: Towards a Reappraisal', *Revue des Études Juives*, 143 (1984), 59–82. Baron consciously tried to separate his study from the apologetic trend: 'the term "factor" still seems preferable to the usual phraseology of "Jewish contributions to medieval civilization" which, without being less ambiguous, has decidedly apologetic overtones' ('The Jewish Factor in Medieval Civilization', 2). Yet, he too utilized the expression 'cultural contributions' (p. 24), and the use of the word 'factor' does not prevent his article from conforming to the conventions of contribution discourse.

[9] The following analysis is my attempt to develop further and apply the theories presented in Floyd James Davis, *Minority-Dominant Relations: A Sociological Analysis* (Arlington Heights, Ill., 1978), and J. Milton Yinger, 'Contraculture and Subculture', *American Sociological Review*, 25 (1960), 625–35, as well as his *Countercultures: The Promise and Peril of a World Turned Upside Down* (New York, 1982), esp. 18–50. In the later work Yinger, over-influenced, I think, by the popular use of the term 'counterculture' in the United States at the time, saw countercultures as 'emergent phenomena not rooted in traditional subsocieties, ethnic communities, occupational groups, or other fairly stable social structures', although he admitted that subcultures and countercultures 'are sometimes empirically mixed' (*Countercultures*, 41, and cf. 89–113). The earlier article, in which he theorized less concerning contemporary developments, is more useful for historical application. Cf. Milton M. Gordon, *Assimilation in American Life* (New York, 1964), esp. 38–51, 68–74, 105–9, 126–9; Minako Kurokawa (ed.), *Minority Responses* (New York, 1970); Floyd James Davis (ed.), *Understanding Minority-Dominant Relations: Sociological Contributions* (Arlington Heights, Ill., 1979); Russell A. Kazal, 'Revisiting Assimilation: The Rise, Fall, and Reappraisal of a Concept in American Ethnic History', *American Historical Review*, 100 (Apr. 1995), 437–71, esp. 439–40, 443–51.

practices.[10] The contradiction between these two tendencies is seldom fully resolved, with the ultimate status of the minority within the larger society usually dependent on the balance achieved between them.

When the second tactic, exclusion, is primary and the minority finds itself in constant conflict with the majority, facing frustration in its attempts to realize a comfortable identity as a subculture, the result often is that the *sub*-culture becomes a *counter*culture where a central element of the normative system of the group is in conflict with the values of the majority society it is in. The counterculture defines itself largely by virtue of its contradictions with respect to the majority.[11]

By mutual, if tacit, agreement between Christians and Jews, medieval European Jewry was a marginal group in northern European society. Having been subject to many legal, economic, social, and cultural restrictions in the Middle Ages, one important process of modernity for the Jews was 'emancipation'—their release from these limitations. Simultaneously, Jewish attitudes and cultural devices, such as ritual laws and communal discipline which promoted Jewish segregation, were also eroded by a process of acculturation. Through emancipation and acculturation, Jews in the modern period moved progressively from the margins of society towards its centre, although throughout the modern period Jewish identity never shed all of its distinctive characteristics. One might portray this trajectory of modernity (in my view roughly 1650–1950[12]) as Jews evolving from a counterculture to a subculture.[13]

In the course of the transition from counterculture to subculture Jews adopted more and more of the values of majority society, but they also utilized various forms of covert aggression to combat continuing manifestations of majority hostility and the desire to keep them marginalized. In the custom of minority groups, one important form of this covert aggression was expressive hostility—verbally denigrating and otherwise casting aspersions on the majority group. One type of expressive hostility is ethnocentric

[10] The phenomenon of multiculturalism, where society rejects the notion of a core, hegemonic culture to which others are expected to assimilate to some degree, and attempts to arrange intercultural interaction in a non-hierarchical and non-power-related way, is a rather recent, and one might say experimental, development in Western society; for how it has affected historical and sociological analysis of the past, see Kazal, 'Revisiting Assimilation', 437–8, 441, 448–62, 470–1.

[11] Yinger, 'Contraculture and Subculture', 628–30, 632–3, 635.

[12] For the rationale behind this periodization, see Moshe Rosman, 'Defining the Post-Modern Period in Jewish History', in Eli Lederhendler and Jack Wertheimer (eds), *Text and Context: Essays in Modern Jewish History and Historiography in Honor of Ismar Schorsch* (New York, 2005).

[13] See e.g. the analysis of how modern German Jewry became a subculture in David Sorkin, *The Transformation of German Jewry, 1780–1840* (New York, 1987), esp. introduction and conclusion.

interpretation of both history and current events. Minorities often create myths, asserting, appearances to the contrary notwithstanding, that they stand at the centre of events, wield unseen power over the majority, and in some significant measure determine society's fate.[14] Consider, for example, the various Jewish stories about how Jews influenced or controlled royal policy in Poland, or even the monarchy itself; or the Jewish claim that Poland was partitioned by its neighbours as punishment for its Jewish policies.[15]

This kind of ethnocentrism is intended to affirm the minority's importance in society; this society needs us; we make a crucial difference; we are part of you; by discounting us the majority impoverishes itself and works counter to its own interests. Such expressive hostility also subtly indicates the minority's *desire* to be important in a given society. It is an expression of the minority's internalization of majority values as well as an assertion of the minority's right to internalize them; it means minority members believe they should belong. In addition, this ethnocentrism is a counter-reaction to the majority's continued exclusionary practices—its apparent preference that the minority remain a counterculture rather than a subculture.

By stipulating that it is a founder of the culture or that it exercises a determinative influence on events, the minority is declaring that it cannot possibly be excluded; it is an intrinsic, coherent component of the whole. This declaration is part of the larger attempt to establish a modus vivendi (or to re-establish one that has been ruptured) between majority and minority that both sides can live with. While implicitly conceding the primacy of the majority culture, the minority members are also trying to bolster their own self-image and to convince the majority of their loyalty and utility so that they might be granted security and acceptance.

Contribution discourse is a form of ethnocentric expressive hostility. By proving how valuable minority members—in this case Jews—were to society, indeed to civilization as a whole, the apologists were trying to convince their non-Jewish interlocutors of the indispensable role that Jews play in society. They were also trying to provide Jews themselves with confidence-building facts that would help them in their fight for full-fledged membership (as opposed to mere citizenship) in society. Perhaps, most of all, they were demonstrating to both the non-Jews and themselves how much they

[14] Cf. Davis, *Minority-Dominant Relations*, 50, 131–2, 138, 145; Robert A. LeVine and Donald T. Campbell, *Ethnocentrism: Theories of Conflict, Ethnic Attitudes, and Group Behavior* (New York, 1972), p. 33, theorem 3.10; p. 68, theorems 5.1, 5.1.2. Like the quasi-racist claims noted earlier, this too was an ironic echo of a primary antisemitic assertion, that Jews dominated government, culture, and the economy; see Shmuel Ettinger, *Modern Anti-Semitism: Studies and Essays* (Heb.) (Tel Aviv, 1978), 1–12 and *passim*.

[15] Haya Bar-Itzhak, *Jewish Poland: Legends of Origins* (Detroit, 2001); Ber Birkenthal, *The Memoirs of Ber of Bolechow*, ed. Mark Vishnitzer (London, 1922; repr. New York, 1973), 149–51.

really had adopted and internalized general Western categories of value and how much they believed in the truth of this way of life and wanted to adhere to it.

OLDER VERSIONS OF CONTRIBUTION DISCOURSE

When viewed as a type of expressive hostility, however, contribution discourse has a much longer history than the period coinciding with the rise of modern antisemitism and the prelude to and aftermath of the Second World War. It is at least as old as the modern period itself, beginning when some Jews first realized that it was possible—and decided that it was desirable—to be an integral component of European or Western society. It has reappeared whenever that desire was obstructed—up until the present day.

This discourse began in the early modern period when secularizing, rationalizing trends in Europe undermined the old religion-based evaluation of many cultural conventions, including the status of the Jews in society. Once religion ceased to be the only authoritative guide to formulating an attitude towards the Jews, new possibilities developed. If, for example, it was *raison d'état*, and not Christianity, that was to determine the value of a group or an idea, then Jews, who brought economic advantage to the state, might be seen as an asset worth cultivating. Rather than remain a pariah to be tolerated so as to serve as an object lesson in the consequences of failure to recognize theological truth, or so as to be relegated to performing socially undesirable functions like moneylending or high-risk entrepreneurship, Jews might be transformed into constructive, contributing members of society.[16]

The possibility of such a transformation was, to be sure, not a foregone conclusion. All three leading early Enlightenment theorists of toleration, Benedict Spinoza, John Locke, and Pierre Bayle, came to the conclusion that Judaism was 'fundamentally intolerant—and thus inevitably also in some sense intolerable', while adherence to this Judaism and the exceptional historical circumstances surrounding Jewish existence prevented inclusion of the Jews on an equal basis in enlightened society.[17] Deist doctrine, in general, though often considered to contain the seeds of Jewish rehabilitation, was nonetheless profoundly hostile to Jews and Judaism, supplying—according to Shmuel Ettinger—'an important link in the development of modern anti-Semitism'. Most of the enlightened thinkers of the seventeenth century were still of the opinion that even under the newly formulated conceptions

[16] Jonathan I. Israel, *European Jewry in the Age of Mercantilism, 1550–1750* (Oxford, 1985), 35–69.

[17] Adam Sutcliffe, 'Enlightenment and Exclusion: Judaism and Toleration in Spinoza, Locke and Bayle', *Jewish Culture and History*, 2/1 (1999), 40.

of society the Jews would perforce continue to serve as civilization's nemesis, thwarting its good intentions and undermining its institutions at many opportunities. For its own reasons, the emerging secular state could no more rely on Jews' loyalty or trust their intentions than could the receding religious one.[18]

It was left to Jews to be the first to theorize on the possibilities of the new secularizing world-view for changing the perception of the Jews and making a positive place for them in society. To persuade their non-Jewish readers (all of the famous Jewish tracts on this subject were written in European languages) that Jewish status should be ameliorated, they resorted to contribution discourse. The seventeenth-century Jewish thinkers Simone Luzzatto, Manasseh b. Israel, and Isaac Cardoso all insisted that the Jews did not need to be improved or reformed; they were already fine, upstanding, noble, even superior, people.[19] Emphasizing mercantilist arguments, Luzzatto and Manasseh b. Israel enumerated the myriad ways Jews contributed to the welfare—especially economic—of the places where they resided. Cardoso averred that Jews were actually the best of people. Discrimination against them hurt the discriminators, made no rational sense, and was unjust. Effacing barriers would enable Jews to make a tremendous contribution wherever they lived.[20]

[18] Shmuel Ettinger, 'The Position of the Deists on Judaism and its Influence on the Jews' (Heb.), in Ettinger, *Studies in Modern Jewish History*, i: *History and Historians* (Jerusalem, 1992), 224.

[19] Simone Luzzatto, *Discorso circa il stato de gl'hebrei: Et in particolar dimoranti nell'inclita città di Venetia* (Venice, 1638); Manasseh b. Israel, *Menasseh ben Israel's Mission to Oliver Cromwell: Being a reprint of the pamphlets published by Menasseh ben Israel to promote the re-admission of the Jews to England, 1649–1656*, ed. Lucien Wolf [London, 1901]; Isaac Cardoso, *Las excelencias de los hebreos* (Amsterdam, 1679).

[20] For analyses of these apologia, see Benjamin C. I. Ravid, *Economics and Toleration in Seventeenth Century Venice: The Background and Context of the 'Discorso' of Simone Luzzatto* (Jerusalem, 1978); id., '"How profitable the nation of the Jewes are": The *Humble Addresses* of Menasseh ben Israel and the *Discorso* of Simone Luzzatto', in Jehuda Reinharz and Daniel Swetschinski (eds), *Mystics, Philosophers, and Politicians: Essays in Jewish Intellectual History in Honor of Alexander Altmann* (Durham, NC, 1982); Lester W. Roubey, 'Simeone Luzzatto's *Discorso* (1638): An Early Contribution to Apologetic Literature', *Journal of Reform Judaism*, 28 (1981), 57–63; Ismar Schorsch, 'From Messianism to Realpolitik: Menasseh ben Israel and the Readmission of the Jews to England', *Proceedings of the American Academy for Jewish Research*, 45 (1978), 187–209; Yosef H. Yerushalmi, *From Spanish Court to Italian Ghetto: A Study in Seventeenth-Century Marranism and Jewish Apologetics* (New York, 1971), 350–472; cf. Richard I. Cohen's discussion of these and other writings contemporary with them in his chapter in this volume. To the apologetic works listed here one might add Leon Modena's *Historia degli riti hebraici* (Paris, 1637), although it was more concerned with defending Judaism as a non-superstitious religion than with the issue of Jews' contribution; see Mark R. Cohen, 'Leone de Modena's Riti: A Seventeenth-Century Plea for Social Toleration of Jews', *Jewish Social Studies*, 34 (1972), 287–319.

Even those Christian Europeans who eventually were willing to entertain new attitudes towards the Jews[21] were not so confident as the Jewish writers that the Jews were a latent, powerful, positive force needing only to be unbound. Their point of departure was that currently Jews were a problematic presence in society, but they postulated that the Jews might make a positive contribution if properly refined. The argument was over how to do so, whether by giving them maximum freedom or by supervising their progress through the imposition of restrictions that would be gradually abolished as the Jews proved their worthiness.[22] The basic premiss was clear: any improvement in Jewish status, any move to integrate Jews into society, was a function of the supposition that they had a positive contribution to make. Early modern Jewish apologists welcomed the opportunity to prove the point.

By the nineteenth century the terms of the argument over Jewish integration had shifted. The Romantic, progress-preoccupied, culturally arrogant nineteenth century virtually dared Jews to demonstrate how they—never feeling at home in a world they did not create, constituting a state within the state, incapable of loving justice, mankind, and truth, utilizing their privileges in order to exploit their fellow citizens—could be part of the grand projects of its civilization.[23] As other chapters in this volume demonstrate, Jews responded in several ways.[24] Whether by internalization and self-application of non-Jewish critiques of Jews and Judaism, development of Jewish mission theory, 'missionizing' European culture to 'uncivilized' Jews, or impudent insistence that actually it was the Jews who laid the foundations for civilization (which Christianity in many ways subverted), Jewish apologists sought to prove that Jews could be and had indeed become contributing

[21] Shmuel Ettinger, 'The Beginning of Change in the Attitude of European Society towards the Jews', *Scripta Hierosolymitana*, 7 (1961), 193–219.

[22] Compare, for example, the proposals for Jewish integration made by John Toland, *Reasons for Naturalizing the Jews in Great Britain and Ireland* (London, 1714), and Christian Wilhelm von Dohm, *Über die bürgerliche Verbesserung der Juden* (Berlin, 1781), conveniently excerpted in Paul R. Mendes-Flohr and Jehuda Reinharz (eds), *The Jew in the Modern World: A Documentary History* (Oxford, 1995), 13–17, 28–36. Note especially Toland: 'In a word they ought to be so naturaliz'd in *Great Britain* and *Ireland*, as, like the Quakers, to be incapacitated in nothing but where they incapacitate themselves' (Mendes-Flohr and Reinharz (eds), *The Jew in the Modern World*, 16); versus Dohm: 'it would even be permissible, at least in the beginning, to restrict the number of Jews active in commerce, or subject them to special taxes. . . . But impartiality would demand that if a Jewish and a Christian applicant show equal capability, the latter deserves preference. This seems to be an obvious right of the majority in the nation—at least until the Jews by wiser treatment are changed into entirely equal citizens and all differences polished off' (ibid. 33).

[23] See the excerpts from writers of the first half of the 19th century brought by Mendes-Flohr and Reinharz (eds), *The Jew in the Modern World*, 309–13, 321–31, 334–6.

[24] See the chapters by Richard I. Cohen and David N. Myers in this volume and references there.

members of civilization. They were not only civilized, but forgers of civilized culture.

If I am correct that contribution discourse is part of Jews' effort, within the new parameters of modernity, to move from the status of counterculture to that of subculture, then discussion of Jews' contribution was also a component in the attempt to formulate a new definition of Jewishness that would be appropriate in the modern world. In the early modern period, people like Luzzatto, Manasseh b. Israel, and Cardoso saw the Jews as a semi-autonomous ethnos who contributed as a coherent community to the larger society in which they lived. Nineteenth-century German, French, and English Jews held Jews to be members of a different, but vital and essential, religion. This meant that they could contribute by applying the positive religious values and insights of Judaism to social life and that there was no impediment to their contributing as individuals to general civil life as any other citizen might.

In the second half of the nineteenth century, with the world continually subdividing into nation-states, another definition of Jewishness was proffered as the means by which Jews could lay claim to a place in the developing Western, or world, civilization. Since the world was being organized according to nation-states, it was only within the framework of a political state that Jews could take their rightful place in civilization and make their dutiful and proper contribution alongside other nation-states to the furthering of human progress and whatever was necessary for the advancement of enlightened civilization. Only as a nation, asserted some early Jewish nationalists, could Jews carve out a role and contribute on an equal basis with everyone else. Thus, although not usually categorized this way, early Jewish nationalist assertions can also be seen as a version of contribution discourse.

The classic Jewish nationalist theorists Lev Pinsker and Theodor Herzl saw Jewish nationalism as an antidote to the anomalous nature of Jewish existence as a minority, eternally unwanted by its host nations. For them, Jewish nationalism would solve, primarily, the so-called Jewish problem, i.e. on what basis could the Jews attain a normal existence in the world. Indeed, both believed that Jewish nationalism would be enthusiastically accepted by non-Jews as well as Jews because it would alleviate the *non-Jews'* problem with the Jews.

In contrast, earlier theorists such as Judah Alkalai, Moses Hess, Peretz Smolenskin, and Moses Leib Lilienblum, with various individual codicils and nuances, all saw the Jewish national state as providing a natural platform, in parallel to the other nation-states, for enabling and launching the Jews' substantial contribution to the world order. Organized as a state, the Jewish nation could finally assume its rights, but also its duties, in the world.[25] As

[25] See e.g. the chapters treating each of these figures in Arthur Hertzberg, *The Zionist Idea: A Historical Analysis and Reader* (New York, 1959), and Shlomo Avineri, *Varieties of Zionist Thought* (Heb.) (Tel Aviv, 1980).

they saw it, the issue was not the current impossibility of the Jews' circumstances, but the desirability of creating new conditions that would facilitate the Jews' reaching their full potential.

Hess, for example, vigorously advocated Jewish nationalism as the *sina qua non* for Jewish partnership in a better world:

> The contemporary movements for national self-realization do not only not exclude a concern for all humanity but strongly assert it. These movements are a wholesome reaction, not against universalism but against the things that would encroach upon it and cause it degeneration . . . and it is only against these destructive forces that I appeal to the power of Jewish nationalism . . . all political and social progress must necessarily be preceded by national independence. . . . The Jewish people will participate in the great historical movement of present-day humanity only when it will have its own father-land.[26]

CONTEMPORARY CONTRIBUTION DISCOURSE

Over the last generation or so academic experts in Jewish Studies have tended to disparage the investigation of 'the Jewish contribution to civilization'. Its overt apologetic nature and vulgar ethnocentrism are pathetic, embarrassing, and silly in a context where Jews have 'made it' as part of the academic and other establishments. Having gained full acceptance, having assured themselves that they indeed belong to the general culture and society, Jews have no need to prove their worthiness. As if to drive this home, many Jewish academics revel in a new-found capacity to explicate Jewish foibles, misdeeds, and mistreatment of others; which explication, among other things, testifies to Jewish security and self-confidence.

Almost half a century ago, it was Jacob Katz, an Israeli scholar, safely ensconced in the Jewish state (at the time boasting its ability to allow the Jews to be themselves without regard to 'what the *goyim* might say'), who was the first to state unambiguously that traditional Jewish society practised a double standard of morality in its dealings with non-Jews. Even in 1958 this threatened to serve as confirmation of a standard antisemitic canard.[27] Today, however, most Jewish scholars feel so safely embedded in their social

[26] Hertzberg, *The Zionist Idea*, 130, 136, 137.

[27] Jacob Katz, *Tradition and Crisis: Jewish Society at the End of the Middle Ages*, trans. and with afterword by Bernard D. Cooperman (New York, 1993; first pub. in Heb., Jerusalem, 1958), 32–4. In his autobiography, *With My Own Eyes: The Autobiography of a Historian*, trans. Ann Brenner and Zipora Brody (Hanover, NH, 1995), 147, Katz himself noted that his continued demonstration in his second book, *Exclusiveness and Tolerance*, 'that traditional Judaism upheld neither absolute religious tolerance nor a universalist code of morality' led to hesitations on the part of its publisher because of fears 'that the book might provide ammunition for the enemies of the Jewish people'.

and cultural environments, wherever they may be, that they are convinced that skeletons in the Jewish collective closet will not be held against them, and they certainly do not hesitate to expose blemishes. Conversely, when the subject of 'Jewish contribution' is discussed, it is often placed in quotation marks, as in the titles of this chapter and of the conference that spawned this volume, to emphasize that modern Jewish scholarship has moved beyond apologetics and to denote the ironic posture preferable for treating a topic whose time has passed.

But has it? As a means for an insecure minority to justify its position, contribution discourse is still very much with us, albeit in a new incarnation. Postmodernism and multiculturalism have once again shaken Jews' confidence that they belong. Multiculturalist critics consistently speak about Jews, Judaism, and Jewishness as conservative, even reactionary and oppressive, aligned with the established powers of hegemony that seek to exclude and disempower people of colour and other minorities.[28] This gives rise to feelings of hurt, frustration, resentment, and anger among Jews. Once again, they have become an anomalous minority: establishment in the eyes of other minorities; still not completely at one with the majority monoculture.

Some Jews feel cheated because the goalposts have been moved in the middle of the game. For three or four generations they were taught that they could integrate by adopting a pluralist ethos—assimilating to the majority's monoculture, while maintaining, with majority approval, distinctive minority cultural norms in private and within the minority community. Witness to occasional transvaluation of their own culture to the point where it influenced the majority, they understood that the price of such acceptance was full internalization of majority monoculture. After successfully negotiating the barriers to this internaliza-tion and to cultivating a pluralist stance, they have suddenly learned that pluralism is no longer desirable. Having mastered the construct of subculture, these Jews now discover that to gain postmodern legitimacy it is preferable to be a counterculture—precisely the circumstance that was abandoned with so much effort.[29]

[28] Edward Alexander, 'Multiculturalism's Jewish Problem', [*American Jewish*] *Congress Monthly* (Nov.–Dec. 1991), 7–10; Stephen Whitfield, 'Multiculturalism and American Jews', *Congress Monthly* (Sept.–Oct. 1995), 7–10; Mitchell Cohen, 'In Defense of Shaatnez: A Politics for Jews in a Multicultural America', in David Biale, Michael Galchinsky, and Susannah Heschel (eds), *Insider/Outsider: American Jews and Multiculturalism* (Berkeley, 1998), 45.

[29] For an interesting example of Jewish attempts to adopt a pluralist stance in the past, see Nadia Malinovich, 'Orientalism and the Construction of Jewish Identity in France, 1900–1932', *Jewish Culture and History*, 2/1 (1999), 1–25. Diana Pinto—in *A New Identity for Post-1989 Europe*, JPR/Policy Paper 1 (London, 1996); 'The New Jewish Europe: Challenges and Responsibilities', *European Judaism*, 31/2 (1998), 1–15; 'The Jewish Challenges in the New Europe', in Daniel Levy and Yfaat Weiss (eds), *Challenging Ethnic Citizenship: German and Israeli Perspectives on Immigration* (New York, 2002)—passionately advocates a pluralist position for Jews in Europe today (in my view, hers is an illustration of the argument delineated

Cultural evolution has reached the stage of multiculturalism, defined as, for example, 'pluralism without the element of public conformity and without pluralism's optimism of ultimate inclusion for all . . . a nation of disparate entities sharing public power but existing, immutably, as separate and autonomous units'. Multiculturalism, unlike pluralism, sees no virtue in acculturation. There is no hierarchy of cultures; no majority–minority; no general and sub. The only accommodations cultures might make should be pragmatic to allow peaceful coexistence. Substantive accommodation in the form of assimilation is unnecessary and even undesirable. Jews as the avatars of pluralism cannot fit easily into the multicultural matrix.[30]

Other Jews are willing to turn their back on pluralism and adopt the multicultural paradigm; they believe that in a world organized as 'a community of communities and a culture of cultures' Jewish culture and the Jewish community can assume a respected place. Jewishness, as the product of so much historical multicultural experience, might even be emblematic of multiculturalism, with 'multicultural theory itself [lying] at the heart of modern Jewish experience'.[31]

Responses to this thesis from the multiculturalists are often, however, in the nature of: your culture was too complicit in the formation of the oppressive monoculture for you now to claim membership in—much less leadership of—the ranks of the oppressed; however you might construe your history in the past, today you are aligned with the white elite; you are no longer vulnerable (if indeed you ever were); you are not outsiders; contrary to your claims, there is no valid multiculturalism inherent in Jewishness.[32]

towards the beginning of this chapter that 'it [is] paramount that Jews themselves have a sense of their own value and importance if they [are] to morally convince or legally coerce others to recognize finally that they really [belong]'). In her writings, Pinto emphasizes again and again that the Jews in Europe do now 'belong'. For Pinto's critique of multiculturalism, see Pinto, *A New Identity for Post-1989 Europe*, 13; id., 'The Jewish Challenges in the New Europe', 248–50.

30 David Biale, Michael Galchinsky, and Susannah Heschel, 'Introduction: The Dialectic of Jewish Enlightenment', in Biale et al. (eds), *Insider/Outsider*, 3–7; Cheryl Greenberg, 'Pluralism and its Discontents: The Case of Blacks and Jews', ibid.; cf. David T. Goldberg, 'Introduction: Multicultural Conditions', in Goldberg (ed.), *Multiculturalism: A Critical Reader* (Cambridge, Mass., 1994).

31 Biale et al., 'Introduction: The Dialectic of Jewish Enlightenment', 8–12 (the quotation is on p. 12), and Susannah Heschel, 'Jewish Studies as Counterhistory', in Biale et al. (eds), *Insider/Outsider*, 113; Dan Diner, 'Geschichte der Juden—Paradigma einer europaïschen Geschichtsschreibung', *Gedachtniszeiten* (Munich, 2003), 246–62.

32 Greenberg, 'Pluralism and its Discontents', 78–9; Amy Newman, 'The Idea of Judaism in Feminism and Afrocentrism', in Biale et al. (eds), *Insider/Outsider*, esp. 152, 154, 160, 161, 167, 174, 176; Susannah Heschel, 'Configurations of Patriarchy, Judaism and Nazism in German Feminist Thought', in Tamar Rudavsky (ed.), *Gender and Judaism* (New York, 1995); id., 'Anti-Judaism in Christian Feminist Theology', *Tikkun*, 5/3 (1990), 25–8, 95–7; Sander Gilman, *Jews in Today's German Culture* (Bloomington, Ind., 1995), 4, 35–6. On the 'occlusion of Jewish otherness', see Jonathan Boyarin, 'The Other Within and the Other Without', in Laurence J.

This is most poignantly and vociferously expressed in the so-called new academy, the stronghold and fountainhead of multiculturalism. Jewish academics who thought that Jewish Studies belonged in a framework dedicated to entitling every tile in the cultural mosaic to full visibility are rudely awakened to their exclusion.[33] They are left out and, like Jews legally emancipated but socially discriminated against, they protest that they deserve to belong. In time-honoured fashion, their argument for inclusion in the hegemonic group concentrates on the contribution Jewishness can make to the dominant discourse and ethos, now connected to multiculturalism.

This new discourse on the contribution of Jews to multicultural civilization has two main vectors. One version (popular among some non-Jewish theorists as well as Jews) is to regard Jews, whose identity is always in flux, as an allegory, metaphor, or trope representing all of the people sinned against by modern Western civilization and summarizing all of the ways in which they have been harmed. 'The Jew' (often in quotation marks and sometimes with lower case 'j') *stands for* all of those in diaspora, all victims, all Others, 'the outsiders, the nonconformists: the artists, anarchists, blacks, homeless, Arabs, etc.—and the Jews'.[34]

Silberstein and Robert L. Cohn (eds), *The Other in Jewish Thought and History: Constructions of Jewish Culture and Identity* (New York, 1994), esp. 430–5.

[33] Sara R. Horowitz, 'The Paradox of Jewish Studies in the New Academy', in Biale et al. (eds), *Insider/Outsider*; Arnold Eisen, 'Jews, Jewish Studies, and the American Humanities', *Tikkun*, 45 (1989), 23–9; Laurence J. Silberstein, 'Benign Transmission versus Conflicted Discourse: Jewish Studies and the Crisis of the Humanities', *Soundings*, 74 (1991), 485–507; Boyarin, 'The Other Within and the Other Without'. In contrast, what might be termed celebration of Jewish Studies' acceptance by the 'old academy' is represented by Ismar Schorsch, 'The Place of Jewish Studies in Contemporary Scholarship', and Jaroslav Pelikan, 'Judaism and the Humanities', both in Shaye J. D. Cohen and Edward L. Greenstein (eds), *The State of Jewish Studies* (Detroit, 1990).

[34] Jean-François Lyotard, *Heidegger and 'the Jews'*, trans. A. Michel and M. S. Roberts (Minneapolis, 1990), as cited in Daniel Boyarin and Jonathan Boyarin, 'Diaspora: Generation and the Ground of Jewish Identity', *Critical Inquiry*, 19 (1993), 700, and see pp. 697–701 for presentation of other theorists of the 'Jew-as-trope' school. See also Bryan Cheyette and Laura Marcus (eds), *Modernity, Culture, and 'the Jew'* (Cambridge, 1998), a collection of essays where this position is very much in evidence, as is its editors' attempt to problematize it. While Pinto urges that European Jews must 'transcend' the Holocaust ('The New Jewish Europe: Challenges and Responsibilities', 9; 'The Jewish Challenges in the New Europe', 243) and 'regard themselves not as victims, but as a vibrant force' (*A New Identity for Post-1989 Europe*, 1), she speaks of 'their inherent "belonging", if only through suffering' (ibid. 3) and shares the supposition that it is the Holocaust experience and its incorporation into European consciousness that has largely qualified the Jews truly to 'belong' to the new European society and culture and toassume a central role in fashioning these (see ibid. 1, 3, 4, and *passim*; 'The New Jewish Europe: Challenges and Responsibilities', 6–7, 10; 'The Jewish Challenges in the New Europe', 242–3). Cf. Dan Michman, 'A Third Partner of World Jewry? The Role of Memory of the Shoah in the Search for a New Present-Day European Jewish Identity', in Konrad Kwiet and

This 'Jewish' victim was and is always both a passive receptacle of injustice, persecution, and suffering as well as a hybrid, even chameleon-like, cultural creature, lacking a fixed content. Aside from victimhood, its one constant distinguishing feature is the ability to continually disrupt and confound the hegemonic culture. For scholarship (especially in its social criticism mode) the 'jew' is the location from which the critique of and the battle against what Homi Bhabha called 'lethal modernity' begin and are conducted.[35]

Thus the Jewish experience is shorthand for the universal experience of all hybridized, colonized, alterior people who have suffered at the hand of modern civilization because they disconcert it. It is studied as an introduction to the need for multiculturalism and for the way in which it problematizes hegemony. It has no intrinsic value, or even significant content, beyond its representative potential and its power to discomfit.

This depriving Jewish identity of particularist substance (essence?) has elicited a strong reaction from some academics whose main occupation is the study of Jewish texts and Jewish experiences, yet who are committed to a multicultural perspective. They reject the presumption that Jewishness has no content valuable in and of itself or that the attempt to assure the deracialization of Jewishness requires its deracination as well. Daniel and Jonathan Boyarin, for example, perhaps the most accomplished syndics of Jewish Studies to the curia of postmodernism, justified their critique of the-Jew-as-trope on the basis of one of multiculturalism's most hallowed precepts, the right to be different:

Although well intentioned, any such allegorization of *Jew* is problematic in the extreme for the way that it deprives those who have historically grounded identi-

Jurgen Matthaus (eds), *Contemporary Responses to the Holocaust* (Westport, Conn., 2004); Moshe Rosman, 'Hybrid with What? The Variable Contexts of Polish Jewish Culture: Their Implications for Jewish Cultural History and Jewish Studies', in Yaron Eliav and Anita Norich (eds), *Jewish Cultures and Literatures* (Providence, RI, 2007).

[35] Cheyette and Marcus (eds), *Modernity, Culture, and 'the Jew'*, pp. xv–xvi. Cf. Silberstein's summary of the 'antiessentialistic, constructionist approach to Jewish identity', in 'Others Within and Others Without: Rethinking Jewish Identity and Culture', which serves as an introduction to Silberstein and Cohn (eds), *The Other in Jewish Thought and History*, and also his 'Mapping, Not Tracing: Opening Reflection', the introductory chapter in his edited book *Mapping Jewish Identities* (New York, 2000). Silberstein's insistence on dichotomizing essentialist versus constructionist approaches easily leads into the Jew-as-trope rhetoric. In my opinion one can agree that Jewish culture and identity are constantly under construction, yet still ask if there aren't some fixed, if flexible, features that enable all of the various constructions to be grouped under the genus of Jewish (see my 'Hybrid with What', and the discussion there of polythetic definition). The Boyarins trace the view of the Jew-as-trope, i.e. the Jew 'as both signifier of unruly difference and symbol of universalism', to Paul and early Christianity; noting that 'once Paul succeeded, "real Jews" ended up being only a trope. They have remained such for European discourse down to the present . . .' ('Diaspora', 697).

ties in those material signifiers of the power to speak for themselves and remain different. In this sense the 'progressive' idealization of *Jew* and *woman*, or more usually, *jew* and *Woman*, ultimately deprives difference of the right to be different . . . We will suggest that a Jewish subject-position founded on generational connection and its attendant anamnestic responsibilities and pleasures affords the possibility of a flexible and nonhermetic critical Jewish identity.[36]

This second vector of the new Jewish contribution discourse sees the Jews, not as trope, but as model; that is the Jewish experience and Jewish texts have something to teach—to *contribute*—to contemporary, multiculturalist-governed, discourse. For the advocates of Jew-as-trope the Jewish contribution lies in 'the Jew' being a background concept for use in interpretation and criticism and not in any specific, concrete Jewish idea or action (except, perhaps, as a special—Holocaust-legitimized—protagonist within the larger struggle for equality and multiculturalism—or pluralism[37]); so the Jewish contribution is rather amorphous. The proponents of Jews-as-model, who contend that Jews and Judaism possess precious and powerful cultural treasures, propose many concrete ways for Jews to contribute (sometimes they actually use the word); some examples:

Indeed we would suggest that Diaspora, and not monotheism, may be the most important contribution that Judaism has to make to the world . . .[38]

My aim is to describe multiculturalism as a workable social system. . . . The experience of American Jews may be of some help here . . .[39]

Both the examples of the Jews and Jewish studies as a field can make a theoretical contribution to the development of the multicultural academy.[40]

What can [Jewish Studies'] perspectives contribute to a rethinking and reshaping of cultural studies?[41]

. . . Kafka may even help us to understand how Jewish identity and Jewish difference are bound up with the unpredictable future of our planet.[42]

36 Boyarin and Boyarin, 'Diaspora', 697–701: 697, 701; see also Boyarin, 'The Other Within and the Other Without'.

37 Cf. the writings by Pinto cited in nn. 29, 34.

38 Boyarin and Boyarin, 'Diaspora', 723. For their development of the idea of diaspora as a theoretical and historical model to replace national self-determination (and especially Zionism), see ibid. 706–23.

39 Michael Walzer, 'Multiculturalism and the Politics of Interest', in Biale et al. (eds), *Insider/Outsider*, 91.

40 Heschel, 'Jewish Studies as Counterhistory', 112.

41 Horowitz, 'The Paradox of Jewish Studies in the New Academy', 123; on pp. 124–9 there are detailed answers to this question.

42 Boyarin, 'The Other Within and the Other Without', 446.

By engaging in systematic comparisons of their condition with the analogous conditions of postcolonial diasporas, American Jews may be able both to learn from and to contribute to dialogues of inordinate importance in a time of global population shifts and the thrilling but frightening restructuring of nations.[43]

The presence of Jews and Judaism in the academy, then . . . may contribute to debate within the academy about the nature and purpose of humanistic learning.[44]

Jews, in many ways the prototype of the new European, have the chance to *belong* in Europe as never before. . . . The Jewish contribution to the fostering of a tolerant, pluralist, European democratic identity is best fulfilled by drawing the widest possible conclusions from the positive developments of the post-war Jewish experience in Europe. . . . Other groups could also profit from the Jewish precedent. . . . Jews can make an important contribution in this realm for, in this tragic century, they experienced both the attractions and dangers of acculturation.[45]

I have no doubt that each of these scholars is correct and the paths of enquiry or action suggested by them all have merit. The point in the present context, however, is not really the fact that Jewish Studies can enlighten an array of cognate and general subjects or that Jews can make a prodigious contribution to the formation of culture, but the perception of the necessity to justify the utility of the endeavour. In this these academics leave us with the impression that their circumstances are more akin to those of Jacobs and Roth, or even much earlier contribution explicators, than they might care to acknowledge.

[43] Michael Galchinsky, 'Scattered Seeds: A Dialogue of Diasporas', in Biale et al. (eds), *Insider/Outsider*, 187.

[44] Eisen, 'Jews, Jewish Studies, and the American Humanities', 29.

[45] Pinto, 'The New Jewish Europe: Challenges and Responsibilities', 9, 12, 13. Pinto also calls for European Jewry 'to contribute positively and meaningfully to world Judaism, and to Israel's own tormented crisis of identity' (ibid. 3); but, despite advocating a pluralist approach to Judaism and the evolution of a protean Jewish identity where Jews can define themselves in whatever—religious, cultural, intellectual, ethnic, political—terms they desire (*A New Identity for Post-1989 Europe*, 6, 8; 'The New Jewish Europe: Challenges and Responsibilities', 8; 'The Jewish Challenges in the New Europe', 248), she does consistently assign European Jewishness an indispensable, 'essential' content (one is tempted to say *mitsvah*): 'responsibility' for 'promoting historical, national and religious reconciliation and fighting for a tolerant democratic pluralism' ('The New Jewish Europe: Challenges and Responsibilities', 9; see, similarly: *A New Identity for Post-1989 Europe*, 1, 5, 6, 8; 'The New Jewish Europe: Challenges and Responsibilities', 4–5, 11, 12, 14; 'The Jewish Challenges in the New Europe', 247–8). Despite her protestations, this is reminiscent of various universalist Jewish political and social programmes proposed over the past 250 years or so; by her lights, any particularist content to Judaism is, by implication, negotiable—at most. I should emphasize again (see n. 29) that in line with her vision of a pan-European identity, and unlike the authors of the other quotations adduced here, Pinto sees the Jewish contribution in a pluralist—i.e. subcultural—context and not a multicultural one.

If multiculturalism is the contemporary analogue to nineteenth-century 'civilization', then the two approaches of Jew-as-trope and Jews-as-model might be roughly analogous to the Alliance Israélite Universelle declaring that it could spread civilization better than anyone, while Abraham Geiger asserted that Judaism contains the essence of civilization and the Christians would do well to stop perverting this essence and try to learn from it. The trope school offers the Jews and Judaism as a felicitous vehicle for conducting multicultural discourse. The model school contends that multicultural discourse has much to learn from the Jewish model. Both seek acceptance, legitimacy, and validation.

The question of Jewish contribution to civilization is, then, once again relevant. As before, a certain unease prompts Jewish intellectuals to try to prove Jewish bona fides to the world. Make no mistake, however. Whatever its genesis, like its predecessors, this discourse will most assuredly produce some works of lasting scholarly value and probably even a master narrative of Jewish history in the multicultural key that will take its place alongside the nationalist and acculturationalist metahistories that have developed over the past century and a half. Only when the multicultural challenge to Jews' position in the society and culture is somehow resolved is a new perspective apt to emerge.

PART II

JUDAISM AND OTHER CULTURES

FOUR

Day of Gladness or Day of Madness? Modern Discussions of the Ancient Sabbath

ELLIOTT HOROWITZ

THE SUBLIME LEGISLATION

In the first edition of his *Social and Religious History of the Jews*, published in 1937, Salo Baron acknowledged that the 'obvious origin' of the Jewish sabbath had been in ancient Babylonian astronomy, but asserted, perhaps with a measure of particularistic pride, that it 'had received quite a novel and profound sanctification by virtue of its connection with the beginnings of all history—the day chosen by God for rest after his labors of creation'. The Galician-born and Vienna-educated historian who had arrived in the United States just over a decade earlier went so far, in fact, as to claim that 'nowhere else, except in Judaism and its daughter religion, had the Sabbath received this character of holy and absolute rest'.[1] Despite its Babylonian origins, then, the sabbath, for Baron, was to be considered a Judaeo-Christian contribution to civilization. He was careful, however, to avoid the two 'C' words 'Christianity' and 'civilization', though both were central to his thesis. Christianity was the daughter of Judaism, and civilization was, by extension, its grandchild.

A year later, as much of civilized Europe was sinking further into barbarism, the Anglo-Jewish scholar Cecil Roth, who had competed (unsuccessfully) with Baron for the chair in Jewish History at Columbia University, published *The Jewish Contribution to Civilisation*, in which, as might be expected, the sabbath was included among the various gifts imparted by his co-religionists to the civilized world—side by side with those imparted by Christianity, which he also placed within the 'Hebraic tradition'. For both Baron and Roth, writing in the years after Hitler's rise to power, Christianity itself was implicitly one of the lasting Jewish contributions to civilization, though each found a different way of conveying that timely message.

[1] Salo W. Baron, *A Social and Religious History of the Jews*, 3 vols (New York, 1937), i. 6.

'Men need a vision which gives meaning to moral striving,' wrote Roth in 1938, adding that this vision could 'take the form of one of two ideals', either that of 'a perfected social order', or that of 'a perfected individual life-style', both of which, he claimed, 'took shape in the Hebraic tradition, the former receiving more stress in Judaism, the latter in Christianity'. Although it is reasonably clear what he thought was praiseworthy in the Jewish ideal of social order, Roth prudently chose not to specify what he found superior in the Christian ideal of the 'perfected individual life-style'. To these two ideals Roth added a third, derived from 'the Old Testament', which, like the other two, still had 'a role to play' in what he called 'our civilisation'. This was the institution of the sabbath, which, he asserted, was 'nothing other than the voluntary limitation of the hours of labour, which raises man above the beasts and asserts man's moral dignity as a human being'.[2] As Roth certainly knew, a similar argument had been put forward nearly a century earlier by one of the characters in Benjamin Disraeli's novel *Tancred* (1847): 'The life and property of England are protected by the laws of Sinai. The hard-working people of England are secured in every seven days of rest by the laws of Sinai. And yet they persecute the Jews . . . to whom they are indebted for the sublime legislation which alleviates the inevitable lot of the labouring multitude.'[3]

And, as Disraeli certainly knew, his own father, Isaac D'Israeli, had asserted, in his anonymous work *The Genius of Judaism* (1833), that 'an entire cessation from all the affairs of life on each seventh day is a Jewish institution, and is not prescribed by the laws of any other people'. The latter claim had been made in response to the pan-Egyptian arguments of the great Cambridge Hebraist John Spencer (1630–93), who had suggested in his *De Legibus Hebraeorum* that the sabbath had originated with the ancient Egyptians, who passed it on, like circumcision, to the Hebrews.[4] Yet at the same time Isaac, a former member of London's Bevis Marks synagogue who in 1817 left the Anglo-Jewish community and had all four of his children—including Benjamin—baptized, expressed nothing but scorn in that same work for the 'scrupulous superstitions' that had been added by the 'Rabbinical Pharisees' to the observance of sabbath: 'What was sacred,' wrote D'Israeli (anonymously), 'they have made ridiculous.'[5] These two points raised in 1833 by the father of England's future prime minister continued to be debated, with varying degrees of immediacy and intensity, over

[2] Cecil Roth, *The Jewish Contribution to Civilisation*, 2nd edn (Oxford, 1943), 159.

[3] Quoted by Cecil Roth, *Benjamin Disraeli: Earl of Beaconsfield* (New York, 1952), 73.

[4] On Spencer, see Jan Assman, *Moses the Egyptian: The Memory of Egypt in Western Monotheism* (Cambridge, Mass., 1997), 55–79.

[5] Isaac D'Israeli, *The Genius of Judaism* (London, 1833), 126, 133. On that work and D'Israeli's earlier departure from the Bevis Marks congregation, see, among others, Jane Ridley, *The Young Disraeli* (London, 1995), 18–19.

the next dozen decades: Was the sabbath a distinctly Hebrew contribution to civilization, and did the rabbis make that day of gladness into a day of madness?

The latter claim had, as we shall see, a distinguished history in Christian scholarship on Second Temple and rabbinic Judaism. Already in the seventeenth century Spencer's older contemporary and fellow Cambridge graduate John Lightfoot (1602–75) had commented, in connection with the 'Sabbath's day journey' referred to in the book of Acts (1: 12), on the 'pleasant art' the rabbis had 'of working anything out of anything' (*fabricandi quidlibet ex quolibet*). Early in the twentieth century the British biblical scholar Samuel Rolles Driver (1846–1914) cited Lightfoot's comment in his enormously erudite (and equally ambivalent) entry on 'Sabbath' for the multi-volume *Dictionary of the Bible* edited by James Hastings. The 'Jewish legalists', Driver asserted there, 'developed and systematized' the biblical regulations respecting the sabbath 'to an extent which has made their rules on the subject a byword for extravagance and absurdity'.[6] Later in the same century, the eminent German New Testament scholar and theologian Rudolf Bultmann (1884–1976) cited the sabbath, in his *Primitive Christianity* (which originally appeared in 1949), as one of those instances in which the regulations imposed by the Pharisees 'went into detail to the point of absurdity'.[7]

Whether or not a German scholar should have had second thoughts about propagating this platitude in the aftermath of the Holocaust is not a question to be pursued here, but Bultmann's comments, no less than those of D'Israeli or Driver, indicate to what extent the sabbath was seen, for better or worse, as a synecdoche for Judaism. The sabbath's own journey among the Jews from the sublime to the ridiculous was seen as reflecting a broader narrative, and when Solomon Schechter set out heroically, in the late nineteenth century, to challenge that narrative, he did so largely by recasting the sabbath of the rabbis as 'a day of rest and joy, of pleasure and delight, a day in which man enjoys some presentiment of the pure bliss and happiness which are stored up for the righteous in the world to come'[8]—a description that Driver dutifully quoted

[6] S. R. Driver, 'Sabbath', in James Hastings (ed.), *Dictionary of the Bible*, 5 vols (New York, 1911–12), iv. 320–1. See also Marcus Jastrow, *Hebrew and Babylonian Traditions* (New York, 1914), on the 'species of casuistry' employed by the rabbis to extend the distance one might walk on the sabbath; and T. J. Meek, 'The Sabbath in the Old Testament', *Journal of Biblical Literature*, 33 (1914), 211–12, who asserted that in rabbinic times 'the Sabbath lost completely its early joyousness and festivity and came finally to be the severest kind of burden, fettered by every mannner of restriction and loaded down with ritual'.

[7] R. Bultmann, *Primitive Christianity in its Contemporary Setting*, trans. R. H. Fuller (London, 1956), 65. I thank David Berger for bringing this passage to my attention, which was brought to his attention by the late Gerson Cohen.

[8] S. Schechter, 'The Law and Recent Criticism', *Jewish Quarterly Review*, os 3 (1891), 763, repr. slightly rev. in Schechter, *Studies in Judaism*, i (Philadelphia, 1896). For the quotation, see there, p. 245.

in his aforementioned entry. This, however, did not stop Driver, who had served simultaneously as Regius Professor of Hebrew at Oxford and Canon of Christ Church since 1883, from writing in that very same entry that 'as time went on, an anxious and ultimately a superstitious dread of profaning the Sabbath asserted itself, the spiritual was subordinated to the formal, restrictions were multiplied, till at length those which were really important were buried beneath a crowd of regulations of the pettiest description'.[9]

Driver also devoted part of his entry to what he carefully called 'Speculations on the Origin of the Sabbath', wherein he reported with donnish diffidence that 'it is not improbable that the sabbath is ultimately of Babylonian origin'. When writing, as we have seen, of the subordination of the spiritual to the formal in rabbinic Judaism, the Canon of Christ Church did not hide behind such circumlocutions, but the Babylonian origins of the sabbath clearly did not sit as well with his theological convictions—or those of his imagined audience, before whom he felt comfortable referring to Jesus as 'Our Lord'.[10] Moreover, as a British Protestant he may well have felt a particular bond with the sabbath. 'There are few things in ecclesiastical history more remarkable', the Irish essayist and historian William Lecky had memorably written in 1896, 'than the speed and power with which the Puritan doctrine of the Sabbath pervaded British Protestantism'[11]—a subject to which we shall return. Nonetheless, as a responsible Semitic scholar he could not simply ignore the results of the past several decades of archaeological and philological research.

ISRAEL VERSUS BABYLONIA

Already in the 1870s the British Assyriologist George Smith, one of the first scholars to decipher the cuneiform tablets found at Nineveh, reported that he had recently discovered 'a curious religious calendar of the Assyrians, in which every month is divided into four weeks, and the seventh days, or "Sabbaths" are marked out as days on which no work should be undertaken'.[12] Although Smith died tragically in 1876, at the age of 36, the torch of Assyriological Studies in England was soon picked up by Archibald Sayce of Oxford (1845–1933), who published a panoply of popular books on the ancient Near East, some of which were published by the Religious Tract Society. In *Assyria: Its Princes, Priests, and Peoples*, first published in 1885, he asserted that 'the very name of Sabattu, or Sabbath, was employed by the

[9] Driver, 'Sabbath', 321–2.

[10] Ibid. 319, 322.

[11] W. E. H. Lecky, *Democracy and Liberty*, 2 vols (New York, 1896), ii. 106.

[12] G. Smith, *Assyrian Discoveries: An Account of the Explorations and Discoveries on the Site of Nineveh*, 2nd edn (London, 1875), 12.

Assyrians, and is defined as "a day of rest for the heart"'. This 'Sabbath', Sayce explained in his *Social Life Among the Assyrians and Babylonians* (1893), was observed five times each month (on the seventh, fourteenth, nineteenth, twenty-first, and twenty-eighth) 'and on it all kinds of work were disallowed'. The sabbath on the nineteenth, he explained in *Babylonians and Assyrians* (1899), marked 'the end of the seventh week from the first day of the previous month'. On all five of these sabbaths, he again asserted, 'no work was permitted to be done'.[13] Sayce had by then risen from Deputy Professor of Philology at Oxford (1876–90) to become (in 1891) the university's first Professor of Assyriology, which may explain why he was emboldened in his next popular work, *The Religions of Egypt and Babylonia* (1902), to state explicitly what had been merely implicit in the previous ones, namely that 'the Sabbath rest was essentially of Babylonian origin'.[14]

Sayce's unequivocating boldness in attributing the origins of the sabbath rest to ancient Babylonia may be contrasted with the more tentative position of his learned colleague Samuel Driver, who had been chosen over him, partially for reasons of purported orthodoxy, for the coveted Regius Professorship of Hebrew at Oxford. Just before Christmas of 1881, perhaps in anticipation of the death of the octogenarian E. P. Pusey, who had been Regius Professor of Hebrew and Canon of Christ Church (the two positions were customarily linked) since 1828, Driver was ordained a deacon by the Bishop of Salisbury. A year later, following the passing of Pusey—who had been famously hostile to German biblical scholarship—Driver was ordained an Anglican priest in Salisbury, thus allowing him to be admitted in July of 1883 as Canon of Christ Church and to assume his professorship at Oxford.[15]

In an essay published in 1899 entitled 'Hebrew Authority', Driver conceded that it was 'difficult not to agree' with such Assyriologists as Sayce

[13] A. H. Sayce, *Assyria: Its Princes, Priests, and Peoples*, 2nd edn (London, 1926), 92; id., *Lectures on the Origin and Growth of Religion as Illustrated by the Religion of the Ancient Babylonians* (London, 1887), 76–7; id., *Social Life among the Assyrians and Babylonians* (London, 1893), 121; id., *Babylonians and Assyrians: Life and Customs* (London, 1899), 245. For the critical reaction of the French Jewish orientalist Joseph Halévy to Sayce's argument about the Babylonian origins of the sabbath, see Halévy, 'La Religion des anciens babyloniens et son plus récent historien M. Sayce', *Revue de l'Histoire des Religions*, 9/1 (1888), 184. For the reaction of Ahad Ha'am (Asher Ginzberg), see the essays from *Hashiloaḥ* reprinted in *Kol kitvei aḥad ha'am* (Tel Aviv, 1947), 286–7, 301–3, and S. J. Zipperstein, *Elusive Prophet: Ahad Ha'am and the Origins of Zionism* (Berkeley, 1993), 127.

[14] A. H. Sayce, *The Religions of Egypt and Babylonia* (Edinburgh, 1902), 476. On Sayce and his career, see his autobiography, *Reminiscences* (London, 1923), and the necrological essay by Stephen Langdon, 'Archibald Henry Sayce as Assyriologist', *Journal of the Royal Asiatic Society of Great Britain and Ireland for 1933* (1933), 499–503.

[15] On Driver, see J. A. Emerton, 'Samuel Rolles Driver', in C. E. Bosworth (ed.), *A Century of British Orientalists, 1902–2001* (Oxford, 2001).

who saw 'the week of seven days, ended by the sabbath, as an institution of Babylonian origin'. Yet it was clearly important for the Canon of Christ Church to add that, in contrast to the Babylonians, for whom the seventh day had primarily mystical and superstitious associations, the Hebrews had divested the sabbath 'of its heathen associations and made it subservient to ethical and religious ends'. Driver, however, had by that point demonstrated (to the probable dismay of the departed Pusey) that he was fundamentally in agreement with the methods and assumptions of German biblical scholarship, and thus he noted, less piously, that if the sabbath did indeed originate in Babylonia, 'its sanctity is explained unhistorically' in the book of Genesis:

> Instead of the sabbath, closing the week, being sacred because God rested upon it after His six days' work of Creation, the work of Creation was distributed among six days, followed by a day of rest, *because* the week, ended by the Sabbath, already existed as an institution, and the writer wished to adjust artificially the work of Creation to it.[16]

In 1899, the year in which Driver's essay appeared, the Germans, who had previously lagged behind the British and French in archaeological research—and thus had less non-literary material for orientalists to study—initiated their first excavations (at Babylon), sponsored by the German Oriental Society and under the auspices of Kaiser Wilhelm II. One of the founders of the Oriental Society was Friedrich Delitzsch (1850–1922) of Berlin, who in January of 1902, shortly after returning from a review of the Mesopotamian excavations, delivered before its members the first of his 'Babel und Bibel' lectures. Their stated purpose was 'to show in how many and various questions of a geographical, historical, chronological, linguistic, and archaeological type Babylon proves itself an interpreter and illustrator of the Bible'. On 1 February the first lecture was repeated, at the Kaiser's request, at the royal palace in Berlin.[17]

'What is the reason for these efforts in remote, inhospitable, and dangerous lands?', asked Delitzsch in his opening paragraph. 'What is the reason

[16] S. R. Driver, 'Hebrew Authority', in D. G. Hogarth (ed.), *Authority and Archaeology, Sacred and Profane: Essays on the Relation of Monuments to Biblical and Classical Literature* (London, 1899), 17–18. Both the emphasis and the sometimes puzzling orthography (one 'Sabbath' capitalized and the other not; 'Creation' capitalized but not 'writer') appear in the original. For an attempt by an American Jewish scholar to distinguish between the Babylonian sabbath and that of the Hebrews, which he saw as having emerged independently, see Morris Jastrow, 'The Original Character of the Hebrew Sabbath', *American Journal of Theology*, 2 (1898), 312–52; id., 'The Hebrew and Babylonian Accounts of Creation', *Jewish Quarterly Review*, OS 8 (1901), 649.

[17] See H. B. Huffmon, '*Babel und Bibel*: The Encounter between Babylon and the Bible', in M. P. O'Connor and D. N. Freedman (eds), *Backgrounds for the Bible* (Winona Lake, Ind., 1987), 125–6; M. T. Larsen, 'The "Babel/Bibel" Controversy and its Aftermath', in Jack Sasson (ed.), *Civilizations of the Ancient Near East*, i (New York, 1995), 95 ff.

for the competition among nations to secure excavation rights to these deserted mounds, and the more the better?' To these and other questions about the 'ever-increasing, self-sacrificing interest, on both sides of the Atlantic', allotted to the excavations in Mesopotamia, Delitzsch asserted that there was 'one answer . . . which points to what is for the most part the motive and the goal'. That answer, in a word, was 'the Bible'.[18] However, as Herbert Huffmon and others have noted, in the course of the first lecture it became clear that Delitzsch was interested not merely in 'parallels between Babylonia and the Bible', but, rather, in establishing the former as 'the source of many of the key ideas and institutions in the Bible'.[19] Thus, regarding the sabbath, he asserted in the first lecture that 'the Babylonians also had a Sabbath day, on which, for the purpose of conciliating the gods, there was a festival—that is to say, no work was to be done'. Delitzsch added that 'it is scarcely possible for us to doubt that we owe the blessings decreed in the Sabbath or Sunday rest, in the last resort, to that ancient and civilized race on the Euphrates and the Tigris'—as opposed, it was clearly implied, to that considerably less civilized race of former nomads in Palestine.[20]

Although the views expressed by Delitzsch in his lectures were not, at base, fundamentally different from those that British colleagues, such as Sayce, had been expressing for over a decade, they were presented in a far more provocative manner. In the preface to the second lecture Delitzsch wrote, for example, that the deeper he immersed himself 'in the spirit of the prophetic literature of the Old Testament, the greater becomes my mistrust of Yahweh, who butchers the peoples with the sword of his insatiable anger; who has but one favorite child, while he consigns all other nations to darkness, shame, and ruin'.[21] The distinguished German historian Edouard Meyer, after hearing the second lecture, wrote to a colleague that Delitzsch had demonstrated 'the religious, political, and intellectual inferiority of the Old Testament with such vigor as I would never have expected'.[22] As may be expected, there were hundreds of responses to the published 'Babel und Bibel' lectures, especially after the first two were translated into six other European languages—English, Italian, Danish, Swedish, Hungarian, and Czech.[23]

[18] Quoted by Huffmon, '*Babel und Bibel*', 127; Larsen, 'The "Babel/Bibel" Controversy', 97. The first two lectures appeared in English in 1903 in two separate translations, one by C. H. W. Johns, and the other by T. J. McCormack and W. H. Carruth.

[19] Huffmon, '*Babel und Bibel*', 128. See also, more recently, B. T. Arnold and D. B. Weisberg, 'A Centennial Review of Friedrich Delitzsch's *Babel und Bibel* Lectures', *Journal of Biblical Literature*, 121 (2002), 441–57; Yaacov Shavit and Mordecai Eran, *The War of the Tablets* (Heb.) (Tel Aviv, 2003).

[20] F. Delitzsch, *Babel and Bible*, ed. C. H. W. Johns (New York, 1903), 40–1.

[21] Quoted by Huffmon, '*Babel und Bibel*', 130.

[22] Quoted by Larsen, 'The "Babel/Bibel" Controversy', 101.

[23] Huffmon, '*Babel und Bibel*', 132.

KOHLER, SCHECHTER, MONTEFIORE

One of the few immediate responses by a Jewish scholar was that by the American Reform rabbi Kaufmann Kohler (1843–1923) in his essay 'Assyriology and the Bible', which he published in 1903, the same year in which he was appointed president of the Hebrew Union College. The Bavarian-born Kohler, who had also been educated in Germany, had previously served congregations in Chicago (where he introduced Sunday services in 1874), Detroit, and New York. In his 1903 essay, which was published in the *Yearbook of the Central Conference of American Rabbis*, Kohler responded primarily to the recently published lectures of Delitzsch, including his comments regarding the sabbath. He was willing to concede that although 'convincing proof' had not yet been adduced, 'it may be assumed as certain that the Sabbath, as a day of rest, originated in Babylonia'. However, Kohler argued that the sabbath of the Babylonians and the sabbath of the Hebrews were fundamentally different institutions. The former, he asserted, 'was a day of fear and gloom . . . observed only as a day on which no work should be undertaken by king or priest from dread of the unlucky seven stars'. The Jewish sabbath, by contrast, 'was rendered a day of rejoicing and uplifting for the people, for both master and servant, man and beast', and was thus 'a real day of God'.[24]

This description of the Jewish sabbath would seem to echo the writings of two of Kohler's contemporaries, Solomon Schechter, whom he had met in Cambridge shortly prior to the latter's recent arrival in New York to head the (Conservative) Jewish Theological Seminary,[25] and Schechter's friend, student, and benefactor Claude Goldsmid Montefiore, whom Kohler had presumably also met during his 1901 visit to England. In 1891 Schechter had published a powerfully polemical essay in the recently founded *Jewish Quarterly Review*, co-edited by Montefiore and Israel Abrahams, in which he used the sabbath as a 'fair example' of the way in which scholars of early Christianity commonly presented Jewish life 'under the Law' when the latter was still understood in its onerously literal sense.

This day [he wrote] is described by almost every modern writer in the most gloomy colours, and long lists are given of the minute observances connected with it, easily to be transgressed, which would necessarily make of the Sabbath, instead of a day of rest, a day of sorrow and anxiety, almost worse than the Scotch Sunday as depicted by continental writers.[26]

[24] K. Kohler, 'Assyriology and the Bible', *Yearbook of the Central Conference of American Rabbis*, 13 (1903), 110–11.

[25] See Solomon Schechter, 'Higher Criticism—Higher Anti-Semitism', in Schechter, *Seminary Addresses and Other Papers*, ed. Louis Finkelstein (New York, 1959), 35.

[26] See above, n. 8.

Among the 'modern writers' Schechter had in mind was certainly Emil Schürer of Göttingen, author of a multi-volume *History of the Jewish People in the Time of Jesus Christ* (originally published in German, 1874) that included an infamous chapter entitled 'Life under the Law'.[27] But it is likely that he was also thinking of his recently deceased former co-religionist Alfred Edersheim (1825–89), who had been born a Jew in Vienna but had become first a Presbyterian divine, serving for twelve years as minister of Aberdeen's Free Church, and finally an Episcopalian priest in England. It was during his years as vicar of Loders (in Dorset) that Edersheim completed his popular two-volume study *The Life and Times of Jesus the Messiah* (1883), which contained a long appendix entitled 'The Ordinances and Law of the Sabbath as Laid Down in the Mishnah and the Jerusalem Talmud'. Edersheim, perhaps thinking also of his Viennese youth, referred to the 'terribly exaggerated views of the Rabbis, and their endless, burdensome rules about the Sabbath', which ultimately 'changed the spiritual import of its rest into a complicated code of external and burdensome ordinances'.[28]

In contrast to the assertions of such Protestant scholars as Schürer and Edersheim, Schechter stressed that 'the Sabbath is celebrated by the very people who did observe it in hundreds of hymns . . . as a day of rest and joy, of pleasure and delight'.[29] Kohler, in describing the Babylonian sabbath as a day of 'fear and gloom', seems to have simply transposed the negative depiction of the Jewish sabbath countered by Schechter in his 1891 essay (which had since been reprinted in his *Studies in Judaism*), and in describing the Hebrew sabbath as, by contrast, 'a day of rejoicing' he seems to have drawn upon Schechter's by then classic essay as well.

Kohler's emphasis upon the Jewish sabbath as applying to both 'master and servant, man and beast' would seem to echo the comments of Montefiore in his *Bible for Home Reading*, first published in 1896. In that immensely popular work the Balliol-educated liberal theologian discussed the Fourth Commandment from both human and divine perspectives. From the former perspective he saw it, coming as he did from a wealthy and aristocratic family, as a kind of *noblesse oblige*:

> People who have the full and unimpeded control of their own lives and actions might, if they please, make a day of rest for themselves, but those who are the

[27] See Israel Abrahams, 'Professor Schürer on Life under Jewish Law', *Jewish Quarterly Review*, OS 11 (1898–9), 626–42; Elliott Horowitz, '*Jewish Life in the Middle Ages* and the Jewish Life of Israel Abrahams', in D. N. Myers and D. B. Ruderman (eds), *The Jewish Past Revisited: Reflections on Modern Jewish Historians* (New Haven, 1998), 145–6.

[28] A. Edersheim, *The Life and Times of Jesus the Messiah*, American edn (repr. Grand Rapids, Mich., 1950), ii. 52, 777–87. On Edersheim, see S. R. Driver, 'Edersheim, Alfred', in *Dictionary of National Biography*, xxii, suppl. 1 (London, 1901), 600–1.

[29] See above, n. 8.

servants of others, employed by them in their houses or shops or offices or factories, whose lives and actions are not wholly under their own control and disposal . . . could not, even if they wished it, make such an arrangement for themselves. So here the Sabbath law steps in and seeks to make an arrangement for them. No diviner enactment has ever been given than this rule of one day's rest in seven.[30]

Montefiore stressed, furthermore, that part of the sabbath's divine character lay in its separation of man from machines, on the one hand, and beasts, on the other, neither of which had control over their own time.[31] He was also eager to point out that the biblically enjoined sabbath rest not only separated man from animals but also extended to the latter, 'without whose strength and endurance and ability our civilization would never have come to be what it is'.[32] This characteristic of the biblical sabbath, as well as its application to both master and servant, would later be stressed by Kohler in his 1903 reply to Delitzsch.

In that same year Morris Joseph published his *Judaism as Creed and Life*. Joseph, one of the few Anglo-Jewish clergyman who moved in both traditional and liberal circles,[33] stressed the benefits of the sabbath for both humans and beasts. 'No one can go on toiling uninterruptedly day after day and year after year without impairing sooner or later his powers of body or mind,' wrote the Revd Joseph. 'Rest is essential to health, and its good effects are most marked when it is periodical, when it comes at regular intervals. This is, doubtless, the great secret of the power of the Sabbath as a restorer of our jaded energies.' He noted, as had Montefiore, that its 'merciful character' extended also to the 'toiling animals', taking the opportunity to stress that this was 'one of many examples of that tender consideration for the brute which the Hebrew Bible, almost alone among ancient religious codes, so consistently displays'.[34]

Another feature that the presentations of the sabbath by Montefiore and Joseph had in common was their stress, in the wake of Schechter's influential essay, upon its character as a day of joy and delight. 'The Sabbath', wrote the

[30] C. G. Montefiore, *The Bible for Home Reading*, 2 vols (London, 1909), i. 86.

[31] 'The Sabbath is one of the glories of our humanity. For if to labour is noble, of our own free will to pause in that labour . . . may be nobler still. Ants and bees labour, but the ants and bees have no Sabbath. To dedicate one day a week to rest and to God, this is the prerogative and privilege of man alone' (ibid. 89).

[32] Ibid. 86.

[33] Joseph's wife had been one of the four friends who reviewed Montefiore's book before its publication. On Joseph, see David Cesarani, *The Jewish Chronicle and Anglo-Jewry, 1841–1991* (Cambridge, 1994), 92.

[34] M. Joseph, *Judaism as Creed and Life*, 2nd edn (London, 1910), 153. The Revd Joseph's eagerness to stress 'that tender consideration for the brute' in Jewish tradition may well have been a response to the report of the Admiralty Committee on Humane Slaughtering which was highly critical of *shehitah*. See V. D. Lipman, *Social History of the Jews in England, 1850–1950* (London, 1954), 125–6; Cesarani, *The Jewish Chronicle and Anglo-Jewry*, 110.

former, 'is called in the Bible a day of delight. Now pure inaction is not delight, except to some very hard-worked persons. So our rest must be so spent that it is delightful.'[35] And Joseph, whose popular book was also reprinted many times, pointed out that the rabbis, too, were interested not merely in defining the forms of prohibited work, but also in emphasizing the 'higher character' of the sabbath. 'For them,' he wrote, 'it is a day of joy, a day, above all, of religious joy . . . a foretaste of heaven.'[36]

All three of these authors—Montefiore, Joseph, and Kohler—alluded, in writing about the sabbath, to Schechter's revisionist essay of 1891, which, as we shall see, had an impact upon Christian writers as well. But neither of the first two made any attempt to engage recent claims about the Babylonian origins of the sabbath, although in their own country such claims had circulated widely since 1875, and Kohler, who devoted an entire essay to 'Assyriology and the Bible', published it 'in house' (in the *Yearbook of the Central Conference of American Rabbis*), rather than in a periodical such as the *Journal of Biblical Literature* that non-Jewish scholars such as Sayce and Delitzsch could hardly ignore.

In March 1903 Solomon Schechter, speaking at a banquet held in Kohler's honour shortly after his appointment as president of the (rival) Hebrew Union College in Cincinnati, famously attacked 'higher' biblical criticism as 'higher anti-Semitism'. He claimed, furthermore, without referring explicitly to Delitzsch, that it had 'reached its climax' in the more recent trend (associated with the latter) in which 'every discovery . . . is called to bear witness against us and to accuse us of spiritual larceny'. Schechter saw this denigration of Hebrew originality as 'denying all our claims for the past, and leaving us without hope for the future'. The Bible, he asserted dramatically, 'is our patent of nobility granted to us by the Almighty God, and if we disown the Bible . . . the world will disown us'. It was therefore necessary to fight fire with fire. 'This intellectual persecution', exhorted the newly appointed president of the Jewish Theological Seminary, 'can only be fought by intellectual weapons', and it was necessary, consequently, to make a serious effort not only 'to recover our Bible' but also to rethink Jewish theology:

> A mere protest in the pulpit or a vigorous editorial in a paper, or an amateur essay in a monthly, or even a special monograph will not help us. We have to create a really living, great literature, and to do the same for the subjects of theology and the Bible that Europe has done for Jewish history and philology.

Yet although Schechter gallantly used the pronoun 'we', his clear intention was to hit the ball (a metaphor he would not have liked) into his competitor's court.

[35] Montefiore, *The Bible for Home Reading*, i. 87. [36] Joseph, *Judaism as Creed and Life*, 155.

He hailed Kohler's election 'as a happy event in the annals of American Jewry' and expressed his confidence that under the latter's guidance 'Cincinnati, will, in good time, contribute its share to this great "battle of duty".'[37]

THE SABBATH IN ANGLO-AMERICAN SCHOLARSHIP

In fact, however, although serious and sustained efforts were made by Jewish scholars to show that 'life under the Law', including the laws of the sabbath, was hardly devoid of joy and spirituality, until the rise of Nazism in the 1930s they made only lame and sporadic efforts to reclaim the sabbath as the exclusive contribution of the Hebrews to Western civilization. Those who did rise to the challenge during the early years of the twentieth century were typically Protestant orientalists such as Albert Clay of the University of Pennsylvania, who in 1909 published *Amurru, the Home of the Northern Semites*, based on a series of lectures he had delivered at the Protestant Episcopal Theological Seminary in Virginia. Although Clay's title suggested another soporific Semitic monograph, his polemical subtitle (*A Study Showing that the Religion and Culture of Israel Are Not of Babylonian Origin*) clearly signalled that the Pennsylvania professor was squaring off for a fight. 'The Sabbath as a day of rest, observed every seven days, has not been found', Clay emphatically asserted, 'in the Babylonian literature.' Moreover, he wrote at the end of his chapter on the sabbath, 'knowing what this institution was to the Hebrew . . . a day of consecration . . . a day of rest for slave, stranger, and even the beast', and bearing in mind that 'it was an institution without parallel in ancient as well as modern times', it seemed evident 'that the Pan-Babylonists, and others who hold similar views, are mistaken when they find the origin of the institution in Babylonia'.[38]

Some scholars, such as Charles Foster Kent of Yale, argued that it was more probable that the Jews inherited the sabbath 'from the agricultural Canaanites' than from the Babylonians. Ultimately, however, in Kent's view, the origins of the sabbath were to be 'traced back to those nomadic ancestors of the Hebrews and Canaanites, who paid chief homage to the moon, whose benign light guided them in their night journeys over the plains of Northern Arabia'.[39] During the early years of the twentieth century a somewhat differ-

[37] Schechter, 'Higher Criticism—Higher Anti-Semitism', 36–8.

[38] A. T. Clay, *Amurru, the Home of the Northern Semites* (Philadelphia, 1909), 61–2. See also Jastrow, *Hebrew and Babylonian Traditions*, 154, who in 1914 reiterated his earlier expressed view (see above, n. 16) that 'the Hebrew Sabbath is an expression of religious ideas and of a conception of divine government utterly distinct from that which we find in the religion of Babylonia and Assyria'.

[39] C. F. Kent, *Israel's Laws and Legal Precedents: From the Days of Moses to the Closing of the Legal Canon* (New York, 1907), 257. This view was later seconded by Meek; see 'The Sabbath in the Old Testament', 201–2.

ent 'lunar theory' of the sabbath's origins was advanced by the German scholars Heinrich Zimmern and Johannes Meinhold, particularly in the latter's *Sabbat und Woche im Alten Testament* (1905).[40] According to this theory, the sabbath was originally a full-moon day among the ancient Babylonians, and in that form was absorbed by the Hebrews, who in post-exilic times transformed it into a weekly observance. Yet even some who accepted this lunar theory, such as the Swiss scholar Karl Marti of Berne, nevertheless stressed that by adding the notion of 'absolute rest' to the Babylonian sabbath the Hebrews gave it 'an entirely different character'.[41]

The counter-attack of Clay and others upon the pan-Babylonists evidently had an impact upon Samuel Driver of Oxford, who in his entry on the sabbath for the *Dictionary of the Bible* dithered, as we have seen, even more donnishly than he had in his 1899 essay 'Hebrew Authority'. Whereas in that earlier essay he had asserted that the sabbath was 'in all probability an institution ultimately of Babylonian origin', a dozen years later, in his entry on the sabbath, this was demoted by Driver to 'at least a plausible conjecture'.[42]

Why was the possible, or probable, Babylonian origin of the sabbath so painful a subject for Driver, driving him to seek refuge in such prim circumlocutions as 'it is difficult not to agree' or 'it is not improbable'? For one, Professor Driver, as noted above, was also Canon Driver, and although 'the Jewish sabbath', as he wrote, 'like other Jewish ceremonial observances . . . was abrogated under the Christian dispensation', it had originally, even according to liberal Anglican belief, been part of the divinely inspired Decalogue—not developed by what Delitzsch had called 'that ancient and civilized race on the Euphrates and the Tigris'. Furthermore, the special role played by the sabbath (observed on Sunday) in British life—as noted by Disraeli and others—may have heightened the intuitive sense on Driver's part that it was, at base, a biblical rather than Babylonian institution.

The Calvinist Scots, of course, had always been strict about observing Sunday as a sabbath,[43] but during the nineteenth century English Sabbatarianism had increased in power and influence. In 1831 the Lord's Day

[40] Johannes Meinhold, *Sabbat und Woche im Alten Testament* (Göttingen, 1905). For Zimmern, see his contribution to Eberhard Schrader, *Die Keilinschriften und das Alte Testament*, ed. H. Zimmern and H. Winckler, 3rd edn (Berlin, 1903), 592–94.

[41] K. Marti, *The Religion of the Old Testament*, trans. G. A. Bienemann (London, 1907), 15. See also Meek, 'Sabbath in the Old Testament', 201; Karl Budde, 'The Old Testament and the Excavations', *American Journal of Theology*, 6 (1902), 685–708; id., 'The Sabbath and the Week', *Journal of Theological Studies*, 30 (1928), 8.

[42] Driver, 'Sabbath', 319.

[43] The Scottish barrister William Rae Wilson (1772–1849), who early in the 1820s found himself in Marseilles on his way to the Holy Land, wrote that it was 'lamentable to find in this place, that on the Lord's day, as in other parts of the Continent which I have visited, the Catholics gave themselves to all kinds of sensual gratification; in fact, every species of folly, buffoonery, and amusement was indulged in' (William Rae Wilson, *Travels in the Holy Land: Egypt*, 3rd edn, 2 vols (London, 1831), i. 3).

Observance Society was founded by Anglican evangelicals, whose major successes came, however, just after mid-century. In 1854 the Wilson-Patten Act was passed, which closed English drinking places on Sunday between 2.30 and 6 p.m., and again after ten in the evening (they were already closed all day in 'dry' Scotland). Two years later both the British Museum and the National Gallery were closed on Sundays—a policy that remained in effect for forty years.[44]

In 1855 the Sunday Trading Bill forbade all Sunday trading in London, with the exception of meat and fish sold before 9 a.m., and newspapers and cooked food sold before 10 a.m.[45] Although the bill had negative consequences for many English Jews, Abraham Benisch, the Bohemian-born editor of the *Jewish Chronicle*, initially urged political cooperation between Jews and the Protestant Dissenters who were promoting Sabbatarian legislation. During the following decade, however, as Scottish Sabbatarians increasingly claimed the authority of Jewish tradition for abstinence from work on Sunday, Benisch devoted four consecutive editorials in early 1866 to combating the movement. In the last of them he wrote: 'If the controversy on the Sabbath is to be continued, let the disputants either altogether abstain from unnecessarily dragging in Jews and Judaism, or, if references to them be expedient, let them be represented in their true light.'[46]

Three decades later the influential essayist and historian William Lecky wrote confidently that

> No one who knows England will doubt that the existence of an enforced holiday, primarily devoted to religious worship, has contributed enormously to strengthen the moral fibre of the nation, to give depth, seriousness, and sobriety to the national character, and to save it from being wholly sunk in selfish pursuits and material aims.[47]

And precisely three decades later the Cambridge historian G. M. Trevelyan, who had almost certainly read Lecky, commented in his monumental *History of England* on the relatively strict observance of Sunday in that country (as

[44] Brian Harrison, 'The Sunday Trading Riots of 1855', *Historical Journal*, 8 (1965), 220; James Obelkevich, 'Religion', in F. M. L. Thompson (ed.), *The Cambridge Social History of Britain, 1750–1950*, 3 vols (Cambridge, 1990), iii. 346; D. A. Reid, 'Playing and Praying', in M. Daunton (ed.), *The Cambridge Urban History of Britain*, iii (Cambridge, 2000), 752. Lecky had noted in 1892 that the Vice-President of the Council of Education, who was in favour of Sunday openings of museums, replied to a deputation: 'I understand that in Birmingham certain persons of the Jewish denomination, who have their Sabbath on the Saturday . . . give their services on what to them is a week-day, for the purpose of assisting in the museum and library' (Lecky, *Democracy and Liberty*, ii. 117 n. 1). This may be the first recorded instance of a 'Sunday Jew'!

[45] Harrison, 'The Sunday Trading Riots', 221.

[46] See Cesarani, *The Jewish Chronicle and Anglo-Jewry*, 37, and the sources cited there, as well as L. P. Gartner, *The Jewish Immigrant in England, 1870–1914* (Detroit, 1960), 62.

[47] Lecky, *Democracy and Liberty*, ii. 112.

opposed to the Continent), and observed that 'the good and ill effects of this self-imposed discipline of a whole nation, in abstaining from organized amusement as well as from work on every seventh day, still awaits the dispassionate study of the social historian'.[48] It would appear that the effects of that 'self-imposed discipline' have some relevance also for the intellectual historian. The difference between Britain and the Continent with regard to abstaining from 'organized amusement' and similar pleasures had also been evident, as we have seen, to Solomon Schechter, who noted acerbically that the rabbinic sabbath 'is described by almost every modern writer' in such a manner that it made it seem 'almost worse than the Scotch Sunday as depicted by continental writers'.[49]

Schechter's revisionist essay had an impact not only on Driver, as we have seen, but also on his own Cambridge colleague William Robertson Smith (1846–94), who, together with his student and successor Stanley Cook, composed the entry on the sabbath for the justly celebrated eleventh edition of the *Encyclopaedia Britannica.* The rabbinic sabbath, they wrote, 'observed in accordance with the rules of the Scribes, was a very peculiar institution, and formed one of the most marked distinctions between the Hebrews and other nations'. One of its most 'peculiar' features was the enumeration of 'thirty-nine main kinds of work forbidden on the Sabbath, and each of these prohibitions gave rise to new subtleties'. Citing Schechter's essay, however, they stated quite unequivocally that 'In actual life the Sabbath was often far from being the burden which the Rabbinical enactments would have led us to expect.'[50]

Late in the second decade of the twentieth century Israel Abrahams, who had taken over Schechter's readership at Cambridge upon the latter's departure for New York,[51] contributed the section 'Sabbath (Jewish)' to the multipartite entry on the sabbath in the monumental *Encyclopaedia of Religion and Ethics* edited by James Hastings. Abrahams, who had also been co-editor of the *Jewish Quarterly Review* when Schechter's essay 'The Law and Recent Criticism' originally appeared there in 1891, stressed the role of that essay in dispelling the stereotypical notion of the rabbinic sabbath. 'The idea that the Sabbath was felt as a burden has no foundation whatsoever,' he wrote, adding that 'once and for all this misconception was dispelled by S. Schechter'.[52]

[48] Quoted by D. S. Katz, *Sabbath and Sectarianism in Seventeenth-Century England* (Oxford, 1988), 6 n. 27.

[49] See above, n. 8.

[50] W. Robertson Smith and S. A. Cook, 'Sabbath', in *Encyclopaedia Britannica*, 11th edn, xxiii (Cambridge, 1911). Schechter's essay is also quoted by Hutton Webster, *Rest Days: A Study in Early Law and Morality* (New York, 1916), 265–6.

[51] On this subject, see most recently D. B. Starr, 'The Importance of Being Frank: Solomon Schechter's Departure from Cambridge', *Jewish Quarterly Review*, 94 (2004), 12–18.

[52] Israel Abrahams, 'Sabbath (Jewish)', in James Hastings (ed.), *Encyclopaedia of Religion and Ethics*, x (Edinburgh, 1919), 892.

A few years earlier Morris Jastrow of the University of Pennsylvania was invited to deliver the Haskell Lectures at Oberlin College. Jastrow (1861–1922), who was the son of a noted Philadelphia rabbi and had done his doctorate at Leipzig, devoted one of the five lectures to 'the Hebrew and Babylonian Sabbath'. Although the scope of the lectures, published in 1914 under the title *Hebrew and Babylonian Traditions*, did not suggest that talmudic Judaism would be treated, Jastrow made a point of stressing that 'we must be careful not to conclude from the elaborate discussions in the Talmud as to the precise manner in which detailed observances had to be carried out, that the spiritual influence of the Sabbath was lost upon its pious observers'. He also emphasized, albeit somewhat sermonizingly, the Hebrew sabbath's relevance for modern man in that 'it gives to labour a dignity that places it far above the merely material necessity or the desire for material gain, and thus directs man to the path along which he is to proceed to reach his destined goal'.[53] Apologetics of this sort became increasingly common, as we shall see, in the early decades of the twentieth century.

Schechter's revisionist portrayal of the rabbinic sabbath was influentially echoed in George Foot Moore's pioneering study *Judaism in the First Centuries of the Christian Era* (1927–30). Moore, who had gone to Harvard in 1902—the same year in which Schechter went to New York's Jewish Theological Seminary—adhered closely to the latter's views, both on the nature of the sabbath and on the skewed presentation of Judaism by Christian scholars. He described the sabbath of the rabbis as a day 'of recreation and good cheer' that also allowed ample room for 'religious instruction and edification'. He then added, in a clear nod to Schechter (whom he had movingly eulogized), that it would be 'a stupendous error to concentrate attention on the micrologic casuistry of external restrictions . . . ignoring the real significance of the day for religion itself'.[54]

RABBIS AND LABOUR LEADERS IN ALLIANCE

Ironically, however, just as the tarnished reputation of the rabbinic sabbath was being restored by renowned Ivy League professors, American rabbis of various denominations were waking up to the fact that, as one of them, Israel Herbert Levinthal, frankly acknowledged in 1925, 'we have lost our

[53] Jastrow, *Hebrew and Babylonian Traditions*, 191, 194.

[54] G. F. Moore, *Judaism in the First Centuries of the Christian Era*, 3 vols (Cambridge, Mass., 1927–30), ii. 39. For Moore's high estimate of Schechter and his work, see 'Solomon Schechter: Scholar and Humanist', *Menorah Journal*, 2 (1916), 1–6. On Moore's work and its influence, see the cantankerous but nonetheless valuable essay by Jacob Neusner, '"Judaism" after Moore: A Programmatic Statement', *Journal of Jewish Studies*, 31 (1980), 141–56.

Sabbath'.[55] In that same year representatives of Orthodox, Reform, and Conservative organizations met in New York for the purpose of furthering 'the five-day week in American industry'. The Vilna-born and Columbia-educated Levinthal, who had been rabbi of the (Conservative) Brooklyn Jewish Center since 1919, and his colleagues in the Interdenominational Committee established by the Jewish Sabbath Alliance of America joined forces with labour leaders who were working towards the 'progressive shortening of the hours of labor', and presented the sabbath in light of those aims. 'I can see but one way to save the Sabbath for the Jew,' Levinthal told the *New York Times* in 1925, 'and that is through the establishment of the five-day week,' which, he claimed, he would favour even if he were not interested in preserving the Jewish sabbath, 'because it would add health and strength to the American people. It would promote the home and home life, giving the father added opportunity to become more acquainted with . . . his children.'[56]

A decade earlier Levinthal's Orthodox colleague (and fellow Columbia graduate) Bernard Drachman of Manhattan's Oheb Zedek congregation, who was president both of the Jewish Sabbath Alliance and of the Union of Orthodox Jewish Congregations, had presented the case for a five-day working week before a convention of Christians in Oakland, California. This was particularly difficult terrain, since, as Drachman acknowledged, many Christians had supported 'blue laws' in various states prohibiting the conduct of business on Sundays, making Jewish sabbath observance particularly difficult. Yet Drachman, who after Columbia had earned a doctorate at Heidelberg, proved himself quite equal to the task, appealing, on the one hand, to his audience's belief in the importance of protecting religious freedom and, on the other, to its fear, in the period framed by the Haymarket Affair of 1886 and the Sacco and Vanzetti case of 1920, of godless anarchism gaining force in America. 'How', he asked, 'can an American state say to its citizens of Hebrew faith: "You must revere and observe the day consecrated to the memorial of the resurrection of the Nazarene." Yet this is exactly what it is doing when it compels the observance of Sunday by Jews.' Playing to the fears of his conservative Christian audience shortly after Eugene Debs, who

[55] Quoted (from the *New York Times*, 10 Jan. 1925) by B. K. Hunnicutt, 'The Jewish Sabbath Movement in the Early Twentieth Century', *American Jewish Historical Quarterly*, 69 (1979–80), 197. Levinthal had argued that 'if we see Jewish life crumbling before our eyes in America it is mainly due to the fact that we have lost our Sabbath'. On the connection between sabbath and Jewish survival, see also the 1898 essay by Ahad Ha'am, 'Shabat vetsiyonut', *Kol kitvei aḥad ha'am*, 286–7, and H. N. Bialik's 1929 speech in Tel Aviv, published posthumously in id., *Devarim shebe'al peh*, 2 vols (Tel Aviv, 1935), 163.

[56] Quoted in 'Hunnicutt, 'The Jewish Sabbath Movement', 206–7. On Levinthal, see most recently Kimmy Caplan, 'The Life and Sermons of Israel Herbert Levinthal (1882–1982)', *American Jewish History*, 87 (1999), 1–27.

had been one of the founders in 1905 of the (anarchist) Industrial Workers of the World, won 6 per cent of the popular vote as the Socialist Party's candidate for president in 1912, Drachman asserted that 'the compulsory observance of Sunday by Jews leads to results which should be deemed undesirable by state and church, as well as by loyal Jews'. In an age of 'fierce economic competition', he argued, Jews could not possibly sacrifice two days weekly from their vocational pursuits, and would become alienated from their religion—with dangerous consequences for all:

> Once the Sabbath is gone, irreligion follows, which may then lead, in individual instances, to atheism and anarchism. Why should any Christian desire to break down the religious sentiments of his Jewish fellow-citizens? . . . I would certainly prefer to see a Christian loyal to his faith rather than an infidel, and I should think Christians would feel the same towards us.[57]

Rabbi Drachman did not have to mention the names of Emma Goldman, the founding editor of *Mother Earth*, who had become an anarchist in the aftermath of Chicago's Haymarket Affair, or other American Jewish immigrant radicals,[58] in order for his Christian audience to understand why Jewish observance of the sabbath was good for America.

A decade later, however, the Sabbath Alliance's Interdenominational Committee, of which Drachman himself was a member, pursued a rather different strategy, working in tandem with such labour leaders as Sidney Hillman of the Amalgamated Clothing Workers of America to promote a five-day working week. By 1934 Drachman had fully mastered the liberal discourse of labour economists, arguing that 'under modern methods of production' the 'rate of natural consumption' would lag chronically behind that of production, leading to mass unemployment—unless structural changes were made to the hours and days of the working week. In his *Looking at America*, published a year into Franklin Delano Roosevelt's New Deal presidency, Drachman asserted that he supported 'the idea of the shorter work week, not only on economic grounds, but also on social, cultural, and spiritual grounds'.[59]

In doing so Drachman was echoing the views expressed several years earlier by his younger Reform colleague Abba Hillel Silver of Cleveland, who, in supporting the 'progressive shortening of the hours of labor', had promoted

[57] Hunnicutt, 'The Jewish Sabbath Movement in the Early Twentieth Century', 219–21. On Drachman, see the latter's autobiography, *The Unfailing Light: Memoirs of an American Rabbi* (New York, 1948), as well as J. S. Gurock, 'From Exception to Role Model: Bernard Drachman and the Evolution of Jewish Religious Life in America, 1880–1920', *American Jewish History*, 76 (1986–7), 456–84, and the sources cited there.

[58] See David Waldstreicher, 'Radicalism, Religion, Jewishness: The Case of Emma Goldman', *American Jewish History*, 80 (1990), 74–92, and more generally Gerald Sorin, *The Prophetic Minority: American Jewish Immigrant Radicals, 1880–1920* (Bloomington, Ind., 1985).

[59] Bernard Drachman, *Looking at America* (New York, 1934); Hunnicutt, 'The Jewish Sabbath Movement in the Early Twentieth Century', 204–5, 208–9.

the sabbath as a bulwark against the 'philistine' gospel of consumption that he felt (prophetically) was victimizing the American people. 'We must say to ourselves,' wrote Silver in 1927, 'so far shall I go in my pursuit of the things of life and no further. Beyond that I am a free man, a child of God.'[60]

The notion of the sabbath as the protector of man's freedom and dignity, especially those of the working man, was also the central theme of Judah Leo Landau's contribution to a volume published in London in 1925 called *The Real Jew: Some Aspects of the Jewish Contribution to Civilization*. In that volume, which carried a prefatory note by Chief Rabbi Joseph Hertz and an introduction by Israel Zangwill, the Galician-born Landau, who had been serving as a rabbi in Johannesburg for more than two decades, wrote that 'the main object' of both the biblical sabbath and of the sabbatical year 'was to impress every Jew with the idea of personal freedom, of his higher mission as a member of the human race, and thus also with the idea of the equality of all men'.[61] In his essay, which had originally been delivered (in 1923) before the Working Men's Educational Union of Johannesburg, Landau, who was also an accomplished writer (primarily in Hebrew), powerfully, if somewhat purplishly, described how the sabbath rest served to raise the working man from his wretchedness:

> To the rich every day is a festive day. He often finds the day too long, and tries to kill time by various amusements. But the labourer whose hand has to raise the heaving hammer for many hours or to lead the plough and to swing the pruning-knife in the burning sun, or to expose his face to the irritating glow of the furnace, he who sits bent over his work for hours and hours, and for days and days, so that his bent back aches, and his sore eyes burn with pain; all those poor men and women who return to their desolate homes and hard couches worn and weary, unable to turn their thoughts to any subject that demands a clear and rested mind; all those wretched human beings who sink gradually but surely deeper and deeper into the morass of sensualism . . . they alone are able to appreciate a whole day devoted to rest, rest of body and mind.[62]

THE BATTLE FOR THE SABBATH

By 1925 the 'battle for the sabbath' had taken on international dimensions, largely in response to the activities of the Special Committee of Inquiry into the Reform of the Calendar established by the fledgling League of Nations

[60] Hunnicutt, 'The Jewish Sabbath Movement in the Early Twentieth Century', 213–14.

[61] J. L. Landau, 'The Sabbath', in Landau, *Judaism in Life and Literature* (London, 1936); from H. Newman (ed.), *The Real Jew: Some Aspects of the Jewish Contribution to Civilization* (London, 1925), 63.

[62] Ibid. 65–6. On Landau as Hebrew writer, see e.g. Veronica Belling, '"Ahavat Yehonatan": A Poem by Judah Leo Landau', *Polin*, 15 (2002), 243–8.

in 1923. The timing, as the British chief rabbi, Hertz, later remarked in his participant–observer account 'The Battle for the Sabbath at Geneva', was somewhat ironic, since during the preceding decade the Gregorian calendar, first established in the late sixteenth century, had finally been adopted by some of the major countries still holding out against it—China, Turkey, Russia, and, in 1923, Greece. As Hertz wrote with his customary causticity, 'In that very year . . . when the whole civilised world had at long last acknowledged allegiance to *one* calendar, the League decided to start a new era of confusion for humanity.'[63]

The 'impetus to the whole venture', Hertz argued, 'was due solely to American commercial and financial interests', led by Mr M. B. Cotsworth, the 'determined apostle' of a thirteen-month year in which all months would comprise exactly twenty-eight days, and the thirteenth would close with an eight-day week—the last day of which would simply be blank. Hertz, who had studied at New York's City College before receiving his ordination from the Jewish Theological Seminary, did not fail to note that a prime supporter of Cotsworth's plan had been George Eastman, founder of Kodak, 'who supplied the very ample funds required for world-wide propaganda'.[64] Hertz clearly intended to suggest that whereas the traditional sabbath was the friend of the working man, the reformed calendar was the ally of world capitalism.

In February of 1925 the British and French chief rabbis, together with two other European rabbinical colleagues, appeared before the League's Committee of Inquiry into the Reform of the Calendar. Their delegation was joined by Lucien Wolf of London, who was its concluding speaker. 'In view of the present chaotic conditions in Eastern Europe,' Wolf argued, 'no thinking man can contemplate without anxiety a measure which is calculated at once to undermine the moral anchorages of a large and stable element of the population, and to aggravate the economic difficulties of those who wish to remain true to the teachings of a sound polity.'[65] Shortly afterwards, upon his return to England, Rabbi Hertz addressed a meeting of the Hampstead Literary Society on the subject of calendar reform.[66]

In 1931, the same year in which Hertz and his European colleagues established the Jewish Calendar Committee, the League for Safeguarding the Fixity of the Sabbath was established in New York, headed by Rabbi Moses Hyamson of Congregation Orach Chaim on Lexington Avenue. Rabbi Hyamson had formerly been dayan of the London Beth Din, but departed in disappointment for the United States in 1913 after Hertz had been brought

[63] J. H. Hertz, 'The Battle for the Sabbath at Geneva', repr. (without notes) in Hertz, *Sermons, Addresses, and Studies*, 3 vols (London, 1938), ii; from *Transactions of the Jewish Historical Society of England*, 13 (1932–5), 190. [64] Ibid. 192. [65] Ibid. 192–3.

[66] Joseph Hertz, 'Calendar Reform', *Jewish Guardian*, 6 Mar. 1925.

to England to replace Chief Rabbi Hermann Adler, who had died two years earlier. It is hardly surprising that the two headed separate committees that were established for the same purpose.

During the early 1930s, partly as an extension of the activities of the League for Safeguarding the Fixity of the Sabbath, and partly in response to new social and economic circumstances precipitated by the Depression (including the five-day working week), Jewish organizations in the United States began to cooperate in an effort they called 'Sabbath Recovery'. In his contribution to a symposium on the subject in the *Jewish Forum*, Cyrus Adler, then president of the Jewish Theological Seminary, wrote:

> It has always seemed to me axiomatic that without the Sabbath, Jewish life could not continue for any length of time . . . I regard the Sabbath not only as the foundation of the Synagogue but also of Jewish family life . . . The United Synagogue of America has taken an excellent first step in calling the National Recovery Assembly, which has inaugurated an effort to make the Sabbath more widely observed. I hope that other organizations will join them and that out of our common efforts, the Sabbath may be re-established in America.[67]

One might think that such a bipartisan effort would be welcomed by both lay and religious leaders of American Jewry, and indeed it was supported by the presidents of B'nai B'rith, the National Council of Young Israel, the Union of Orthodox Jewish Congregations of America, and the Women's Branch of the Union of Orthodox Jewish Congregations. However, Rabbi Leo Jung, then president of that same union's Rabbinical Council, found reason to dissent. 'The five-day working week', he wrote, 'may become a source of blessing through its releasing tens of thousands of Jewish workingmen from Sabbath work.' The Moravian-born Jung, who was then rabbi of Manhattan's Jewish Center and Professor of Jewish Ethics at Yeshiva University, feared, however, that the five-day week could also 'become a source of great danger, perhaps of the greatest menace facing Judaism in our country'. How?

> Until now, the Sabbath desecrator appeased his conscience by looking upon himself as an *Anuss* [*sic*], one forced by economic stress to work on the Holy Day. Unless orthodox Jewry will immediately devise means for legitimate Sabbath occupation our liberated working-men will become frequenters of the movies and of the football fields, with their wives patronizing shops and spending the Sabbath in complete week-day manner.[68]

In 1933, the same year in which Jung and others contributed to the *Jewish Forum*'s symposium, his older contemporary Hayyim Schauss published a

[67] Cyrus Adler, 'Sabbath Recovery in American in Jewish Life', *Jewish Forum*, 16/4 (Dec. 1933), 127–8.

[68] Ibid. 129.

Yiddish book on the Jewish holidays, which appeared five years later in English as *The Jewish Festivals: From their Beginnings to our Own Day*. In his book Schauss, who had emigrated to the United States from Lithuania (where he had been born in 1884), noted mournfully that 'for about twenty-three hundred years, from the time of Ezra and Nehemiah, the Sabbath stood as fast and firm as a rock, until it was washed away by the mighty waves of the new economic life of the nineteenth century'. Schauss noted that in America and western Europe not only were 'religiously indifferent' Jews desecrating the sabbath, but even many of those who were otherwise quite Orthodox kept their stores open on Saturdays. 'It is not an infrequent occurrence in small congregations in America,' he reported, 'that there are no *Kohanim* . . . to pronounce the ancient priestly blessing on holidays. If the only *Kohanim* present work on the Sabbath they consider themselves unfit to perform this ceremony.'[69] Like earlier Jewish apologists, Schauss stressed that in contrast to its Babylonian cousin (the *Shabbatum*), the biblical sabbath prohibited work not for superstitious reasons, but out of humanitarian motives—so 'that thine ox and thine ass may have rest, and the son of thy handmaid and the stranger may be refreshed'. And, like some of his distinguished predecessors, he also proudly asserted that 'the Sabbath, as a day of rest in each week, was thus a genuinely Jewish institution'.[70]

Similarly, in a posthumously published essay written sometime before 1942, Jacob Lauterbach, another transplanted European Jew who fell somehow into the lap of the American Reform movement, described the sabbath as 'a unique institution conceived and developed by the Jewish genius, without any equivalent among the similar institutions of other people'. Lauterbach, who had been born in Galicia and ordained at the Orthodox seminary in Berlin before emigrating to the United States, where he served as rabbi of traditional congregations in Peoria and Rochester as well as a Reform congregation in Alabama, later joining the faculty of Hebrew Union College, went so far as to claim that 'our spiritual as well as material life is to be made richer, more pleasant and more delightful by our leisure on the Sabbath day and by the observance of its ceremony'.[71] The latter assertion seems to have been motivated, however, less by recent threats to the sabbath posed by calendar reform, than by those posed by the gradual withering away of traditional observance.

[69] Hayyim Schauss, *The Jewish Festivals: From their Beginnings to our Own Day*, trans. Samuel Jaffe (New York, 1938), 29.

[70] Ibid. 4–5.

[71] J. Z. Lauterbach, *Rabbinic Essays* (Cincinnati, 1951), 437, 440, 445. Echoing Schechter's famous essay, Lauterbach also stressed that 'the Jewish Sabbath is not a Puritan Sabbath; it is not a gloomy or a sad day. It is a day of joy and pleasure' (ibid. 444). See also, similarly, Landau, 'The Sabbath', 68.

Lauterbach's fellow Galician emigrant Salo Baron had also stressed, as we have seen, the 'novel and profound sanctification' of the sabbath among the ancient Jews, asserting that 'nowhere else, except in Judaism and its daughter religion, had the Sabbath received this character of holy and absolute rest'.[72] And, like the Lithuanian-born Schauss, the great historian Baron, though he himself was not sabbath-observant, was nonetheless saddened by the precipitous decline of the sabbath in his new country of residence. 'The degeneration of orthodox Jewish life in America', wrote Baron on the eve of the Second World War, in the epilogue to the first edition of his *Social and Religious History*, 'has gone so far as to enable officers of orthodox congregations to openly pursue their business on the Sabbath.'[73]

What disturbed him even more than the open transgression of the sabbath, however, was the rampant inconsistency of standards among 'orthodox persons throughout the world', who were forced increasingly to invent compromises of their own:

> One man carries money and purchases food, but refrains from writing on the Sabbath. Another regards writing as a smaller transgression than purchasing necessities.

Baron saw similar patterns in other aspects of contemporary Jewish observance:

> One consumes all ritually prohibited food but does not eat pork; another draws a distinction between roast pork, of which he cannot think without nausea, and ham and bacon in which he willingly and regularly indulges. In short, everyone composes a new unwritten Shulhan Aruk for his private benefit, and whimsically acknowledges or repudiates its authority thereafter.[74]

Yet in the twenty-first century there may be those who would proudly display this whimsical attitude towards authority as yet another Jewish contribution to civilization which, as Baron's contemporary Cecil Roth wrote of the sabbath, 'asserts man's moral dignity as a human being'.

[72] Above, n. 1.

[73] Baron, *Social and Religious History of the Jews*, ii. 389.

[74] Ibid. On these ostensibly arbitrary dietary distinctions, see now G. Tuchman and H. G. Levine, '"Safe Treyf": New York Jews and Chinese Food', *Contemporary Ethnography*, 22 (1992), 382–407, repr. in B. C. Shortridge and J. R. Shortridge (eds), *The Taste of American Place* (Lanham, Md., 1997).

FIVE

The 'Jewish Contribution' to Christianity

DAVID BERGER

FROM the late nineteenth until the middle of the twentieth century, Jews and their sympathizers devoted considerable research, energy, and ingenuity to the documentation of signal Jewish contributions to Western civilization. Whatever objections critics might have raised regarding the extent of the Jewish role, the positive assessment of the discipline, field, or ideal to which Jews had allegedly contributed was not usually a matter of controversy, so that the authors of this literature generally take the intrinsic value of the 'contribution' for granted.

In 1921 an American Christian recounting what 'the Jew has done for the world' listed patriotism, the prophet Samuel's 'argument that battered down the enslaving doctrine of Divine Right of kings', involvement in the discovery of America, science, mathematics, medicine, politics, poetry, philology, and law-abiding behaviour.[1] Four years later another book of this genre provided chapters on Jewish contributions to education, folklore, literature, philosophy, the law, scientific research, medicine, chemistry, infant welfare, art, music, drama, athletics, Eastern exploration, and citizenship. Still, even such lists, read at a later time, reveal unsuspected layers of complexity. Thus, a heading that I have skipped, 'Jewish Pioneers of British Dominion', was of course seen by the author as unequivocally positive; in our age, with its deep reservations about imperialism, that chapter inadvertently alerts us to the value judgements that underlie and potentially bedevil aspects of this enterprise, a point already evident if we contemplate how a seventeenth-century European would have reacted to the assertion that the Jewish Bible undermines the divine right of kings.[2] Indeed, since the Bible is the primary source

[1] Madison C. Peters, *Justice to the Jew: The Story of What He Has Done for the World* (New York, 1921), 23.

[2] H. Newman (ed.), *The Real Jew: Some Aspects of the Jewish Contribution to Civilization* (London, 1925). Needless to say, this is not the only assumption in such a book that can render a contemporary reader uneasy. Here is a description of Jewish athletic aptitude: 'The highly emotional and excitable temperament characteristic of the Jew is singularly adapted to enable the possessor to excel. . . . The alert Jewish mind is well suited to boxing and sprinting. Moreover, the Jewish mentality, the morbid anticipation that precedes competition, the almost

of the doctrine *affirming* the divine right of kings, the tendentiousness of the argument that a single speech in the book of Samuel establishes Jewish responsibility for undermining that doctrine is particularly striking. As late as 1951 we find a shorter but similar list pointing to Jewish contributions to achievements understood as self-evidently meritorious: democracy, science, medicine, exploration, and the military.[3]

So far, with the exception of the reference to Samuel, we have looked at headings that are relentlessly secular, and even the apparent exception congratulates Jews for a political contribution that liberated its beneficiaries from the shackles of a religious conception. But a discussion of Jewish contributions omitting the religious dimension is a quintessential example of the Hebrew adage *Ha'ikar ḥaser min hasefer* ('The main element is missing from the book'). As soon as we turn our attention to that dimension, the valuation assigned to both the Jewish characteristic and its purported consequence becomes anything but self-evident, and we are propelled into a fascinating arena of warring values and competing perceptions.

Nonetheless, even on the religious front, we find efforts to produce lists of Jewish influences on Christianity intended to sound soothing and uncontroversial, describing religions whose essential approaches are the very quintessence of harmony. A Christian writer, in a chapter entitled 'The Fountainhead of Western Religion', asserted that 'much that came to be called Christian was, in fact, the lengthening shadows of Hebraic ideas and influences'. His bill of particulars includes a sense of destiny and the unification of morals and religion, even the identity of Judaism's and medieval Catholicism's list of cardinal sins, to wit, 'the shedding of blood, sexual impurity, and apostasy'.[4] That 'apostasy' for Jews included the embrace of medieval Catholicism goes unmentioned.

Cecil Roth's *Jewish Contribution to Civilization* (1940), a classic work on our theme by a prominent historian, concentrates on the secular areas typical of this genre, but the introductory chapter underlines Jewish

uncanny knack of seizing opportunities are admirable. The certainty the Jew has of rising to the occasion . . . his overwhelming self-appreciation and confidence—what qualities can be more calculated to enable a man to achieve high athletic distinction? The Jew born of Jewish parents possesses physical qualities and mental qualities well suited to athletic success' (Harold M. Abrahams, 'The Jew and Athletics', in Newman (ed.), *The Real Jew*, 248–9). On the other hand, Charles and Dorothea Singer, in one of the best books of the 'Jewish contribution' genre, assert—albeit with some hesitation—that there is no Jewish race. See their 'The Jewish Factor in Medieval Thought', in Edwyn R. Bevan and Charles Singer (eds), *The Legacy of Israel* (Oxford, 1927), 180.

3 Dagobert Runes (ed.), *The Hebrew Impact on Western Civilization*, abr. edn (New York, 1951).

4 Vergilius Fern, 'The Fountainhead of Western Religion', in Runes (ed.), *The Hebrew Impact on Western Civilization*.

contributions to Christianity itself, and through it, to the world at large: monotheism, the value of human life, the sanctity of the home, the dignity of the marital relationship, equality of all before the one God, the messianic vision, prayer, even Christian ceremonial (baptism, Communion (from the Passover *seder*), lectionaries, and the liturgical use of Psalms).[5] Perhaps the lengthiest list of this sort was compiled by Joseph Jacobs in 1919, and despite its general tone of apodictic certainty, it includes occasional qualifications that, once again, provide some hint of the problematics of this enterprise. In the realm of practice: prayer (especially the Psalter), the Mass or Communion, baptism, bishops (from the synagogue position of *gabai*), charity boxes, ordination of priests, religious schools, the missionary character of early Christianity (borrowed from the missionary spirit of the Judaism of the time), aspects of canon law. In the realm of theology: the kingdom of heaven, original sin ('though it must be allowed that it has received much more elaborate development in Church doctrine', while Judaism mitigated its harshness with 'original virtue', to wit, the merit of the fathers), special grace to God's favourites, the Fatherhood of God (and even, to some degree, 'the analogous conception of the Son of God'), the chosen people, resurrection, hell (though Christianity laid greater emphasis on this), repentance, confession of sin, the Messiah, the Golden Rule (though this is more practical in its negative, Jewish form), the dicta of the Sermon on the Mount, the Lord's Prayer, and the importance of the Law to Jesus.[6] Jacobs does add that while the only difference between primitive Christianity and developed Judaism is the vague one of Jesus's personality, three major distinctions eventually emerged: the Law, image worship, and the doctrine of a Man-God.

One suspects that Jacobs was well aware that some items on his list of contributions bore a more mixed message than he acknowledged. Thus, Jewish apologists generally denied the existence of any serious concept of original sin in Judaism, pointing *inter alia* to a Jewish prayer beginning, 'My God, the soul that you have given me is pure,' and minimizing the lasting effect of the sin of Adam and Eve on the spiritual nature of their descendants. Like Roth, he does not inform us that Jews through the ages, like the early Calvinists, perceived the Catholic Mass as an idolatrous ceremony, whatever its original connection to the Passover *seder*, and he does not acknowledge what Jews saw as the critical distinction between confessing one's sins to God and con-

[5] Cecil Roth, *The Jewish Contribution to Civilization* (Cincinnati, 1940), 4–13. Leon Roth, *Jewish Thought as a Factor in Civilization* (Paris, 1954), lists the messianic idea, the return to Hebrew Scriptures in Christian Reform movements, the Psalter, even the sense of sin and divine punish-ment.

[6] Joseph Jacobs, *Jewish Contributions to Civilization: An Estimate* (Philadelphia, 1919), 91–100. Some of the last items should arguably have been classified as practice rather than theology. The unelaborated reference to the Sermon on the Mount relies, says Jacobs, on Gerald Friedlander's *The Jewish Sources of the Sermon on the Mount* (New York, 1911).

fessing them to a human being.[7] He was surely not interested in noting the interesting irony that while Jews had decidedly 'contributed' the idea of the Messiah to Christianity, Reform Judaism, by abandoning belief in a personal Messiah, had recently moved away from a central element of that concept, which was precisely the one that Christians had placed at centre stage. Finally, I suspect that one of the items on his list was intended as a subtle critique of Christianity, though he deliberately left the implication unspoken. For a Jew to include 'the chosen people' in an accounting of Jewish contributions to Christianity is to underscore the argument that Christian stereotypes of narrow Jewish particularism versus Christian universalism obscure the reality that Christendom has identified itself as the new chosen people to the exclusion and perhaps damnation of the rest of humanity.[8]

The tendency of authors writing in this genre to avoid highlighting the Jewish clash with Christianity is sharply illustrated in Louis Finkelstein's classic, monumental *The Jews: Their History, Culture and Religion* (1949). His work is far more than an exemplar of the typical effort to establish a Jewish contribution to civilization, but this is surely a major component of its mission. In its four massive volumes, we look in vain for any serious discussion of the relationship between Judaism and Christianity. The brief allusion to Christian ethics in Mordecai Kaplan's contribution affirms, as we shall see, complete commonality between the two faiths. And the editor's own, even briefer, comment on Jewish attitudes towards Christianity is quite remarkable: 'Rabbi Jacob Emden (1697–1771), one of the foremost teachers in the history of Judaism, summarized the general Jewish view regarding Christianity in the following words . . . "[Jesus] did a double kindness to the world by supporting the Torah for Jews and teaching Gentiles to abandon idolatry and observe the seven Noahide commandments"'.[9] And that is all. So does one of the most strikingly positive—and highly atypical—Jewish assessments of Christianity ever proffered by a traditional rabbi become 'the general Jewish view'.

It is worth noting that Jewish scholars and apologists during the period in question frequently affirmed that another atypical Jewish view of Christianity

[7] For a particularly sharp medieval example of this Jewish critique of Christianity, see my *The Jewish–Christian Debate in the High Middle Ages: A Critical Edition of the 'Nizzahon Vetus' with an Introduction, Translation, and Commentary* (Philadelphia, 1979), 22–3 and n. 60, 223–4, 339.

[8] As we shall see more strikingly in our discussion of Leo Baeck, the assertion that Jews contributed the missionary spirit to Christianity is also noteworthy and by no means typical.

[9] Louis Finkelstein (ed.), *The Jews: Their History, Culture and Religion*, 4 vols (Philadelphia, 1949), iv. 1347. On the rarest of occasions, we find a Jewish scholar writing during the period under discussion who exaggerates Jewish *hostility* to Christianity. Thus, Samuel Krauss asserts that 'Jesus' illegitimate birth was always a firmly held dogma in Judaism' ('The Jews in the Works of the Church Fathers', *Jewish Quarterly Review*, OS 5 (1892), 143).

was in fact standard. Rabbi Menahem Hameiri of late thirteenth- and early fourteenth-century Perpignan had taken the position that Christianity is not to be seen as idolatry at all and that its adherents are entitled to full equality with Jews in matters of civil law because they are among the 'nations bound by the ways of religions'. Though elements of this position were shared by other medieval and early modern authorities, it is profoundly misleading to describe it as typical. Nonetheless, distinguished Jewish authors, for reasons that are not difficult to discern, often described it as such—sometimes, I suspect, in full sincerity.[10]

If the only dynamic in play were the assessment of the Jewish contribution to civilization, it might have been possible to sidestep the major tensions between the two faiths and affirm the Jewish contribution to Christianity by recording the bland commonalities that we have already noted—or by resorting to the silence and disingenuousness of Finkelstein's work. But during the period in which this enterprise was at its height, a period that I will delineate for the purposes of this chapter as roughly the 1890s to the middle of the twentieth century, a related dynamic was also at its height: the depiction by Christian scholars and theologians of a sharp contrast between rabbinic Judaism and Christianity, and the consequent need for a Jewish response.[11]

[10] Cf. my observations in 'Jacob Katz on Jews and Christians in the Middle Ages', in Jay M. Harris (ed.), *The Pride of Jacob: Essays on Jacob Katz and his Work* (Cambridge, Mass., 2002), 42–4. On Hameiri, see Moshe Halbertal, *Between Torah and Wisdom: Rabbi Menachem Hameiri and the Maimonidean Halakhists in Provence* (Heb.) (Jerusalem, 2000). An English translation of much of the relevant chapter appeared in the online *Edah Journal*, 1 (2000), <http://www.edah.org/backend/JournalArticle/ halbertal.pdf>, accessed 11 Sept. 2006.

[11] A substantial scholarly literature has developed around this confrontation, providing analysis of the earlier part of the 19th century as well as the period of direct concern to us. First and foremost is the brilliant work of Uriel Tal, *Christians and Jews in Germany: Religion, Politics and Ideology in the Second Reich, 1870–1914* (Ithaca, NY, 1975). Susannah Heschel addressed the content and impact of a seminal Jewish figure's perception of Jesus in *Abraham Geiger and the Jewish Jesus* (Chicago, 1998). Christian Wiese's important study *Wissenschaft des Judentums und protestantische Theologie in wilhelminischen Deutschland* (Tübingen, 1999) is highly relevant in its entirety; chapter 4, which deals with particularism versus universalism, ethics versus law, and love versus fear in the context of the debate surrounding Wilhelm Bousset's *Die Religion des Judentums im neutestamentalischen Zeitalter* (Berlin, 1903), bears most directly on our concerns. (An English translation has now been published: Christian Wiese, *Challenging Colonial Discourse: Jewish Studies and Protestant Theology in Wilhelmine Germany*, trans. Barbara Harshav and Christian Wiese (Leiden, 2005).) Ismar Schorsch, *Jewish Reactions to German Anti-Semitism, 1870–1914* (New York, 1972), 169–77, provides a succinct summary of Jewish concerns from an institutional perspective. Overviews of modern Jewish assessments of Jesus and Christianity include Gosta Lindeskog, *Die Jesusfrage im neuzeitlichen Judentum. Ein Beitrag zur Geschichte der Leben-Jesu-Forschung* (Uppsala, 1938); Jacob Fleischmann, *The Problem of Christianity in Modern Jewish Thought (1770–1929)* (Heb.) (Jerusalem, 1964); Walter Jacob, *Christianity through Jewish Eyes: The Quest for Common Ground* (Cincinnati, 1974); Donald A. Hagner, *The Jewish Reclamation of Jesus* (Grand Rapids, Mich., 1984).

During the course of the late nineteenth century, the maturation of both liberal Protestantism and biblical criticism produced a concerted attack on classical Judaism. Since many liberal Protestants no longer believed the standard dogmas of Christianity, they shifted their faith's centre of gravity to the arena of ethical teaching and an intense spiritual relationship to God. The trajectory of pre-Christian Israelite–Jewish religion came to be seen roughly as follows: The early Pentateuchal documents affirmed by adherents of the newly regnant critical hypothesis reflected a naive, rather primitive perception of a God who was accessible in an immediate, almost tangible sense and whose ethical character left much to be desired. With the rise of the literary prophets, both the moral and theological understanding of God reached unprecedented heights. At the same time, the transcendent theology expressed in what the critics identified as the Priestly document of the exilic period produced a remote Deity and came to be associated with overemphasis on ritual, legalism, and arid genealogies, while in the quintessential cases of Ezra and Esther, late biblical Judaism degenerated into extreme, chauvinistic exclusivism. It is these characteristics that persisted into what came to be described as Late Judaism, that is, the Judaism of Jesus's time. Jesus himself, and Christianity after him, not only restored the highest form of religion found in the Hebrew Bible but transcended it, combining ethical selflessness with a fresh, direct experience of God without sacrificing the essence of monotheism.

Needless to say, Jews could not allow this portrait to go unchallenged. Much has been written about the Jewish indictment of Christian scholars for distorting rabbinic Judaism out of both malice and ignorance, and I will not reiterate this aspect of the argument in detail. These Jewish reactions were not without their effect; nonetheless, the old critique of the rabbis persisted in some circles into the mid-twentieth century despite all the efforts of Jewish apologists and sympathetic Christian scholars. Thus, no less a theologian than Rudolf Bultmann, notwithstanding a few pro forma qualifications, produced a chapter entitled 'Jewish Legalism' in his *Primitive Christianity* that could have been written in the 1890s. He informs us that ritual in Judaism became more important than morality, 'with the result that men lost sight of their social and cultural responsibilities'. Precepts that had become meaningless 'still had to be obeyed unquestioningly. . . . Regulations went into detail to the point of absurdity . . . This ritualism . . . sanctified the life of the community, but that sanctity was an entirely negative affair.' And on and on.[12]

Consequently, from the late nineteenth century until the middle of the twentieth, Jews faced the delicate, challenging task of balancing a complex of

[12] Rudolf Bultmann, 'Jewish Legalism', in Bultmann, *Primitive Christianity* (New York, 1956). I was first alerted to this chapter in graduate school as a result of a passing remark by Gerson Cohen.

objectives that were often in tension with one another. They surely wanted to demonstrate that Judaism played a central role in the rise of Christianity. After all, no Jewish contribution to Western civilization could be clearer than this. At the same time, they did not want to erase the line between the religions. They did not want to offend Christians, but they did not want to absorb the indictment of Judaism supinely. They wanted to embrace Jesus as their own without accepting him as a Jewish authority or granting Jewish legitimacy to the religion that he founded (or, perhaps, did not found).

In this daunting enterprise, their religious and ethical perspectives came to be deeply engaged. One of the most intriguing aspects of this study is the light shone by the historical and apologetic works of these Jews on their own differing values. What some Jews considered quintessentially Christian, others saw as a Jewish influence; what some saw as an admirable Christian belief, others saw as an unfortunate deviation; what some saw as central to Judaism, others saw as problematic and dispensable. Nonetheless, there are also broad and deep commonalities marking the Jewish assessments of the relationship between the religions.

While the range of issues marking these controversies covers a broad spectrum, several stand out in bold relief. These include the Law, particularism and universalism, ethics, the experience and conception of God, and the view of redemption and redeemer. It is to these that we now turn our attention.

On one level, Jews had long argued—inconsistently to be sure—that Jesus himself did not reject the Law.[13] In the modern period, the perception of a 'Jewish' Jesus became dominant, to the point where the distinguished German Reform rabbi Leo Baeck eloquently, though no doubt tendentiously, produced an 'original Gospel' consisting entirely of Jewish elements.[14] Beyond this point, Jews needed to defend the role of law in rabbinic Judaism itself. Two of the most distinguished Jewish scholars in Britain turned their attention to this task: Israel Abrahams in his classic essay on Emil Schürer's caricature of rabbinic law and Solomon Schechter in his encomium to the sabbath and, more briefly, to the donning of tefillin.[15] Wilhelm Bousset's invidious characterization of Judaism generated several

[13] See my 'On the Uses of History in Medieval Jewish Polemic against Christianity: The Search for the Historical Jesus', in Elisheva Carlebach, John M. Efron, and David N. Myers (eds), *Jewish History and Jewish Memory: Essays in Honor of Yosef Hayim Yerushalmi* (Hanover, NH, 1998).

[14] Leo Baeck, *Judaism and Christianity* (Philadelphia, 1960), 98–136. This volume, published shortly after Baeck's death in 1956, contains English translations of works written several decades earlier.

[15] Israel Abrahams, 'Professor Schürer on Life under the Jewish Law', *Jewish Quarterly Review*, OS 11 (1899), 626–42; Solomon Schechter, 'The Law and Recent Criticism', *Jewish Quarterly Review*, OS 3 (1891), 754–66.

Jewish reactions, most fully and notably by Felix Perles, who underscored the deep spirituality of the rabbinic concept of repentance, the joy attendant upon fulfilling the commandments (*simḥah shel mitsvah*), and the understanding of the Law as an expression of divine love.[16] The essential argument of these works was repeated decades later in a lesser-known essay by the Edinburgh rabbi Salis Daiches, who remarked that to those who know Judaism from within, depicting it as legalism standing in contrast to spirituality 'appears not only unfounded but also unintelligible'.[17]

In an ambitious, systematic response to Adolf Harnack's *The Essence of Christianity* (*Das Wesen des Christentums*, 1900), the Berlin rabbi Joseph Eschelbacher not only composed a paean of praise to the halakhah but also formulated a sharp riposte. Scholastic argument, he noted, developed Christian dogmatics through the ages. In our time, Julius Wellhausen has agreed that the basic teachings of Jesus can be found in Jewish sources but has insisted that they are submerged by a legal system in which everything is equal. Well, said Eschelbacher, did not Christian dogmatics do to the message of Jesus precisely what Wellhausen ascribes to the Jewish legal system?[18]

In a different mode, Moritz Güdemann argued in 1892 that the depiction of Jewish adherence to the letter rather than the spirit is itself an unfair caricature. Jewish contemporaries of Paul would not have quarrelled with the assertion that 'the letter killeth but the spirit giveth life' since the letter of various biblical laws from the *lex talionis* to the year of release were in effect set aside by rabbis in favour of the spirit. While Güdemann had no intention here of fully homogenizing Christian and Jewish attitudes towards the Law, this is a striking instance of taking a liberal understanding of the operation of rabbinic law, placing it into a conceptual framework that the rabbis themselves would not have endorsed—and thereby neutralizing a Christian objection to Jewish legalism.[19]

A disturbing problem for some Jews engaged in apologetics regarding the Law was generated by the fact that some of them adhered to Reform, or Liberal, Judaism, so that they rejected elements of the ceremonial law for reasons not very different from those proffered by Christian critics.[20] In

[16] See Felix Perles, *Boussets 'Religion des Judentums im neutestamentalischen Zeitalter kritisch untersucht'* (Berlin, 1903), and the discussion and references in Wiese, *Wissenschaft des Judentums und protestantische Theologie*, 161.

[17] Salis Daiches, 'Judaism as the Religion of the Law', in Newman (ed.), *The Real Jew*.

[18] Joseph Eschelbacher, *Das Judentum und das Wesen des Christentums* (Berlin, 1908), 27–8.

[19] Moritz Güdemann, 'Spirit and Letter in Judaism and Christianity', *Jewish Quarterly Review*, OS 4 (1892), 352–3. Though this article appeared in an English journal, Güdemann resided in Vienna, where he pursued a distinguished rabbinic and scholarly career.

[20] I made this point in 'Religion, Nationalism, and Historiography: Yehezkel Kaufmann's Account of Jesus and Early Christianity', in Leo Landman (ed.), *Scholars and Scholarship: The*

1907 the Reform rabbi Israel Goldschmidt, in another of the book-length Jewish responses to Harnack, wrote an entire appendix to demonstrate that the differences between Orthodoxy and Reform do not undermine a proper analysis of the contrast between Judaism and Christianity. He provided an abstract, highly philosophical account of those differences, and that account enabled him to argue that the essence of Judaism is unaffected by the Orthodox–Reform divide. For him, the basic difference between the Jewish movements is not the Law per se but Orthodoxy's assertion that the bond between God and Israel was formed in a supernatural fashion versus the Reform understanding that sees it in terms of historical evolution.[21]

This approach, however, by avoiding a direct confrontation with the question of the Law, left the issues raised by the Christian critique unresolved. The most striking example of a Liberal Jewish move in the direction of the Christian position on this issue appears in Claude G. Montefiore's 1927 commentary to the Synoptic Gospels. Not surprisingly, the passage in question was noted both by Lou Silberman in his Prolegomenon to the 1968 Ktav reprint of Montefiore's work and by Donald Hagner in his evangelically oriented analysis of Jewish approaches to Jesus, though neither of them quite captures its full radicalism.[22] The Gospel text in question is Mark 7: 15: 'There is nothing outside a man, which entering into him can make him unclean, but the things which come out of a man, these are what make him unclean.' Montefiore asserted that this is one of the two chief justifications for Liberal Judaism's view of 'the old ceremonial law'. First, the 'old prophets' said that 'the true service of God is not ceremonial, but moral'. But they dealt with the ceremonial laws that were supposed to affect God. Jesus's observation, on the other hand, deals with those ceremonial laws that were supposed to affect man. 'Upon these two doctrines, the doctrine of Hosea . . . and the doctrine of Jesus . . . the new attitude of Liberal Judaism toward the ceremonial Law depends.'[23] Montefiore hastened to add that Liberal Judaism takes the further step of retaining the ceremonies that it values; nonetheless, we find here a remarkable citation of Jesus as an authority on a par with Hosea in undermining the binding character of sections of the Torah. While this is extraordinary and atypical, it underscores with ruthless candour a central dynamic in the Reform Jewish discourse on Christianity and the Law.

Interaction between Judaism and Other Cultures (New York, 1990), 154. See now Wiese, *Wissenschaft des Judentums und protestantische Theologie*, 162.

[21] Joseph Goldschmidt, *Das Wesen des Judentums* (Frankfurt am Main, 1907), 218–19.

[22] Claude G. Montefiore, *The Synoptic Gospels* (first pub. 1927; New York, 1968), Prolegomenon by Lou Silberman, 11–13; Hagner, *The Jewish Reclamation of Jesus*, 114–15.

[23] Montefiore, *The Synoptic Gospels*, 131–2.

A secondary but revealing point that emerges from this discussion is Montefiore's distinction between ceremonial laws that were supposed to affect God and those intended to affect man. The former category presumably refers to sacrifices, which are ostensibly subjected to criticism in several notable passages in the literary prophets. It is highly unlikely that any pre-modern Jew would have adopted this classification except in a kabbalistic context, where other commandments as well could affect the upper worlds. Sacrifices, whatever their precise purpose, were designed to affect human beings no less than God. For Montefiore, however, they are a reflection of a primitive religious mentality in which God's behaviour is directly changed by propitiatory offerings. The prophets took one step towards a more elevated religious sensibility by decrying this crude ceremonial practice; it was left for Jesus to discern the triviality and inappropriateness of ceremonies whose theological primitivism is less evident. Perhaps, then, one should say not that Jesus is on a par with Hosea but that he stands on a higher rung than the prophet on the ladder of spiritual development.

It is a matter of no small interest that Martin Buber, who did not have a high regard for the ceremonial law, nonetheless saw both biblical sacrifice and the prophetic criticism directed against it through a very different lens.

> One of the two fundamental elements in biblical animal sacrifice is the sacralization of the natural life: he who slaughters an animal consecrates a part of it to God, and so doing hallows his eating of it. The second fundamental element is the sacramentalization of the complete surrender of life; to this element belong those types of sacrifice in which the person who offers the sacrifice puts his hands on the head of the animal in order to identify himself with it; in doing so he gives physical expression to the thought that he is bringing himself to be sacrificed in the person of the animal. He who performs these sacrifices without having this intention in his soul makes the cult meaningless, yes, absurd; it was against him that the prophets directed their fight against the sacrificial service which had been emptied of its core.[24]

With respect to the central issue before us, Buber's dismissive attitude towards the legal component of Judaism placed him in agreement with the liberal Protestant critique. He dealt with this, as Ekkehard Stegemann has pointed out in a perceptive analysis, by identifying Jesus as a perfectly good Jew who indeed recaptured the prophetic, ethically resonant dimension of Judaism, while describing Paul as one who transformed this message into 'the sweet poison of faith'. Thus, historic Judaism contains whatever is valuable in Christianity and justly rejects that which is distinctively

[24] Martin Buber, 'The Two Foci of the Jewish Soul', in Fritz A. Rothschild (ed.), *Jewish Perspectives on Christianity: Leo Baeck, Martin Buber, Franz Rosenzweig, Will Herberg, and Abraham J. Heschel* (New York, 1990), 126.

Christian.[25] Through this approach, Buber, at least in his own mind, rendered unnecessary the defence of the ceremonial law that presented such a daunting challenge to Liberal Jewish apologists.

We have already noted Eschelbacher's structural analogy between the Law in Judaism and dogmatics in Christianity. Montefiore provided the more direct analogy between Jewish law and Christian *ritual*. Thus, John would have objected to the abolition of baptism and the Eucharist just as Philo objected to the abolition of Pentateuchal Law.[26] Similarly, Yehezkel Kaufmann, whose brilliant and original œuvre addressed not only biblical religion but the entire span of the Jewish experience, argued that Christianity could not have prevailed over Judaism because of its rejection of the Law since Christianity itself is replete with ritual.[27]

Leo Baeck, however, emphasized not the similarity but the disparity between Jewish law and Christian ritual. Paul left Judaism when he embraced *sola fide* and moved from there to dogma and sacrament. Sacrament is not law in the Jewish sense; it is mystery made tangible. What then is the Law to the Liberal rabbi? In one place it is exemplified by ethics. But at the end of the essay he moves to the sabbath. 'The Law, and quite especially the Sabbatical element in it—has educated that capacity in man which is born of the depth of life—the capacity to be different.' From here he returns to his earlier emphasis on Judaism as a special synthesis of mystery and commandment. 'This is the gift and possession of Judaism.'[28] This last sentence encapsulates perfectly the challenge at the heart of the discourse regarding 'the Jewish contribution' to Christianity and perhaps to civilization as a whole. Jews wanted to show that they have provided a gift—but that it is still their special possession. The sabbath is an ideal vehicle for the realization of Baeck's objectives. It is an embodiment of law, but it can be affirmed without all the details of the Law; it is a gift to the world, yet it remains uniquely Jewish.

While this aspect of Baeck's argument, for all the originality of his formulation, is consistent with the mainstream Jewish attitude towards Christianity, he also proffers a highly unusual approach to the relationship between Judaism and Christian antinomianism. A talmudic statement affirmed that the world would last 6,000 years: 2,000 desolation, 2,000 Torah, and 2,000 the messianic age. Since the late twelfth century, Christians had cited this statement to demonstrate that the Torah would be annulled in the

[25] See Stegemann's introduction to the selections from Buber in Rothschild (ed.), *Jewish Perspectives on Christianity*, 115–16.

[26] Claude G. Montefiore, 'Notes on the Religious Value of the Fourth Gospel', *Jewish Quarterly Review*, OS 7 (1895), 46.

[27] This is part of a larger analysis of the success of Christianity in Yehezkel Kaufmann, *Exile and Alien Lands* (Heb.) (Tel Aviv, 1929), i. 292–301.

[28] Baeck, *Judaism and Christianity*, 177, 175, 184.

messianic age, and since the thirteenth, Jews had struggled to show that this conclusion did not follow. Baeck adduced this rabbinic passage along with some other evidence to establish precisely what Christians had affirmed all along—that the messianic age is not an age of Torah. He proceeded to argue that since this was the standard Jewish view in antiquity, Paul's rejection of the Law was deeply Jewish. His only innovation was his conviction that the final age had already arrived. In other words, Paul's belief in Jesus's messiahship required him—on Jewish grounds—to affirm the abolition of the Law. Christian antinomianism is itself a Jewish contribution to the new faith.[29]

Adherence to the Law was often seen as a manifestation of Jewish particularism. Christians had criticized Jews for this presumed failing as early as the Middle Ages; in early modern times, the issue rose to greater prominence, and by our period it was almost ubiquitous. A central explanation—so it was said—of Christendom's victory over Jewry is that the former bore a universalistic message while the latter was concerned only with itself. Here again Jews and their supporters demurred, but in very different ways. One approach was to emphasize the particularism of Jesus himself, who did not want to cast his pearls before non-Jewish swine and who was sent only to the lost sheep of the House of Israel.[30] With respect to the broader arena, a Christian writing enthusiastically of the Jewish struggle against paganism in a book bearing a philosemitic message would only affirm that Judaism had the *potential* to become a world religion, but, he said, the rabbis robbed it of its vital force through a policy of isolation. Thus, 'the role which it might have filled was handed over to Christianity'.[31] Yehezkel Kaufmann agreed with the final sentence but strongly rejected the reason. Judaism, he argued, was thoroughly universalist, providing everyone the option to enter the Jewish people through conversion. It was not particularism or even Jewish ethnicity per se that caused Judaism to miss its opportunity. Rather, it was the historical accident of exile that transformed this ethnicity into an insuperable obstacle. Non-Jews would have joined the Jewish people, but not a defeated Jewish people. It was the Jewish message of universalist monotheism—and that message alone—that accounted for the sweeping triumph of Christianity and then of Islam. The tragedy of Jewish history is that this victory was achieved only by proxy.[32]

Some Jews went even further by arguing that Judaism is more universalist than Christianity. For Israel Goldschmidt, the concept of a church is

[29] Ibid. 154, 161–4, 241–2.

[30] See e.g. Samuel S. Cohon, 'The Place of Jesus in the Religious Life of his Day', *Journal of Biblical Literature*, 48 (1929), 89, citing also Joseph Klausner and Montefiore.

[31] George H. Box, 'How Judaism Fought Paganism', in Newman (ed.), *The Real Jew*, 34.

[32] See my discussion in 'Religion, Nationalism, and Historiography', 159–68.

particularistic in the extreme. Unlike Christianity, Judaism is a *Schule* or an *Orden*, a school of thought or an order, rather than a *Kirche*.[33] Montefiore, conceding Jewish particularism, dealt with it through his openness to religious development: 'Jewish particularism is very objectionable . . . but it was happily not part and parcel of the real Jewish creed. It could be, and has been, easily got rid of.' On the other hand, John's division of humanity into saved Christians and damned others is deeply embedded in the creed, and thus harder to exorcise. If the rabbis restricted the dictum 'Thou shalt love thy neighbour as thyself' to Jews—at least to some degree—John restricts it to Christians. Is this really an improvement?[34] Similarly, but without any overt reference to Christianity, the British rabbi and scholar Abraham Cohen affirmed that the brotherhood of man, including the salvation of righteous Gentiles, is essential to Judaism, which does not 'stipulate the necessity of a uniform creed for all'.[35] Needless to say, this argument goes back at least to Moses Mendelssohn and served as the stock in trade of many Jewish apologists throughout modern times.

Montefiore himself took the denial of a relationship between faith and salvation to an extreme that can be explained only by his commitment to Liberal Judaism combined with his desire to maintain what was for him a crucial contrast between Judaism and Christianity:

> To all Jews, presumably to all liberal Christians, the action of God on man is not determined by the accuracy of his belief about God. We do not believe that the relation of God to man is different in the case of a Jew and in the case of a Christian. We realize that varying religious beliefs may and do have varying effects upon character, but so far as God is concerned we do not believe that he has other laws of influence and judgment for those who believe concerning him more truly or less truly, or even for those who have failed to find him altogether. Least of all do we believe that these variations of belief affect the destiny of the soul beyond the grave. . . . But inconsistently, as we believe, with the justice of God and the universalism of his providence, the author of the Fourth Gospel did presumably believe that the result of true belief . . . is the prerogative of eternal life.[36]

'All Jews', then, in 1895, presumably including the traditionalist masses of eastern Europe and the Muslim world, as well as their rabbinic leaders, rejected Maimonides' assertion that denial of his principles deprived the non-believer of a portion in the world to come. It is hard to envision a more striking example of parochialism than Montefiore's blinkered vision of the Jewish world in which he lived. Moreover, even if his presentation of the

[33] Goldschmidt, *Das Wesen des Judentums*, pp. vi–vii, 214.
[34] Montefiore, 'Notes on the Religious Value of the Fourth Gospel', 41, 43.
[35] Abraham Cohen, 'Great Jewish Thoughts', in Newman (ed.), *The Real Jew*, 25.
[36] Montefiore, 'Notes on the Religious Value of the Fourth Gospel', 32–3.

theology of his contemporary co-religionists had been accurate, there is a transparent element of unfairness in comparing the views of the Fourth Gospel on a point like this with the Judaism of the 1890s rather than that of the first and second century.

And then there was the argument for Jewish nationalism, which in some sense affirmed the value of parochialism. The paradigmatic exemplar of this approach in our context is Joseph Klausner, a fervent Zionist who regularly utilized his scholarship as a handmaiden of his ideological commitments. Klausner insisted that monotheism itself could be preserved only through Jewish adherence to a particular national identity. Abandonment of that identity would have caused Israel—and its unadulterated monotheism—to have been swallowed up by the far more numerous nations.[37]

The contrast between universalism and particularism is not unrelated to the evaluation of Jewish versus Christian ethics. I have already alluded to Mordecai Kaplan's avoidance of any contrast between the ethics of the two faiths in his contribution to Finkelstein's *The Jews*. 'The Christian Gospel . . . not only retained the confidence the Jews had had in their own way of life, as well as the original emphasis upon the primacy and divine character of the ethical, but it also possessed the irresistible vigor and impetus of a new revelation.' Thus, it saved 'the ethical emphasis of Judaism from being confined to the Jewish people'. Monotheism made Judaism's teachings acceptable to the sophisticated as well as the unlettered, and 'the same is true of Christianity'.[38]

This irenic, contrast-free presentation is, however, highly atypical. For both liberal Protestants and Liberal Jews, a key factor, perhaps *the* key factor, defining the quintessential character of their respective religions was ethics. Since Liberal Jews were no longer committed to traditional Jewish law, and liberal Christians, as I have already noted, were no longer committed to traditional Christian dogma, it followed that unless their ethical teachings

[37] Joseph Klausner, *From Jesus to Paul* (Heb.) (Tel Aviv, 1940), ii. 220–1. The full discussion fades, as best as I can see, into near incoherence, but I hope I have captured its recoverable essence. It is no accident that, in a quite different context, the argument from the need for national survival was invoked by the Zionist historian to defend acts that raise moral questions of the most serious sort. The Hasmonean expulsion of pagans and occasional acts of forcible conversion appear unjust, says Klausner, but a different policy would have led to the destruction of Judaea and the end of the Jewish people. Faced with such a prospect, 'the moral criterion *cannot help* but retreat, and in its place there comes another criterion: *the possibility of survival*'. See *History of the Second Temple*, 2nd edn, 5 vols (Jerusalem, 1951), iii. 65–6. I discuss this and other aspects of Klausner's Zionist historiography in 'Maccabees, Zealots, and Josephus: The Impact of Zionism on Joseph Klausner's *History of the Second Temple*', in Shaye J. D. Cohen and Joshua Schwartz (eds), *Studies in Josephus and the Varieties of Ancient Judaism: Louis H. Feldman Jubilee Volume* (Leiden, 2006).

[38] Mordecai Kaplan, 'The Contribution of Judaism to World Ethics', in Finkelstein (ed.), *The Jews*, ii. 686–7.

could be distinguished from those of rival religions, their own faith's *raison d'être* was called into question.

That this dynamic operates even in the absence of any ill will towards the Other was brought home to me with particular force in a contemporary context quite different from that of late nineteenth- and early twentieth-century Europe. The State of California was preparing a religion curriculum for its schools, and a still unfinished textbook in the history of religions prepared for this purpose had elicited criticism from Jewish organizations (and, not surprisingly, from other groups as well). The Jewish concerns centred on the depiction of Judaism in the time of Jesus. I was asked to comment on these criticisms and quickly realized that, *mutatis mutandis*, I had been transported back into the days of Schürer, Bousset, Harnack, Eschelbacher, Abrahams, Perles, et al. This time not a trace of antisemitism could reasonably be attributed to the authors, and yet they faced an intractable dilemma. How are the career and significance of Jesus of Nazareth to be presented in a school textbook? Separation of Church and State precludes the affirmation that he was the Messiah and Son of God who died for our sins. At the same time, the United States is a predominantly Christian country, so that Jesus cannot be presented simply as a charismatic preacher who taught more or less what his contemporaries taught but somehow so inspired his disciples that they succeeded in founding a religion centred upon him. What remains is precisely what remained for liberal Protestants in Europe a century earlier: a depiction of Jesus as the bearer of an ethical message distinct from that of his surroundings and markedly superior to it. While many of those liberal Protestants went well beyond what this structural dilemma had forced upon them, to a significant degree they had little choice.

Perhaps the most systematic—and one of the most combative—Jewish works arguing that whatever is admirable in Jesus's ethics is Jewish, while the rest is not particularly admirable, was Gerald Friedlander's *The Jewish Sources of the Sermon on the Mount* (1911).[39] It is worth noting in this connection that scholars, both Christian and Jewish, of the early twentieth century were not unaware of a methodological issue that has attained particular prominence in our own generation, to wit, the problem of using rabbinic materials, which have come down to us in a literary form that does not predate the second century, to characterize first-century Judaism. Friedlander cites several Christians who made this point with respect to various concepts, most notably the Fatherhood of God, but he argues vigorously, in part by resort to New Testament criticism, that the evidence of rabbinic texts and liturgy can justly be used to argue for Jewish priority.[40]

[39] See n. 6.

[40] Friedlander, *The Jewish Sources of the Sermon on the Mount*, 129–34.

Joseph Klausner also asserted that the key ethical categories of Judaism are equal or superior to those of Christianity. Thus, Paul's *agape* is simply Jewish love; indeed, he may have refrained from ascribing the principle of loving one's neighbour specifically to Jesus (Rom. 13: 8–10; Gal. 5: 13–14) precisely because he knew that this emphasis was already that of Hillel. At the same time, excessive emphasis on love can eclipse justice, so that Pauline love may be appropriate for the individual, but it cannot serve as the basis for social or national life. I think it is fair to maintain that Klausner and other Jews saw justice as a quintessential Jewish contribution to civilization but did not see it as mediated through Christianity except perhaps in the technical sense that Christians served as a conduit for the Hebrew Bible. I am tempted to say, in a reversal of the medieval Christian assertion, that Christians served as the book-bearers of the Jews.

Yehezkel Kaufmann, in his argument that Christian ethics did not provide the attraction that accounted for its victory over Judaism, made the particularly acute point that if Christians were so ethically sensitive they would have chosen Jewish civil and criminal law over the torture-ridden Roman *corpus iuris*.[41] But the most striking Jewish reversal of the argument from Christian ethical superiority was made by Leo Baeck. Christianity, he asserted, is the ultimate romantic religion, and the romantic stays away from law, from commandment, from the sphere of good and evil—and hence from ethical action as the highest ideal. Indeed, for Paul and Luther faith is counterposed to all works, not just the ceremonial. Paul made moral demands because he was rooted in Judaism, but ethics are merely an appendage to his religion as well as to that of later Christians. 'In the Church, ethics has basically always caused embarrassment. It was there—it had been introduced by the Old Testament which had been accepted as part of the Bible—but the faith lacked any organic relation to it.'[42]

Despite the centrality of the ethical moment, liberal Christians who had forsaken much of Christian dogma did not rest their case for Christianity on ethics alone. Harnack's famous account of the essence of Christianity spoke also of the kingdom of God, the Fatherhood of God, and the infinite value of the human soul, and especially emphasized the immediacy of Jesus's relationship with God. Eschelbacher's is the most detailed, systematic Jewish response to these assertions, appealing both to the biblical prophets and to rabbinic aggadah to establish the vibrancy of the Jewish encounter with the divine.[43]

[41] Kaufmann, *Exile and Alien Lands*, i. 405–6, noted in my 'Religion, Nationalism, and Historiography', 166.

[42] Baeck, *Judaism and Christianity*, 192–3, 249–51, 256. The standard approach of Jewish apologists in the exchange about ethics is exemplified by Moritz Lazarus, *Die Ethik des Judentums* (Frankfurt am Main, 1898, 1911).

[43] Eschelbacher, *Das Judentum und das Wesen des Christentums*, *passim*.

Buber made a major point of insisting on the reality of the Jew's immediate personal relationship with an imageless God.[44] And Montefiore insisted with vigour and eloquence that the doctrine of the Incarnation was not needed to bridge the gap between God and man. Jews 'from Isaiah to Jesus and from Jesus to Mendelssohn' did not feel what a Christian writer described as 'despair at the seemingly hopeless task of climbing the heavens and finding the unapproachable God'. Indeed, says Montefiore in a somewhat different context, the complete incarnation of the Logos at a particular time and place substitutes 'something mechanical, sensuous, spasmodic, magical' for the gradual unfolding of God's plan for the world.[45]

Finally, a word about eschatology. That Judaism 'contributed' to Christianity its concept of a redeemer hardly needs to be said.[46] Jews through the ages concentrated on stressing the differences between the Jewish criteria for identifying the Messiah and those of Christianity, not the obvious commonalities. Thus, *inter alia*, the Jewish Messiah is a human being, not a denizen of the heavens. But the genre we are examining can produce, as we have already seen, some surprising assertions of influence. In this case, Leo Baeck, while of course rejecting the conception of a fully divine redeemer, insisted that the concept of a supernatural Messiah was indeed borrowed from Judaism. Baeck was convinced that the figure 'like a [son of] man' in Daniel 7 who comes with the clouds of heaven is in fact the pre-existent Messiah. Thus, 'faith had long raised the figure of the Messiah beyond all human limitations into a supra-historical, supra-terrestrial sphere. He was endowed with the radiance of the heavens and transfigured above the earth.' Buber maintained that the son of man in Daniel is a 'still indefinite image', and even this is too strong a depiction of a figure who is almost certainly nothing more than a symbol. But Baeck sees him as a supernatural Messiah, so that the basic building block of the Christian messianic conception is not merely in extra-biblical apocalypses but in the Jewish Bible itself.[47] Baeck does, however, make a point of noting that the Greek word *soter*, or saviour, which is applied by Luke to Jesus, is a term whose Hebrew equivalent is used in the Jewish Bible about God alone.[48]

44 Martin Buber, *Two Types of Faith* (New York, 1951), 130–1. A Christian scholar writing in our genre also stressed that 'the Fatherhood of God' is a Jewish term, but could not refrain from adding a qualification about the fresh vitality infused into it by Jesus. See Francis C. Burkitt, 'The Debt of Christianity to Judaism', in Bevan and Singer (eds), *The Legacy of Israel*, 72.

45 Montefiore, 'Notes on the Religious Value of the Fourth Gospel', 66–7, 40.

46 Burkitt, 'The Debt of Christianity to Judaism', 95–6, makes the related observation that 'the reality and eternal significance of time', the awareness that reality is a grand drama to be played out but once, is a lesson learned from Judaism by all forms of Christianity.

47 Baeck, *Judaism and Christianity*, 66, 148; Buber, *Two Types of Faith*, 112.

48 I cannot resist noting a personal experience with the term *soter* in the context of Jewish–Christian relations. In 1995 the Open University in Israel distributed an eight-part

No less surprising is Baeck's identification of the Christian missionary spirit as a function of Jewish influence. The modern affirmation of Jewish universalism and tolerance, going back to Mendelssohn's emphasis on the portion of ethical non-Jews in the world to come, led Jews to characterize Christian mission as a function of a regrettably intolerant spirit. Not so Baeck. Romantic religion, he says, looks inward, possessing the promise as a gift. It was the Jewish element in Paul, with its 'confidence in the meaning of man's exertions', that gave Christianity its missionary impulse, which remains strongest in those Christian groups who are closest to Judaism and the Old Testament.[49]

The project of demonstrating the Jewish contribution to civilization was simultaneously easiest and most difficult when the object of Jewish beneficence was Christianity. Jews wanted to show that they had enriched the world through their daughter religion, but they did not want to render her as attractive as her parent. What is Jewish and what is not, what is Christian and what is not, what is legalistic and what is not, what is ethical and what is not, what is particularistic and what is not—these questions and more provide a window not only into the dynamics of Judaism's encounter with a dominant faith but into its struggle to define its own contours and to penetrate the depths of its soul.

video of discussions between Yeshayahu Leibowitz and Marcel Dubois about Judaism and Christianity that had taken place in 1992 (*In Two Octaves*). The conversations were held in Hebrew, and the video supplied English subtitles. I was asked to comment on two of the instalments when the series was shown on a cable TV channel in New York, and so I read the English carefully. Near the end of the second programme, Leibowitz tells Dubois that Paul did a terrible thing by denying halakhah and insisting that everything depends on the *soter*. The term recurs about five times at the end of that instalment and the beginning of the third. The translator, who knew Hebrew and English but had no understanding of theology or of Greek, recognized *soter* as a perfectly good Hebrew word, and repeatedly provided the incoherent translation 'refuter' or 'refutation'. When I noted this, I had to struggle to convince the moderator that the translation was incorrect.

[49] Baeck, *Judaism and Christianity*, 284–9. We recall that Joseph Jacobs had also included Christian missionizing in his lengthy list of Jewish influences on Christianity. See n. 6.

SIX

Judaism, Islam, and Hellenism: The Conflict in Germany over the Origins of Kultur

SUSANNAH HESCHEL

JEWS did not simply 'contribute to civilization', they gave birth to it. That, at least, was the dominant rhetoric of most modern Jewish thinkers in Europe. While 'civilization' was equated principally with Europe, at least in the eyes of Europeans, Jews expanded the rubric to include eras of Islamic efflorescence, and even contrasted a tolerant, scientifically sophisticated, and morally upright Muslim culture with an intolerant, backward, and morally degenerate Christian culture. The mode of measurement in both cases was the extent to which the two daughter religions of Judaism deviated from the mother: by mixing Jewish monotheism with pagan ideas, Christianity had lost its moral bearings, whereas Islam, by virtue of its stricter monotheism, had not strayed as far from the moral righteousness of Jewish teaching. That, however, was the viewpoint of Jewish thinkers, hardly widespread in Christian Europe.

Norbert Elias has called attention to the particular German understanding of 'civilization'. For the English and French, 'civilization' expresses 'their pride in the significance of their own nations for the progress of the West and of mankind'. For Germans, by contrast, 'civilization' is a term that, he writes, 'is indeed useful, but nevertheless only a value of the second rank, comprising only the outer appearance of human beings, the surface of human existence. The word through which Germans interpret themselves, which more than any other expresses their pride in their own achievement and their own being, is *Kultur*.'[1] *Kultur* was linked in the German imagination to spiritual origins stemming from classical Greece, and was part of what E. M. Butler termed the 'tyranny of Greece over Germany' that flour-

[1] Norbert Elias, *The Civilizing Process*, trans. Edmund Jephcott (New York, 1978); first pub. as *Über den Prozess der Zivilisation. Soziogenetische und psychogenetische Untersuchungen* (Basel, 1936).

ished in the eighteenth and nineteenth centuries.[2] Romantic thinkers in several countries in Europe, most notably Johann Gottfried Herder, Matthew Arnold, and Ernest Renan, emphasized the Hellenic as the cultural ideal, defining it in opposition to 'Hebraism', each for different motives. As Tessa Rajak writes, 'The Greeks are understood as being what the Hebrews are understood as not being.'[3] In each case, the Hellenic was that which the Hebraic was not, which encouraged a negative or at least inferior depiction of Hebraism and raised questions regarding early Christianity as repository of both traditions, the Greek thought of Paul and the Hebraic religion of the Old Testament. The smooth flow of divine revelation from Old to New Testament, exemplified in the studies of mid-nineteenth-century theologians as religiously divergent as the highly conservative Ernst Hengstenberg and the liberal Karl von Hase, was interrupted by Hellenic–Hebraic dichotomy.

That dichotomy, in turn, set the stage for Jewish thinkers, who argued for Judaism's centrality within Western civilization as the 'mother religion' of three great monotheisms. Their argument was that Western civilization originated with Judaism's monotheism and emphasis on the ethical, and that Christianity and Islam were derivative religions that strayed, to a greater or lesser degree, from the purity of Judaism. The two models of argumentation played an important role in Protestant theological developments in Germany, in which Christianity (like the Hellenic) was placed in opposition to Judaism, and Western *Kultur* was defined as originally and essentially Aryan, in opposition to the Semitic. By the decades just before the Third Reich, a group of Protestant theologians in Germany sought to recover the Aryan identity of Christianity through a process of de-Judaization, a theological adaptation of racial theory.

Starting in the early nineteenth century, Jews questioned how Scripture, especially the Old Testament, could compete with the great works of classical Hellenic culture. Hellenism was widely identified in Germany with ethics, beauty, nature, culture, and philosophy, leaving the Hebraic (Jewish) side of the equation with the negative attributes traditionally assigned by Christian thought. The initial strategy of Jewish thinkers was to adopt Herder's aesthetic defence of Hebrew poetics, which had little impact on subsequent Christian scholarship. Herder was extended and modified within the early Wissenschaft des Judentums by Abraham Geiger's identification of

[2] E. M. Butler, *The Tyranny of Greece over Germany: A Study of the Influence Exercised by Greek Art and Poetry over the Great German Writers of the Eighteenth, Nineteenth and Twentieth Centuries* (Cambridge, 1935).

[3] Tessa Rajak, 'Jews and Greeks: The Invention and Exploitation of Polarities in the Nineteenth Century', in Rajak, *The Jewish Dialogue with Greece and Rome: Studies in Cultural and Social Interaction* (Leiden, 2001), 539.

the 'religious genius' of the Hebrew soul. The Greeks had an inborn genius for philosophy, while the Jews invented religion, he wrote in an argument resonant among many German Jews. Geiger went further, juxtaposing the figure of Jesus, as a singular Jew claimed by Christian theologians to have had a unique religious consciousness, with the extraordinary religiosity of the collective Jewish people. Even as Geiger claimed there was nothing new in Jesus's message, that it was entirely derived from Pharisaic Judaism, he invented the religion of the Jewish people along the model of liberal Protestants, and created the Pharisees in the image of the Protestant Jesus, part of a broader trend that was later criticized by Franz Rosenzweig in his essay 'Atheistic Theology'.[4]

While Jewish texts since antiquity had mocked various aspects of Christianity, from the life of Jesus to Church dogma, Jewish thought in the modern period walked a finer tightrope, affirming Christianity's central role in European civilization and yet at the same time claiming that Christianity, at its origins, was derived from Judaism. The Hellenic, in Jewish thought, was given a secondary role in the shaping of Europe, because its opposition to Judaism was too deeply ingrained to be overcome, and no claim for Jewish influence over the Hellenic could be established. Indeed, one senses a concern that Germany's love of the Hellenic has led to a neglect of Judaism, and a desire to repair that imbalance by showing the superiority or at least parity of Jewish genius to Greek.

JEWS, HELLENISM, ISLAM, AND *KULTUR*

'Athens and Jerusalem' is a phrase that runs as a motto over the course of 2,000 years of Jewish self-understanding, and in a variety of Jewish literatures—historiographical, political, literary—has long served as a metaphor for Jewish relations with the non-Jewish world. Indeed, the term 'Judaism' is used for the first time in contrast to Hellenism, in 2 Maccabees 4, and ever since then Judaism has been defined in nearly every generation as a kind of inverse of Hellenism—Torah versus Homer—with all the affinities implied by mirror images.[5] A shift, however, comes in Jewish discussions from classical Greece to Hellenism more generally, and the latter is most often presented as a degenerative movement that demonstrates the inability of classical Greek civilization to maintain its purity over the centuries and after

[4] Franz Rosenzweig, 'Atheistic Theology: From the Old to the New Way of Thinking', trans. Robert G. Goldy and H. Frederick Holch, *Canadian Journal of Theology*, 14/2 (1968), 79–88. See also Susannah Heschel, *Abraham Geiger and the Jewish Jesus* (Chicago, 1998).

[5] Mishnah *Yadayim* contrasts Homeric writings with Torah over the question of which text conveys ritual impurity. The question is debated by Sadducees and Pharisees. See the excellent, thorough study by Yaacov Shavit, *Athens in Jerusalem: Classical Antiquity and Hellenism in the Making of the Modern Secular Jew*, trans. Chaya Naor and Niki Werner (London, 1997).

it is exported throughout the Mediterranean basin. While classical Greece gives evidence for a Greek genius for philosophy and the plastic arts, Geiger writes, the Hellenism carried by Alexander had become aged.[6]

It is striking that the mode of Jewish claims to civilizational priority was primarily the discipline of history. Historicism was not only on the rise in Europe, it was identified as a quintessentially European project, distinguishing the colonizer from the colonized. Historicism was the discipline through which civilized status was demonstrated and legitimized; as Dipesh Chakrabarty has argued: 'Historicism enabled European domination of the world in the nineteenth century.'[7] As much as theology gave rise to historicism, it was through the great nineteenth-century historicist project of determining the origins and originality of Christianity that Judaism's 'inferiority' was transferred from the theological to the historicist realm, and that the religions of the colonized were invented—Hinduism, Buddhism, Taoism, Confucianism, and so forth.[8] In grasping the reins of historicism, Jewish scholars in Europe were not only engaging in theological polemics that had been transferred to a new discipline, but were also taking a political stance, using historicism as a tool to combat Christian Europe's political as well as intellectual imperialism.

During the nineteenth century, as Jewish historical scholarship first took shape, Hellenism, as Tessa Rajak has shown, became a template for a variety of relations with the outside world, all of which served to define in turn the nature of Judaism and Jewish identity, just as Hellenism functioned as a template for describing Western *Kultur*.[9] The most passionate and dramatic debate in the past hundred years has been geographical: was Hellenism limited to the Diaspora, or did Hellenism extend its reach into Jewish Palestine, and how much did it infiltrate? In the German Jewish historical narratives of the nineteenth century, Hellenism functions as the danger from without that challenges the integrity of Jewish religious belief and practice. The Hellenism of the Syrians that threatened Palestine in the second century BCE and was supposedly defeated by the Maccabean revolt is defined as a degenerate Hellenism, whereas that of Egypt, with its sizeable Jewish communities, especially in Alexandria, is given greater respect and viewed not as a danger, but as an opportunity for Jewish religious growth. Why, Heinrich Graetz asks, did the classical Greek civilization die out, despite its creativity, while the Hebrew survived? The Greeks had 'no determined, self-conscious

[6] Abraham Geiger, *Das Judenthum und seine Geschichte bis zur Zerstörung des zweiten Tempels* (Breslau, 1865), 78.

[7] Dipesh Chakrabarty, *Provincializing Europe: Postcolonial Thought and Historical Difference* (Princeton, 2000), 7.

[8] Peter Harison, *Religion and the Religions in the English Enlightenment* (New York, 1990).

[9] See Rajak, 'Jews and Greeks'.

life task. The Hebrew people, however, had a life task that united them and strengthened and preserved them in terrible times.'[10]

While undertones of the debates over political emancipation and assimilation affected Jewish scholarship during the nineteenth century, there was an additional context. Both the Christian fascination with Greece and the Jewish response to it may have been motivated by a search for cultural roots and their contemporary manifestation, but Jewish scholarship took on a different configuration. Examination of Jewish scholarship reveals that the rise of 'orientalism' in Europe that was identified by Edward Said took a very different direction among Jewish thinkers. The attributes of 'orientalism' were applied by Jewish scholars not to Islam but to Hellenism. In similar fashion, Jewish scholarship lends support to Martin Bernal's claim that European constructions of 'Hellenism' were projections of Christian cultural and racial superiority; for Jewish scholars, the attributes associated with Hellenic civilization were applied instead to Islam. Each group constructed the Hellenic and the Islamic in its own image, and the two came into being as a result of theological polemics and political self-definitions of both Christians and Jews, illustrating Anthony Grafton's point that 'From Wolf at the beginning of the century to Wilamowitz at the end, influential scholars set out research programmes that called for a rigorous historicism, but insisted on their personal allegiance to the unique superiority of Hellenism.'[11]

The European Jewish search for cultural roots in the nineteenth century was aimed at affinities between Jewish and Islamic civilizations. The philhellenism that imbued Germany was replaced among German Jews by a philislamism, and much of the rhetoric of 'orientalism' developed by non-Jewish Europe can be found in Jewish scholarship applied to Hellenistic culture, rather than Muslim. Hellenistic Jewish civilization was received with ambivalence, as a cultural moment in which most Jews abandoned Judaism, whereas Jews within Islamic civilization had an opportunity to bring into Hebrew discourse new philosophical and scientific methods that deepened Judaism's self-understanding. In addition, Jewish philislamism was part of an ongoing polemic by Jewish theologians against Christianity's historic intolerance towards Jews. Jews presented Islam as superior to Christianity because of its greater historic tolerance of Jews; the myth of a Golden Age of Spain and a symbiosis of Jewish and Muslim culture was invented by German Jewish historians as a model not so much of what Germany might become as of what Jews (west European Jews at least) were capable of achieving within a tolerant society.[12]

[10] Heinrich Graetz, *Geschichte der Juden* (Berlin, 2002), i. 21.

[11] Anthony Grafton, 'Germany and the West 1830–1900', in K. J. Dover (ed.), *Perceptions of Ancient Greece* (Oxford, 1992), 239.

[12] Daniel Schroeter notes that German Jews, in their disdain for their east European counterparts, labelled them as 'oriental'. See Daniel J. Schroeter, 'Orientalism and the Jews of the Mediterranean', *Journal of Mediterranean Studies*, 4/2 (1994), 183–96.

Jewish scholarship, in other words, transferred the rhetoric of 'orientalism' to Hellenistic civilization, and transferred the Christian adoration of classical Hellenic culture to Islamic civilization. The Jewish criticisms of Hellenism became a kind of inverse apologetic for the lack of Jewish status in the eyes of Western civilization, focusing most of its claims on the allegedly inferior morals of Hellenists compared to those of the Jews, particularly on sexual issues. To accomplish that, it was easy to draw on classical Jewish texts to describe Hellenism in the feminine metaphors frequently employed in orientalist rhetoric, as seductive, sexual, beautiful, concerned with the arts, wine, and women, and so forth, to enhance the masculine status of Jewish culture. That tradition extends to the Mishnah itself, in its feminine metaphors for Hellenism. For example, the Nasi Gamaliel II, when asked why he bathed at a public bath at Acco in which there was a statue of Aphrodite, replied, 'I did not come into her domain, she came into mine.'[13]

The overarching historiographical tension in the study of Hellenism, however, was between Jewish and Christian theologians over the question of the origins of Christianity—Greek or Jewish—and, by implication, the origins and nature of west European civilization. In commencing their efforts to write a history of Christian origins, Protestant theologians in nineteenth-century Germany were faced with a dilemma. Demonstrating the novelty and singularity of the Christian message was the obligation of historians, who had to present the context with which Christianity broke, but which also provided the occasion for its occurrence. Writing the history of Christianity meant establishing that which gave rise to it and that which it superseded. The nature of that historical moment was crucial for the theological claim to Christian originality, but establishing that originality also meant establishing that which Jesus rejected; i.e. what was wrong with Judaism. This in turn engendered the dilemma that plagues much New Testament scholarship to this day: is the historical authenticity of sayings attributed to Jesus to be determined by their similarity with other teachings of the same era, or by what Norman Perrin later termed the 'criterion of dissimilarity'?

Determining originality revolved primarily around the two poles of Judaism and Hellenism: which exerted the greater influence in the teachings of Jesus, Paul, and the early Christian community, and with which did they break most definitively? The definition of the newness of the Christian message rested on the way the large Jewish and Hellenistic contexts were defined. In most Protestant interpretations, Jesus's faith was what Judaism was not, and Hellenism was the vehicle by which he exited from the Jewish context. In most Jewish interpretations, Jesus's faith was simply the common Pharisaic religion

[13] Mishnah *AZ* 3: 4.

of his day, while Paul became the founder of Christianity by mixing Judaism with Hellenistic religious ideas—a betrayal of Jesus's own Judaism and the reason for the ultimate Christian break with Judaism.

The development of Judaism was given a different historical path. Modern Jewish theologians were united in their insistence on Judaism as originary and resistant. The traditional rabbinic view was that the Greeks learned their wisdom from Judaism: 'Pythagoras, Socrates and Plato followed in Moses' footsteps,' says Aristobulos, and Philo added the Athenian legislators. To this argument was added a rivalry: the Greeks had a genius for philosophy, the Jews had a genius for religion; Graetz writes that 'Greeks and Hebrews are alone as creators and founders of higher cultures.'[14] The question posed by Jewish writers was: which kind of genius produces and sustains a moral order in society? The answer was everywhere the same. Geiger writes that the Greeks have an imperfect idea of deity, with crude religious conceptions.[15] Unable to grow and be transformed, Greek culture became exhausted.[16] While the Greeks produced artists, Jews produced prophets.[17] The Greeks spoke of taming one's passions, while Judaism speaks of moral elevation.[18] In Hellenism, the 'worth of woman according to her true character has not been properly appreciated', while 'noble pictures of woman . . . [are found] throughout Jewish literature'.[19] Similarly, for Graetz the Greeks lacked morality and were imbued with concerns for the physical and aesthetic, which he regarded as superficial and lacking moral purpose. He writes contemptuously, 'The ideal of the Greek was beauty and science; but this ideal only served them for comfort, pleasure, and enjoyment. Did they ever show any self-sacrifice or produce any martyrs for these ideals?'[20] Underlying the question of morality in Judaism and Hellenism is actually the question of morality in Judaism and Christianity, a motif at the centre of modern Jewish theology. Graetz is quite explicit: while Judaism is distinguished by its morality, Christianity was contaminated by paganism, leading to the immorality of modern European society.[21] Similar views were expressed by Leo Baeck a generation later in his distinction between ethical religion, Judaism, and romantic religion, Christianity.

Just as Jewish thinkers presented Hellenic culture as declining into a corrupt Hellenism with its geographic dispersion, Christianity, too, was presented as a decline from the pure Jewish teachings of Jesus to a pagan-inflected doctrinal system once it left Palestine. Christianity took Greek

[14] Graetz, *Geschichte der Juden*, i. 19. [15] Geiger, *Das Judenthum und seine Geschichte*, 19.
[16] Ibid. 19. [17] Ibid. 34.
[18] Ibid. 19. [19] Ibid. 44.
[20] Graetz, 'Historical Parallels in Jewish History', in Graetz, *The Structure of Jewish History and Other Essays*, ed. and trans. Ismar Schorsch (New York, 1975), 265.
[21] Graetz, 'The Significance of Judaism for the Present and Future', ibid. 283.

ideas such as the Logos, divine transcendence, the son of God, and divine sacrificial death from a Hellenized Jewish thought, and Paul brought those ideas to the non-Jews, with the idea that Jewish law should be abolished. Like Jesus, Islam was said to stand within Judaism; the important difference is that Islam did not become a persecutory religion. Geiger writes, 'Whatever good elements Islam contains, whatever enduring idea appears in it, it has taken over from Judaism [the unity of God] . . . It is the only fruit-bearing and world-conquering thought contained in Islam.'[22] In their later development, however, both Islam and Christianity drew from Hellenism as well as Judaism, but in different ways. Islam, Geiger writes, 'availed itself of those resources and formed a connection with them. The Koran had drawn from Judaism and its Bible the best and noblest contents. The literature of the Muslims following thereafter leaned especially upon the monuments of Greek literature which came to them in translations.'[23]

In contrast to the persecution endured by Jews within Christian Europe, the Arab world is portrayed as a sanctuary shared by two Semitic peoples; indeed, Graetz writes that Jews in Spain reached their highest pinnacle of culture and knowledge and that Islam 'has exercised an immense influence on the course of Jewish history and on the evolution of Judaism'.[24]

Such attitudes were in sharp contrast to non-Jewish attitudes. Scholars and publicists of the Enlightenment in France and Germany regularly spoke of Muhammad as a hypocrite, deceiver, and fanatic, a *Schwärmer*; Voltaire called him 'a bloodthirsty rogue', and scholars of the nineteenth century indulged in similar epithets, calling him treacherous, cunning, selfish, and a deceptive fraud, although the views of English scholars, such as George Sale and Simon Ockley, as well as Thomas Carlyle, were far more positive. As Albert Hourani notes, Islam was viewed as both the enemy and the rival of Christianity.[25] For most Christian theologians in Germany, Islam lacked truth and originality, and was either the product of Christian heretical movements in Arabia, or else a parasitic growth (*Schmarotzergewächs*) of 'late Judaism', as Hubert Grimme wrote in 1902.[26] Yet, as colonizing and missionary activity grew in the nineteenth century, Christian theologians asked if the success of Islam might be a divine judgement against Christians of the East, who were easy targets for conversion to Islam as a result of their weak Christianity. Perhaps, as F. D. Maurice, the nineteenth-century Christian

[22] Geiger, *Das Judenthum und seine Geschichte*, 156.

[23] Geiger, *Das Judenthum und seine Geschichte bis zum Ende des zwölften Jahrhunderts* (Breslau, 1865), 96.

[24] Graetz, *Geschichte der Juden*, v. 100.

[25] Albert Hourani, *Islam in European Thought* (Cambridge, 1991), 16.

[26] Hubert Grimme, Review of A. Geiger, *Was hat Muhammed*, *Orientalistische Literatur-Zeitung*, 7 Jahrgang, No. 6 (June 1904), 226–8.

socialist, argued, Islam functioned to deter Christians from sinking into paganism.[27]

By contrast, for Jewish theologians, Islam was neither an enemy nor a rival. In theology and practice, it was the product of Judaism and remained its great friend, sharing its strict monotheism, morality, and respect for religious law, but also providing an open and tolerant cultural and political environment for Jews during most of the periods and places of its rule. Geiger described Muhammad as a 'genuine enthusiast who was himself convinced of his divine mission, and to whom the union of all religions appeared necessary for the welfare of mankind'.[28] Geiger demonstrated parallels between rabbinic and Koranic literature, to argue for Islamic derivation from Judaism—and not from a Christian heretical sect, as had been assumed since the days of John of Damascus (675–749)—and Jewish historians described a 'creative symbiosis' that emerged between medieval Jewish and Muslim cultures.[29] All depicted Jewish life in Muslim Spain as a Golden Age in which Jewish communal and cultural life flourished and was fully integrated into the larger society, with Jews and Muslims working closely together to produce great monumental works of science, philosophy, theology, and poetry—in sharp contrast to their descriptions of impoverished, isolated, and pious Jewish life in medieval Christian Europe, with little contact other than periods of persecution. Indeed, most German Jewish historians of the nineteenth century blame Christian intolerance for the rise of Jewish rabbinic narrowness, legal pettiness, and kabbalistic nonsense. Graetz writes:

From the decrepitude, ossification, and senility of the inner relations among Jews in the Occident one turns with delight to the freshness and youthfulness of the communities in Guadalquivir and Guadiana. Knowledge itself was neither one-sided nor dry, but rather filled itself with healthy juices and strove to remain fresh

[27] Grimme, Review of Geiger, 222.

[28] The many distinguished Jewish scholars of Islam included, in addition to Geiger, Isaac Gastfreund, Gustav Weil, Hartwig Hirschfeld, Israel Schapiro, Hayim Zeev Hirschberg, David Künstlinger, Rudolf Lesczynsky, and Ignaz Goldziher, to name a partial list.

[29] Hartwig Hirschfeld, 'Essai sur l'histoire des Juifs de Médine', 2 pts., *Revue des Études Juives*, 7 (1883), 167–93; 10 (1885), 10–31; id., *Beiträgen zur Erklärung des Koran* (Leipzig, 1886); also see his *Jüdische Elemente im Koran. Ein Beitrag zur Koranforschung* (Berlin, 1878). See also Israel Schapiro, *Die haggadischen Elemente im erzählenden Teil des Korans*, i (Leipzig, 1907); Victor Aptowitzer, *Kain und Abel in der Agada, den Apokryphen, der hellenistischen, christlichen und muhammedanischen Literatur* (Vienna, 1922); Gustav Weil, *Mohammed der Prophet. Sein Leben und Seine Lehre. Aus handschriftlichen Quellen und dem Koran geschöpft und dargestellt* (Stuttgart, 1843); *Historisch-kritische Einleitung in den Koran* (Bielefeld, 1844); *Biblische Legenden der Muselmänner. Aus arabischen Quellen zusammengetragen und mit jüdischen Sagen verglichen* (Frankfurt am Main, 1845). See Rudi Paret's evaluation of Geiger in *The Study of Arabic and Islam at German Universities: German Orientalists since Theodor Nöldeke* (Wiesbaden, 1968), 9–10.

and enjoyable. The educated Jews of Andalusia spoke and wrote the language of the land with as much purity as their Arabic co-inhabitants, and they were proud to count Jewish poets in their ranks.[30]

More than simply political and religious freedom, Muslim Spain was said to have offered Jews the opportunity for a cultural symbiosis and indicated through its tolerance and encouragement of intellectual and theological exploration the superiority of Islam to Christianity. While both Islam and Christianity stemmed from Judaism, only Islam exerted a constructive influence on Judaism, according to Graetz:

Thanks to their Semitic origins the Jews of Arabia had many points of contact with those born in the land. Their language was related to Arabic, their customs, in so far as they were not generated by the religion, were not all that different from those of the sons of Arabs. The Jews Arabized themselves so completely that they could only be distinguished from the inhabitants of the land through their religious beliefs. Ties of marriage between the two strengthened the similarities in character between the two groups.[31]

Moreover, the relationship was two-sided. Graetz writes that Islam 'was inspired by Judaism to bring into the world a new religious form with political foundations, which one calls Islam, and it in turn exerted a powerful impact on Jewish history and the development of Judaism'.[32]

In presenting Islam as religiously and politically superior to European Christian culture, Jews were searching for previous eras in which they were able to create Jewish philosophy, literature, and scholarship in a free and open atmosphere, without the pressures of narrow-minded Orthodox rabbis. Islam was credited as tolerant, pluralistic, and intellectually far more advanced than the Christian culture of the same era, as part of a larger polemical effort against Christianity as well as the Orthodox rabbinate.

Similar polemics were articulated a generation later by Ignaz Goldziher, the Hungarian Jew who came to be recognized as one of Europe's greatest scholars of Islam. Profoundly influenced in his study of the Hadith by the methods developed by Geiger in his study of rabbinic and targumic literature, Goldziher also was in accord with Geiger's efforts at reform of Judaism and his polemics against Christianity.[33] Through Geiger's work, Goldziher came to understand the radically historicist methods of the Tübingen School, though it was only after reading Strauss and Baur that Goldziher, he writes, 'began to understand Geiger's message'.[34]

30 Graetz, *Geschichte der Juden*, v. 370. 31 Ibid. 76. 32 Ibid. 101.

33 Robert Simon, *Ignac Goldziher: His Life and Scholarship as Reflected in his Works and Correspondence* (Leiden, 1986), 101.

34 Ignaz Goldziher, *Tagebuch* (Leiden, 1978), 39; cited by Simon, *Ignac Goldziher*, 134.

Christianity, Goldziher wrote, was bankrupt: 'What has this system with its nineteen hundred year history of world conquest brought forth? Dogmas and pyres.'[35] Islam was superior to Judaism as well as Christianity: 'My ideal was to elevate Judaism to a similar rational level.'[36] By contrast, Goldziher called Christianity an 'abominable religion, which invented the Christian blood libel. . . . The forehead of a whore, that is the forehead of Christianity.'[37]

The myth of the Golden Age of Jewish–Muslim intellectual and religious cooperation, however discredited today, was created in the nineteenth century to provide a 'stately new model' for Jewish contributions to modern European society. Golden Age Jews assimilated without losing their sense of Jewish identity, and their contributions to intellectual life were extraordinary. Yet the myth also functioned as a polemic, primarily, as John Efron has described, in denigrating Christianity as an intolerant religion in comparison to Islam, and also in rejecting Orthodoxy as a barrier to full participation in intellectual and cultural life.

CHRISTIANITY AND GERMAN NATIONALISM

Even as Jewish thinkers were disparaging Hellenism and depicting Judaism and its monotheism as the font of Western civilization, Christian thinkers moved to assert the originality of Christianity and its autonomy from Jewish influences. The search for a German *Kultur* was bound up, of course, with the German search for national identity and the concomitant racial dimensions that became part of that search. The centrality of religion, specifically German Protestantism, in the formation of the German nation is well known, as is the *Kulturkampf* that left Catholic membership in the German nation queasy. Protestant theology, in turn, increased its nationalist overtones by the late nineteenth century, a phenomenon well explored by historians. Often neglected in analyses of the complex of nation formation, however, are the role of theology in the construction of race and the role of race in the development of modern German Protestantism. Indeed, there remains in general an underexamined and undertheorized relationship between religion and race.

Protestantism was not simply a theological matter, but a national project, and scholarship on Jesus, as Albert Schweitzer once wrote, was a Germanic

[35] Goldziher, *Tagebuch*, 284; cited by John Efron, 'From Mitteleuropa to the Middle East', *Jewish Quarterly Review*, 94/3 (2004), 518.

[36] Goldziher, *Tagebuch*, 59; cited by Efron, 'From Mitteleuropa to the Middle East', 514.

[37] Raphael Patai, *Ignaz Goldziher and his Oriental Diary* (Detroit, 1987), 21; cited by Efron, 'Orientalism and the Jewish Historical Gaze', in Ivan Davidson Kalmar and Derek J. Penslar (eds), *Orientalism and the Jews* (Hanover, NH, 2005), 92.

activity. It was in Germany where scholarship on the Bible was concentrated throughout the nineteenth century and up to the Second World War, in part stimulated by the Lutheran quest for the authentic biblical text. D. F. Strauss entitled his 1864 life of Jesus 'for the German *Volk*'. A special affinity between the Germans and Christianity, especially Protestantism, was asserted by figures as diverse as Paul de Lagarde, Jacob Grimm, and Artur Bonus, but both realms of German and Christian civilization required cleansing of Jewish accretions, to complete the task Luther had begun. Fichte, in his 1807 *Reden an die deutsche Nation*, hailed Martin Luther himself as a kind of Christ figure: Luther 'became the pattern for all generations to come and died for us all'. Luther and his Reformation expressed the 'characteristic of the German spirit'.[38] Karl von Hase called Luther a *Volksheilige*,[39] Heinrich von Treitschke called him a 'Christian–Germanic *Kampfgenossen*',[40] and the 1910 edition of the important lexicon *Religion in Geschichte und Gegenwart* stated that Luther had Germanized Christianity.[41] Finally, Siegfried Leffler, a leader of the pro-Nazi German Christian Movement, declared in 1935 that Hitler stood in a direct line with Luther. Both had brought about a national revival, which Leffler interpreted as a part of religious history, and were conflated: 'So we cannot think of Adolf Hitler without Martin Luther.'[42] Ultimately, one slogan of the German Christians (the Deutsche Christen) became: 'With Luther and Hitler for Faith and *Volkstum*!' The conflation of nationalism and religion was soon joined by race. Gobineau's assertion that the Germanic race was the highest, but that

[38] J. G. Fichte, *Addresses to the German Nation*, trans. R. F. Jones and G. H. Turnbull (Chicago, 1922), 97. 'Es bleibt auch bei diesem Evangelisten immer zweifelhaft, ob Jesus aus jüdischem Stamme sei, oder, falls er es doch etwa wäre, wie es mit seiner Abstammung sich eigentlich verhalte' (*J. G. Fichte Werke*, ed. Fritz Medicus, iv (Leipzig, 1912), 105; cited by Alan T. Davies, 'The Aryan Christ: A Motif in Christian Anti-Semitism', *Journal of Ecumenical Studies*, 12 (Fall 1975), 569–79).

[39] Karl von Hase, *Handbuch der protestantische Polemik gegen die römisch-katholische Kirche* (Leipzig, 1862), 589–90; cited by Hedda Gramley, *Propheten des deutschen Nationalismus. Theologen, Historiker und Nationalökonomen 1848–1880* (Frankfurt am Main, 2001), 95.

[40] Wolfgang Tilgner, 'Volk, Nation und Vaterland im protestantischen Denken zwischen Kaiserreich und Nationalsozialismus (ca. 1870–1933)', in Horst Zilleßen (ed.), *Volk—Nation—Vaterland. Der deutsche Protestantismus und der Nationalismus* (Gütersloh, 1970), 140. The classic analyses of German *völkisch* thought are George L. Mosse, *The Crisis of German Ideology: The Intellectual Origins of the Third Reich* (New York, 1964); Fritz Stern, *The Politics of Cultural Despair: A Study in the Rise of the Germanic Ideology* (New York, 1961). See also Uwe Puschner, *Die völkische Bewegung im wilhelminischen Kaiserreich. Sprache—Rasse—Religion* (Darmstadt, 2001), and Uwe Puschner, Walter Schmitz, and Justus H. Ulbright (eds), *Handbuch zur völkischen Bewegung, 1871–1918* (Munich, 1996).

[41] Eva-Maria Kaffanke, *Der deutsche Heiland. Christusdarstellungen um 1900 im Kontext der völkischen Bewegung* (Frankfurt am Main, 2001), 152–3.

[42] Siegfried Leffler, *Christus im dritten Reich der Deutschen. Wesen, Weg und Ziel der Kirchenbewegung 'Deutsche Christen'* (Weimar, n.d., foreword dated 1935), 75.

today's Germans were a mongrel race superseded by the English, annoyed the *völkisch* movement, which sought to prove the superiority of present-day Germans and to purify Germany of any threats to that superiority.

The celebration of the Lutheran jubilee in 1917 in the midst of the First World War further reinforced the alliance between Protestantism and German nationalism that had taken formal shape in the last decades of the nineteenth century, as Thomas Nipperdey has described, and that had become, by the 1890s, an 'emotional *Akklamationsnationalismus*' with the slogan 'Ein Volk, Ein Reich, Ein Gott' ('One Race, One Empire, One God').[43] Indeed, in 1896, Artur Bonus, a pastor in Niederlausitz, West Prussia, called for an active Germanization of Christianity,[44] six years after the Protestant theologian Otto Pfleiderer had written that the German *Volk* was 'predestined for Protestant Christianity'.[45] To Germanize Christianity meant to purify it by removing non-German, Jewish accretions.[46] Indeed, an entire generation of pre-First World War German youth was exposed in academic and theological circles to a national Protestant theology and to an idea of a Christian German unified culture.[47] Just as a unique 'third way' for German politics was promoted during the interwar period, a unique, Germanic path for Christian theology was also promoted.[48]

Nationalism, Theology, and Race

The relationship between German Protestantism and race is not simply a matter of theology responding to changing political winds, whether nationalism or fascism, but a deeper intellectual affinity between theology and race. Central to modern race theory, as it emerges out of eighteenth-century materialism, was not the inferiority of certain peoples' bodies, but the degeneracy of their morality and spirituality and the alleged threat posed by such degeneracy to superior races. Physiognomy did not stand alone; rather, the body was seen as a carrier of the soul, of moral and spiritual potencies. It was the spiritual threat of lesser races and especially the Jews that racists

[43] Thomas Nipperdey, *Religion im Umbruch. Deutschland 1870–1918* (Munich, 1988), 98.

[44] *Von Stöcker zu Naumann. Ein Wort z. Germanisierung des Christentums* (1896); Artur Bonus, *Zur Germanisierung des Christentums* (Jena, 1911), 66–7.

[45] Otto Pfleiderer, *Das deutsche Nationalbewußtsein in Vergangenheit und Gegenwart. Rede zur Feier des Geburtstages Seiner Majestät des Kaisers und Königs am 27. Januar 1893* (Berlin, 1895), 27; cited by Tilgner, 'Volk, Nation und Vaterland', 139.

[46] Paul Graue, *Deutsch-evangelisch* (Stuttgart, 1894); id., *Unabhängiges Christentum* (Berlin, 1904); Georg Schneider, *Der Heiland Deutsch. Eine gegenwartsnahe Darleitung der Botschaft Jesu* (Stuttgart, 1935).

[47] Tilgner, 'Volk, Nation und Vaterland', 139.

[48] Karl Dietrich Bracher, *Die deutsche Diktatur. Entstehung Struktur Folgen des Nationalsozialismus* (Frankfurt am Main, 1979), 21–3; George L. Mosse, *Die völkische Revolution. Über die geistigen Wurzeln des Nationalsozialismus* (Frankfurt am Main, 1991), 121–2, 287, esp. 295–308.

worried about; the inferior bodies of those races were reflections of their corrupt spirits, not causes of the corruption. The crucial relationship between body and soul that characterizes racist discourse is a mirror of the body–soul dilemma at the heart of Christian metaphysics, and precisely the stamp that Christianity has placed on Western philosophy.[49]

Race, as Richard Dyer has argued, is about incarnation: 'For all the emphasis on the body in Christianity, the point is the spirit that is "in" the body. What has made Christianity compelling and fascinating is precisely the mystery that it posits, that somehow there is in the body something that is not of the body which may be variously termed spirit, mind, soul or God.'[50] Race, like Christianity, Dyer argues, is a theology not of materialism or spiritualism but of embodiment and incarnation, and it is precisely Christian iconography and the sacramental system of the body that marks the Christian contrast to Judaism and Islam and forms the basis of Europe's racial thinking. In the Christological schema well through the nineteenth century, it is Jesus's body that constitutes his Jewishness, while his Christianity lies in his spirit.

Yet not only did Christianity promote a theology of embodiment and incarnation, it is itself an incarnate religion, that is, a religion whose founder, Jesus, is the embodiment of his father, the transcendent God; a religion that embodies in the Church the teachings of Jesus; and yet a religion that disembodies the teachings of the Old Testament by spiritualizing them in the New Testament. The ambiguity remains: is Christianity the body of the spiritual teaching, or is it the spiritual transformation of the materialist revelation? The confusion is never resolved, making Christian identity unstable, unfixed: that is both its strength and its weakness. As unstable, Christianity can be an apparently attainable, flexible, variable religion, open to a multitude of adherents and interpretations, yet in that destabilized position it is plagued by unclear, undefined boundaries.

Its instability was brought to light both by the rise of theological historicism and by the question pursued by Jewish theologians of the nineteenth century: where, in fact, does Christianity begin and Judaism end? The very figure of Jesus creates the aporia: he is at once a Jew and the founder of Christianity. Jesus begins his life as a Jew but ends his life as a Christian. Christianity itself is achieved, the narrative of his life implies, through a process of emergence, a religious purification that rids the Jewish from the Christian. The Jewish is neither wholly carnal nor spiritual, but is an undefined threat that can purge either body or soul, and enter the one through the other—polluting the body through a corruption of the mind. Purity of the self can be achieved through a Christianization of the self, a removal of

[49] David L. Hodge, 'Domination and the Will in Western Thought and Culture', in John L. Hodge, Donald K. Struckmann, and Lynn Dorland Trost (eds), *Cultural Bases of Racism and Group Oppression* (Berkeley, 1975).

[50] Richard Dyer, *White* (London, 1997), 16.

the Jewish, just as purification from the Jewish marks the creation of the Christian. Thus the emergence in the early decades of the twentieth century of a racialized Protestant theology should be viewed not only as a response to political developments in Germany, but as a recognition of the aporia of Jesus brought into focus by the claims of Jewish historical scholarship to have created Christianity.

The central task of theology, as it was proclaimed by the mid-nineteenth century, was determining the origins of the particular religion, Judaism or Christianity, yet the quest for the historical Jesus led, above all, to the problem of his Jewishness, a theme Jewish scholars eagerly exploited. By placing his teachings within the context of Pharisaic religion they could prove that he said nothing unique or original and they could also make Jewish historiography determinative of Christian originality. The question was whether Jesus had ever left Judaism and become a Christian, and the narrative lives of Jesus are simultaneously metaphorical narratives of European identity and origins, rehearsing issues of culture, nation, patrimony, and race. Had Jesus always been a Christian even among the Jews or did he undergo a conversion process? Such questions gave rise, in turn, to the issue of Paul's Jewishness, brought to the fore by Paul de Lagarde, who accused him of Judaizing Christianity. By the 1930s the Nazi racial laws made Paul's conversion impossible and some theologians sought to substitute the Gospel of John for the Pauline epistles.

Christian anxieties over the presence of Judaism at the very heart of its religion were goaded by the Wissenschaft des Judentums, eager to dismantle Christian hegemony over European culture and emancipate Jews from the position of politically, theologically, and culturally colonized. It is striking to note how many Jewish historians focused their scholarship on Second Temple Judaism and the origins of Christianity; among others, Isaac Jost, Abraham Geiger, Heinrich Graetz, Levi Herzfeld, Joseph Derenbourg, Daniel Chwolsohn, Leo Baeck, Joseph Eschelbacher, and Felix Perles. Studies of the Jewish context of early Christianity were no apolitical scholarly endeavour, but were motivated by a Jewish colonial revolt against Christianity, which proceeded as an effort to assert the Jewish presence within Christianity all the more strongly, as an act of dismembering the colonizer from the inside. By affirming Jesus's Jewishness and demonstrating the irrefutable parallels between Jesus's teachings and those of the rabbis of his day, Jewish historians sought to sever the connection between Christianity and the New Testament: the New Testament was a Jewish book, and Christianity was merely a dogma subsequently constructed around it. If liberal Protestantism, in rejecting the dogma, miracles, and everything supernatural claimed by the New Testament and subsequent Christian theology, claimed to be the religion *of* Jesus, rather than the religion *about* Jesus, then Jewish historians replied by demonstrating that the religion of Jesus was Judaism—liberal Pharisaic Judaism, as Geiger argued. That same liberal Pharisaism did not disappear with the destruction of the Jerusalem Temple in 70 CE, but went underground and was being revived by the Reform Judaism of nineteenth-century European Jews. If true Christianity meant following the faith of Jesus, Pharisaic Judaism, then being a Christian ought to lead to conversion to Reform Judaism.[51]

The work of Jewish historians was widely known and often praised by New Testament scholars in Europe. Authors of lives of Jesus, including Renan, Daniel Schenkel, Adolf Hausrath, Theodor Keim, and Heinrich Ewald, among others, conceded the historical legitimacy of Geiger's arguments, but then sought ways to preserve Jesus's Christian identity. Renan's *Life of Jesus*, proclaimed 'one of the events of the century'[52] when it was published in 1863, created a sensation throughout a Christian Europe disturbed by debates over the legal emancipation of the Jews and increasingly anxious over the presence of Judaism at the heart of Christianity. Renan depicted a Jesus who undergoes a transformation from Jew to Christian, and a Christianity that emerges from Judaism to become Aryan. These transformations structure the narrative of his *Life of Jesus*. Whereas Jesus was born into the Jewish milieu and practised Judaism, his greatness, for Renan, lay in his ability to overcome his Jewishness. Hailed by the Galileans, whose Jewishness was minimal or even dubious, Jesus was condemned by the Jews of Jewish Judaea. After visiting Jerusalem, Renan writes, Jesus himself 'appears no more as a Jewish reformer, but as a destroyer of Judaism. . . . Jesus was no longer a Jew.'[53] Jesus was from Galilee, a distinct region whose population was not immersed in Jewish learning and legalistic religious practice and hence was open to the spiritual teachings of Jesus. Similarly, argues Renan, whereas Christianity originally was 'Jewish to the core, over time [it] rid itself of nearly everything it took from the race'.[54] The transformation of Jesus is recapitulated by the structure of Renan's own book, which moves increasingly away from Jewish references during the course of his narrative of Jesus's life.

In Renan's version, as in many of the lives of Jesus from the 1860s onward, Jesus and Christianity were distinguished and deemed qualitatively superior

[51] For further discussion, see Heschel, *Abraham Geiger*.

[52] Bernard Reardon, *Liberalism and Tradition: Aspects of Catholic Thought in Nineteenth-Century France* (Cambridge, 1975), 296; cited by Terence R. Wright, 'The Letter and the Spirit: Deconstructing Renan's *Life of Jesus* and the Assumptions of Modernity', *Religion and Literature*, 26/2 (Summer 1994), 55–71.

[53] Ernest Renan, *The Life of Jesus*, trans. Charles Edwin Wilbour (New York, 1864), 224–5.

[54] Ernest Renan, *Œuvres complètes*, ed. Henriette Psichari, 10 vols (Paris, 1947–61), v. 1142; cited by Maurice Olender, *The Languages of Paradise: Race, Religion and Philology in the Nineteenth Century*, trans. Arthur Goldhammer (Cambridge, Mass., 1992), 70.

not simply on the basis of more accurate or insightful religious teaching. Rather, Jesus transformed himself into a qualitatively higher being, both physically and spiritually, thereby overcoming his Semitic origins and launching a new, superior race of beings—his followers—into the world. The racial component of Renan's analyses was already clear by 1855: 'I am the first to recognize', he declared, 'that the Semitic race compared to the Indo-European race represents in reality an inferior composition of human nature.'[55]

In Renan's schema, one was not necessarily born an Aryan, but became an Aryan—through conquest of the Jewish, following the example of Jesus. Race, despite assumptions to the contrary, was not inevitably fixed, but mutable. As Ann Stoler has noted, 'the force of racial discourse is precisely in the double-vision it allows, in the fact that it combines notions of fixity and fluidity in ways that are basic to its dynamic'.[56] The instability of race, not its immutability, lies at the heart of its invention.

The discomfort over Jesus's Jewishness was narratively transformed by Renan into a further indication of the Aryan genius, which knew how to convert an odious Hebrew monotheism into a glorious Christianity. The cleverness of Renan's argument was that it made room for viewing monotheism as a divine gift and Christianity as the successful human activity of transforming it; elements of the supernatural, racial, and historical could go hand in hand.

The quest for the historical Jesus thus became a tool, along with philology and archaeology, for describing the evolution of Christianity as the origins of the Aryans and, hence, of Germany's *Kultur*. The effort gives added weight to Benedict Anderson's observation that racism functions not to cross national boundaries but as 'domestic repression and domination'. The quest for the historical Jesus became a quest for the Aryan Jesus, that is, a search for the Aryan roots of European civilization, which then could be used to exclude those Semites who did not belong in its midst. Already with Renan, the shift from the Hellenic–Semitic distinction to the Aryan–Jewish distinction is evident. His writings on the origins of the Semitic languages make a sharp distinction between Greek and Hebrew that draw not only on linguistic properties but on cultural attributes. The distinction encouraged a link between Greek and German as part of the Aryan language family, a linguistic family identified by Max Müller, though he repudiated any racial implications. Distancing Jesus from the Hebraic, Semitic, and Jewish allowed a closer affiliation of the German with the Hellenic and, by easy elision, with

55 Ernest Renan, *Histoire générale et système comparé des langues sémitiques*, 5th edn (Paris, 1893), 4.

56 Ann Stoler, 'Racial Histories and their Regimes of Truth', *Political Power and Social Theory*, 11 (1997), 198.

the Aryan; a comparable identification of the English with the Hellenic and Indo-European is found in Matthew Arnold.[57]

Jesus, Nationalism, and Hitler

The German nation could not be represented through a Jewish Jesus, who was both Jewish and mortal, but only through a historically transcendent, unique Christ. The representation by German nationalists of Germany in terms of the Christ story grew stronger in the twentieth century. Some divorced Christ from the Jesus of the Bible, making him instead an 'eternal idea', not limited by biblical history, just as they presented the German nation as a transcendent idea unbound by political conventions. It seemed intolerable that European Christians worshipped a Jewish Jesus rather than the God of the young, vigorous Indo-Europeans. Germany itself came to be identified in the Nazi era as Christ: crucified during the First World War and resurrected by Adolf Hitler, who was described by some theologians and Church leaders in messianic terms as the Second Coming: through the 'faith of Adolf Hitler . . . the German path of suffering and death can be transformed into a resurrection' and 'the Golgotha of the world war can be transformed through the faith of Adolf Hitler into a path of resurrection of the German nation. . . . In the person of the Führer we see the one sent by God who places Germany before the Lord of history.'[58]

The rise of Oriental Studies in the last two decades of the nineteenth century began to change the terms of scholarship on Judaism. The Wissenschaft des Judentums was able to engage Protestant theologians in debates about Judaism's influence on the early Christian movement, but the Jewish polemics remained stuck in theological discourse and failed to respond adequately to the new methods. The Jewish historical construction of *Kultur* that had set itself in counterpoint to the philhellenism of Germany found a more formidable opponent in what Suzanne Marchand has identified as the 'Furor Orientalis' of the late nineteenth century.[59] Marchand has described the new enthusiasm, starting in the 1880s and 1890s, of collecting oriental manuscripts and artefacts, pursuing archaeological expeditions, and looking East, not West, for religious influences. Not monotheistic ideas but ritual practices were now investigated to find parallels to Christian culture—and these were then deemed influences of the Orient on the West.

[57] See Rajak, 'Jews and Greeks', 552.

[58] Julius Leutheuser, *Die deutsche Christusgemeinde* (Weimar, 1935), 4–7, 12; Siegfried Leffler, *Christus im Dritten Reich der Deutschen. Wesen, Weg und Zielsetzung der Kirchenbewegung Deutsche Christen* (Weimar, 1935), 29–30.

[59] Suzanne Marchand, 'Philhellenism and the *Furor Orientalis*', *Modern Intellectual History*, 1 (Nov. 2004), 331–58.

Oriental Studies soon found a counterpart within theology as History of Religions, which began with Adolf Hilgenfeld but entered scholarship more forcefully with Wilhelm Bousset. While theologians had been critically investigating the biblical texts from within, the History of Religions school introduced a new body of texts—from the ancient Near East, India, Persia—that called into question the originality of Scripture and the location of the New Testament within a Hebraic tradition. Not bound by doctrinal loyalties to the Church, the History of Religions school claimed its independence from Christian dogma along with its enthusiasm for non-Western traditions. Neither Germany's philhellenism nor its Lutheran *sola scriptura* could have the final word. Babylonian exile was increasingly viewed as an era for the transmission of allegedly Aryan traditions through Persian and Indian Buddhism that arrived in Palestine and then moved into the Hellenistic and Christian world. 'Aryan' manifestations were said to include apocalypticism, which supplanted monotheism as the interesting religious attribute to investigate. Methodologically, texts were read as a window into the religious culture that they presumably reflected, rather than constituting a chain of theology. Most in the History of Religions school followed Ferdinand Weber in viewing Judaism and Christianity as two contrasting, opposing types of religions.[60]

The History of Religions school, well into its Bultmann days, was not interested in the historical figure of Jesus, and indeed suggested that the quest was irrelevant, further undermining the need for Christian scholarship on Judaism. What mattered was not what Jesus said or did, but how he was shaped in the religious imagination of the early Christian community. In his *Commentary on Revelation* (1896), Bousset argued that the early Church had simply clothed Jesus in the theological garments of the religious milieu, and his study of the Antichrist legend compared it to myths of a primordial dragon.[61] Some members of the History of Religions school attempted to sever the connection between Jesus and the Messiah anticipated in Jewish Scriptures. Gustav Dalman argued that the 'son of God' was not a conventional messianic title in pre-Christian Judaism, based on his analysis of Jewish biblical and rabbinic texts, so that the appellation was not meant to signify Jesus's messianic identity.[62] Similarly, Bousset argued in *Die Religion des Judentums* (1903) that 'son of man' was not a title found or even anticipated within Judaism, but stemmed from a syncretistic religious milieu

[60] Ferdinand Wilhelm Weber, *System der altsynagogalen Palästinischen Theologie. Aus Targum, Midrasch, und Talmud* (Leipzig, 1880). For a discussion of Weber's impact, see E. P. Sanders, *Paul and Palestinian Judaism: A Comparison of Patterns of Religion* (Philadelphia, 1977).

[61] Wilhelm Bousset, *Der Antichrist in der Überlieferung des Judentums, des Neuen Testaments, und der alten Kirche* (Göttingen, 1895).

[62] Gustav Dalman, *Worte Jesu*, i (Leipzig, 1898), 223.

within Hellenism—a category the History of Religions employed to serve as a kind of witch's brew of religious notions from India, Persia, Greece. Bousset identified a 'Primal Man' in Gnostic texts and also in the Rig Veda, which, he argued, was modified through contact with Hellenism and given its eschatological valence through contact with Judaism, ultimately emerging as the son of man figure of the New Testament.[63] As Karen King has commented, Bousset did not trace the genealogy of the motif in order to reduce its meaning to that of an ancient fertility rite, but used genealogy to enrich the motif through vast associations beyond the limited realm of the New Testament.[64] However, Bousset was also providing a genealogy for Europe and its putative Aryan origins, reinforced by his presentation of Jesus as 'a heroic figure with a daring faith in God that led him to stand uncompromisingly against the false piety of his day'.[65] Indeed, the faith of Jesus's environment, Judaism, was portrayed by Bousset, like Weber, as a religion diametrically opposed to Christianity.

Until the 1910s and 1920s Jewish scholars did not keep pace methodologically with the History of Religions, nor recognize its *völkisch* implications; their response focused instead on liberal theologians, not realizing that their discourse was outmoded and undermined by the new History of Religions scholarship. The numerous critical responses to Bousset formulated by Jewish scholars complained of bias and simply reiterated the demand for greater attention to rabbinic texts. Yet the Jewish scholars generally failed to recognize the diversity of early Judaism and the possibilities of external influences in its development recognized by History of Religions scholars, and they ignored Wellhausen's warning that late redaction made the Mishnah a dubious source for early first-century Pharisaism. In general, they were reluctant to abandon their own theologically rooted claim that a normative Judaism could be traced from the Bible through the talmudic era, consisting of ethical monotheism and shunting apocalypticism to a marginal role. Jewish historians were also slow to follow the changing scholarly understanding of the nature of religion, from text to ritual practice, theology to popular belief, philosophy to piety. In so doing, Jewish scholars failed to recognize both the larger cultural and political motivations of Oriental Studies: its fight against Hellenic primacy in shaping German *Kultur*, the growing popular enthusiasm for orientalism, and the identification of nationalism with primitivism.

Jewish historians who had hoped rabbinic literature might find a place in the canon of Christian theological historicism now discovered that the

[63] Bousset, *Die Religion des Judentums*, 267.

[64] Karen King, *What is Gnosticism?* (Cambridge, Mass., 2003), 9.

[65] Wilhelm Bousset, *Kyrios Christos. Geschichte des Christusglaubens von den Anfänge des Christentums bis Irenaeus* (Göttingen, 1913), 116–17; cited in King, *What Is Gnosticism?*, 93.

pseudepigrapha and the Zend-Avesta had become more intriguing to scholars. Moreover, even as Jewish scholars had attempted to demolish the originality of Christianity, they now found the Old Testament under attack on the same grounds, as Old Testament scholars were fascinated by the decipherment of cuneiform, the discovery of the Code of Hammurabi (1901–2), and of the Tel Amarna letters (1887–8), while scholars of New Testament were debating the primacy of Hellenistic or Persian influences on early Judaism. Did Parseeism depend upon Judaism, as James Darmesteter argued, or did Jewish popular religion emerge from Parseeism, as Bousset argued? At stake was the question of what constituted the essential elements of the Jewish religion—biblical monotheism, eschatological beliefs, or primitive legends and rituals?

Nor were the History of Religions scholars dismayed by Jewish attacks on Jesus's originality, as the liberal Protestant theologians had been; the historical Jesus was not the issue, but the religious forces that shaped the early belief in him. Just as the pan-Babylonian controversy reached popular attention through the Kaiser's attendance at Friedrich Delitzsch's Babel und Bibel lectures in 1903, as Yaacov Shavit has shown,[66] the Aryan Jesus grew in popularity after Houston Stewart Chamberlain's *Foundations of the Nineteenth Century* (1899) became a best-seller. If the liberal Protestant theologian Adolf Harnack called Jesus a Jew who transcended Judaism spiritually, the Kaiser felt it would be easy to win him over to Chamberlain's Galilean Jesus. Traditional German New Testament scholarship in the early decades of the twentieth century stagnated, while growing popular enthusiasm for the oriental over the Hellenic led to a flood of publications comparing Jesus to both Indian and Teutonic deities. Soon the Wissenschaft des Judentums found itself facing a racialized Christianity in thrall to nationalism and, ultimately, Nazism.

Renan's notion of Christianity emerging out of Judaism, purifying itself from Jewish elements, was reversed. Now Jesus was proclaimed an Aryan who rejected Judaism, but after his death early Christianity had become falsified by Judaizations. Once Chamberlain proclaimed Jesus an Aryan, calls came for a rejection of Christianity as a non-Germanic religion while others wanted a sanitization of Christianity from Jewish elements and a return to the originally Aryan Jesus. In 1917 the Flensburg pastor Friedrich Andersen, in collaboration with several *völkisch* writers, published *95 Theses for Reshaping the Church*,[67] and in 1921 he and several others formed the Bund

[66] Yaacov Shavit and Mordecai Eran, *The War of the Tablets: The Defence of the Bible in the 19th Century and the Babel–Bibel Controversy* (Heb.) (Tel Aviv, 2003).

[67] *Deutschchristentum auf rein-evangelischer Grundlage. 95 Leitsätze zum Reformationsfest 1917*, by Hauptpastor Friedrich Andersen in Flensburg, Professor Adolf Bartels in Weimar, Kirchenrath D. Dr. Ernst Katzer in Oberloßnitz bei Dresden, and Hans Paul Freiherr von Wolzogen in Bayreuth (Leipzig, 1917). Note that Bartels and von Wolzogen later became involved in Grundmann's institute.

für deutsche Kirche, calling for a German Christianity that would proclaim a pure teaching of salvation without 'Jewish obfuscation'. By 1927 the scholar of early Christianity Walter Bauer distinguished between a Pharisaic Judaea and an un-Jewish, syncretistic Galilee where Jesus won his supporters and where Jewish religious belief and practice exerted negligible influence. As a result, 'Christian faith had overflowed the boundaries of Judaism long before the fossilization of Jewish Christianity into Judaism could paralyse its wings and could destroy its mobility.'[68] That Jewish Christians 'paralysed' and 'destroyed' Christian faith gave scholarly legitimization to the efforts of the Nazi era.

Christian De-Judaization in the Third Reich

By 1932 such ideas were represented by the German Christian Movement, initially led by Joachim Hossenfelder, representing the Nazi Party within the Church. Yet could Christianity be de-Judaized? Alfred Rosenberg insisted that nothing would be left once the Jewish elements were removed, and for Wilhelm Hauer, Professor of Indology at the University of Tübingen and leader of the German Faith Movement of the 1930s, neo-pagans were not inventing but restoring older Germanic or even ancient Nordic concepts of divinity that had parallels with Indic divinities. In response, the German Christian Movement became increasingly radicalized, maintaining that the tools of scholarship allowed them to recognize and eradicate Jewish falsifications and create a Aryan Christianity, and that government measures against Jews were mandated by Christianity. According to the minutes of a meeting held in February 1936, at which the more radical Thuringian German Christians explained their views to representatives of the Saxonian Church, Julius Leffler called for murdering the Jews:

> In a Christian life, the heart always has to be disposed toward the Jew, and that's how it has to be. As a Christian, I can, I must and I ought always to have or to find a bridge to the Jew in my heart. But as a Christian, I also have to follow the laws of my nation [*Volk*], which are often presented in a very cruel way, so that again I am brought into the harshest of conflicts with the Jew. Even if I know 'thou shalt not kill' is a commandment of God or 'thou shalt love the Jew' because he too is a child of the eternal Father, I am able to know as well that I have to kill him, I have to shoot him, and I can only do that if I am permitted to say: Christ.[69]

[68] Walter Bauer, 'Jesus der Galiläer', in *Festgabe für Adolf Jülicher* (Tübingen, 1927); repr. in Bauer, *Aufsätze und Kleine Schriften*, ed. Georg Strecker (Tübingen, 1967), 108.

[69] Akte Thüringisches Volksbildungsministerium Signatur A 1400, Blatt 293. The meeting was held on 24–5 February 1936. Present: Paul Althaus, Martin Dörne, Erich Fascher, Meyer Erlach, Dedo Müller (pastors and church superintendents); and Siegfried Leffler, Julius Leutheuser, Hugo Hahn from Dresden (Bekenende Kirch), and Grundmann. It is striking that

The formal expurgation of Judaism from Christianity, which became the central goal of the German Christian Movement, was taken up by the Protestant Church as a whole in 1939. On 6 May 1939 several hundred Protestant theologians—professors, bishops, pastors, all sympathetic to the pro-Nazi German Christian movement—gathered at Wartburg Castle, with its strong Lutheran and German nationalist heritage, to inaugurate the Institut zur Erforschung und Beseitigung des jüdischen Einflusses auf das deutsche kirchliche Leben (Institute for the Study and Eradication of Jewish Influence on German Religious Life).[70] With a membership of approximately sixty professors of theology at universities throughout the Reich, a sizeable percentage of the academic community, the Institute represented efforts that were already occurring in the university theological faculties and in the scholarship being published. At the University of Jena, one of the most Nazified, Hebrew study was made optional, courses on *völkisch* religiosity replaced dogmatics, and doctoral dissertations were failed for not following racial theory.[71]

Institute members set to work immediately, publishing a de-Judaized hymnal and New Testament, a catechism proclaiming Jesus the Messiah of Aryans, and a slew of theological materials detailing the violent degeneracy of Judaism. These were not merely theological but political interests: 'We know that the Jews want the destruction of Germany,'[72] proclaimed Walter Grundmann in 1938, Professor of New Testament at the University of Jena and academic director of the Institute. According to the Institute's catechism, published in 1941, 'To this day the Jews persecute Jesus and all who follow him with irreconcilable hatred.'[73] Opening a 1941 Institute conference, Grundmann declared: 'Our *Volk*, which stands above all else in a struggle against the satanic powers of world Judaism for the order and life of this

Rinnen does not cite this document, and that Hugo Hahn, who attended the meeting, does not mention Leffler's comments in his memoir. See Hahn, *Kämpfer Wider Willen. Erinnerungen aus dem Kirchenkampf 1933–1945*, ed. Georg Prater (Metzingen, 1969).

[70] Susannah Heschel, 'When Jesus Was an Aryan: The Protestant Church and Antisemitic Propaganda', in Robert Ericksen and Susannah Heschel (eds), *Betrayal: The German Churches and the Holocaust* (Minneapolis, 1999). The best study of the Deutsche Christen is Doris L. Bergen, *Twisted Cross: The German Christian Movement in the Third Reich* (Chapel Hill, NC, 1996).

[71] Susannah Heschel, 'The Theological Faculty at the University of Jena as a "Stronghold of National Socialism"', in Uwe Hoßfeld, Jürgen John, and Rüdiger Stutz (eds), *Kämpferische Wissenschaft. Studien zur Universität Jena im Nationalsozialismus* (Cologne, 2003).

[72] Walter Grundmann, 'Das Heil kommt von den Juden. Eine Schicksalsfrage an die Christen deutscher Nation', *Deutsche Frömmigkeit*, 6 (Sept. 1938), 1.

[73] *Deutsche mit Gott. Ein deutsches Glaubensbuch* (Weimar, 1941), 46. 'Vorwort' signed by Grundmann, Wilhelm Büchner, Paul Gimpel, Hans Pribnow, Kurt Thieme, Max Adolf Wagenführer, Heinrich Weinmann, and Hermann Werdermann.

world, dismisses Jesus, because it cannot struggle against the Jews and open its heart to the king of the Jews.'[74]

Descriptions of Judaism as morally and religiously degenerate were common in nineteenth- and early twentieth-century Protestant theological literature, but the emphasis on Judaism's violence is new to the Nazi era and central to the Institute. The fate of German *Kultur* was in the hands of the Nazis and depended on purging the Jewish from Germany—both Jews as people and the Jewish from Christianity. In *Das religiöse Gesicht des Judentums*, a 1942 book on Judaism, Grundmann and Karl Euler, a *Dozent* in theology at the University of Giessen and member of the Institute, made their political intentions clear:

> This text will be an attempt to answer the question of the rise of Judaism and of its manner, as it appears everywhere, in a generally understandable form. But the one fact remains through all time incontrovertible (*unverrückbar*): a healthy *Volk* must and will reject Judaism in every form. This fact is justified before history and through history. *If one is upset at Germany's treatment of the Jews, Germany has the historical authorization and historical justification for the fight against the Jews on its side!* To prove this sentence is the particular concern of this text; and no subsequent research can alter this! So this work serves as the great struggle of fate of the German nation for its political and economic, spiritual and cultural, and also its religious freedom.[75]

The Institute, whose members remained leading theological figures after the war, demonstrates the triumph of the most radical, Thuringian wing of the German Christian Movement and its ability to take control not only of most of the regional churches but also of the theological faculties and scholarly organs (e.g. *Zeitschrift für alttestamentliche Wissenschaft*, whose editor, Johannes Hempel, Professor of Old Testament at the University of Berlin, helped establish the Institute). Most of the Protestant theologians in Germany and Scandinavia with training in early Judaism were collaborators with the Institute and its members, including Georg Beer, Johannes Leipoldt, Paul Fiebig, Gerhard Kittel, Hugo Odeberg, Ethelbert Stauffer, Georg Bertram. Both senior and junior faculty were involved, and they represented all fields within theology—Martin Redeker, Schleiermacher scholar in Kiel, Theodor Odenwald, Nietzsche scholar in Heidelberg, Herbert Preisker in New Testament at Breslau, Hans Opitz in Church

[74] Walter Grundmann, 'Das Messiasproblem', in Grundmann (ed.), *Germanentum, Christentum und Judentum*, Studien zur Erforschung ihres gegenseitigen Verhältnisses, Sitzungsberichte der zweiten Arbeitstagung des Instituts zur Erforschung des jüdischen Einflusses auf das deutsche kirchliche Leben vom 3. bis 5. März 1941 in Eisenach (Leipzig, 1942), 381.

[75] Walter Grundmann and Karl Friedrich Euler, *Das religiöse Gesicht des Judentums. Entstehung und Art* (Leipzig, 1942).

History at Vienna. They found a Christian community quickly receptive to its first two concerns, establishing that Jesus was not a Jew but an Aryan, and that Judaism was a violent, degenerate religion, though it encountered resistance to its third effort, replacing the epistles of Paul (who could not be declared an Aryan) with the Gospel of John. Bishop Walther Schultz of Mecklenburg, one of the early and most enthusiastic supporters of the Institute, wrote that the elimination of Paul was 'absolutely devious and therefore an insult to our *Volk*, whom one indirectly accuses, in its pathetic narrowness and lack of instinct, of having been duped for 1500 years by some stinking Jew'.[76]

In the Institute's de-Judaized New Testament, *Die Botschaft Gottes*, which appeared in 1940, passages describing Jesus's genealogical descent from Old Testament figures (the Old Testament, in turn, had already been eliminated from the Bible), and references to Zion, Jerusalem, and the Temple, were removed. To distance Jesus from Judaism, the sabbath was called 'Feiertag', and Passover was called 'Osterfest'. Apocalyptic ideas were removed, as well as terms such as 'sin', 'righteousness', and 'penance'. Records show that hundreds of thousands of copies of the de-Judaized Bible and hymnal were sold to churches throughout the Reich.

The Institute published its hymnal in 1941, under the title *Grosser Gott Wir Loben Dich* (Great God We Praise Thee). The book contained 339 hymns, all purged of references to the Old Testament or Judaism, and presenting a militarized tone in several hymns. Jewish words, such as 'Hallelujah', were eliminated. Bach's well-known hymn 'Wake up, the voice calls us' ('Wachet auf, ruft uns die Stimme') was drastically altered to eliminate the first two stanzas entirely, since the first contained references to Jerusalem and 'Hallelujah', and the second stanza spoke of Zion and 'Hosanna'. The third stanza was retained, but the word 'Hallelujah' was replaced with 'song of praise and thanks' ('Lob und Danklied'). 'Silent Night' ('Stille Nacht') retained the reference to Bethlehem, since Grundmann had determined that a second Bethlehem existed in non-Jewish Galilee, but the word 'Hallelujah' was removed. Samples of the hymnal were sent to church communities throughout Thuringia, so that they could decide whether to purchase copies for their congregations.[77] Sales were excellent; churches throughout the Reich, north and south, in cities and villages, bought copies.

The 'Entjudungsinstitut' (De-Judaization Institute) as it was colloquially known in Church circles, flourished through the war years, coming to an end only in the fall of 1945 when Church leaders in Thuringia declined to

[76] Letter from Schultz to Rönck, 2 Aug. 1944, Landeskirchenarchiv Thüringen, Eisenach.

[77] Bishop Sasse in Bestand 1941-B, Nr. 15, p. 111, Landeskirchenarchiv Thüringen, Eisenach.

maintain it, for the stated reason of financial limitations. Members of the Institute retained their positions, as academics and Church leaders, in both East and West Germany, some of them rising to positions of prominence, and German Christian ideas continued to circulate after the war in German theological writings. Some lost their positions at universities during de-Nazification proceedings, but none lost a position within the Church. It was easy for Institute members, after the war, to claim that their work had been purely scientific, not Nazi, and that it fell within the rubrics of the classical Christian theological effort to define itself in opposition to Judaism.

CONCLUSION

The classic contrast between Athens and Jerusalem, Hellenism and Judaism, was shared by modern Jewish and Christian thinkers, but with very different cultural consequences and political implications. For Germans, starting in the late eighteenth century, classical Hellenic civilization formed the ideal of the modern state and the origins of German *Kultur*. The rise of Oriental Studies in the late nineteenth century sought to dethrone Hellenic hegemony in favour of what sometimes became a pan-Babylonian origin of the West, while Jewish thinkers around the same period presented Judaism as the font of Western civilization and its monotheisms. In the Jewish perspective, Judaism formed the basis of a moral society by producing Christianity and Islam, and its two daughter religions declined only when they veered substantially from their mother religion. With the rise of nationalism and racism, and as theology came to be racialized itself, the Aryan became the substitute for the non-Jewish, whether Hellenic, Germanic, or Babylonian.

As much as Christianity sought to eradicate Judaism in order to establish its own self-sufficiency, it could not eradicate a more troubling awareness: that Judaism is the archive of Christianity, and *Kultur* is the archive of the nation. Judaism's texts and scholars have their own intimate knowledge of Christianity and its origins, and preserve that knowledge as long as they exist. Taking control of scholarship on Judaism, then, also had an internal, psycho-theological motivation, the recognition that Judaism is Christianity's archive. To understand the words and deeds of Jesus, it is necessary to place them in Jewish context, to locate them in the archive of Jewish debates over the Temple, sabbath observance, and the end of times, in order to determine whether Jesus was a Jew who became a Christian, or an Aryan who was falsely Judaized. The narrative is a metaphor for Germany, as nationalists debated whether German *Kultur* consisted of classical Hellenic and Christian values overrun by Jews, or Aryan and Teutonic, Judaized by Christianity.

The problem was that Judaism functions as Christianity's archive, in Derrida's sense of archive, the 'archiviolithic force' that 'not only incites forgetfulness, amnesia, the annihilation of memory, as mneme or anamnesis, but also commands the radical effacement, in truth the eradication, of that which can never be reduced to mneme or to anamnesis, that is, the archive'. The aporia of Christianity is its claim that Jesus founded a new religion, despite being immersed throughout his life in Judaism, its practices and beliefs. Arguing that he was an Aryan still requires a comparable attention to Judaism, constructing it as opposite of Jesus. Either Jesus's historical reality as a Jew or Judaism's historical reality within the first century must be eradicated by Christian theology if its claim to be a new religion is to have any meaning. Jesus's Jewishness must be relegated to the archive, the storage that provides the contextualization for Jesus's religious messages even as its context must be annihilated for Jesus's originality to make its claim. Thus, by the logic of the phenomenon, the Christian theologian cannot recognize its archive without destroying itself.[78]

Treitschke, Susanne Zantop notes, speaks of a mature, virile German state taking possession of virgin territories,[79] and elsewhere she describes an 'erotics of conquest' in German literary texts.[80] Christianity, too, is described as untainted and virginal: Gustav Volkmar, a prominent member of the Tübingen School, writes, the Judaism that formed the religious background to Jesus and Christianity was not the Pharisaic Judaism dominant during the Second Temple era, but 'the virgin lap of the God of Judaism'.[81] He is the God worshipped by Judaism, but not the creator of Judaism. God's virginity means that Christianity has no older sibling; it is God's only child.

Volkmar's metaphor, that the mother lap from which Christianity emerged was 'the virgin lap' of the God of Judaism, expresses the archive of German Protestantism quite clearly: Christianity was derived from Judaism, and superseded it, but Judaism was not the offspring of God, who remained a virgin until giving birth to his first child, Christianity. Christianity is the first-born son of the virgin, Christ himself. Yet even in denying that Judaism is a divinely revealed religion, Volkmar is unable to remove it from Christian genealogy. It is the archive as circumcision, in Derrida's term,[82] Judaism leaving its indelible presence in the flesh of Christian theology.

[78] Jacques Derrida, *Archive Fever: A Freudian Impression*, trans. Eric Prenowitz (Chicago, 1996), 12.

[79] Susanne Zantop, *Colonial Fantasies: Conquest, Family, and Nation in Precolonial Germany* (Durham, NC, 1997), 199.

[80] Ibid. 101.

[81] Gustav Volkmar, *Die Religion Jesu und ihre erste Entwicklung nach dem gegenwärtigen Stande der Wissenschaft* (Leipzig, 1857), 52. Quoted in Heschel, *Abraham Geiger*, 161.

[82] Derrida, *Archive Fever*, 26.

SEVEN

From Sephardi to Oriental: The 'Decline' Theory of Jewish Civilization in the Middle East and North Africa

DANIEL SCHROETER

EUROPE AND THE SEPHARDI 'GOLDEN AGE'

SINCE the birth of modern Jewish historiography, scholars have situated the apogee of medieval Jewish civilization in the Muslim world, and in particular in Spain. 'The height of culture which the nations of modern times are striving to attain, was reached by the Jews of Spain in their most flourishing period,' writes Heinrich Graetz.[1] Graetz, and other nineteenth-century founders of modern Jewish historiography, sought to elevate Jewish history to the level of an important national history like other nations, countering an often expressed Christian view that denied Jews a legitimate history after the Second Temple period.[2] Graetz insisted on the fundamental influence of Jews on general history—their contribution to civilization. So significant was the Jewish role in the history of Spanish civilization that their expulsion in 1492 led to Iberian decline. 'With the discovery of America, the Jews might have lifted Spain to the rank of the wealthiest, the most prosperous and enduring of states . . . Talent, activity, and prosperous civilization passed with them from the country.'[3] Graetz's notion of the great contribution of Jews in Spanish civilization, and the subsequent decline of Spain resulting from the expulsion, was already a theme in apologetic writing in the seventeenth and eighteenth centuries, suggested, for example, in Manasseh b. Israel's mercantilist arguments for the readmission of the Jews into England, in which he proposes, in his appeal to Oliver Cromwell in

[1] Heinrich Graetz, *History of the Jews*, 6 vols (Philadelphia, 1956; first pub. in Eng., 1891), iii. 236.

[2] Editor's introduction to Heinrich Graetz, *The Structure of Jewish History and Other Essays*, ed. Ismar Schorsch (New York, 1975), 46–51.

[3] Graetz, *History of the Jews*, iv. 353. The expulsion of the Jews had only a minor economic impact. See Henry Kamen, *The Spanish Inquisition* (New Haven, 1997), 25–7.

1655, that the Jews who fled Spain brought prosperity to the countries where they settled. This is echoed in John Toland's advocacy for the naturalization of Jews in his 1714 pamphlet, where he attributes Spain's decline to the expulsion of the Jews and Moors and the Inquisition.[4]

In Graetz's cyclical view of civilization, the end of the tenth century marked the decay of the Jews in Babylonia and the ascendancy of the Jews of Andalusia.[5] Graetz was not alone in his view of the Jews of the Muslim world and Spain; other Jewish scholars of the nineteenth century wrote very favourably about Jewish civilization in Islam, contrasting a relatively positive view of Islam with an often clear antipathy towards Christianity, in what became a widely accepted understanding of the Jewish experience.[6] What particularly distinguished Jews in the Muslim world, in contrast to medieval Christendom, was the degree to which Jews were a part of the wider civilization, nourished by the cultural and intellectual climate of Islamic civilization. The term 'symbiosis' has often been applied in reference to the Jews of the Muslim world. Compared to the more insular Jewish communities of Christian Europe, Jews in Islamic civilization were cosmopolitan, interacting with the rich Arab–Islamic civilization responsible for preserving and developing classical culture that had long disappeared from the heirs to the barbarian states in Europe.

The measure particular to this 'Golden Age' was the intellectual contribution of Jews to Arab civilization. Islam was also seen as a religion of much greater tolerance than Christendom, fostering a symbiosis—for some, an 'interfaith utopia'—not possible in the medieval Christian world.[7] The Golden Age idea has been firmly entrenched since the nineteenth century when European Jewish scholars, Germans and central Europeans especially, sought to find a more palatable model of Jewish–non-Jewish relations than the more bitter history of persecution in medieval Christian Europe. Furthermore, the Sephardim represented a model of a Diaspora community that remained attached to Judaism while, at the same time, participating in

[4] [John Toland], *Reasons for Naturalizing the Jews in Great Britain and Ireland* (London, 1714), 17. Manasseh b. Israel and John Toland's texts are excerpted in Paul R. Mendes-Flohr and Jehuda Reinharz (eds), *The Jew in the Modern World: A Documentary History* (New York, 1980), 9–15.

[5] Graetz, *History of the Jews*, iii. 234.

[6] John M. Efron, 'From Mitteleuropa to the Middle East: Orientalism through a Jewish Lens', *Jewish Quarterly Review*, 94 (2004), 490–520.

[7] See Mark R. Cohen, *Under Crescent and Cross* (Princeton, 1994), 3–5. This book explicitly analyses and compares persecution and its absence in the Muslim and Christian worlds; elsewhere Cohen refers to this symbiosis as 'cultural embeddedness'. See id., 'Medieval Jewry in the World of Islam', in Martin Goodman (ed.), *The Oxford Handbook of Jewish Studies* (Oxford, 2002), 194. On the sympathetic, idealized attitude of European Jews towards Islam and the Turks, and the development of Islamic Studies among Jewish scholars, see Bernard Lewis, 'The Pro-Islamic Jews', *Judaism*, 17 (1968), 391–404.

the surrounding secular culture with a high level of cultural openness.[8] Moreover, as racial theories developed in the last decades of the nineteenth century, a biological argument on the ideal Sephardi type was adopted to counter antisemitic charges of Jewish degeneracy: the Sephardim represented the 'original Jews', linked to the ancient past and as a model projected for the rejuvenation of the Jews in the future.[9]

The growing immigration of east European Jews (Ostjuden) to western Europe was another reason for this focus on the Sephardim. The Ostjuden caused increased anxiety among the already established communities since the new immigrants were seen as a potential obstacle to the assimilationist agenda. It was from their 'oriental' customs and practices, of which antisemites were all too eager to remind Jews that these constituted their essential characteristics, that Western Jews sought to distance themselves.[10] Appropriating the term 'oriental' to refer to the idealized model of the Sephardim in the Islamic world,[11] where Jews kept their Judaism yet were much a part of the wider civilization, Graetz could counter the negative oriental stereotypes of the east European Jews, with their backward, pre-emancipation religious practices. 'Paradoxically,' writes Ismar Schorsch, 'the contact with Islam had made Judaism part of the Western world.'[12]

It is, in a sense, a double paradox, for it was not the encounter with contemporary Islam, the site of a decayed civilization in the minds of nineteenth-century Europeans, that could in any way serve as a model for the integration of Jews in the West. 'Eastern' Jews, now in contact with their Western co-religionists through European Jewish organizations or colonial rule, were associated with the stagnation and decay of the Middle East and North Africa as if they had no connection with the culture of their ancestors in the same region, the very civilization that Western Jews sought to

[8] On the idealization of Sephardim, see Ismar Schorsch, 'The Myth of Sephardic Superiority', *Leo Baeck Institute Year Book*, 34 (1989), 47–66; Ivan G. Marcus, 'Beyond the Sephardic Mystique', *Orim*, 1 (1985), 35–8. For some of the same reasons that European Jews idealized the Sephardim, Yitzhak Baer disparaged them: external influence corrupted the Jews of Spain. For an analysis of the ideological underpinnings in Baer's work, see the discussion by David N. Myers, *Reinventing the Jewish Past* (New York, 1995), 121–4. Most scholars of Spain, however, continued to idealize Jewish existence there (see e.g. Eliyahu Ashtor, *The Jews of Moslem Spain*, 3 vols (Philadelphia, 1973).

[9] John M. Efron, 'Scientific Racism and the Mystique of Sephardic Racial Superiority', *Leo Baeck Institute Year Book*, 38 (1993), 75–96.

[10] Paul Mendes-Flohr, 'Fin de Siècle Orientalism, the Ostjuden, and the Aesthetics of Jewish Self Affirmation', in Mendes-Flohr, *Divided Passions: Jewish Intellectuals and the Experience of Modernity* (Detroit, 1991), 81–3; see also John M. Efron, 'Orientalism and the Jewish Historical Gaze', in Ivan Davidson Kalmar and Derek J. Penslar (eds), *Orientalism and the Jews* (Hanover, NH, 2004), 86–7.

[11] See Efron, 'From Mitteleuropa to the Middle East', 506.

[12] Schorsch, 'The Myth of Sephardic Superiority', 66.

emulate. In nineteenth-century Europe, Western Jews were admittedly anxious to assimilate their east European co-religionists; yet with the French colonization of Algeria (and later of Tunisia and Morocco), and with the British occupation of Egypt, they encountered another kind of oriental Jew that needed to be transformed. West European Jewry believed that the Jews of North Africa and the Middle East were negatively affected by the obscurantist and decayed milieu of the contemporary Muslim world. Thus, Western and especially French Jews, under the aegis of colonialism, sought to assimilate Eastern Jews through education and emancipation, legitimized by the universal principles of the French Revolution. Oriental Jews would, like their occidental counterparts in an earlier period, abandon their traditional life for modern ways,[13] undergoing the revolutionary transformative process of 'regeneration', a requisite of citizenship.

While this model of a Jewish society involved in secular culture ended in a sense for the Sephardi Diaspora in the southern Mediterranean, it was somewhat of a different matter for the Sephardim of western Europe.[14] Well into the twentieth century, Spain continued to be used as a model for living in the Diaspora. Owing to the relatively lower degrees of persecution and isolation that they experienced in non-Jewish society, Sephardim were perceived as better able than Ashkenazim to integrate their Jewishness with secularism.[15]

The study of this 'culture of tolerance', including the focus on Jewish contributions to medieval civilization in Spain and the Islamic world, has endured for reasons also rooted in the contemporary world of the last few decades. Again, it offers a counter-history to either the notion of Muslims and Jews as implacable enemies, or the 'clash of civilization' model, the supposed fault line between major civilizational entities in which Islam and the West figure most prominently, especially 'post-9/11'.[16]

[13] Cf. Michel Abitbol, 'The Encounter between French Jewry and the Jews of North Africa: Analysis of a Discourse (1830–1914)', in Frances Malino and Bernard Wasserstein (eds), *The Jews in Modern France* (Hanover, NH, 1985).

[14] Yosef Kaplan, *An Alternative Path to Modernity: The Sephardi Diaspora in Western Europe* (Leiden, 2000), 1 ff.

[15] For an uncritical review of literature that proposes this comparative model, see Abraham D. Lavendar, 'Arabic-Islamic and Spanish Mediterranean Influences on "the Jewish Mind": A Comparison to European-Christian Influence', *Journal of Ethnic Studies*, 8/4 (1981), 25–35.

[16] The 'clash of civilizations' refers to the much critiqued model of Samuel P. Huntington, *The Clash of Civilizations and the Remaking of World Order* (New York, 1996). A postscript to a book written shortly before 9/11 reflects on the relevance of Spain's history of tolerance: Maria Rosa Menocal, *The Ornament of the World: How Muslims, Jews, and Christians Created a Culture of Tolerance in Medieval Spain* (Boston, 2002).

SYMBIOSIS AND THE DECLINE THEORY OF ISLAMIC CIVILIZATION

While the use of the 'Golden Age' concept in Jewish historiography has often been analysed and criticized, the reverse side of the coin—the 'decline theory' of Jewish civilization in the Middle East and North Africa—has not been subjected to the same scrutiny. World history scholars have for decades questioned and criticized the use of the 'rise of the West' model (which presumes that the 'East' was in decline). These discussions, which offer a very different view of Asia and Africa, have gone largely unnoticed in recent Jewish historiography. Rather, the 'Jewish contribution to civilization' model continues to shape studies on Asian and African Jewish culture and history, which assumes a kind of rise and decline theory of Jewish civilization that is indebted to nineteenth-century European historiography and orientalist scholarship on the Islamic world.

Orientalist scholarship here refers to the tradition of the critical study of texts in 'oriental' languages, and the various kinds of studies that this produced. The orientalist tradition in history, which has examined a range of phenomena from intellectual culture, ideas, art, and religion, is influenced by the nineteenth-century focus on the rise and fall of civilizations as the basic historical model. Civilization also has an essential kind of unity, and in the study of Islamic civilization the first four to five centuries are considered to be the period of 'classical' Islam. Despite the political fragmentation that began in the very first Islamic centuries, an essential civilizational unity existed until the Abbasid Caliphate came to an end with the conquest of Baghdad by the Mongols in 1258.[17] After the decline of classical Islam, the next 300 years are often represented as a period of stagnation and decline, until the Ottoman efflorescence of the sixteenth century. Ottoman rise, however, was short-lived, followed by its rapid demise in the seventeenth and eighteenth centuries. In this construction of Islam as civilization, with its rise and decline, its successes and failures are measured against the civilization of the West. The theory of Islamic decline is dependent on a largely negative view of Islamic civilization in the post-classical age, a civilization, according to this perspective, which lacked the intrinsic qualities that

[17] See e.g. G. E. von Grunebaum, *Classical Islam: A History, 600–1258* (London, 1970). The critique of orientalism is best known through the book of Edward W. Said, *Orientalism* (New York, 1978). It is important, however, to point out that scholars before Said's work had already begun to examine Middle Eastern history through analytical lenses that departed from the approaches that Said criticized. See e.g. Maxime Rodinson, 'The Western Image and Western Studies of Islam', in Joseph Schacht and C. E. Bosworth (eds), *The Legacy of Islam* (Oxford, 1974); and Roger Owen's review of *The Cambridge History of Islam*, *Journal of Interdisciplinary History*, 4 (1973), 287–98.

allowed for European progress. This comparative model is also found in Max Weber, who analyses Islamic society in terms of the absence of civic and other institutions that developed in western Europe.[18] In modern history, Middle Eastern Islamic civilization is analysed not on its own terms but in terms of the impact that the West had on society.

While this approach to the study of the Islamic world has been greatly revised in the last two to three decades, studies on the 'Jews of Islam', or 'oriental' Jewry, continue to be shaped by this civilization model of historical inquiry, with its emphasis on rise and inevitable decline. The view on when this decline among the Jews of the East began depends somewhat on the context of what is being studied. In the Graetz tradition, decline started shortly after the death of Maimonides, the demise of rationalist discourse combined with the increase of persecution. In a different context, the persecution, Inquisition, and ultimately expulsion from Spain in 1492 marked the next point of decline. In what clearly constitutes the most voluminous and detailed study of Jewish communities in the medieval Muslim world, Shlomo Dov Goitein sets the trend with his idea of 'creative symbiosis'.[19] Goitein depicts a highly mobile and cosmopolitan society of Jews, coexisting with Muslims, which he likens to his experience with the laissez-faire, free-enterprise system in the United States.[20] Yet this period of creative symbiosis lasted until about 1300, about the time when the Geniza era ends. From this period on, Goitein argues, 'Arabs faded out from world history, and Oriental Jews from Jewish history.'[21]

This model of cosmopolitanism and coexistence, followed by decline, has shaped many scholarly discussions. Bernard Lewis refers to the cultural exchange between Muslims and Jews as 'Judaeo-Islamic', and, adopting the model of symbiosis, refers to a cosmopolitan bourgeoisie, but also sees in the later Middle Ages a period of decline.[22] Goitein has also had an influence beyond historians of Jewish history. In an influential counter-history to the Eurocentric explanations of the rise of the West theory, Janet Abu-Lughod writes, based in part on Goitein's work (anachronistically, I should add, because she refers to the period after the 'Geniza people', about which Goitein writes), on a kind of near-world system of exchange of which one of its most important centres was in the Muslim Mediterranean. In constructing a model of a world economy from 1250 to 1350, 'before European hegemony', Abu-Lughod explains that there was no intrinsic reason why

[18] Bryan S. Turner, *Weber and Islam* (London, 1974).

[19] Use of the concept of symbiosis is examined by Steven M. Wasserstrom, *Between Muslim and Jew: The Problem of Symbiosis under Early Islam* (Princeton, 1995).

[20] S. D. Goitein, *A Mediterranean Society*, i: *Economic Foundations* (Berkeley, 1967), p. ix.

[21] S. D. Goitein, *Jews and Arabs: Their Contacts through the Ages* (New York, 1955), 10–11.

[22] Bernard Lewis, *The Jews of Islam* (Princeton, 1984), 67–8, 77–8, 88.

the West became hegemonic, as portrayed by Wallerstein's 'modern world system' in the sixteenth century (countering the argument that sees the sixteenth century as the first world system). After the mid-fourteenth century, this 'Eastern' world system declined because of the simultaneous convergence of economic and political difficulties in the various subsystems of the world economy, though scholars more recently have challenged Wallerstein's model from the other end, questioning the extent to which European hegemony applied to Asia in the sixteenth, seventeenth, and even eighteenth centuries.[23]

It should be noted here that there is another, broader context to this periodization of decline. For those who focus on the 'Arab' Islamic world, Islamic decline set in much earlier, around 1200 according to the traditional understanding, or a century or so later according to Abu-Lughod. If one were to focus on non-Arab Islam (Ottomans, Safavid, and Mughal empires), then the sixteenth century was an era of great expansion for Islamic civilization, a period of Muslim pre-eminence, as Marshall Hodgson argues.[24] The decline relative to the ascendancy of Europe, according to this model, began to set in during this period, but began truly in the seventeenth century.

In Jewish historiography, the decline theory is based on a number of assumptions, but with somewhat different criteria. Goitein was following the conventional model of orientalist scholars who saw the Mamluk period as marking Arab decline, characterized by cultural, intellectual, and scientific stagnation in contrast to the emergence of European culture in the Renaissance. Also implicit in his analysis, though it lacks a 'world system' interpretation, is the assumption that the cosmopolitan milieu of highly mobile Jewish merchants deteriorated. Thus, there is a convergence between intellectual or cultural contributions to civilization and the mobility and prosperity of Jewish merchants. Corresponding to this decline was the growth of persecution, or at least, the much harsher application of the prohibitions associated with the Jews' *dhimmi* status (literally 'protected person' status, implying the legal status of members of legitimate religions, especially Jews and Christians, in Islam).[25] Most accounts of Middle Eastern Jewry pay scant attention to the next 300 years of history (the decline period), picking up the threads when the Ottomans came to rule the Middle East. The decline in the position of the Jews in the previous period is therefore, for a period of time, reversed by Ottoman expansion of the fifteenth and sixteenth centuries,

[23] Andre Gunder Frank, *ReOrient: Global Economy in the Asian Age* (Berkeley, 1998).

[24] Marshall Hodgson, *The Venture of Islam: Conscience and History in a World Civilization*, 3 vols (Chicago, 1974), ii. 570–4; iii. 3 ff.

[25] On the stricter enforcement of the Pact of Umar that defined the status of *dhimmis* during the Mamluk period, see Norman A. Stillman, *The Jews of Arab Lands: A History and Source Book* (Philadelphia, 1979), 68–75.

which made use of the skills offered by the Sephardi immigrants. According to Bernard Lewis, this resurgence of Jewish life was not evident in the peripheries of the Islamic world, and he points to the Shi'ites in Safavid Iran and sharifian Morocco, where, in the latter case, Jews were forced to live in ghettos (*mellahs*) in many locations.[26]

Where Lewis detects decline in the Moroccan 'periphery' from the seventeenth century on, Haïm Zafrani paints a broad landscape of Judaeo–Muslim symbiosis. Interestingly, this does not deter Zafrani from concurring with the idea that the 'Hispano-Maghribi' Golden Age declined and was followed by a period of impoverishment, isolation, and stagnation. Yet it is precisely about this period of decadence that Zafrani writes, a period in which his whole œuvre portrays the rich cultural symbiosis between Muslims and Jews in Morocco, demonstrating the creativity and contributions that Moroccan Jews made to civilization.[27] Although both the trade routes and political structures had changed since the eleventh century, the kind of highly mobile, mercantile bourgeoisie, much like in Goitein's 'Geniza people', was in evidence from the Marinid period on, when Moroccan Jews fostered commercial ties with West Africa, the Middle East, and Europe. This is equally true for other parts of the Middle East, but this has not prevented scholars from describing these later periods in terms of decline.

The periodization of decline in the Jewish historiography of Spain and the Sephardim is somewhat different from the Arab Middle East. A number of distinctive periods of decline are proposed, though for some scholars the impact of the earlier Golden Age in Muslim Spain continued in Christian Spain. Recent scholarship has challenged the still widely accepted narrative, mainly established by Yitzhak Baer, of the fourteenth- and fifteenth-century decline of the Jews in Christian Spain, culminating in the expulsion of 1492, that largely neglects the resurgence of Jews in the fifteenth century.[28]

26 Lewis, *Jews of Islam*, 148–53. A recent example that subscribes to this decline theory is Jane S. Gerber, 'History of the Jews in the Middle East and North Africa from the Rise of Islam until 1700', in Reeva Spector Simon, Michael Menachem Laskier, and Sara Reguer (eds), *The Jews of the Middle East and North Africa in Modern Times* (New York, 2003). While following closely the decline after the fall of the caliphate model, Michel Abitbol, in contrast to Lewis, refers to the revival of Maghribi Jewry during this period, but then reverts to the decline theory (*Le Passé d'une discorde Juifs et Arabes du VIIᵉ siècle à nos jours* (Paris, 2003), 66 ff.).

27 Haïm Zafrani, *Études et recherches sur la vie intellectuelle juive au Maroc de la fin du 15ᵉ au début du 20ᵉ siècle*, 3 vols (Paris, 1972–80); id., *Mille ans de vie juive au Maroc* (Paris, 1983), 290.

28 Mark D. Meyerson, *A Jewish Renaissance in Fifteenth-Century Spain* (Princeton, 2004), 1–12. This refers to Yitzhak Baer, *A History of the Jews in Christian Spain* (Philadelphia, 1961). It should be noted, as David N. Myers has analysed, that in his rejection of the Enlightenment and assimilation model of his 19th-century predecessors, Baer departs from the 'Golden Age' idealization model, portraying negatively the external influences that Arab culture had in undermining Judaism, and comparing Sephardi Judaism unfavourably with the supposedly more pious Ashkenazim (*Re-Inventing the Jewish Past* (New York, 1995), 122–4).

Studies in recent decades debate the relative degree of tolerance or intolerance in Spain, or, indeed, the interdependency between violence and coexistence.[29] Yet the notion of the Golden Age of Spain, characterized by interfaith coexistence (*convivencia*), despite the acknowledgement by most scholars of the decline in the last Jewish period, continues to shape historical inquiry.[30] While some might situate the end of the Jewish Golden Age to the incursions of the less tolerant Almoravids and Almohads, others have sought to minimize the impact of these Moroccan-based dynasties.[31] Furthermore, the political fragmentation of Spain, first between the Muslim 'party kings' and then between Muslim and Christian kingdoms during the centuries of the Reconquista, did not entail the decline of Jewish culture in the eyes of many scholars. Historians continue to examine Jewish contributions to civilization as the main subject of inquiry. And while many standard accounts, following Baer's interpretation, still contend that the fourteenth and fifteenth centuries were marked by decline, many scholars focus on the thriving Jewish culture that continued in Christian Spain, even with the growing persecution in the last two periods before the expulsion. The richness of Jewish culture has remained at the centre of scholarly inquiry.[32]

THE OTTOMAN 'GOLDEN AGE' AND DECLINE

The continued efflorescence of Jewish culture in Spain and, as Goitein puts it, the 'fading of Oriental Jews from Jewish history', come together in a sense as a way to explain the contributions of Jews to the Ottoman Empire in its heyday. The once Arab, now Hispanic, Jewish communities living in Spain in the fifteenth century infused the expanding Ottoman Empire with new European Jewish blood after the expulsion of 1492. Wherever the Sephardim settled, according to this model, they became the social and religious leaders of the Jewish communities, clinging tenaciously to their language and sense of a superior culture. 'Thus,' writes Graetz, 'thousands

[29] David Nirenberg, *Communities of Violence: Persecution of Minorities in the Middle Ages* (Princeton, 1996).

[30] See e.g. a book that accompanied an exhibition at the Jewish Museum, New York: Vivian B. Mann, Thomas F. Glick, and Jerrilynn D. Dodds (eds), *Convivencia: Jews, Muslims, and Christians in Medieval Spain* (New York, 1992).

[31] Norman Roth, 'The Jews in Spain in the Time of Maimonides', in Eric L. Ormsby (ed.), *Moses Maimonides and his Time* (Washington, DC, 1989), 15–17; id., *Conversos, Inquisition and the Expulsion of the Jews from Spain* (Madison, 1995), pp. xi–xv. David Corcos argues that the duration of Almohad persecution was relatively short-lived: 'The Attitude of the Almohadic Rulers towards the Jews' (Heb.), *Zion*, 32 (1967), 137–60.

[32] See e.g. Benjamin R. Gampel, 'A Letter to a Wayward Teacher: The Transformations of Sephardic Culture in Christian Iberia', in David Biale (ed.), *Cultures of the Jews: A New History* (New York, 2002); Yom Tov Assis, 'The Judeo-Arabic Tradition in Christian Spain', in Daniel Frank (ed.), *The Jews of Medieval Islam: Community, Society, and Identity* (Leiden, 1995).

of Spanish Jews settled in Turkey, and before a generation had passed they had taken the lead among the Turkish Jews, *and made Turkey a kind of Eastern Spain*.'[33] Jews in the Ottoman Empire in the fifteenth and sixteenth centuries prospered as merchants and craftsmen, and because of the skills brought from Spain and Portugal, they were able to serve the sultans as influential financiers, merchants, customs agents, tax farmers, arms manufacturers, and physicians. In the 'Golden Age' of prosperity and scholarly achievement, the Ottoman authorities were able to maintain peace between the various religious groups. The image here is that of an intellectually and culturally superior European Sephardi Jewry immigrating to the more tolerant Ottoman Empire. The Sephardi Jews not only brought technical and scientific skills that helped the Ottomans expand in power, but they also caused the resurgence of Middle Eastern Jewish culture that had been in decay.[34]

While it is commonly recognized that Sephardi Jews made an important contribution to the Ottoman state, this has generally been understood in terms of external stimuli, rather than as a development emerging from internal dynamics of the Ottoman Empire. While intellectual and religious movements in Palestine are studied, these are usually approached only as a part of the history of Jewish ideas and religion rather than as a part of Ottoman history (unlike corresponding phenomena in Spain, where almost all historians study Jewish culture as the product of interaction with Muslim society). General histories of the Jews, with the major exception of Salo W. Baron's,[35] do not consider the Ottoman Empire as an important centre of Jewish civilization, instead shifting attention to an emerging east European Jewry, or the Sephardi dispersion in western Europe. In a world history context, this is consistent with the older, largely abandoned historiography that recognizes the military prowess of the Ottoman Empire but regards the Turks as barbarians, with little or nothing to contribute to civilization, unlike the Arabs in the 'classical' age.

In an effort to correct that image, recent works on the Jews of the Ottoman Empire by Ottomanists have used the terms 'symbiosis' or 'Golden Age' to

[33] Graetz, *History of the Jews*, iv. 364; my italics.

[34] Not everyone is in agreement that culture flourished in North Africa and the Middle East, even for a brief period following the expulsion. Norman Roth, for examples, refers to this as a 'popular myth' (*Conversos*, p. xv). The assumption that the position of the Ottoman rulers towards the Jews was positive, and the general Jewish experience in the Ottoman Empire was peaceful, is challenged by Joseph R. Hacker, 'Ottoman Policy toward the Jews and Jewish Attitudes toward the Ottomans during the Fifteenth Century', in Benjamin Braude and Bernard Lewis (eds), *Christians and Jews in the Ottoman Empire*, 2 vols (New York, 1982), i.

[35] 'Turkey's Golden Age' is the title of Baron's chapter dealing with the Jews of the 16th-century Ottoman Empire in *A Social and Religious History of the Jews*, 2nd edn, xviii (New York, 1983).

describe Jewish life in the fifteenth- and sixteenth-century Ottoman Empire, and the various contributions that Jews have made to Ottoman civilization.[36] Though they depart from the Arab centrism of orientalist scholarship (the decline of 'classical' Islam) by focusing on a genuine Judaeo-Ottoman culture that emerged, an idealized Golden Age concept of civilization remains, nevertheless, the category of analysis. 'Jewish culture and intellectual life flourished as brightly in Ottoman times as in the greatest days of Islamic Spain,' asserts Stanford Shaw.[37] Glossing over linguistic and cultural differences in the many parts of the Ottoman Empire, Shaw paints a picture of an idealized Golden Age when the ingathering of Jews to the empire produced an essential unity among the Ottoman Jewish communities, through the assimilating impact of Judaeo-Spanish, 'which gradually brought the national and regional groups together'. This cultural unity stemming from language was supported by the sharing of a common ruler, a common Middle Eastern civilization and way of life, and the reconciliation of separate legal interpretations.[38]

The flourishing of Jewish culture in the sixteenth century corresponded to the Ottoman Golden Age, the expansion of the empire that culminated in the idealized reign of Süleyman I (1520–66). Following this Golden Age, according to this 'decline paradigm' the empire began its inexorable deterioration beset by military and institutional decay.[39] In accounts of Middle Eastern 'decline' in the seventeenth and eighteenth centuries, Ottoman decay is measured against the expansion of European power, or intellectual developments and the scientific revolution in western Europe.[40] In recent years, the theory of Ottoman decline has come under serious criticism, and some historians argue that the state and society were able to transform themselves. Yet orientalists have based their assumptions on the decay of the empire, not only in relation to the expansion of European power, but also on expressions of decline found among contemporary Ottoman writers in the late sixteenth and seventeenth centuries, who focused on the inability of the sultans to maintain the foundations of the state. Yet these transformations, though interpreted as decline, can in another light, even in Western terms,

36 Avigdor Levy, *The Sephardim in the Ottoman Empire* (Princeton, 1992), 13–15. See also Halil Inalcik, 'Foundations of Ottoman–Jewish Cooperation', in Avigdor Levy (ed.), *Jews, Turks, Ottomans: As Shared History, Fifteenth through the Twentieth Century* (Syracuse, NY, 2002), 3–14.

37 Stanford J. Shaw, *The Jews of the Ottoman Empire and the Turkish Republic* (New York, 1991), 97.

38 Ibid. 56.

39 Jane Hathaway, 'Problems of Periodization in Ottoman History: The Fifteenth through the Eighteenth Centuries', *Turkish Studies Association Bulletin*, 20/2 (Fall 1996), 25–31; id., 'Rewriting Eighteenth-Century Ottoman History', *Mediterranean Historical Review*, 19/1 (June 2004), 29–52.

40 See e.g. Halil Inalcik, 'The Heyday and Decline of the Ottoman Empire', in P. M. Holt, Ann K. S. Lambton, and Bernard Lewis (eds), *The Cambridge History of Islam*, 2 vols, i: *The Central Islamic Lands* (Cambridge, 1970).

be otherwise interpreted as signs of adaptation, modernization, and progress. It can be demonstrated that well into the eighteenth century the empire was prospering, with growth in agriculture, industry, and international commerce.[41]

For historians of Ottoman Jewry, the older decline of civilization model continues to set the tone of inquiry: the sixteenth and first half of the seventeenth century is followed by a period of economic and cultural decay and stagnation, closely connected to the fate of the Ottoman state. As Avigdor Levy writes: 'The lot of Ottoman Jewry was always closely interwoven with that of the Ottoman state. Where Ottoman fortunes declined, so did those of its Jewish population.'[42] In a very apologetic tone, Stanford Shaw attributes in part this decline of the Jews, worse than for other major communities, to the importation of Christian antisemitism (in part brought by converted *devflirme* Christians who retained the antisemitism of the lands of their birth,[43] and in part by European merchants and diplomats), rather than to the Ottomans.[44] Harking back to the rationalist critique of mysticism found in the nineteenth-century Wissenschaft des Judentums' historiographical tradition, scholars have pointed to the kabbalah and the Shabatean movement as evidence of decline in the Ottoman Empire.[45] Culturally, the turn towards kabbalah and the Shabatean movement was evidence of a decline in intellectual culture; fervent pietism and superstitious practices prevailed. The communities themselves were taken over by an autocratic leadership of rabbis and notables who despotically enforced a rigorous and detailed code of moral discipline, eschewing luxury and regulating every minutia of daily life.[46] All of this Shaw contrasts with the progress of Europe:

Europe now was beginning to enter onto the path of rationalism and enlightenment, but Ottoman Judaism remained dominated by religion. While the Jews of Germany and France emancipated themselves under the influence of Mendelsohn [*sic*] and the *Encyclopédie*, the overpowering and depressing combination of Ottoman disintegration and abuses, violent community strife, economic decline and

[41] See Hathaway, 'Problems of Periodization in Ottoman History', 25–31; Daniel Goffman, *The Ottoman Empire and Early Modern Europe* (Cambridge, 2002), 112–13, 123–7; Linda T. Darling, 'Rethinking Europe and the Islamic World in the Age of Exploration', *Journal of Early Modern History*, 2 (1998), 221–46; Sevket Pamuk, 'The Ottoman Empire in the Eighteenth Century', *Itinerario*, 24/3–4 (2000), 104–15.

[42] Levy, *The Sephardim in the Ottoman Empire*, 71. This chapter is entitled 'The Era of Standstill and Decline 1580–1826'.

[43] *Devflirme* refers to the child levy system, which converted young Christians to Islam and brought them into the sultan's service in high administrative or military positions.

[44] Shaw, *The Jews of the Ottoman Empire and the Turkish Republic*, 119.

[45] Jacob Barnai, 'The Jews of Muslim Countries in Modern Times and the "Jerusalem School of History"' (Heb.), *Pe'amim*, 92 (2002), 98–9.

[46] Ibid. 127–39.

poverty, and the domination of life by rabbinical authorities led most Ottoman Jews to withdraw away from active participation in society altogether. The schools which had long perpetuated the culture and progressive thought brought from Spain declined and for the most part closed. Ignorance and superstition replaced knowledge and thought.[47]

For Michel Abitbol, this decline of the Jewish communities was evidenced throughout the Muslim world in the seventeenth century, 'the end of the era' as he calls his chapter:

From Fez to Jerusalem, passing through Istanbul, Salonika, Cairo, or Aleppo, the impression that emerges from reading the historical sources concerning the Jews in the land of Islam, between the 17th and the 18th centuries, is of communities in an advanced state of physical and intellectual exhaustion. The short-lived Sephardi 'embellishment' due to the arrival of the *megorashim* [those expelled from Spain] is nothing but a distant memory; the disciples of the great masters who came from Spain ended up transforming into a sort of closed religious oligarchy, undistinguished as spiritual leaders apart from a few rare cases, and self-perpetuating from generation to generation.[48]

Implicit in this analysis is that, after the sixteenth-century hiatus, the Middle East returns to its post-classical decay, and the Sephardim mostly disappear as a force in history, both in the Arabic-speaking parts of the empire and in the Judaeo-Spanish culture area of the eastern Mediterranean and the Balkans, as if they were absorbed into Eastern decay.[49] In this way, the Sephardim of North Africa and the eastern Mediterranean became orientals, dissociated from the Sephardim of western Europe.

In the period characterized by Ottoman decline, scholars continue to examine the contribution of Sephardim to Western civilization.[50] Sephardi Jews in western Europe, some of whom had been educated in Iberian universities ostensibly as new Christians and then re-emerged as Jews in the major intellectual and commercial centres of Europe, continued to contribute to the progress of Western civilization, and were at the forefront of new ideas and philosophies, or were crucial in the development of a new, world capitalist economy, which, unlike in Goitein's Geniza period, now included the Americas. Jews, in the minds of some Europeans, were the founders of modern capitalism because of the extensive Sephardi global commercial network.

[47] Shaw, *The Jews of the Ottoman Empire and the Turkish Republic*, 131. There is little evidence to support the idea of the growth of an autocratic rabbinical leadership. See Levy, *The Sephardim in the Ottoman Empire*, 87–8.

[48] Abitbol, *Le Passé d'une discorde*, 114.

[49] For a corrective of this view, see Esther Benbassa and Aron Rodrigue, *A History of the Judeo-Spanish Community, 14th–20th Centuries* (Berkeley, 2000), pp. xx–xxi.

[50] Yosef Kaplan, 'Bom Judesmo: The Western Sephardic Diaspora', in Biale (ed.), *Cultures of the Jews*.

From the late sixteenth and especially in the seventeenth century, Sephardi Jews were welcomed by north European rulers because of their experience in world trade and their network of connections stretching from the Iberian Peninsula to the New World.[51] The great Dutch success and Iberian decline in the seventeenth century were attributed to the expulsion of the Jews from Spain and Portugal and subsequent oppression, and the contribution that Sephardim made to the Netherlands.[52] Advocates of mercantilism who sought the readmission of Jews to west European countries where they had been excluded adopted this argument. The exaggerated and historically inaccurate theory of the preponderance of Sephardim in the development of capitalism was echoed in Werner Sombart's thesis *Die Juden und das Wirtschaftsleben*, published at the beginning of the twentieth century.[53]

The Atlantic world dominated by European nation-states was not necessarily the most important place of Jewish life in the seventeenth and eighteenth centuries, when the Mediterranean remained an important centre for trade and intellectual culture—even if Jews were never again to play such a major role for the Ottoman rulers. Jews lost their pre-eminent position in the Ottoman state in the latter decades of the seventeenth century, owing, on the one hand, to imperial support for a reformist movement of Muslim pietists and the concurrent effort to convert non-Muslims, and, on the other hand, to the growth in European support for Orthodox Christians that made the latter more valuable than Jews.[54] But Jews were not entirely supplanted from positions of influence in the Porte, and they continued to thrive in the Mediterranean world of commerce. Sephardi Jews were central in Algiers, Tunis, and Tripoli as middlemen between the Regencies and Europe, and as key intermediaries in the diplomatic and commercial ties with Britain, the Netherlands, and the Italian ports.[55] Moroccan Jews in the

[51] This is analysed in detail in Jonathan I. Israel, *European Jewry in the Age of Mercantilism, 1550–1750* (Oxford, 1985); see also Yosef Kaplan, 'The Self-Definition of the Sephardic Jews of Western Europe and their Relation to the Alien and the Stranger', in Benjamin R. Gampel (ed.), *Crisis and Creativity in the Sephardic World, 1391–1648* (New York, 1997), 121.

[52] In much of the traditional historiography, Spain's great empire in the 16th century proved to be a false start, hence the 17th-century decline. See Henry Kamen, 'The Decline of Spain: A Historical Myth?', *Past and Present*, 81 (Nov. 1978), 24–50.

[53] Leipzig, 1911; analysed by Freddy Raphäel, *Judaïsme et capitalisme: Essai sur la controverse entre Max Weber et Werner Sombart* (Paris, 1982).

[54] Marc David Baer, 'The 1660 Fire and the Islamization of Space in Istanbul', *International Journal of Middle East Studies*, 36 (2004), 162–3.

[55] Richard Ayoun and Bernard Cohen, *Les Juifs d'Algérie: Deux mille ans d'histoire* (Paris, 1982), 79; M. Eisenbeth, 'Les Juifs en Algérie et en Tunisie à l'époque turque (1516–1830)', *Revue Africaine*, 96 (1952), 347–50; H. Z. Hirschberg, *A History of the Jews in North Africa*, 2 vols (Leiden, 1974–81), ii. 11–28, 165–71; Paul Sebag, *Histoire des Juifs de Tunisie: Des origines à nos jours* (Paris, 1991), 82–9; Renzo de Felice, *Jews in an Arab Land: Libya, 1835–1970* (Austin, Tex., 1985), 6–8; Harvey E. Goldberg, *Jewish Life in Muslim Libya: Rivals and Relatives* (Chicago, 1990), 18–23.

Sa'dian period of the sixteenth century and in the Alawid period from the seventeenth century on were crucial in the Atlantic and Mediterranean trade with Europe.[56] Seventeenth-century Livorno became in the seventeenth century the most important port for Sephardi Jewry, not only constituting a major Jewish community, but also sending forth a large dispersion of 'Livornese' merchants and scholars throughout the southern Mediterranean basin.[57]

FROM SEPHARDI TO ORIENTAL IN THE MEDITERRANEAN WORLD

There were a number of important Jewish centres—some of which were situated in the Middle East and North Africa—and until the late eighteenth century it would be difficult to establish that the western Atlantic was dominant. But Jewish historiography continues to focus on Jewish merchants and scholars in the European and Atlantic worlds, contributing to the notion of 'oriental' decline in the Mediterranean basin. The west European Sephardim themselves contributed to this myth of superiority, in their assertion of belonging to a kind of supranational Spanish and Portuguese Nação

[56] Hirschberg, *A History of the Jews in North Africa*, ii. 236–72. Scattered throughout the series Les Sources inédites de l'histoire du Maroc, drawn from the European archives, is evidence of the role that Jewish merchants played in the international trade of the 16th and 17th centuries. See also Johan de Bakker, 'Slaves, Arms, and Holy War: Moroccan Policy vis-à-vis the Dutch Republic during the Establishment of the 'Alawi Dynasty', Ph.D. diss. (University of Amsterdam, 1991). For a detailed analysis of the world of Moroccan international merchants in the 16th and 17th centuries, see Mercedes García-Arenal and Gerard Wiegers, *A Man of Three Worlds: Samuel Pallache, a Moroccan Jew in Catholic and Protestant Europe* (Baltimore, 2003); for the late 18th and early 19th centuries, see Daniel J. Schroeter, *The Sultan's Jew: Morocco and the Sephardi World* (Stanford, Calif., 2002), and id., 'Royal Power and the Economy in Precolonial Morocco: Jews and the Legitimation of Foreign Trade', in Rahma Bourqia and Susan Gilson Miller (eds), *In the Shadow of the Sultan: Culture, Power, and Politics in Morocco* (Cambridge, Mass., 1999).

[57] On the development of the Jews of Livorno and the diaspora of Livornese Jews, see Israel, *European Jewry in the Age of Mercantilism*, 113, 164, 175, 238; Jean-Pierre Filippini, 'Les Juifs d'Afrique du Nord et la communauté de Livourne au XVIIIe siècle', in Jean-Louis Miège (ed.), *Les Relations intercommunautaires juives en Méditerranée occidentale, XIIIe–XXe siècles* (Paris, 1984); id., 'Les Négociants juifs de Livourne au XVIIIe siècle', *Revue des Études Juives*, 132 (1973), 672–3; id., 'Le Rôle des négociants et des banquiers juifs de Livourne dans le grand commerce international en Méditerranée au XVIIIe siècle', in Ariel Toaff and Simon Schwarzfuchs (eds), *The Mediterranean and the Jews: Banking, Finance and International Trade, XVI–XVIII Centuries* (Ramat Gan, 1989); Renzo Toaff, 'La nazione ebrea de Livorno dal 1591 al 1715 nascita e sviluppo di una comunità di mercanti', in Toaff and Schwarzfuchs (eds), *The Mediterranean and the Jews*; Richard Ayoun, 'Les Juifs livournais en Afrique du Nord', *La Rassegna Mensile di Israel*, 50 (1984), 650–705; Minna Rozen, 'The Leghorn Merchants in Tunis and their Trade with Marseilles at the End of the 17th Century', in Miège (ed.), *Les Relations intercommunautaires*.

(Nation), with Amsterdam as its epicentre.[58] Though historically linked to the Sephardim of the Levant and the Maghrib, members of the Nação were condescending towards their more 'Turkish' co-religionists from the Ottoman Empire, or designated those Jews coming from the Maghrib as a separate category, called Berberiscos (i.e. the Jews coming from the Barbary Coast), and were contemptuous of their 'oriental' religious practices. With the growing number of foreign Sephardi poor arriving in London and Amsterdam, the Spanish and Portuguese Nação began to pay them to leave the country to migrate to other parts of the Sephardi Diaspora in the Mediterranean or New World.[59] No less significantly, Jews from eastern Europe, who began arriving in much larger numbers in the eighteenth century and who soon outstripped the Sephardim, were viewed with even greater disdain for their Eastern ways.[60] Although in western Europe the Sephardim had gained privileges not enjoyed by other Jews in most other countries, belonging to a larger network of Sephardim was arguably more important than belonging to the nations among whom they lived.

The growing contempt of Western Sephardim towards their 'oriental' co-religionists was reflected in a shift in European attitudes towards the East. It is important to note, however, that during the European Enlightenment a more sympathetic examination of Islam developed in contrast to the medieval period, when Islam was seen as the enemy of Christianity. The rationalist ideas of the Enlightenment, together with the critique of Christianity, led some Enlightenment thinkers to view Islam as a tolerant religion. However, by the late eighteenth century, as the Ottomans were in clear decline as a world power, the more hostile view of Muslims and Islam became prevalent, though in ways distinct from the Middle Ages. Hostility towards contemporary Muslims as ignorant, irrational, incapable of scientific thinking, and living under the yoke of despotic rulers—hence, in a state of arrested development—contrasted with the progress of European civilization in the age of developing nationalism. It was believed that though 'classical' Islam had made great achievements in the past, its civilization had decayed.[61]

European Jews began to reflect these attitudes of superiority towards their co-religionists of the Middle East and North Africa in the decades before

[58] Miriam Bodian, *Hebrews of the Portuguese Nation* (Bloomington, Ind., 1997).

[59] See Todd M. Endelman, *The Jews of Georgian England, 1714–1830* (Philadelphia, 1979), 168–9; Robert Cohen, 'Passage to a New World: The Sephardi Poor of Eighteenth Century Amsterdam', in Lea Dasberg and Jonathan N. Cohen (eds), *Neveh Ya'akov: Jubilee Volume Presented to Dr. Jaap Meijer on the Occasion of his Seventieth Birthday* (Assen, 1982), 34–5; Schroeter, *The Sultan's Jew*, 65–7.

[60] On the exclusiveness of members of the Nação of western Europe towards other Jews, see Kaplan, 'The Self-Definition of the Sephardic Jews of Western Europe'.

[61] Maxime Rodinson, *Europe and the Mystique of Islam* (Seattle, 1987); Ann Thomas, *Barbary and Enlightenment: European Attitudes towards the Maghreb in the Nineteenth Century* (Leiden, 1987).

emancipation, even though their co-religionists in the 'East' often enjoyed a more secure and superior position in society than Jews in many places in Europe. Yet there was a growing awareness of an ascendant European society and the growing disparity of power between Europe and the Islamic world. European Jewry was positioning itself on the side of a 'superior' Europe, anticipating the betterment of its legal status and social standing, soon to be radically transformed by emancipation. The lines between Western and Eastern Jews were being drawn, even before new identities connected to the modern European nation-state were forged. European Jews began to view Sephardi Jews of Asia and Africa as a different branch of Judaism, more associated to their oriental ways than their Spanish heritage.[62] These new attitudes were being shaped in a period when the wider network of Sephardi merchants in international trade was losing ground. The intellectual culture of the Spanish and Portuguese Naçao also seemed to be in decline in the eighteenth century, while assimilation and conversion in western Europe increased.[63]

The Sephardi Jew of the Mediterranean world had become an oriental in the minds of European Jewry, legitimized in nineteenth-century notions of decline of the Middle East and North Africa. While distinctions between Sephardim and Ashkenazim in Europe remained, increasingly what mattered was affiliation to the nation-state. A new kind of dichotomy emerged between emancipated and unemancipated Jews. This included not only the Arabic-speaking Jews of the southern Mediterranean, but the Judaeo-Spanish communities of the Levant and northern Mediterranean who were exoticized as part of the Middle East: their history has also largely been ignored.[64]

European Jews saw in colonialism the opportunity to save their less fortunate co-religionists from a moral and spiritual decline that was not so much of their own making but the result of the backwardness of the countries in which they lived, the oppressive nature of Muslim society, and the despotic governments to which they passively submitted. No longer were Mediterranean and Middle Eastern Jews part of the same Jewish world, except through ties to their ancient or medieval past from which modern Western Jews sought to refashion their new-found ethnic identities.

In this sense, then, the concept of the Jewish contribution to medieval Islamic and Spanish civilization and the decline theory become inextricably linked. It provided the legitimizing principle by which Western Jews

[62] See Daniel J. Schroeter, 'Orientalism and the Jews of the Mediterranean', *Journal of Mediterranean Studies*, 4 (1994), 183–5.

[63] Kaplan, 'Bom Judesmo', 666–7. On England, see Todd M. Endelmann, *Radical Assimilation in English History* (Bloomington, Ind., 1990), 9–33.

[64] Benbassa and Rodrigue, *A History of the Judeo-Spanish Community*, pp. xx–xxi.

supported the cause of emancipation of Asian and African Jewry as if to extract them from their decline. In their advocacy of emancipation, west European Jews saw little value in the culture of their contemporaries, but sought to retrieve from the usable past a long-decayed cultural heritage.[65]

West European Jews therefore supported 'colonial emancipation', which was distinct from the cause of emancipation in Europe. Rather than calling for Jews to become citizens in the countries where they lived, European advocates of emancipation called for granting them citizen rights of the colonizing power. Support for colonial emancipation was rooted in the very insecurities that Jews in the new nations of Europe felt. Jews were viewed, in another sense, as the oriental within European society, and both advocates and detractors of the Jews' emancipation in the eighteenth century saw the Jews as degenerate, either capable of moral improvement if they were to obtain civil rights (and, in this sense, needing to be 'colonized') or intrinsically different, anticipating the debates of the nineteenth century over the wisdom of emancipation. Even after emancipation, the 'oriental' character of the Jews was still believed by many to be their essence, which accounted for their stubborn adherence to Mosaic law, or as the immutable character of Jews and Judaism as an obstacle to the Jewish ability to self-emancipate.[66]

THE DECLINE IN THE MODERN PERIOD?

The complicated ideological background to the relationship between 'Western' and 'oriental' Jews in the modern period offers an explanation for the almost total absence of scholarship on the contributions of modern Middle Eastern and North African Jewries to civilization in the modern period. To the extent that studies were undertaken, Jews have rarely been represented as agents in their own histories, but rather as recipients of Westernizing reforms through the aegis of European Jewish education (especially the Alliance Israélite Universelle) and colonial institutions, or participants in political movements extraneous to their own societies: Zionism or patriotism to the colonizing power.[67] This teleology pointed to

[65] Schroeter, 'Orientalism and the Jews of the Mediterranean', 190–1.

[66] Jonathan M. Hess, 'Johann David Michaelis and the Colonial Imaginary: Orientalism and the Emergence of Racial Antisemitism in Eighteenth-Century Germany', *Jewish Social Studies*, 6 (2001), 56–101; James Pasto, 'Islam's "Strange Secret Sharer": Orientalism, Judaism, and the Jewish Question', *Comparative Studies in Society and History*, 40 (1998), 437–74.

[67] This is clearly the approach of André Chouraqui, *Marche vers l'Occident: Les Juifs d'Afrique du Nord* (Paris, 1952). The focus of many of the pioneering studies on the Middle East and North Africa has been on the enormous influence of the Alliance Israélite Universelle in the Mediterranean communities. See especially Michael M. Laskier, *The Alliance Israélite Universelle and the Jewish Communities of Morocco, 1862–1962* (Albany, NY, 1983). For the impact of the Alliance on Turkish Jewry, see Aron Rodrigue, *French Jews, Turkish Jews: The*

the eventual decline and dissolution of all but a trace of these Jewish communities in the second half of the twentieth century: the 'end of the tradition', as Bernard Lewis entitles the last chapter of *The Jews of Islam*, about the history of the nineteenth and twentieth centuries.[68] In some ways, this theory is indebted to an outmoded scholarship referred to as 'modernization' theory that assumes a Western trajectory of modernization in developing countries and societies. In this model, tradition and modernity are analysed as dichotomous, and modernization leads inevitably to the disintegration of traditional society.[69] Oriental Jewish communities in the modern period have also been analysed in these terms. Following Jacob Katz, who argued that all traditional Jewish communities shared an essentially uniform social structure,[70] the Jewish communities of the Middle East and North Africa have also been classified as 'traditional societies', until the penetration of Western influence, sometimes well into the twentieth century.[71] The oriental Jewish communities, thus, lag behind their European counterparts, but, consistent with the notion of the essential unity of Jewish history characteristic of the 'Jerusalem School', are nevertheless part of the same historical process of modernization, meaning west European modernity. Much of this scholarship echoes the modernizing discourse of the colonizing powers and their Jewish supporters, especially the vast network of Jewish educators of the Alliance Israélite Universelle, who saw traditional Jewish society as an integral part of the decayed and stagnant Middle East. Shmuel Ettinger, the most influential figure in the Jerusalem School, clearly articulated the theory of decline of the Jewish communities of Islam in the modern period, in contrast to the Golden Age of Spain or to European Jewry in the modern period. For Ettinger, the histories of the oriental communities were shaped in the modern period by west European influence, but changes were constrained by the absence of integration and modernization in their societies, which provoked a crisis in Muslim–Jewish relations, again implying a contrast with the process that took place in Europe. While a Westernized elite emerged, they largely abandoned the masses, who, attracted to Zionism

Alliance Israélite Universelle and the Politics of Jewish Schooling in Turkey, 1860–1925 (Bloomington, Ind., 1990). For a synthesis of this first generation of studies on the modern period, see Norman A. Stillman, *The Jews of Arab Lands in Modern Times* (Philadelphia, 1991).

[68] See n. 22.

[69] For the classic and influential study that applied modernization theory to the Middle East, see Daniel Lerner, *The Passing of Traditional Society* (New York, 1958).

[70] Jacob Katz, 'Traditional Jewish Society and Modern Society', in Shlomo Deshen and Walter P. Zenner (eds), *Jews among Muslims: Communities in the Precolonial Middle East* (Houndmills, 1996).

[71] Walter P. Zenner and Shlomo Deshen, 'Jews among Muslims in Precolonial Times: An Introductory Survey', in Deshen and Zenner (eds), *Jews among Muslims*, 6.

by their traditional messianic longings, were rescued by Israel.[72] In the period of mass emigration of Jews from Muslim countries, it was indeed a kind of 'rescue research' that motivated the first generation of scholars, who, with a sense of urgency, sought to study the traditional culture of Sephardi and oriental Jewry before it was too late.[73]

The decline theory of oriental Jewry also became an integral part of Israeli and Zionist historical discourse, which could serve the purpose of absorbing the Asian and African communities into the dominant, 'modern' society as represented by Jews of European origin. The idea that all Jewish communities were in essence the same, and that the ethnic differences that existed between Asian and African immigrants and European Jews were produced by a cultural gap, legitimized the absorption of immigrants from Middle Eastern and North African countries in the national society. Thus, modernization theory, as applied to these immigrants, saw a linear process of transformation from traditional to modern Israeli society.[74] The push for integration in Israel from the mid-1960s and even more from the 1970s, reflected in educational policy, led to the growth of academic institutions and scholarship on oriental Jewish history.[75] Goitein's early studies on the Jews of Yemen, and H. Z. Hirschberg's studies on the history of North African Jewry, represent the first important scholarly efforts to study the communities that had settled in Israel in the first two decades (or before statehood, in the case of the Yemenites), yet when writing about the contemporary period, their work tended to be more ethnographic or folkloric, based on their own observations and travels or the travelogues of others. Goitein's serious historical work concentrated on the medieval Geniza period, while Hirschberg's two-volume narrative on the Jews of North Africa gives very short shrift to the nineteenth and twentieth centuries, a period that culminated in the emigration of these communities.[76]

[72] Ettinger frames these ideas in his introduction to volumes I and II of what became a standard textbook on the Jews of Islam in the modern period, in *History of the Jews in the Islamic Countries* (Heb.), 3 vols (Jerusalem, 1986), discussed critically in Barnai, 'The Jews of Muslim Countries in Modern Times and the "Jerusalem School of History"', 88–92; and Yaron Tsur, 'Israeli Historiography and the Ethnic Problem' (Heb.), *Pe'amim*, 94–5 (2003), 26–33.

[73] Norman A. Stillman, 'From Oriental Studies and Wissenschaft des Judentums to Interdisciplinarity' (Heb.), *Pe'amim*, 92 (2002), 66–71.

[74] On the relationship between ethnic problems and historiography, see Tsur, 'Israeli Historiography and the Ethnic Problem'. This theme is taken up, but with a somewhat more narrow and tendentious focus on the critique of orientalism, by Gabriel Piterberg, 'Domestic Orientalism: The Representation of "Oriental" Jews in Zionist/Israeli Historiography', *British Journal of Middle Eastern Studies*, 23 (1996), 125–45.

[75] Barnai, 'The Jews of Muslim Countries in Modern Times and the "Jerusalem School of History"', 105–7.

[76] See S. D. Goitein, *From the Land of Sheba: Tales of the Jews of Yemen* (New York, 1947; rev. edn, 1973). In Goitein's revised edition, he writes of the 'fantastic achievement' of Operation

The tendency to inscribe oriental Jewry into the Zionist, 'end of exile' tradition has produced, broadly speaking, two counter-narratives to this civilization and decline model. One focuses on the persecution of oriental Jewry in Arab lands, challenging the notion of tolerance in Islam. Implicit in this argument is that, like Ashkenazi Jews, oriental Jews suffered from 'antisemitism' or were victims of 'pogroms'. Rather than a focus on periods of tolerance followed by decline, the whole experience of 'Jews of Islam' is essentialized as one of persecution, referred to by Marc Cohen as a kind of 'neo-lachrymose conception of Jewish–Arab history'.[77] Thus, the legal status of Jews in the Islamic world, *dhimmi* status, becomes understood as an epithet of discrimination as second-class citizenship.[78] In this model there is little distinction between periods, but, rather, an effort is made to trace the unfolding of antisemitic violence. The notion of synthesis is absent; instead one is left with totally separate and antagonistic cultures (Jews and Muslims). This perspective offered a way for Jews from Asia and Africa, with their sense of marginalization and discrimination in Israeli society, to integrate themselves into the dominant nationalist Ashkenazi ideology of antisemitism and rebirth in the Land of Israel.

The efforts led by intellectuals of Middle Eastern and North African immigrant backgrounds to integrate their history into the dominant historical narrative is reflected in the Israeli school curriculum. While earlier textbooks mainly ignored 'oriental' Jewish history after the expulsion from Spain, or else portrayed oriental Jewish communities as essentially backward, frozen in the past, more recent historiography portrays Asian and African communities as 'proto-Zionist', without examining the communities on their own terms.[79]

The second counter-narrative is a total contrast to the one of separation and persecution. Invoking Goitein and his 'Geniza world', Ammiel Alcalay finds a world of mobility and fluidity, a crossover of Jewish and Arab cultures that is a model for the contemporary world of 'Levantine' culture. In his paradigm, there is a quantum leap from medieval Spain's Golden Age and

Magic Carpet from Yemen to Israel in 1949–50, and of the good adaptation of the Yemenites to Israel (preface, p. ix). See also Hayyim Habshush, *Travels in Yemen: An Account of Joseph Halevy's Journey to Najran in the Year 1870*, ed. S. D. Goitein (1939; Jerusalem, 1941). H. Z. Hirschberg, *A History of the Jews in North Africa: From Antiquity to our Time* (Heb.) (Jerusalem, 1965; Eng. trans., Leiden, 1974–81); Hirschberg's travel account on the Jews of Morocco was published shortly before the emigration of many of the communities he visited: *Inside Maghreb: The Jews in North Africa* (Heb.) (Jerusalem, 1957). See the discussion on Goitein and Hirschberg in Tsur, 'Israeli Historiography and the Ethnic Problem', 17–19.

77 Cohen, *Under Crescent and Cross*, 9.

78 Bat Ye'or, *The Dhimmi: Jews and Christians under Islam* (Rutherford, NJ, 1985).

79 Avner Ben-Amos, 'An Impossible Pluralism? European Jews and Oriental Jews in the Israeli History Curriculum', *History of European Ideas*, 18 (1994), 48–9.

Goitein's Geniza world (epitomized, at one point, by the appearance of Dunash b. Labrat's famous wine song) to the world of the twentieth century (exemplified in the Yemenite poems written in Israeli transit camps in 1951), with no intervening period of decline.[80] In contrast to Lewis's 'end of the tradition', Alcalay retrieves lost voices from the Levant that suggest a vibrant Jewish culture embedded in the Arab world in the modern period. However, the period of decline was produced by the state of Israel with its class and ethnic divisions, which eroded the 'mobility, diversity, autonomy, and translatability possessed by the Jews of the Levant', for this long stretch of time.[81] In this critical, post-Zionist model, inter-ethnic tensions produced either by religious differences in the medieval period or by new nationalist identities in the modern era are minimized, and medieval and modern history are bridged into an essentialized Levantine civilization. Implicit also is the possibility of peaceful coexistence in a post-national world, or, as James Clifford (based on Alcalay's invocation of Goitein) suggests, 'the Sephardi strand offers a specific counter history of Arab/Jewish coexistence and crossover'.[82] While clearly rejecting the negative stereotypes in orientalist views of Levantine civilization, Alcalay returns in a sense to the older, nineteenth-century Wissenschaft des Judentums model of idealizing a past—yet, a past that, in contrast to the older civilization model, has extended up through modern times.

With the formation of classical Andalusian culture in tenth-century Spain, and its subsequent influence throughout the Levant writ large (which would include present-day Portugal, Spain, southern France and Italy, the Balkans, Greece, Turkey, Iran, Iraq, Yemen, Syria, Lebanon, Cyprus, Israel–Palestine, Egypt, Morocco, Tunisia, Algeria, Libya, and even parts of West Africa and India), Jewish creativity also extended itself, sometimes following, sometimes leading. This remains true right up until the full or partial dissolution of these Sephardi, Levantine, Ottoman, Arab, and Persian Jewish communities and their massive transfer to Israel in the 1950s.[83]

Alcalay's work, however, does serve as a corrective to those studies that analyse Jewish society in the modern period in terms of communities in decline, with no dynamic culture of their own.[84] A number of recent studies

[80] Ammiel Alcalay, *After Jews and Arabs: Remaking Levantine Culture* (Minneapolis, 1993), 27–8.

[81] Ibid. 28.

[82] James Clifford, *Routes: Travel and Translation in the Late Twentieth Century* (Cambridge, Mass., 1997), 274.

[83] Alcalay, *After Jews and Arabs*, 21. In a similar vein, Ella Shohat laments the loss of Arabness after Zionism and the displacements caused by immigration to Israel. 'Rupture and Return: Zionist Discourse and the Study of Arab Jews', *Social Text* 75, 21/2 (Summer 2003), 49–74.

[84] See Alcalay's chapter 'Intellectual Life', in Simon et al. (eds), *The Jews of the Middle East and North Africa in Modern Times*. Also other chapters in the book explore different aspects of Jewish cultural production in the modern period.

have approached the question of modernization in a much more complex manner, analysing Asian, African, and Mediterranean Jews not simply as 'a people without history', prone simply to outside influence, but as multiple societies and cultures in their own right, and as agents in their own history.[85] This type of history, too, which focuses on the culture of the Jews of the modern Muslim world, has begun to emerge in the Israeli school curriculum.[86] In this type of history, it is not simply a question of stagnated communities acculturating to Western modernity, but rather of the dynamic interplay between foreign influences and indigenous modernity. Religious thinking in the Middle East and North Africa, for example, responded to the challenges of modernity in innovative ways that need to be understood on its own terms.[87] The development of a Haskalah movement and linguistic transformations in North Africa, or the modern theatre in Morocco, offer further evidence of the internal dynamics of modernization.[88] Such studies do not ignore the fact that western Europe often had a preponderant influence, but are concerned with the internal responses to these influences. Rather than simply looking in an undifferentiated manner at history as a process of acculturation to the West, cultural and religious adaptation is seen

[85] For discussions of some of the recent literature, see Sarah Abrevaya Stein, 'Sephardi and Middle Eastern Jewries since 1492', in Goodman (ed.), *The Oxford Handbook of Jewish Studies*; see also id., *Making Jews Modern: Yiddish and Ladino Newspapers of the Russian and Ottoman Empire* (Bloomington, Ind., 2003); Barnai, 'The Jews of Muslim Countries in Modern Times and the "Jerusalem School of History"', 94–6; see the introduction and chapters in Harvey E. Goldberg (ed.), *Sephardi and Middle Eastern Jewries: History and Culture in the Modern Era* (Bloomington, Ind., 1996); Lucette Valensi, 'Multicultural Visions: The Cultural Tapestry of the Jews of North Africa', in Biale (ed.), *Cultures of the Jews*; Daniel J. Schroeter, 'A Different Road to Modernity: Jewish Identity in the Arab World', in Howard Wettstein (ed.), *Diasporas and Exiles: Varieties of Jewish Identity* (Berkeley, 2002). A number of studies have focused in particular on indigenous religious responses to modernity.

[86] See e.g. Yaron Tsur, *The Evolution of a Culture: The Jews of Tunisia and Other Islamic Countries* (Heb.) (Jerusalem, 2003). Tsur has investigated the question of modernization in the pre-colonial period in 'The Tunisian Jewry at the End of the Pre-Colonial Period' (Heb.), *Mikedem umiyam*, 3 (1990), 77–113.

[87] See Tsevi Zohar, *Tradition and Change: Rabbis in Egypt and Syria Confront the Challenge of Modernization, 1880–1920* (Heb.) (Jerusalem, 1993), id., *Luminous Face of the East: Studies in the Legal and Religious Thought of Sephardic Rabbis of the Middle East* (Heb.) (Tel Aviv, 2001); Norman A. Stillman, *Sephardi Religious Responses to Modernity* (Luxembourg, 1995); Harvey E. Goldberg, 'Religious Responses among North African Jews in the Nineteenth and Twentieth Centuries', in Jack Wertheimer (ed.), *The Uses of Tradition: Jewish Continuity in the Modern Era* (New York, 1992).

[88] Joseph Chetrit, 'Hebrew National Modernity against French Modernity: The Hebrew Haskalah in North Africa at the End of the Nineteenth Century' (Heb.), *Mikedem umiyam*, 3 (1990), 11–76; id., 'Discours et modernité dans les communautés juives d'Afrique du Nord à la fin du XIXe siècle', in Esther Benbassa (ed.), *Transmission et passages en monde juif* (Paris, 1997); id., 'Jewish Theatre: A Chapter in Moroccan Jewry's Wrestle with Modernization' (Heb.), in Haim Saadoun (ed.), *Maroko* (Jerusalem, 2003).

as a dynamic process that comes as a response to both foreign influences and indigenous modernity. Whether the accumulative results of these studies will eventually put the decline theory of Jewish civilization in the Middle East and North Africa to rest waits to be seen.

PART III

JEWS, GERMANS, AMERICANS

EIGHT

From Admission Ticket to Contribution: Remarks on the History of an Apologetic Argument

YAACOV SHAVIT

What does Europe owe to the Jews?
Many things, good and bad . . .

FRIEDRICH NIETZSCHE
Beyond Good and Evil

THE JEWS AND EUROPEAN CULTURE: FROM THE BACK DOOR TO THE FRONT ENTRANCE

NOT long after the idea of culture (*Kultur*)[1] became a key concept, not only as a descriptive term, but also as a term of value, modern Jews began to use it to define the content of their singular heritage, tradition, and identity as Jewish culture. At the same time, they also tried to prove that the intellectual and creative heritage of the Jews, namely, their culture, included all the traits and assets then regarded as an inseparable part of the high culture of a *Kulturnation*.[2] Such proof could serve both those who wanted to depict Judaism as the bearer of a cultural tradition no less rich than the culture they aspired to join, and those who wanted to create a new autonomous, all-inclusive Jewish cultural system.

[1] For my purposes here, the distinction between the terms 'civilization' and 'culture' is not significant, particularly since in the literature of the period the former term generally referred to the material aspect of the culture, not to its intellectual–spiritual aspect. On the other hand, some believe—erroneously, in my view—that the term 'Jewish civilization' is broader and more all-embracing than the term 'Jewish culture'. In the context of this chapter, the distinction between the overall European culture (Western culture), which is a *Weltkultur*, and the specific national cultures of Europe is far more important.

[2] See the programmatic article by Immanuel Wolf (the nom de plume of Immanuel Wohlwill, 1799–1847, one of the founders of Verein für Kultur und Wissenschaft der Juden, the Society for the Culture and Science of the Jews), 'Über den Begriff einer Wissenschaft des Judentums', *Zeitschrift für die Wissenschaft des Judentums*, 1 (1822), 1–24.

The former are the subject of this chapter. They believed that, as a result of the diminishing status and role of religion in European culture, it had become a cultural system in which modern Jews could actively participate, as indeed they did. On the basis of this belief, in 1821 Eduard Gans (1797–1839), one of the founders of the Science of Judaism, expressed the optimistic view that the main entrance, not the back door as in the past, was now open to Jews—specifically, German Jews—allowing them full admission into European society and culture.[3] The hope Gans expressed came out of the belief that modern German society—in his view, the apex of European culture—was now a liberal, open, and secular society, so that all the legal and religious obstacles to the integration (*Verschmelzung*) and even assimilation (*Aufgehen*) of Jews had now disappeared. The special Jewish–German relationship and the influence of Hegelian philosophy gave rise to a rich vocabulary capable of proposing a range of possible models of cultural participation and activity, while also being among the tools of philosophical reasoning and historical metaphysics that explained the necessity—or feasibility—of these models.[4]

There is, however, quite a large gap between the world of ideas and deliberations on the abstract nature of the *Jüdische Geist*, on the one hand, and the actual cultural reality, on the other. In reality, there was a fundamental distinction between participation and contribution in two separate spheres of culture. The first was the 'neutral' area of science, technology, and the learned professions. The other was the area of literary and artistic creation in all of its dimensions. The scientist, the technician, the physician can participate in the culture without coming up against a cultural barrier, or the need for legitimization. Yet such is not the case with the writer, the poet, and the artist. Participation and contribution were problematic in these areas, since both the Romantic and Hegelian concepts held that literary and artistic creative works are a unified whole that expresses the uniqueness and oneness (*Eigenheit* and *Einheit*) of the particular national spirit (*Volksgeist*).[5]

Jews therefore faced a serious problem in attempting to adopt the notion of *Kultur* in its holistic interpretation, which postulated the unity of all manifestations of a cultural system and claimed that they are an expression of a 'spirit' or of an ordering principle (or structural unity). The critical question was: If there existed a *besonderer Volkgeist* (a peculiar national spirit), as Hegel

[3] In Eduard Gans, 'Drei Reden im Kulturverien' (1821); repr. in *Der judische Wille*, 1/1–3 (1919); trans. into Heb. in Paul R. Mendes-Flohr (ed.), *Modern Jewish Studies: Historical and Philosophical Perspectives* (Heb.) (Jerusalem, 1979). Gans's lectures were printed in full only there by Zalman Rubaschoff (Shazar).

[4] See Jacob Toury, 'Emancipation and Assimilation: Concepts and Conditions' (Heb.), *Yalkut Moreshet*, 2 (1964), 167–82.

[5] See E. H. Gombrich, *In Search of Cultural History* (Oxford, 1969).

reasoned, how could Jews, with a peculiar spirit that had created their singular cultural heritage, take part in a culture—or even civilization—that is the product of a totally different *Geist*?

Several solutions were proposed for this dilemma. One could claim participation and partnership in the secular liberal culture and its values, represented by the ideal of *Bildung*, or try to argue—unsuccessfully—that the Jews are not alien to the Germanic national spirit, and even that the Jewish spirit is in harmony with it. In a lecture delivered on 22 January 1919 entitled 'The Future of Jewry', Ismar Freund, a prominent member of the Berlin Jewish community, a scholar and a member of the CV Hauptvortand (Central Verein deutscher Staatsbürger jüdischen Glaubens, the Central Union of Jewish Citizens), defined the harmony between 'Germanness' and Judaism as follows: 'The Deutschtum we love with all our hearts is something holy for us . . . We German Jews are conscious of the fact that we have greatly contributed to what we regard as Deutschtum . . .'.[6] According to another claim, the important role filled by Jewish creators in the modernist movements was unquestionably a result of the fact that such nearly metaphysical integration was impossible, and a consequence of the universal, rather than national, nature of modernism.

Most modern Jews looked forward to a modest, measured degree of integration and acculturation. They sought to preserve the distinctive Jewish tradition and yet, at the same time, to adopt aspects of the non-Jewish environment, to assimilate these into their specific Jewish lifestyle, and to participate in the culture of the non-Jewish society. Such cultural activity grew more and more intensive in the second half of the nineteenth century, constituting one of the important manifestations of the Jewish revolution in the modern era.

BETWEEN PARTICIPATION AND CONTRIBUTION

At the beginning of the nineteenth century, modern Jews began knocking on Europe's door, believing they could see the dawn of a new historical era, and eager to be part of its newly born culture(s). By participating, they meant to be not only passively absorbing consumers of European culture, but active and productive creators in the various fields of the arts, literature, sciences,

[6] Lecture by Ismar Freund, 'Über die Zukunft des Judentums gehalten im Logenhaus am 22 Jan. 1919'; quoted in Jehuda Reinharz, 'The Response of the Zionistische Vereinigung für Deutschland and the Centralverein deutscher Staatsbürger jüdischen Glaubens to Antisemitism during the Weimar Republic' (Heb.), in Abraham Margaliot and Yehoyakim Cohavi (eds), *History of the Holocaust: Germany* (Jerusalem, 1998), 21. I am grateful to Professor Reinharz for his English version.

etc.[7] During the nineteenth century, this *participation* was often defined as a Jewish 'donation', namely, it defined the Jew as a donor and suggested that the recipient was indebted to the Jew.[8]

Participation (or partnership) and *contribution* are, therefore, two concepts that were employed to describe and evaluate a key aspect of the process of the Jews' integration (*Eingliederung*) into the cultures of their non-Jewish environments. However, these concepts embodied two opposites: on the one hand, the awareness that the participants or donors are a distinct group within the larger society, and, on the other, the subjective belief of the group that it is an inseparable part of the surrounding culture, as well as its desire to be seen as such. These two concepts were part of the far larger stock of new formulations and terms that emerged at the beginning of the period of the Haskalah and the emancipation to denote the new character of the relationship between Jews and their surroundings. With the help of this stock of terms, modern Jews tried to clarify for themselves what were the desirable limits of integration and acculturation, what parts of their tradition they would be required to forgo, what type of Jews the non-Jewish society would be prepared to accept, and how the Jews should introduce themselves when they knocked at the gates of European culture and entered through them. In other words, what kind of calling card could serve as an admission ticket for the modern Jew into European societies and their culture.

Of course, it was not ideology that encouraged integration and assimilation or motivated the revolutionary process of Jewish participation in European culture; nor was it formulas that determined the dimensions and boundaries of this participation in the cultural system. But the new concepts did foster a certain pattern of cultural behaviour, gave it legitimacy and described it, and at the same time tried to set the desirable boundaries of the cultural contact between Jews and the surrounding culture. There was an urgent need to set these boundaries, because religious walls were being undermined, if not torn down, and European culture in the West had become, in many aspects, a 'secular' culture, and, according to some, even a 'new paganism'.

This chapter focuses only on one of the calling cards presented by Jews at the gates to European culture, and, leaving aside the metaphor, it is my

[7] See Jacob Katz, 'German Culture and the Jews', in Jehuda Reinharz and Walter Schatzberg (eds), *The Jewish Response to German Culture: From the Enlightenment to the Second World War* (Hanover, NH, 1985).

[8] To the best of my knowledge, the word for contribution (*Beitrag*) appears infrequently in German Jewish literature. The reference is generally to participation (*Anteil*, *Teilnahme*), regardless of whether the subject is 'passive' participation, i.e. as a consumer of culture, or active participation, as a creator of culture. Use of the term 'contribution' was primarily widespread in literature on German Jewry, to stress that this was an act of 'giving' or granting those things that were lacking in the receiving culture.

intent to suggest some headings for the history of the concept of 'Jewish participation in and contribution to European culture' in the nineteenth century, as well as of the uses made of it in the Jewish public discourse before these were appropriated by Jewish historiography. I should point out that the discussion here is limited to contribution in the field of culture and does not deal with the Jewish contribution to other fields (economics, politics, etc.). It is no coincidence that the term 'contribution' always seems to relate to the broad field of culture (including science), and not, for example, to the role filled by Jews in politics or in the revolutionary movements. The stress on 'contribution' in the various fields of cultural creation stemmed from the fact that in Germany (but not only there) national pride and the collective self-esteem emphasized their 'common achievement in science, literature, philosophy and music'.[9] The question of what *really* was the contribution made by Jews to European culture in general, and to specific European cultures in particular, is also outside the purview of this chapter, which deals only with the concept, as well as with the question of what was 'Jewish' in the contribution of the Jews.

APOLOGETICS DIRECTED INWARD AND OUTWARD

Many obstacles stood in the way of the integration of the Jews into European culture (or cultures). One of them was the widespread claim—supported by various pseudo-scientific theories—that the Jews lacked the necessary qualities to participate and create in the various fields of culture. This claim was refuted by what I shall call a polemical or an apologetic strategy. It was directed both inwards, towards those opposed to integration and assimilation, and outwards, towards those non-Jews who spoke about the innate cultural inferiority of the Jews.

In the internal Jewish context, there was a desire to prove to the conservative circles of Jewish society that 'capable' Jews had been active throughout Jewish history in all fields of general culture. Externally, this strategy was part of an apologetic argumentative discourse, for the purpose of showing the surrounding society a calling card that introduced the Jews as the possessors of a rich repertoire of cultural assets: a repertoire that endowed them with the ability as well as the right to take an active part in the culture of modern 'Europe'. This cultural calling card was intended to rebut deeply rooted prejudices and to persuade the non-Jewish society that the Jews did not lack those qualities that characterize a modern *Kulturvolk*; in other words, to claim that they were now entering the gates of modern European

[9] Norbert Elias, *The Germans: Power Struggles and the Development of Habitus in the Nineteenth and Twentieth Centuries*, ed. Michael Schröter, trans. Eric Dunning and Stephen Mennell (New York, 1996), 323.

culture not empty-handed, as cultural beggars, but bringing with them a rich and precious cargo.

In both contexts, there was a need to provide proof from the past. In the former, this proof took the form of discovering, rediscovering, and even inventing forgotten or dormant aspects of Jewish cultural life, mainly its rich cultural productivity throughout the ages. Thus, when the Russian *maskil* Isaac Baer Levinsohn (1788–1860), in his *Te'udah beyisra'el* (A Testimony in Israel, 1828), drew up a long list of rabbis who were engaged in science and philosophy, his aim was to convince traditional Jews that Judaism is not alien to these fields of cultural creativity. In the latter context, which is the subject of this chapter, proof from the past meant contesting the popular dogma of Jews' innate cultural inferiority, which went as far back as the Hellenistic–Roman period. History shows that Jews were always active in almost all those areas of cultural activity considered in the nineteenth century as the vital traits of a *Kulturnation*; hence, they do not immanently lack any of the mental traits or faculties that are the source of this type of creativity.

This dogma concerning the mental inferiority of the Jews was formulated by a number of writers in the Hellenistic–Roman culture. The notorious Apion claimed that the Jews 'have not produced any geniuses, for example, inventors in arts and crafts';[10] Celsus, the anti-Christian pagan philosopher, claimed in *Alethes Logos* (The True Doctrine) that no Jew contributed to philosophy, science, or any of the many practical inventions (Pliny the Elder counts almost 159 such inventions that contributed to the welfare of humanity);[11] the Roman emperor Julian argued in his *Against the Galileans* that the Jews had contributed nothing in the field of culture and science.[12] These claims outlived the Middle Ages and the Renaissance, and were revived at the dawn of the modern era. As one famous example, the French Jansenist *abbé* Henri-Baptiste Grégoire (1750–1831), in his *Essai sur la régénération physique, morale et politique des Juifs* (1789), rejected the idea that the Jews in the Middle Ages were 'princes of the science of medicine', and argued that the Jews had no talent in music, art, or mathematics. However, in his view, this was not an innate flaw and might be corrected by education and by the Jews' self-improvement of their way of life. In the course of the nineteenth century this view became a widespread pseudo-scientific dogma, based on the concepts of 'race' and its 'mental traits', as well as on the morphology of cultures. Again and again, it was stated that the Semitic Jews lacked the capacity for art, science, philosophy, and so on. In an article published in the first issue (1806) of *Sulamith*—a journal that aimed to 'advance culture and

[10] Josephus, *Against Apion*, 2. 135.

[11] From the vast literature on this subject, I will only mention Bezalel Bar-Kochva's article 'The Anti-Jewish Treatise of Apollonius Malon' (Heb.), *Tarbiz*, 69/1 (1999), 6–58.

[12] Julian, *Against the Galileans*, 178 A–B, 216 C–224 D.

humanity among the Jewish people'—the author praised the superiority of Greek culture and argued that Jews 'lack the true spirit of humanity; they did not write poetry, did not create art, etc.'.[13] In a feuilleton written (in Russian) by Ze'ev (Vladimir) Jabotinsky (1880–1940) in 1911, entitled 'An Exchange of Compliments', describing a conversation between a Jewish and a Russian passenger travelling in a train, the Russian claims that the Jews have contributed nothing original to world culture; at the very most, they have served as 'travelling salesmen' who disseminated cultural assets created by others.[14] To sum up, at the gates of modern European culture, Jews encountered the claim that in the past they 'had no art—if we except music—no science, no philosophy'.[15]

One of the ways Jews contested these widespread claims was, of course, to revive old patterns of response, mainly the claim that in fact Jews were the progenitors of many human achievements, and were not strangers to *humanitas*, or *'adab*. Just as Hellenistic Jews responded in *ad maiorem Judaeorum gloriam*, so did modern apologetic Jews in Europe, turning to the old legend 'The Theft of Philosophy' (by the non-Jews).[16] Modern Jewish historical writing—of the Haskalah and of Wissenschaft des Judentums—also undertook to expose and depict the broad field of the Jews' participation in the past in creating and spreading 'alien wisdom'.

PRAISES OF THE ACCOMPLISHMENTS OF THE JEWS

This appeal to the past filled an important role in Jewish rhetoric and apologetics in the nineteenth century, but it does not represent the major strategy that was employed. The important calling card was the present situation, and the present told of the great success Jews had experienced in integrating into all areas of European culture, whose doors were open to them. This is what I. B. Levinsohn wrote in his *Sefer aḥiyah shiloni haḥozeh* (1839):

[13] I. A. L. Richter, 'Worin lag die vorzügliche Kultur der Greichen?', *Sulamith*, 1 (1806), 125–47.

[14] Ze'ev Jabotinsky, 'An Exchange of Compliments' (Heb.), in Jabotinsky, *Nation and Society* (Jerusalem, 1950). The feuilleton was written as part of the debate about the contribution made by Russian Jewry to Russian culture in general and to Russian literature in particular. Also see the article 'Jews and Russian Literature', which he wrote in response to an article of the same title published by Korny Zhukovsky in the newspaper *Svobodnie Mislï* (Free Thoughts) in 1908. It was printed in Ze'ev Jabotinsky, *On Literature and Art* (Heb.) (Jerusalem, 1948), 61–8.

[15] S. H. Butcher, 'Greece and Israel', in Butcher, *Harvard Lectures on Greek Subjects* (London, 1904), 13–14. And see a brief summary on this subject in Yaacov Shavit, 'Have Jews Imagination? Jews and the Creative Arts', in Shavit, *Athens in Jerusalem: Classical Antiquity and Hellenism in the Making of the Modern Secular Jew* (London, 1999), 220–77.

[16] For a catalogue of the claims about Jewish creativity, see Anatole Leroy-Beaulieu, *Israel among the Nations: A Study of Jews and Antisemitism*, trans. Frances Hellmann (New York, 1895).

Let every wise lover of truth among the Christians state whether Jews, in addition to being exceedingly diligent, do not possess intelligence, and whether some among them are not imbued with fine ideas, and others are capable in every branch of learning and science and in all the arts and crafts. How many marvellous artists are there among them today in the world, how many fine musicians skilled in every instrument, and how many have gained wide fame. There is hardly any field of science, art and the crafts, even among the most prestigious and honoured, in which there are no Jews today . . .[17]

Thirty years later, in 1869, the popularizer and historian from Vilna, Kalman Schulman (1819–99), took pride in the speed with which Jews entered into all branches of European culture:

Anyone who sees clearly will gaze with astonishment at the rapid ascent of Jews to the heights in modern times in all areas of wisdom and knowledge, in all arts and crafts. This they achieved in just a short while, whereas other peoples did not succeed in attaining such heights even over a period of many hundreds of years. For no sooner did the kings and counts of the land unloose their bonds and favour them with civil rights and laws, than they opened their treasures and displayed the precious qualities and fine talents that had lain dormant in their souls during the dark years when they were persecuted by their foes, who gave them no rest until they devoured them.

Before many days passed, there arose proudly from their midst great poets, wondrous rhetoricians, lauded authors in all realms, renowned mathematicians and engineers, astronomers, chronologists, men well versed in religion and law, and knowledgeable in all branches of the natural sciences, famous physicians, psalmists, musicians, diplomats, sculptors, visionaries. And there is no wisdom, art or craftsmanship in which the Jews did not engage and become famous in the land for their prowess.[18]

Schulman did not laud the contribution made through this intensive and multi-disciplinary activity of Jews to the development of particularistic modern Jewish culture; rather, he took pride in the presence of Jews in Western culture and in their full integration into it.

In 1864 the poet Judah Leib Gordon (1831–86), a radical *maskil* and Russian patriot, wrote:

Now there is no city or state in which young Jewish men do not draw the clear waters of alien springs . . . You can count the specialist physicians employed by the state . . . how many young Jews you will find today who engage in writing and speak the language of their country fluently, or German and French, and all of them born in the last generation, products of the last decade . . .[19]

[17] I. B. Levinsohn, *The Book of Ahiyah Hashiloni the Visionary* (Heb.) (Leipzig, 1863), 117.
[18] Kalman Schulman, *History of the World* (Heb.), iv (Vilna, 1867), 13–16.
[19] J. L. Gordon, *Letters* (Heb.) (Warsaw, 1893), 90.

Around the same time, in 1858, the Reform leader Abraham Geiger (1810–74) thus tried to dissuade a Jew from converting to Christianity:

Let me tell you—and do not accuse me of arrogance—the Jews are proving an ability to develop that is likely to bring them much favour. For many generations, their human rights have been violated, both the most sublime and the most common, their spiritual development has been hampered and their very existence has been in constant danger. Less than a century has passed since their situation has been considerably eased. And now a totally different generation is quickly springing up! Improving in every sense, enormously energetic in all their aspirations, spiritually alert and making great achievements in all spheres despite the fact that quite a few professions are closed to them. This is not a decadent public; on the contrary, it is brimming with lofty talents . . .[20]

In the eighth letter of his 'Correspondence of an English Lady on Judaism and Semitism' (1883), Heinrich Graetz (1817–91) wrote in the same spirit: 'And now, dear friend, take a look at what the Jews have achieved in less than one century. They perform well in all branches of science and literature and in some they are the leaders.'[21]

This calling card presented not the Jews' real or imaginary achievements in the past, but their ability in the present to become—and in a short period of time—active in every field of cultural activity. There is no reference yet in this picture to the notion of 'Jewish contribution'. It refers only to the fact that—in the words of the Orthodox weekly *Der Israelit*—'since they left the ghetto, the Jews have been active partners in creative works in all walks of life'.[22]

THE NEW CALLING CARD

The words of Geiger and Graetz are no longer apologetic in nature, a change that shows that less than fifty years passed from the time when Jewish apologetics began to present a new calling card that introduced Jews as people capable of being active participants in the surrounding culture. This card stated not only that the Jews are full participants in European culture, but that they are also making a decisive contribution to its creation, and moreover that they have a pre-eminent position in that culture, as the American sociologist Thorstein Veblen put it early in the twentieth century.[23]

[20] A. Geiger, *Über den Austritt aus dem Judenthume. Ein aufgefundener Briefwechsel* (Leipzig, 1858). The letter was printed in a Hebrew translation in Abraham Geiger, *Selected Writing on Religious Reform*, ed. M. A. Meyer, trans. G. Eliashberg (Jerusalem, 1979), 65.

[21] Heinrich Graetz, *The Structure of Jewish History and Other Essays*, ed. and trans. Ismar Schorsch (New York, 1975), 220.

[22] J. Wolff, 'Eine Jahrhundert-Betrachtung', *Der Israelit*, 108 (28 Dec. 1899), 3027–9.

[23] Thorstein Veblen, 'The Intellectual Pre-eminence of Jews in Modern Europe', *Political Science Quarterly*, 34 (1919), 33–42; repr. in M. Lerner (ed.), *The Portable Veblen* (New York, 1959).

Towards the end of the nineteenth century, these concepts, 'Jewish contribution' and 'Jewish excellence', became important elements and motifs, which were permanent and useful in the apologetics and self-consciousness of the Jews. They were perceived not only as part of the self-image, or as a means of defending themselves against prejudicial claims of the cultural inferiority of the Jews, but also as a factual description of the situation, namely of the fact that Jews were not only participating in all fields of culture, but also were over-represented in them and were demonstrating special excellence, demonstrating the quality of the 'Jewish genius'.[24]

What interests me here is not the various explanations given for Jewish 'excellence' in the various spheres of cultural creation. For my purposes, it is important to distinguish between the 'Jewish contribution', on the one hand, and the 'contribution of Jews' as a group or as individuals, on the other. The two terms relate to different things. The former speaks about the contribution of Judaism in the sense of a defined system of ideas and values, in particular the idea of one God and moral rules. The latter assumes that all the Jews who contributed to European culture brought to it a common 'genetic cultural' baggage, which includes a world picture, concepts, values, and faculties. And from this standpoint, we need to define the nature and content of the 'distinctive Jewish cultural traits' that shaped the unique Jewish contribution.

In addition, there were those who related to the Jews as a group and as individuals, whose contribution to the overall culture lacked a shared charac-

[24] In March 1912 the young Jewish journalist Moritz Goldstein published an article entitled 'Deutsch-jüdischer Parnass' in volume 25 (1912) of *Der Kunstwart* (The Art Guard), in which he claimed that the Jews were a dominant factor in the spiritual property of Germany, a country that does not recognize their Germanness. See Moritz Goldstein, 'German Jewry's Dilemma: The Story of a Provocative Essay', *Leo Baeck Institute Yearbook*, 2 (1957), 236–54; Steven E. Aschheim, 'The Publication of Moritz Goldstein's "The German-Jewish Parnassus" Sparks a Debate over Assimilation, German Culture and the Jewish Spirit', in Sander L. Gilman and Jack Zipes (eds), *Yale Companion to Jewish Writing and Thought in German Culture 1096–1996* (New Haven, 1997), 299–305, in which he called it 'an explosive article'. See also id., 'The Jews Within: The Myth of "Judaization" in Germany', in Reinharz and Schatzberg (eds), *Jewish Response to German Culture*. Steven Lowenstein wrote derisively about the idea of a 'collective enterprise' of Jews 'giving a gift to the non-Jewish majority' (Steven M. Lowenstein, 'Jewish Participation in German Culture', in Michael A. Meyer (ed.), *German-Jewish History in Modern Times*, iii: *Integration in Dispute 1871–1918* (New York, 1996–8)). Siegmund Kazenelson edited a collection of articles with the aim of providing an objective description of the situation, but it was banned by the Nazi censor in 1934 (Kazenelson (ed.), *Juden im deutschen Kulturbereich*, 2nd edn. (Berlin, 1959)). See Katz, 'German Culture and the Jews', 91–2; Amos Elon carries on this trend of describing at length the creative activity, in many cases also the pioneering activity, of distinguished Jewish figures in various fields of culture, science, and economics in 19th-century Germany and up to 1933 (A. Elon, *The Pity of It All: A History of Jews in Germany 1743–1933* (New York, 2002)).

teristic and was seen to stem from a changing set of sociological and cultural circumstances that motivated and enabled the Jews to excel.[25]

Nietzsche wrote in 1881 that it was necessary for Jews 'to distinguish themselves in departments of European distinction and to stand in the front rank until they shall have advanced so far as to determine themselves what distinction shall mean'.[26] In this he was referring to the future, as well as to the general character traits of the Jews, which were marked by 'intellectual versatility and shrewdness', and not to the current achievements of Jews. Later he asked, 'What does Europe owe to the Jews?', and answered: 'A lot, for good and bad, and most of all for that one thing that is simultaneously of the worst and the best: for the great moral style, for the awfulness and majesty of the absolute demand . . .'.[27] Although he was speaking here about the Jews as a people, he was actually referring to ideas and values he regarded as Jewish. Similarly, Graetz, when he wrote that it was 'the prophets and the psalmists who brought a breath of fresh air back into European history after the Roman world ended up as a complete swamp', and that, at the beginning of the sixteenth century, it was the 'Hebraic truth' that saved Europe from neo-paganism,[28] he was alluding, not to specific Jews, but to the fundamental ideas and values of Judaism with which they imbued the 'soul of Europe', namely, humanity, monotheism, and religious rationalism.[29] After all, Luther did not need the mediation of Jews to arrive at the *Hebraica veritas* of the Old Testament.

By the same token, when Max Nordau declared in 1903, 'We [Jews] contributed our share to the culture of Europe more than to our own culture; this [European] culture belongs to us as much as it belongs to the German,

[25] Jacob Katz, 'German Culture and the Jews', in Reinharz and Schatzberg (eds), *The Jewish Response to German Culture*; Shulamit Volkov, 'A Stunning Success: The Example of the Jews in Science', in Volkov, *The Magic Circle: Germans, Jews and AntiSemites* (Heb.) (Tel Aviv, 2002), 209–22. For a survey of Jewish participation in all spheres of creation in Germany, see Heinz Mosche Graupe, *Die Entstehung des Modernen Judentums. Geistgeschichte der deutschen Juden 1650–1942*, ii: *Revidierte und erwietere Aufgabe* (Hamburg, 1977), 242–57, and Elon, *The Pity of It All*, 259–95. It is important to note that Orthodox Jews in Germany were primarily consumers of German culture but did not participate in creating it. See Mordecai Breuer, *Modernity within Tradition: The Social History of Orthodox Jewry in Imperial Germany*, trans. Elizabeth Petuchowski (New York, 1992), 162–73.

[26] Friedrich Nietzsche, *The Dawn of Days*, trans. J. M. Kennedy (New York, 1964), 213.

[27] Friedrich Nietzsche, 'Beyond Good and Evil: Volker und Vaterlander', quoted in Josef Simon, 'Nietzsche on Judaism and Europe', trans. John Stanley, in Jacob Golomb (ed.), *Nietzsche and Jewish Culture* (London, 1997), 102–3. The entire article is important for our purposes. See also Walter Kaufman's translation of this section in Nietzsche, *Beyond Good and Evil*, ed. Walter Kaufman (New York, 1989), 185.

[28] Heinrich Graetz, 'Correspondence of an English Lady', in Graetz, *The Structure of Jewish History*, 256.

[29] Heinrich Graetz, 'The Significance of Judaism for the Present and the Future', in Graetz, *The Structure of Jewish History*, 287.

French and English . . .',[30] he too was speaking about the transmission of ideas and values, not about specific contributions by individual Jews. And when Ze'ev Jabotinsky argued that 'from a moral point of view—Europe also belongs to us', he was speaking of a past contribution. The Jews gave birth to Europe, and Europe is in their debt for her social compassion and the idea of progress—for the ideal of a 'golden age' both in the past and in the future; thus, Western culture is a product of the Jewish spirit and genius, and Jerusalem, not Athens, is Europe's alma mater. But modern Europe does not need Jews in order to return to the values of the Bible.[31]

These texts, as well as many others,[32] refer, then, to the contribution of Judaism as a set of formative ideas, or about the contribution of the 'Jewish spirit'—transmitted via a book—and not necessarily about the contribution made by many individuals in the various fields of cultural creation. If that is the case, what about contemporary Jews? Can they take pride only in the fact that they imparted ethical monotheism to European culture via the Hebrew Bible? Is this important and precious asset sufficient to provide them with the highly sought-after admission ticket? One could, after all, argue that one needs no Jews for that contribution. The reply comes in the shape of an emphasis on the fact that present-day Jews are making a contribution in the field of modern culture and in detailed descriptions of this contribution. Lists of 'donors' frequently appear in popular historical literature in the form of books that tell the reader about the activity of Jews in various fields.[33]

THE PRICE OF 'CONTRIBUTION'

The terms 'contribution', or even 'Jewish contribution', can be regarded as reliable descriptions of the reality, or they can be interpreted as expressions of a sense of superiority. However, the frequent use of these terms to

[30] The article, 'Ahad Ha'am über Altneuland', was printed on 13 March in *Die Welt*.

[31] Ze'ev Jabotinsky, 'The East' (Heb.); first pub. in Russian in *Razsvet*, 26 Sept. 1926.

[32] The Jews, Heinrich Heine wrote, gave Europe the 'principle of modernism' (*das moderne Prinzip*); see Heinrich Heine, 'Shakespeares Mädchen und Frauen', in Heine, *Sämtliche Werke*, x (Munich, 1964), 227.

[33] The case of African American society in the United States shows that the concept of contribution did not, nor does it today, serve only the Jews. For example, Gates writes that, during his trip to Africa, he learned about 'the record of black Africans' genuine contribution to civilization', and that 'so many of Africa's genuine contributions have been denied or appropriated by non-Africans' (Henry Louis Gates, Jr., *Wonders of the African World* (New York, 1999), 29, 107). This claim is a central motif in the 'alarming' but popular African American literature that attempts to 'discover' the contribution of the Blacks in Africa to world culture in general, and the contribution of the African Americans to American culture in particular. See also Yaacov Shavit, *History in Black: African-Americans in Search of an Ancient Past* (London, 2001), 16–35.

describe the cultural activity of contemporary Jews probably attests to an awareness of the fact that the Jews' active and creative participation is not a self-evident part of the creative field of overall culture. Hence the need to emphasize it and to speak of Europe's debt to the Jews—not in the past, but in the present—thus also expressing a sense of cultural superiority. When Heinrich Graetz wrote about the 'wondrous Jewish life', and stated that 'they [the Jews] performed well in all branches of science and literature and in some they are the leaders', he referred, among other things, to the great outpouring of creativity on the part of Jews such as David Ricardo, Karl Marx, and Ferdinand LaSalle—pioneers of social science, likely to solve the riddle of the future. Jews, he added, also have an important role in shaping public opinion, as writers of political essays or feuilletons.[34]

Not everyone expressed such admiration for the integration of the Jews, or their contribution and its results. Theodor Herzl (1860–1904), for example, had a disparate view. He accepted the above description that Jews are present in many fields of activity, but he wrote that it is necessary to 'keep the Jews from pushing ahead. They should not make such strides.'[35] And, according to him, the conviction that Jews had indeed gained the admission ticket was but an illusion. To Baron Hirsch he wrote on 3 June 1895 that 'all the engineers, architects, technologists, chemists, physicians, lawyers who have emerged from the ghetto during the last thirty years, and who thought that they would gain their livelihood and their bit of honor outside the higgling and haggling Jewish trade . . . are beginning to constitute a frightful proletariat of intellectuals'.[36] At the same time, Herzl suggested to Baron Hirsch to announce in 'the chief anti-Semitic countries a huge prize for *actions d'éclat*, for deeds of great moral beauty, for courage, self-sacrifice, ethical conduct, great achievements in arts and sciences', and more. This curious suggestion shows that in Herzl's view the majority of the Jews still did not possess the admission ticket to European culture and that only a few of them would gain it.[37]

Was this gloomy picture an objective observation, or was it a justification of his Zionist vision?

JEWS AS INSIDERS AND OUTSIDERS

To summarize this brief history of the concept of Jewish 'contribution', one might argue that this term was used as a mark of pride in the status of Jews as donors to European culture: the target audience for this self-aggrandizement was mainly the Jewish public, although, by the way, it also

[34] In the eighteenth letter of 'The Correspondence', Graetz, *The Structure of Jewish History*, 220.

[35] Theodor Herzl, *The Complete Diaries*, i, ed. Raphael Patai, trans. Harry Zohn (New York, 1960), 23. [36] Ibid. 28. [37] Ibid. 22.

reached non-Jewish ears. The term was intended to repair the image of the Jews as inferior in the sphere of cultural creativity, and to remove the barriers between them and non-Jewish culture by stressing their active role and their achievements. It was used to prove that Jews had gained full membership in Western civilization and were even an asset to it, as well as that they had shared various cultural assets with non-Jews.[38] However, use of the term 'contribution' also emphasized—wittingly or otherwise—the continued existence of these barriers, because it implied that the participation of Jews in European culture was not self-evident. It defined the Jews as both insiders and outsiders, and it reflected both an inferiority complex and a superiority complex. Perhaps the main reason that it continued to be used, even after it became evident that Jewish participation and contribution were a tragic illusion, was a desire to bring the cultural output of the Jews under one roof—even where it had not been created within the framework of Jewish culture. If cultural creativity is evidence of vitality, of accomplishment, and of a creative genius—and if the Jews had disseminated their cultural output in 'alien fields'—it was right to regard the whole of this output as integral to Jewish culture, or Jewish civilization, while also meeting the wider criteria of modern Western culture.

One might regard the rich creative contribution made by Jews to European culture (primarily in Germany) as a vain waste of cultural vitality, and even as a disastrous self-delusion. On this view, the cultural partnership created between the Jews and their environment was not a genuine one since it gave rise to antisemitic claims that the Jews—and 'Jewish values'—had become dominant in European culture, turning it into a Jewish (i.e. alien) culture, or even 'Judaizing' Europe. However, the Jewish contribution might also be perceived as expanding the assets of the universal culture, as well as being intrinsic to the authentic Jewish cultural repertoire, which draws upon the unique 'Jewish spirit'.

38 And, if so, they had met the expectations of Johann Gottfried Herder that 'Jews will live in accordance with European laws and will contribute to the best of the state'; see Alfred D. Low, *Jews in the Eyes of the Germans: From the Enlightenment to Imperial Germany* (Philadelphia, 1979), 61.

NINE

German-Jewish Literature and Culture and the Field of German-Jewish Studies

MARK H. GELBER

> L'interdisciplinaire, dont on parle beaucoup, ne consiste pas à confronter des disciplines déjà constituées (dont, en fait aucune ne consent à *s'abandonner*). Pour faire de l'interdisciplinaire, il ne suffit pas de prendre un 'sujet' (un theme) et de convoquer autour deux ou trois sciences. L'interdisciplinaire consiste à créer un objet nouveau, qui n'appartienne à personne.
>
> Interdisciplinary work, so much discussed these days, is not about confronting already constituted disciplines (none of which, in fact, is willing to *let itself go*). To do something interdisciplinary it's not enough to choose a 'subject' (a theme) and gather around it two or three sciences. Interdisciplinarity consists in creating a new subject that belongs to no one.
>
> ROLAND BARTHES
> 'Jeunes Chercheurs', 1984

I BEGIN with a short anecdote and confession, based on my experience at the German literature archive in Marbach am Neckar, the birthplace of Friedrich Schiller. I have been utilizing the resources of this archive intermittently over the last twenty-five years, that is, since the time I was researching my doctoral dissertation on literary antisemitism in nineteenth-century Germany and Britain. Scholars who visit the archives sign their names in the guest book daily upon arrival, noting also their home city or country, the date, and the specific topic of research. Visitors, if they care, have some sense of the identity of the other colleagues and what they might be researching, thus facilitating conversations during coffee breaks and the like. During an extended research visit in Marbach in 2003–4, I could not help but notice the egregiously disproportionate number of scholars working in the area of German-Jewish literary studies. Although I did not keep an exact record, and even though it may seem at first ludicrous, it would probably be fair to say that about one-third to one-half of the visiting scholars during this period were working on some aspect of the poetry of Paul Celan or another topic related to German literature and the Holocaust. Another quarter, perhaps, were working on topics related to a major figure or topic in

German-Jewish literary or cultural history; for example, Kafka and Walter Benjamin seem to be very popular right now. The rest might be working on any given topic in German or Austrian letters, although only precious few registered that they were researching Goethe or Schiller or the German classical period, which is the glorious, traditional core of the vast archival collection. Researchers were regularly turning to me for advice or with questions about specific German-Jewish authors or about Hebrew language or Yiddish. I found that too much of my time was being spent in this way, and I thought I should begin to avoid the passing glances of my colleagues. The study of German literature seemed to have been displaced by German-Jewish Studies at the very altar of one of its central temples.

In his well-known provocative and controversial polemic of 1912 'Deutsch-jüdischer Parnass', Moritz Goldstein boldly claimed that the Jews in Germany had become the custodians and arbiters of the spiritual—specifically, the literary and cultural—treasures of German society, while, at the same time, it denied them the very right and the capability to fulfil this role.[1] Goldstein waxed enthusiastic about the power of the Jews in the German press, although there was also something ominous in his tone. He also celebrated their dominance in the world of music and public concerts, and their monopoly in the venerable and prestigious German theatre. Not only were high percentages of the theatrical personnel, the directors, playwrights, and actors Jewish (and presumably the theatre critics as well), but also the audiences, in his estimation, were overwhelmingly Jewish in their composition. Furthermore, he opined that the Jews were on the verge of taking undisputed control of German literature and literary studies. There were many Jews to be found among the ranks of Germany's best poets and writers, and, perhaps even more striking, the leading minds in the Germanic seminars at the universities were Jewish. What seemed astonishing to Goldstein was that the Jews could have achieved this remarkable success in face of the relentless and often bitter opposition to them in a society which by and large professed an irrational hatred of Jews and denied them the status of equals. As Goldstein put it: 'Whereas we Jews among ourselves might have the impression that we are speaking as Germans to Germans—no matter how German we feel, they consider us totally un-German (*ganz undeutsch*).'[2] While Goldstein sympathized with Zionist efforts to secure a homeland for the Jewish people and to promote Hebrew language and letters as the honourable future course of the nation, he admitted that this option was not realistic for himself, as it was hopelessly impracticable for the majority of German Jewry. He believed that owing to the close 'communal' ties between Germans and Jews for more than a millennium—'mehr als tausendjährigen

[1] Moritz Goldstein, 'Deutsch-jüdischer Parnass', *Kunstwart*, 25 (1912), 281–94.
[2] Ibid. 286.

Gemeinschaft mit dem Deutschtum'[3]—the two peoples had grown so intimately intertwined at their roots that they could no longer be separated. Whether or not Germans or Jews wished to admit it, for Goldstein, German culture was to a very considerable extent Jewish culture. In fact, for him Europe itself was much more Jewish than one in general cared to know.

The understanding of European culture as largely Jewish, as Goldstein suggested, militates against the idea of a possible Jewish contribution to that culture, because the term 'contribution' appears to make little sense if the Jewish element is the dominant one. The concept of a contribution rests on the notion, or a conceptual model, of a dominant host culture, to which guests might contribute. Given a different model, perhaps a model of fusion, whereby individual cultural strands may be seen to combine their cultural gifts in an integrative manner, the notion of contribution is likewise unsuitable. In any case, the idea of a Jewish contribution to German culture and a notion of Jewish 'participation' in German culture have encountered certain resistance virtually from the time of their inception, dating back at least to the eighteenth century. As the one example of Goldstein illustrates, there were those who viewed the Jewish strand in it to be inseparable from other strands, even while it came to dominate the others. Resistance to the idea of contribution, however, came from without and from within, that is, from without and within Jewry, despite the fact that the ideas of a contribution and active participation in the development of German culture tended to buttress the Jewish case for integration into German and Austrian society and the political entities, that is, the states, these societies encompassed.

The idea of a German-Jewish cooperative cultural enterprise, even along the lines of a 'contribution', or of a possible German–Jewish symbiosis, gained ground in some quarters as an attempt to mediate between exclusionary and inclusionary positions. The progress of this conception can be measured roughly from the time of the first stirrings of emancipation in the German-speaking countries through periods of rising and declining antisemitic resistance, partial or complete integration, and assimilation. Scholarly work by Hans Otto Horch and Andreas Kilcher has documented this process.[4] Whereas the *völkisch*–antisemitic (Adolf Bartels, for example)

[3] Ibid. 291.

[4] Hans Otto Horch, *Deutsch-jüdische Literatur*, Studienbrief. FernUniversität Gesamthochschule in Hagen, pts I and II (Hagen, 1995, 1998); id., 'Was heisst und zu welchem Ende studiert man deutsch-jüdische Literaturgeschichte? Prolegomena zu einem Forschungsprojekt', *German Life and Letters*, NS 49/2 (1996), 124–35; Hans Otto Horch and Itta Schedletzky, 'Die deutsch-jüdische Literatur und ihre Geschichte', in Julius H. Schoeps (ed.), *Neues Lexikon des Judentums* (Gütersloh, 1992), 291–4; Andreas B. Kilcher, 'Was ist deutsch-jüdische Literatur? Eine historische Diskursanalyse', *Weimarer Beiträge*, 45 (1999), 485–517; cf. Andreas B. Kilcher, 'Einleitung', in Kilcher (ed.), *Metzler Lexikon der deutsch-jüdischen Literatur* (Stuttgart, 2000), pp. v–xx.

and Jewish nationalist positions (for instance, Nathan Birnbaum) both tended to emphasize the fundamental cultural incompatibility of Germans and Jews, and thus the very impossibility of a Jewish contribution, large cross-sections of German Jewry affiliated with the ideologies of integration and assimilation tended to argue for the possibility and mutual beneficiality of participation. This was the basis of a working conception of 'contribution', for it provided the foundation and rationale for acceptance of Jews in German society according to guidelines mapped by the host or constructed majority in the society.

During periods of political, social, and economic upheaval in central Europe, lively discussions concerning these issues tended to intensify. The period of the First World War and immediately thereafter seemed especially propitious for producing agonized meditations on the topic of Jewish compatibility or incompatibility with German sensibilities and the question of contributions to or participation in the culture. The writings and literary projects of Moritz Goldstein, Martin Buber, Max Brod, Stefan Zweig, Gustav Krojanker, and Jakob Wassermann, to name but a few, proved to be especially topical in this regard.[5] And the same proved to be the case, before and following the Holocaust, as evidenced by, for example, writings of Julius Bab, Georg Hermann, Sol Lipztin, Hermann Levin Goldschmidt, Margarete Susman, and many more. After the Holocaust, however, the very idea of a Jewish contribution to, or participation of Jews in, German culture has appeared to many observers to be untenable, or even obscene. Writing after the Holocaust, Gershom Scholem, in a manner somewhat reminiscent of Moritz Goldstein, thus denied the very existence of a symbiosis or even a German-Jewish dialogue.[6] Indeed, how could there have been a significant Jewish contribution to a culture, or a serious dialogue with it, when it conspired and partially succeeded to erase brutally the Jewish presence in Europe? For Scholem, a serious dialogue would have had to be founded on a basis of mutual respect, that is, respect for the other, as well as basic self-respect, thus precluding the possibility of what in fact transpired: the Nazi genocide against Jewry. The tragic and devastating recompense of genocide for, or in face of, a substantial cultural contribution, or the idea of it in this sense, boggles the rational mind.

Consequently, a shift in interpretative strategy and denotative vocabulary, not always consistent but nevertheless perceptible, occurred. In lieu of the idea of a Jewish 'contribution', the development and acceptance of a notion

[5] Martin Buber's *Der Jude* serves as an especially interesting source in this regard. Also, the extensive literature published in the German-Jewish press for over two centuries should not be neglected since it provides a wealth of pertinent material.

[6] Gershom Scholem, *On Jews and Judaism in Crisis: Selected Essays*, ed. Werner J. Dannhauser (New York, 1976).

of a Jewish literature and a Jewish voice within German culture gained ground in the latter part of the twentieth century. A strong case has been made that Jews by and large developed their own literature and culture in German-speaking lands over centuries as an independent, mostly autonomous cultural enterprise. Contacts with the surrounding culture might be registered and appreciated within Jewish cultural developments, but nevertheless, according to this model, the structure or the content of Jewish cultural activity throughout German lands would tend to have more in common with Jewish expression in other locales throughout the world than with the local (in this case) German culture, in addition to its constituting a specific tradition in its own right. What appears within this context to be of primary interest is the idea of a specifically Jewish essence in this literature. A good example of this trend is the attempt by Dieter Lamping to document a Jewish discourse in German literature in his book *Von Kafka bis Celan. Jüdischer Diskurs in der deutschen Literatur des 20. Jahrhunderts* (1998).[7]

What has happened, though, roughly since 1980 is that a new academic discipline has come into existence. It is, in Roland Barthes's sense of the term, truly 'interdisciplinary', and it pertains directly to the general discussion of a possible Jewish contribution to German literature and culture. In fact, this is my thesis in this chapter. The discipline 'German-Jewish Studies' began to take shape some time in the late 1970s and early 1980s, although there are a few studies that may be viewed as precursors or harbingers of its formation and that can be dated earlier. My thesis is that a profusion of scholarly interest and writing sought to reorient considerations of German-Jewish literature and culture, together with other related cultural, political, and social factors, and this reorientation allowed this new field to emerge as a discipline in its own right, as a partial answer to the denial of a German-Jewish dialogue before the Holocaust. By creating an independent intellectual framework that transcended, while at the same encompassing, the German and the Jewish, the issue of contribution was rendered feckless and immaterial. Within the short timespan of less than a quarter-century, this discipline not only has come to dominate diverse discussions of literature and culture in central Europe, but it has extended its reach and impact well beyond the boundaries of German-speaking culture. Its leading figures, their writings and careers, discussions of their significance, and theoretical probings based on this literature and cultural productivity constitute a separate industry that has come to figure disproportionately in, or, one might even say, tyrannize to a degree, a wide range of literary and cultural discussions in a global sense.

[7] Dieter Lamping, *Von Kafka bis Celan. Jüdischer Diskurs in der deutschen Literatur des 20. Jahrhunderts* (Göttingen, 1998).

Perhaps just mentioning at the start the names of Walter Benjamin, Franz Kafka, Sigmund Freud, and Paul Celan would suffice to give credence to this bold formulation. One might add, perhaps, a few additional names, for example Karl Marx, Heinrich Heine, Theodor Herzl, Otto Weininger, Arthur Schnitzler, Hannah Arendt, Theodor Adorno, Else Lasker-Schüler, Gershom Scholem, Franz Rosenzweig, and Martin Buber. Of course, this list goes on and on and additional names might be cited, depending on the particular area or endeavour under discussion. However, in terms of comprehending the emergence of a discipline, one would need to take into account and credit a group of scholars and their particular scholarly and editorial activities, which have led to the possibility of the creation of a new discipline. In Germany and the United States one could cite Hans Otto Horch, Sander Gilman, and Jack Zipes: their work in this field has been seminal. Other important scholars in Europe, Australia, and Israel might be added to this very short list. Mark Anderson's recent spirited polemic against the distorted consequences of prioritizing German-Jewish literature (as well as issues related to the Holocaust) within *Germanistik*, while broadly neglecting a range of other worthy areas of inquiry, is one of the surest signs of the field's uncontested domination in the United States.[8]

My view is that German-Jewish Studies should be considered not as a subfield within the purview of *Germanistik*, but rather as a discipline in its own right. This discipline may be discerned between the boundaries of *Germanistik* on one side and Jewish Studies on the other, although such fields as Exile Studies (and Diaspora Studies) and Holocaust Studies (and Memory Studies), which also emerged from and appear to be tangential to German and Jewish Studies respectively, also border on and derive synergistic intellectual energy from German-Jewish Studies. There are some signs that lead me to think that after a quarter-century of fairly intensive scholarly activity an apex of interest in German-Jewish Studies has been recorded, and that scholarly work in this field may soon diminish somewhat. Still, one can expect strong and continued interest in this discipline for some time to come. It appears to me that its ultimate relationship to German Studies—as well as to Jewish Studies—needs to be determined in the future.

In this chapter I divide my presentation into a few parts. Initially, I would like to argue that the idea of German-Jewish Studies as a discipline in its own right provides an alternative conceptual model that solves difficult problems that arise from the conflicted notion of a German–Jewish symbiosis as an explanation of the Jewish contribution to German literature and culture. Secondly, I demonstrate that the discipline developed owing to the

[8] Mark M. Anderson, 'German Intellectuals, Jewish Victims: A Politically Correct Solidarity', *Chronicle of Higher Education*, 19 Oct. 2001, <http://chronicle.com/free/v48/i08/08b00701.htm>, accessed 17 Sept. 2006.

widespread perception of a series of changes taking place in European and Jewish consciousness in the later part of the twentieth century. Thirdly, I suggest that the fantastic success of German-Jewish Studies is a result of its alignment with, and easy suitability to, postmodern discourses and mentalities. Lastly, I wish to enumerate briefly some of the achievements of this field after some twenty years of scholarly activity and speculate momentarily on the future of the discipline.

To call German-Jewish Studies a discipline in its own right must be regarded at this point in time as a daring hypothesis rather than an established fact. By no means is it perceived widely as such in scholarly life, even today. Rather, it is fair to say that it is more often conceived as one particular area of interest within German Studies in general. Some scholars, for example Egon Schwarz, have denied consistently the existence of a German-Jewish literature for years,[9] hence precluding the very possibility of a separate field that might investigate it. In a paper published in 2003, entitled 'Developments in German-Jewish Studies from 1980 to the Present', Noah Isenberg viewed German-Jewish Studies as a subfield of German Studies.[10] However, already in 1997 Sander Gilman and Jack Zipes, editors of the *Yale Companion to Jewish Writing and Thought in German Culture 1096–1996*, perceived acutely that a new and intellectually exciting body of critical and historical scholarship on the culture of the Jews in Germany 'formed a scholarly field of its own. Departing from traditional fields such as literary history and social history, it now takes the complexity of Jewish experience in Germany, Austria, and other central European countries as a model for understanding the diasporic experience of many peoples across many nations.'[11] It appears that this claim by Gilman and Zipes has not been

[9] Egon Schwarz, 'Der "Beitrag" der Juden zur deutschen Literatur', *Literatur und Kritik*, 229–30 (1988), 385–401.

[10] Noah Isenberg, 'Developments in German Jewish Studies from 1980 to the Present', in Peter Uwe Hohendahl (ed.), *German Studies in the United States* (New York, 2003). I would like to thank Dr Manfred Stassen for bringing this short report to my attention in the summer of 2004, after I wrote and delivered the lecture that served as the basis of this chapter. And I would like to thank Noah Isenberg for sending me a copy of it so that I could include it retrospectively in my chapter and bibliography. Although his report focuses on the American situation, Isenberg and I share many of the same ideas regarding this topic, especially the multidisciplinary contours of German Jewish Studies and its elusiveness or lack of clear-cut boundaries. However, it is important to point out that we disagree in at least several specific areas. Most importantly, perhaps, as I have expressed it in the body of my chapter, I do not see German Jewish Studies as a subfield of German Studies, the way that Isenberg does. Concomitantly, I do not view the purpose ('one of the predominant tendencies', according to Isenberg) of German Jewish Studies as to ensure that Jewish writers, thinkers, and others 'become—or, in some cases, become once again—a part of the German literary and cultural pantheon' (p. 304).

[11] Sander L. Gilman and Jack Zipes (eds), *Yale Companion to Jewish Writing and Thought in German Culture, 1096–1996* (New Haven, 1997), p. xv.

widely accepted or absorbed, despite the respectability and popularity of the *Yale Companion*. By focusing in general on an extraordinarily extended sense of Jewish experience and on a model of Jewish diaspora in particular, Gilman and Zipes argued for a cross-disciplinary understanding of the discursive space occupied by Jews in German culture, as a paradigm that would help elucidate diasporic existence. Although the issue of diaspora pertains to the present discussion, it is precisely the possibility of providing a cogent intellectual framework for the appropriation of German-Jewish literature and culture despite the Holocaust and establishing a conceptual model to allow for the possibility of a German-Jewish cultural enterprise that militates in favour of the idea of an independent discipline and makes it so attractive.

The background of the Holocaust and its reception in Western culture must be taken into account in order to understand the genesis and development of German-Jewish Studies. After the Holocaust, it may have appeared highly problematical to some observers to argue conceptually for the appropriation of German-Jewish literature and culture by the very culture that had so recently attempted to eliminate it and its representatives completely. Here one should note that certain post-Holocaust attempts to reformulate and restore a humanist conception of German letters, abandoned or perverted by Nazism or preserved to a degree by a dubious notion of inner exile within Nazi Germany, have had varying degrees of success in terms of their acceptance by different scholars. More importantly still, as a prelude to the establishment of German-Jewish Studies, efforts to construct a new field and conceptual model based on a tradition of German humanism yielded Exile Studies. This endeavour aimed to appropriate and mainstream German (-language) literature and culture produced in opposition to Nazism by its mostly (but not exclusively) Jewish victims, though generally in the name of German humanist values. Scholars have debated the relative importance of the Jewish issue in these frameworks—ranging from those who see it as entirely marginal or irrelevant, to others, including the eminent critic Peter Demetz, who has claimed that the Jewish issue is the most important one facing German Studies today.[12] However, the key point for Demetz, and others such as Klaus Hermsdorf,[13] is that the Jewish issue was and remains part of German Studies and can be approached within the same context and

[12] Peter Demetz, private communication on the occasion of the publication of Mark H. Gelber (ed.), *Confrontations/Accommodations: German-Jewish Literary and Cultural History from Heine to Wassermann* (Tübingen, 2004).

[13] Klaus Hermsdorf, 'Deutsch-jüdische Schriftsteller?', *Zeitschrift für Germanistik*, 3 (1982), 278–92. Hermsdorf argued for a carefully demarcated history of German-Jewish literature within German literary history. See also Jens Stüben and Winfried Wösler (eds) in cooperation with Ernst Löwy, *'Wir tragen den Zettelkasten mit den Steckbriefen unserer Freunde'. Beiträge jüdischer Autoren zur deutschen Literatur seit 1945* (Darmstadt, 1993).

using the same useful methods and critical perspectives that have been applied to other topics in *Germanistik*.

Although it may be fair to say that German-Jewish Studies should theoretically be centred on the hyphenation, that is, on what exactly in specific cases actually links or ties German and Jewish literary, linguistic, historical, and cultural components, sensibilities, and mentalities to one another, in practice it has sometimes appeared to be more concerned with the Jewish dimension in this pairing. While the emphasis on Jewish elements or the tendency to contextualize works by German-Jewish authors within Jewish frameworks had to characterize the scholarly work in this field in order for the discipline to emerge in its own right, there is no reason to suppose that this emphasis would have to continue indefinitely or characterize every example within the field once the parameters for German-Jewish Studies have been established. Nevertheless, the conception of German-Jewish Studies as a discipline in its own right has mostly allowed for the carving out of a discursive space at a distance from Jewish Studies proper, except when the specific topic at hand focuses narrowly on topics of religious or Jewish national concern. This tendency may be partially related to the patent interests, capabilities, and training of those who have become engaged with this field over the last two decades. As an answer to the question of a Jewish contribution to German culture in face of the Holocaust, salvaging and restoring the Jewish component in the pairing as a priority may also have seemed to some observers as a worthy or just or compensatory enterprise. Not only had a large body of German-language literature and culture created by Jews been figuratively and sometimes literally erased, as they and their works were earmarked and then targeted for destruction, but the subsequent dearth of scholars trained to appreciate this cultural production as a phenomenon in its own right contributed to the inertia that almost consigned it or a great part of it to oblivion.

The emergence of German-Jewish Studies in the late 1970s and early 1980s may be linked to the perception and appreciation of new literary and cultural developments in central Europe and beyond. Two are worthy of mention at the start. First, the appearance of a new literature in German produced by young Jews born after the Holocaust, who do not belong to the generation of exile writers, and who had come to maturity in Europe after the war, occasioned perhaps some serious rethinking of the issues of continuity and contribution. Much of the writing in the second half of the twentieth century about the German literature written by Jews before the Second World War adopted as a point of departure the fundamental idea that a German-Jewish expression or tradition had come to an end, that this body of literature could not be revived after the Holocaust. Certainly, the idea of a possible contribution, not only in retrospect after the Holocaust, but as an actual contribution following it in time, that is German-Jewish writers continuing to create in German as a contribution to the German literary and cultural enterprise, seemed scandalous and reprehensible to many observers. Also, the perception of the lack of a critical mass of German Jewry after the Holocaust and its corollary notion, the consequential impossibility of an authentic, variegated, and broad-based German-Jewish experience beyond a narrowly individual or solipsistic one, or one that could not be labelled 'German-Jewish' fairly, could be cited as possible factors. German-Jewish alienation from Germany dominated for an extended period of time. An anthology edited by Henryk Broder and Michel P. Lang, *Fremd im eigenen Land* (1979), gave voice to this view, as did the much debated *Dies ist nicht mein Land. Eine Jüdin verlässt die Bundesrepublik*, written by Lea Fleischmann (1980).[14] But, during the early 1980s, a 'Third Generation' of German-Jewish writers after the Holocaust emerged as a noticeable and perhaps significant cultural presence in Germany and Austria. Karen Remmler has written acutely on this phenomenon, focusing on writers born after 1945 and mentioning Barbara Honigmann, Esther Dischereit, Rafael Seligmann, and Maxim Biller.[15] The subsequent emergence in the 1990s of a separate Austrian-Jewish contingent has also drawn attention. In this connection, one might mention the names of Robert Schindel, Robert Menasse, and Doron Rabinowici. This general phenomenon lends itself naturally to discussions about the possible linkages and plain continuity between the new German-language Jewish literature and the tradition that had established itself well before the Nazi period. A trend in scholarship developed, headed by Sander Gilman, and including Thomas Nolden and Stephan Braese, which saw the blossoming of a new German-Jewish literature in the 1980s and 1990s that forged a link with pre-war German-Jewish expression, guaranteeing continuity in this respect.[16]

Secondly, in the wake of a significant increase in the public interest in the Holocaust in Germany and in the United States, beginning in the late 1970s and continuing unabated into the 1980s and 1990s, a concomitant increase in scholarly interest in German-Jewish literature and culture has been

[14] Henryk Broder and Michel P. Lang (eds), *Fremd im eigenen Land. Juden in der Bundesrepublik* (Frankfurt am Main, 1979); Lea Fleischmann, *Dies ist nicht mein Land. Eine Jüdin verlässt die Bundesrepublik* (Hamburg, 1980).

[15] Karen Remmler, 'The "Third Generation" of Jewish-German Writers after the Shoah Emerges in Germany and Austria', in Gilman and Zipes (eds), *Yale Companion to Jewish Writing and Thought*. Cf. Sander Gilman and Karen Remmler (eds), *Reemerging Jewish Culture in Germany: Life and Literature since 1989* (New York, 1994); Leslie Morris and Karen Remmler (eds), *Contemporary Jewish Writing in Germany: An Anthology* (Lincoln, Nebr., 2002).

[16] Sander L. Gilman, *Jews in Today's German Culture* (Bloomington, Ind., 1995); Thomas Nolden, *Junge jüdische Literatur* (Würzburg, 1995); Stephan Braese, *Die andere Erinnerung. Jüdische Autoren in der Westdeutschen Nachkriegsliteratur* (Vienna, 2001).

registered. Karen Remmler wrote: 'In the 1980s the explosion of commemorative events dedicated to the remembrance of the victims of the Shoah was accompanied by an increase in media attention to Jewish culture and history.'[17] At the same time as 'rites of memorialization' mushroomed, according to Geoffrey Hartman, Jews living in Germany feared a growing indifference among younger generations and a recurrence of antisemitic attacks.[18] As a consequence, perhaps, Jews appeared to take a more active role in the cultural life of Germany, or at least their role received a good amount of media attention, and this public perception may have encouraged the intensification of the scholarly trend that was just beginning. The fantastically successful screening of the American television series *Holocaust* (in the United States and in Germany, 1979) and its reception in Germany and abroad probably served as a catalyst of sorts.

However, other public affairs and scandals that were pertinent to the German-Jewish issue continued unabated, and they received widespread media coverage and academic attention as well. To name but a few: the Bitburg affair, which concerned the controversial visit of former American president Ronald Reagan to a German cemetery where SS soldiers were also buried; the brouhaha surrounding the production of Fassbinder's controversial play *Der Müll, die Stadt und der Tod* (Rubbish, the City, and Death), which had been denounced for its antisemitism; the Waldheim affair, which erupted after the former United Nations Secretary-General's problematical (and hitherto suppressed) war record came to light; the demonstrations at Börneplatz in Frankfurt am Main protesting new construction that would have erased the archaeological remains of the Jewish ghetto there; the famous and protracted 'Historikerstreit', in which numerous historians relativized the Holocaust by comparing it with Stalinist brutality; and, the commemorative events in Germany marking the fiftieth anniversary of the November pogrom called the Reichskristallnacht. All of these and more served to create and maintain an intense, highly charged public atmosphere conducive to literary, cultural, and scholarly confrontations with the heritage of central European Jewry, before and after the Holocaust.

This cycle of recurrent crises which pertain to Jewish issues seems to be a fairly constant feature of post-Holocaust central European society, and in a way it guarantees a vibrant, although sometimes highly charged and tense, public atmosphere for the production and reception of Jewish literary and cultural responses. For example, one might recall the stupendous success in Germany of Daniel Goldhagen, who claimed that the unique perniciousness

[17] Remmler, 'The "Third Generation" of Jewish-German Writers after the Shoah', 796.

[18] Geoffrey H. Hartman (ed.), *Bitburg in Moral and Political Perspective* (Bloomington, Ind., 1986), 1; cf. id., 'Introduction: Darkness Visible', in Hartman (ed.), *Holocaust Remembrance: The Shapes of Memory* (Oxford, 1994).

of German antisemitism helped explain the Holocaust, or the Bubis–Walser controversy, which centred on a public debate between the head of the Jewish community in Germany, Ignaz Bubis, and the well-known German writer Martin Walser, concerning the question of 'how long' modern Germany would continue to bear a special responsibility for the Holocaust. Walser attempted to argue that that period, if it indeed ever existed, could be declared over. That is, for him Germans could no longer be expected to bear special responsibility for the crimes of the previous generations. That era was in the past, and it was high time that Germany moved on in this regard. More recently, but along the same lines, the controversy or controversies surrounding the construction of the major Berlin Holocaust memorial project near the Brandenburg Gate, and the recurrent antisemitically charged public utterances that characterized the minor political scandals associated with the Möllemann and Friedmann affairs, as well as the Hohmann fiasco in 2003, to name just a few, have been headline news, although their individual impact in German society, and also in terms of a possible impact on the German-Jewish issue in general, varies substantially. The point is not that the minor scandals involving Möllemann or Hohmann will be remembered; in fact they are already long forgotten. Rather, it is the ongoing and cumulative impact of antisemitic incidents that endows German-Jewish issues with special urgency and significance.

At the same time that these developments were taking shape and in close conjunction with them, another scholarly field was rapidly coming into existence, namely Holocaust Studies. As it has developed in the last quarter-century, it is only marginally related to German-Jewish Studies, but there are definite areas of overlap. More importantly, the impact of the Holocaust is extraordinarily extensive in numerous cultural contexts and it must be regarded as having exerted certain pressures on the genesis of German-Jewish Studies, as I have indicated. In the domain of literature, certainly, there are numerous important German-Jewish writers of 'Holocaust literature', to employ the term in accordance with S. Lillian Kremer's criteria, which inform the massive (although not definitive) compilation of writers and texts that pertain to this category.[19] In this context, one need only mention Paul Celan, Nelly Sachs, Jakov Lind, Edgar Hilsenrath, Anna Seghers, Manès Sperber, Jean Amery, and Fred Wander, although there are of course many more names that pertain here. Perhaps it is fair to say that the Holocaust looms darkly in the background of German-Jewish Studies, but it does not determine its parameters. There appears to be a modicum of productive synergistic energy emanating from Holocaust Studies, as ironic as this may sound, which

[19] S. Lillian Kremer, Introduction to Kremer (ed.), *Holocaust Literature*, i (New York, 2003), pp. xxi–xlvii.

infuses critical meditations in the area of German-Jewish Studies, but to all intents and purposes the two function as independent scholarly endeavours. The background of the Holocaust lends urgency and primacy to the German-Jewish example, which may be missing from other Jewish diasporic experiences and their reflection in the intellectual discourses that have pursued cultural issues within those contexts.

The central thrust of German-Jewish Studies has been tangential at best to the important items on the agenda of Holocaust Studies, even while the focus of the former has been on literary traditions and culture that were almost eradicated by the Holocaust, but which somehow survived. Even twenty-five to thirty years ago the future of the German (and Austrian) Jewish communities was somewhat in doubt, since the devastation wrought by the Holocaust appeared even then to be perhaps ultimately irreversible or insurmountable. However, with the arrival in the last two decades of significant numbers of former Soviet Jewish immigrants to Germany and the subsequent reinvigoration of organized Jewish community life on the basis of this new and vital infusion, the immediate future of the Jewish communities in Germany (and perhaps in Austria too) now appears assured. Many Jewish communities in Germany are flourishing, even at a time when antisemitism is on the rise. As a matter of fact, in several locations in Germany today, the Jewish communities can boast of larger Jewish populations than the ones that existed before the Nazi period. In a parallel fashion, the apparent continuation of a German-Jewish literary and cultural production also appears secure. The very recent emergence of a new variety of German-Jewish literature penned by immigrants to Germany and Austria from the former Soviet Union seems to corroborate this contention. The writings of Vladimir Kaminer and Vladimir Vertlib, for example, may be cited in this regard.[20]

Although there is no generally accepted opinion about the nature or parameters of the German-Jewish canon or the precise task of the project of a German-Jewish literary history, as Florian Krobb has suggested,[21] German-Jewish Studies have developed into a diverse and challenging international field. Regarding the coalescence of the discipline, the organization

[20] Cf. Vladimir Kaminer, *Russendisko. Mein deutsches Dschungelbuch* (Munich, 2000) and Vladimir Vertlib, *Zwischenstationen* (Munich, 1999).

[21] Florian Krobb, Introduction to *German Life and Letters*, special German Jewish number, 49/2 (1996), 121. Although Liliane Weissberg has recently claimed that it is still too difficult to rethink the original framework of German-Jewish Studies, I submit that this type of rethinking is urgent and must be initiated, even if only tentatively. See Liliane Weissberg, 'Reflecting on the Past, Envisioning the Future: Perspectives for German-Jewish Studies', *German Historical Institute Bulletin*, no. 35 (Fall, 2004), 11–32. I would like to thank Liliane Weissberg for directing me to her essay, which I accessed on the Internet: <http://www.ghi-dc.org/bulletinF04/35.11.pdf>, accessed 17 Sept. 2006.

of international conferences, the publication of anthologies and collections of articles as well as special issues of scholarly journals devoted to this topic, and the compilation of ambitiously conceived lexicons have proven to be decisive factors. Perhaps the foundation for this development had already been laid by the relative success and widespread respectability of yearbooks and periodical literature, which also served as precursors. Specifically, the *Year Book of the Leo Baeck Institute* (London), as well as the now defunct *Bulletin des Leo Baeck Instituts* (Jerusalem) and the *Jahrbuch des Instituts für deutsche Geschichte* (Tel Aviv), later the *Tel Aviver Jahrbuch für deutsche Geschichte*, while mostly focusing on historical aspects of central European Jewry, also published (and continue to publish) important work related to literature and culture. Also, both institutes managed to sponsor independent book publications in German publishing houses, such as J. C. B. Mohr (Siebeck) and Bleicher, respectively, complementing the scholarly publications that appeared in the yearbooks. Concomitantly, the contemporary public discussion pertaining to German-Jewish issues and developments was carried on apace by journals such as *Tribüne*, which also strove to keep scholarly contributions within the spectrum of its publication interests. However, the publication of three special issues of *New German Critique* on Germans and Jews, beginning in 1980, served as a watershed of sorts, even if it appeared to be one-sided in terms of its ideological orientation. Anson Rabinbach and Jack Zipes aimed to place the Holocaust and its lessons at the centre of this discussion, but also claimed that the theme of Germans and Jews, while perhaps implicitly present in the journal since its inception in the early 1970s, was now being given explicit, direct attention.[22] Additionally, they claimed that there was an 'unmistakably Jewish element in critical theory', and that the Frankfurt School's concern with antisemitism, but also its concept of social theory and its debt to Jewish messianism, needed to be accounted for in this context.[23]

A vast amount of scholarly research on German-Jewish historical issues, which has been conducted fruitfully since the Second World War, provided the underpinnings for the blossoming of literary and cultural research in its wake. A certain amount of this work might be labelled 'cultural-historical'. Studies by George Mosse, whose path-breaking volume *Germans and Jews* appeared in 1970, Walter Grab, Jacob Katz, Monika Richarz, Michael Meyer, Ismar Schorsch, and others with pronounced cultural interests, including Fritz Stern, Carl Schorske, and Peter Gay, have probably been decisive in this regard, despite the fact that their individual research projects and presentations on the Jewish presence in central European culture and

[22] Anson G. Rabinbach and Jack Zipes, 'Lessons of the Holocaust', *New German Critique*, no. 19 (1980), 3.
[23] Ibid.

history represent a wide range of different views regarding German–Jewish relations and possibilities for German-Jewish Studies. However, some specific literary-critical contributions, for example by Sol Liptzin, Marcel Reich-Ranicki, Hans Mayer, and George Steiner, probably played especially important roles in terms of the development of German-Jewish literary and cultural studies internationally. But one might cite other authors and contributions, since it is exceedingly difficult to argue for priority here.[24]

As a further development, a series of collections of literary and scholarly essays, some of which were the published lectures of international conferences, began to appear in the late 1970s, and, following a spate of such publications in the early to mid-1980s, a trend developed, serving to inaugurate the field of German-Jewish Studies in its own right. The most important early collections in this regard were Hans Jürgen Schultz's *Mein Judentum* (1978) and David Bronsen's anthology *Jews and Germans from 1860 to 1933: The Problematical Symbiosis* (1979), based on an international symposium that took place at Washington University in St Louis. They were followed by a veritable avalanche of anthologies and conference volumes.[25] This trend reached its first high point with the publication of three thick conference volumes, the now famous Niemeyer Conditio Judaica collections, edited by Hans Otto Horch and Horst Denkler (1988, 1989, 1993), which presented the contributions to three interdisciplinary symposia on German-Jewish literature and culture, sponsored by the Werner-Reimers-Stiftung.

Before the last of the three volumes was published, Hans Otto Horch, who in 1992 was appointed to the first chair in German-Jewish Literary History in Germany (the Ludwig Strauss professorship in German-Jewish Literary History in Aachen), launched a book series, in cooperation with the Israeli scholar Itta Shedletzky, also at Niemeyer, entitled Conditio Judaica.

[24] Cf. Sol Liptzin, *Germany's Stepchildren* (Philadelphia, 1944; repr. 1961); Marcel Reich-Ranicki, *Über Ruhestörer. Juden in der deutschen Literatur* (Munich, 1973); Hans Mayer, *Aussenseiter* (Frankfurt am Main, 1975); and numerous essays by George Steiner. Cf. Hartmut Binder's work on Kafka's relationship to Jewish culture, S. S. Prawer's studies on Heine, Evelyn Torton Beck's published dissertation *Kafka and the Yiddish Theater* (Madison, Wis., 1973), and John Cuddihy's doctoral dissertation on Freud and modern Jewish cultural mediations in Europe, published as *The Ordeal of Civility* (New York, 1974) which focused on Freud, Marx, and Lévi-Strauss.

[25] See e.g. Stéphane Moses and Albrecht Schöne (eds), *Juden in der deutschen Literatur*, proceedings of a German–Israeli symposium, Zur deutsch-jüdischen Literaturgeschichte, the Hebrew University, Jerusalem, 1983 (Frankfurt am Main, 1986); Jehuda Reinharz and Walter Schatzberg (eds), *The Jewish Response to German Culture from the Enlightenment to the Second World War*, proceedings of an international conference held at Clark University, 1983 (Hanover, NH, 1984); Gunter E. Grimm and Hans-Peter Bayerdörfer (eds), *Im Zeichen Hiobs. Jüdische Schriftsteller und deutsche Literatur im 20. Jahrhundert* (Königstein, 1985); and Herbert A. Strauss and Christhard Hoffmann (eds), *Juden und Judentum in der Literatur* (Munich, 1985).

Studien und Quellen zur Deutsch-Jüdischen Literatur- und Kulturgeschichte. Since my edition of its first volume, *The Jewish Reception of Heinrich Heine*, was published in 1992, the series has printed more than sixty volumes on aspects of German-Jewish literature and culture. In 2002 Armin A. Wallas, a highly respected Austrian colleague who passed away in 2003, wrote that this book series had for some time become by far the most important publication forum on themes concerning German-Jewish literary and cultural history.[26] Horch independently initiated numerous scholarly projects and published several important studies focusing on German-Jewish literary and cultural history, one of the most influential of which no doubt for the scholarly community is the 'compact memory' project, which has made a dozen or so German-Jewish periodicals available on the Web to a worldwide audience and community of scholars.[27]

Several German and Austrian publishers, including Wagenbach, Böhlau, the Jüdischer Verlag at Suhrkamp, Athenaeum, Peter Lang, and Aufbau, followed the lead of Niemeyer, where Horch had established German-Jewish scholarship as a priority, or they made independent efforts, albeit with less focused energy and perhaps with fewer resources, ensuring the continuing release of new titles and series pertaining to German-Jewish Studies. In the same framework the establishment in the last quarter-century of new scholarly centres and endowed chairs in Germany and in Israel especially, devoted to German-Jewish History or German-Jewish Literary and Cultural Studies, or to European Jewry and German History with a pronounced interest in the Jewish domain, should be mentioned since they have initiated a range of related scholarly projects and activities. They have also launched new publication series relevant to this topic.[28]

[26] Armin A. Wallas, 'Conditio Judaica', *Mnemosyne*, 28 (2002), 153.

[27] See <http://www.compactmemory.de>, accessed 17 Sept. 2006.

[28] To list some of the most important (in addition to the Leo Baeck Institute and the Institute for German History in Tel Aviv, both already mentioned): the Franz Rosenzweig Center in Jerusalem, the Steinheim Institut in Duisburg, the Moses Mendelssohn Center in Potsdam (with its Haskala Series at Georg Olms Verlag, now numbering some thirty volumes), the Simon Dubnow Institut in Leipzig, the Centre for German Jewish Studies in Sussex, the Wiener Library at the University of Tel Aviv, the Tauber Institute for the Study of European Jewry at Brandeis University, the Braun Chair for the History of the Jews in Prussia at Bar-Ilan University, the Center for German Studies at Ben-Gurion University, and the Bucerius Center for the Study of Contemporary German History and Society at Haifa University. Of course, additional Israeli centres, literature and history departments, and endowed professorships for Austrian Studies, German History, and European Studies have also contributed significantly in this regard. The Center for Austrian Studies at the Hebrew University, headed until recently by Jacob Golomb, should be mentioned in this context. Journals like *Menora*, *Babylon*, *Semit*, *Ashkenaz*, *Jüdischer Almanach*, and *Mnemosyne* have also played an important role in keeping the scholarly and public dimensions of the field alive and lively, especially in central Europe.

Before attempting even briefly to assess this body of work and the nature of the institutions that have been spearheading the current scholarly production, allow me to mention a second high point in the development of the discipline. I am referring to the publication of ambitious lexicons, which have each provided within the covers of one volume general contours for the field of German-Jewish Studies, tantamount to an effort at canon formation. One lexicon, previously mentioned, is the more than 850-page *Yale Companion to Jewish Writing and Thought in German Culture, 1096–1996*, edited by Sander Gilman and Jack Zipes in 1997. Another is the 650-page *Metzler Lexikon der deutsch-jüdischen Literatur*, edited by Andreas Kilcher in 2000.[29] Gilman and Zipes, fully conscious of attempting to provide the first overall guide to Jewish writing in German, saw their task as impossible but necessary. Although designed to provide a loose chronology of the flow of Jewish writing in German-speaking lands, their anthology nevertheless perforce refrained from claiming completeness of coverage. The editors stated clearly that they never meant to imply by it a definite canon, and certain gaps were inevitable.[30] Kilcher also avoided suggesting a canon or claiming completeness in his volume. He sought rather to edit a collection of portraits, forming the potential building blocks for a German-Jewish literary history, even though they inevitably fell short of completeness. Kilcher's conception, drawing on the important essay by Ludwig Geiger 'Die Juden und die deutsche Literatur' (The Jews and German Literature), views German-Jewish literature as a cosmopolitan and intercultural system, 'not as monocultural and national phenomena . . . but rather as plural, discursive fields, on which semiotic systems of different cultures overlap and combine'.[31] For Kilcher, 'German-Jewish' is the product of specific kinds of interpretative enterprise and it is characterized by specific kinds of analytical discourse.

What the essay collections and the lexicons have in common is that they are all typical anthologies produced by an exceedingly diverse international group of scholars, representing a plethora of different methodologies, perspectives, and goals regarding German-Jewish literature and culture. There is no single or even dominant approach or aim, and the patent diversity of the contributors and the multiplicity of the discourses in the contributions appear to be essential aspects of this project, at least in its formative stage. The quality of *Vielstimmigkeit*, praised by Grimm and Bayerdörfer in the

[29] In this connection, one might also mention its companion volume, which is not limited, however, to German-Jewish Studies: Andreas Kilcher and Otfried Fraisse (eds), *Metzler Lexikon jüdischer Philosophen* (Stuttgart, 2003).

[30] Gilman and Zipes (eds), *Yale Companion to Jewish Writing and Thought*, p. xvii.

[31] Kilcher, 'Einleitung', p. v.

introduction to their collection in the mid-1980s,[32] matches the admission or embracement of the same editorial principle in earlier anthologies of this kind, for example Gustav Krojanker's early compilation *Juden in der deutschen Literatur* (1922). There he declared that the contributors to the volume did not share or subscribe to any one particular outlook on the Jewish aspect of their German-Jewish topic, and this diversity was crucial in terms of understanding that it was the existence of the cultural space of the anthology itself that made the discussion of the field possible in the first place. The term Krojanker used was *diskussionsfähig*.[33] Also, it is worth meditating on the fact that despite one or two exceptions (Horch and Hans Schütz, for example, and most recently Willi Jasper in a very problematical study), it is the anthologies, lexicons, and periodical literature that have largely given shape to the field.[34] In an essay entitled 'The Anthological Imagination', David Stern wrote about the canonizing roles of anthologies similar to these, focusing on their authorizing, sacralizing, and legitimizing functions.[35] Albeit without definitiveness or finality, a community of scholars is forged by the editorial project, as a partially rotating community of German-Jewish figures takes centre stage in any given instance. Also, a community of readers comes into play as the last link in a chain of productivity that spans the globe, from centres in Germany, Austria, Israel, and the United States, especially, to others in France, Belgium, and the United Kingdom, to Australia, New Zealand, Japan, and Brazil. The international and multicultural dimension of German-Jewish Studies, with its interdisciplinary interests, is an integral part of the endeavour and it may be related to part of the attractiveness and popularity of the field in an era of globalization.

In effect, by bringing a topic that had been mostly on the margins of intellectual concern to the centre—in order to discuss aspects of a literature and culture with no geographical boundaries (though truly global)—a literature without a fixed canon came into existence, or at least the consciousness of it was bruited and debated. The construction of the discipline engendered borderline and hybrid discourses, enabling the field of German-Jewish

[32] Konrad Kwiet, Gunter E. Grimm, and Hans-Peter Bayerdörfer, 'Einleitung', in Grimm and Bayerdörfer (eds), *Im Zeichen Hiobs. Jüdische Schriftsteller und deutsche Literatur im 20. Jahrhundert* (Königstein, 1985).

[33] Gustav Krojanker (ed.), *Juden in der deutschen Literatur* (Berlin, 1922), 10.

[34] Hans Otto Horch and Andreas Kilcher plan to publish a new German-Jewish literary history. See also Hans Schütz, *Juden in der deutschen Literatur. Eine deutsch-jüdische Literaturgeschichte im Überblick* (Munich, 1992); Willi Jasper, *Deutsch-jüdischer Parnass. Literaturgeschichte eines Mythos* (Berlin, 2004). See also Hans Otto Horch's sharply worded but fair critique of Jasper, 'Bravoröse Wissenschaft?', <http://www.literaturkritik.de/public/rezension.php?rez_id=7135>, accessed 17 Sept. 2006.

[35] David Stern, 'The Anthological Imagination in Jewish Literature', *Prooftexts*, 17/1 (1997), 1–7.

Studies to emerge as the quintessential postmodern field of literary and cultural studies. Its very distrust of meta-narratives, that is, its instinctive critique of 'totalizations', and its avoidance and rejection of attempts to make sense of its own tradition according to some overarching truth appear to be indicative of a postmodern sensibility. The compatibility of German-Jewish Studies with the postmodern impulse or the postmodern condition, as Lyotard put it, may be related to its unprecedented vogue in various literary and cultural discussions today. In a postmodern sense, no coherent picture of the field emerges, and there is no one position from which to assume a superior critical vantage. Attempts to probe the hyphenation of German and Jewish often focus on issues of language, in terms of the way language conditions and enables, while it also delimits, thought. Also, awareness of particular historical, social, and cultural matrices helps observers question norms and categories of race, class, gender, eroticism, identity, and ethnicity from the point of view of difference.

German-Jewish Studies have helped recover, reclaim, and revive, appreciate, and theorize a literature and culture that was almost eradicated by Nazism. Work in this field has encouraged the restoration and republishing of neglected and mostly forgotten writers, from Ludwig Börne to Joseph Roth and Jenny Aloni, who deserve to be read and remembered within a framework that specifically purports to be sensitive to all of their German-Jewish or Austrian-Jewish complexity and uniqueness. German-Jewish Studies have facilitated rereading writers with canonical status in *Germanistik*, for example, in order to understand them in a predominantly German-Jewish light. Sometimes neglected texts of these same canonical writers have been totally re-evaluated in face of this new contextualization, moving from the margin to the centre in this specific sense. One might think of Kafka's thoughts on 'minor literature' in this context, especially in the hands of Gilles Deleuze and Felix Guattari.[36] German-Jewish Studies as an academic discipline have enabled far-reaching discussions about identity and difference, cultural identity politics, memory, exile, diaspora, 'Heimat', antisemitism, racism, and genocide.[37] But, as a new discipline, it has moved well beyond these particular areas of concern to provide an intellectual

[36] Gilles Deleuze and Félix Guattari, *Kafka: Pour une littérature mineure* (Paris, 1975).

[37] Cf. Ritchie Robertson, *The 'Jewish Question' in German Literature 1749–1939* (Oxford, 1999); Paul Mendes-Flohr, *German Jews: A Dual Identity* (New Haven, 1999); Frank Stern, *Dann bin ich um den Schlaf gebracht. Ein Jahrtausend jüdisch-deutsche Kulturgeschichte* (Berlin, 2003); Jost Hermand, *Judentum und deutsche Kultur. Beispiele einer schmerzhaften Symbiose* (Cologne, 1996); Pol O'Dochartaigh (ed.), *Jews in German Literature since 1945: German-Jewish Literature?* (Amsterdam, 2000); Stephen D. Dowden and Meike G. Werner (eds), *German Literature, Jewish Critics: The Brandeis Symposium* (Rochester, NY, 2000). Also, *New German Critique* published a special issue on the Holocaust (*Taboo, Trauma, Holocaust*, no. 90) in fall of 2003, followed by a special issue on Paul Celan (no. 91, Winter 2004).

framework for contemplation of plain human responsibility in a world fraught with contradictions and inhumanity, where critical inquiry can only proceed very tentatively without great hopes of major breakthroughs. Still, that appears to be an ethical stance of sorts, which may prove to be the great contribution of German-Jewish Studies to scholarship, as the field continues to develop in the future.

TEN

Louis Finkelstein, Mordecai Kaplan, and American 'Jewish Contributions to Civilization'

DAVID BIALE

THE modern *topos* of the 'Jewish contribution to civilization' can be traced back at least to Moses Mendelssohn, who argued in his *Jerusalem*[1] that the Jews had anticipated modernity by removing coercion from religion. During the nineteenth century, many other Jewish writers took up the theme as they strove to persuade the majority societies in which they lived—and perhaps equally to persuade themselves—that the Jews deserved to enter Western civilization. But the period of the 1930s created a new urgency in apologetics as Jews faced the Nazi onslaught. Following a venerable tradition in modern antisemitism, the Nazis argued that the Jews contributed nothing positive to civilization and were, instead, a force for 'decomposition'. It was this argument that goaded Cecil Roth to write *The Jewish Contribution to Civilization* in 1938: 'It is alleged by modern anti-Semites . . . that the Jew is essentially a middleman, who has produced nothing; that he is an alien excrescence on Western life; and that the influence which he has had on the world's culture during the past two thousand years has been entirely negative, if not deleterious.'[2] Since the Nazis had forced a racial definition on the Jews, Roth felt justified 'in attempting to evaluate the Jewish contribution in terms of Jews and not of Judaism alone',[3] although he refused to accept the idea that race *caused* culture.

A similar desire to prove the Nazis wrong undergirded a less well-known work with the same title as Roth's. This was a catalogue of books offered for sale by C. A. Stonehill in Birmingham in 1940. In a preface to the catalogue, the Austrian Jewish writer Stefan Zweig specifically mentions the

[1] See Moses Mendelssohn, *Jerusalem or On Religious Power and Judaism*, trans. Allan Arkush (Hanover, NH, 1983), pt. 2.

[2] Cecil Roth, *The Jewish Contribution to Civilization* (New York, 1940; Eng. edn, first pub. London, 1938), p. ix.

[3] Ibid., p. x.

defamation of the Jews for a lack of creativity.[4] The refutation of these accusations lay, according to Zweig, in Stonehill's 'bibliographical survey of the entire contribution made by Jews of all nations to philosophy, literature, art, music and science'. The 2,500 books, while by no means exhausting the Jews' contribution to civilization, nevertheless represented for Zweig the greatest assembly of books under one roof for this express purpose. By 1940, of course, such literary demonstrations of Jewish worthiness were of no practical consequence. And, indeed, two years later Zweig was to take his life in Brazil in a suicide pact with his wife in despair over the fate of Europe.

I begin this discussion of the American Jewish discourse of 'the Jewish contribution to civilization' with these two European examples to highlight an important contrast. As we shall see, the destruction of the European Jews that loomed so large for Roth and Zweig played scarcely any role at all in America, either for those writing before the Holocaust or for those writing immediately after, thus reflecting the general failure of American Jews to respond with great urgency to the European catastrophe.[5] To be sure, as Lloyd Gartner has written on the decade of the 1930s, the rise in American antisemitism during the Depression clearly preoccupied American Jewish intellectuals.[6] But as a new generation of native-born Jews came to prominence in Jewish life and letters, a certain typically American optimism came into play, so that the apologetic character of recounting the Jews' contributions to civilization took on a less desperate tone.

Following the end of the war, American Jewry entered into what Arthur Goren has termed 'the golden decade'.[7] This was the decade that witnessed a dramatic decline in the antisemitism of the inter-war period and the movement of Jews from the cities to the suburbs, a story that has been effectively told by Deborah Dash Moore.[8] Having suffered through the Great Depression, Jews now benefited greatly from the new, post-war prosperity. The ethnic character of the immigrant generations and their children receded, to be replaced by a more narrowly religious definition of Jewish identity. Will Herberg's classic sociological study *Protestant, Catholic, Jew*, published in 1955, seemed to express this development by claiming that the

[4] See Stefan Zweig, Preface to Charles Archibald Stonehill, *The Jewish Contribution to Civilization* (Birmingham, 1940).

[5] See Gulie Ne'eman Arad, *America, Its Jews and the Rise of Nazism* (Bloomington, Ind., 2000).

[6] Lloyd P. Gartner, 'The Midpassage of American Jewry', in Jonathan Sarna (ed.), *The American Jewish Experience*, 2nd edn (New York, 1997).

[7] Arthur Goren, 'A Golden Decade for American Jews: 1945–1955', in Sarna (ed.), *The American Jewish Experience*.

[8] Deborah Dash Moore, *At Home in America: Second Generation New York Jews* (New York, 1981); id., *To the Golden Cities: Pursuing the American Dream in Miami and L.A.* (New York, 1994).

Jews furnished one equal leg of the American religious tripod.[9] And in 1954 Jews celebrated the tercentenary of their presence in North America by congratulating themselves on their integration in American society. Finally, American Jews, having played a role—albeit external—in the creation of the state of Israel, regarded this task as essentially completed, and turned their collective attention elsewhere.

Yet, this 'golden decade' was not without its dark side. In part, this was because the memories of American antisemitism were still so fresh, as was the Holocaust, for which American Jews still did not even have a fixed name. And, antisemitism itself was not yet fully banished to the margins of American life. The trial and execution of the Rosenbergs at the height of the McCarthy period sparked deep anxieties among Jews about accusations of anti-Americanism and communism. In addition, the flight to the suburbs seemed to presage the abandonment of authentic Judaism for a vapid and vacuous imitation of American Christianity. The spectre of assimilation had begun to haunt American Jews.

It was in this climate that Louis Finkelstein, chancellor of the Jewish Theological Seminary of America, assembled thirty-four contributors to produce the first American collaborative history of the Jews. First published in 1949, the second and third volumes of *The Jews: Their History, Culture, and Religion* were entitled *The Role of Judaism in Civilization.*[10] Writing a blurb for his own work, Finkelstein calls it a 'milestone in American Jewish scholarship'. And, indeed, it was, although not entirely for reasons that Finkelstein sets out. At the beginning of his very revealing foreword,[11] which was omitted from later editions, Finkelstein advertises his thirty-four contributors as 'Christian and Jew; Europeans, Israelites and Americans'. A Christian there was, to be sure—William Foxwell Albright—and a number of Europeans as well (but limited to English Jews); and yet, with the exception of one 'Israelite' (a quaint term that reveals that, at least at the Jewish Theological Seminary in 1949, 'Israeli' had not yet become common parlance), all of the other contributors were from the United States. Finkelstein's attempts to solicit Israeli contributions had evidently failed, as he himself admits: Ben Zion Dinaburg (Dinur) had not come through with a history of the Jews of Muslim lands, and another, unnamed contributor, assigned to write on the history of the Yishuv, had his chapter rejected. An essay on Israel finally did appear in a future edition, but written surprisingly

[9] Will Herberg, *Protestant, Catholic, Jew: An Essay in American Religious Sociology* (Garden City, NY, 1955).

[10] Louis Finkelstein (ed.), *The Jews: Their History, Culture, and Religion* (Philadelphia, 1949); page references are to this edn. In the three-volume fourth edition (New York, 1970) *The Jewish Role in Civilization* was to become the third volume.

[11] Ibid., vol. i, pp. xxi–xxxiii.

by an American, Oscar Janowsky of the City College of New York. More surprising still is that this essay appeared in the volume dedicated to the Jews' 'role in civilization', although nothing in the chapter suggested what contribution the state of Israel may have made to 'civilization'—beyond its mere existence.

Finkelstein's foreword tells us a great deal about the thinking in the immediate post-war era of this central figure in American Jewish scholarship, who for many decades stood at the head of the Jewish Theological Seminary. He argues, following a venerable apologetic tradition, that Judaism is 'the unknown religion of our time' and the 'least understood of all major religions'. Indeed, he claims, rather astonishingly right after the Holocaust—which he refers to cryptically as 'the frightful catastrophes of the 1930s'—that a major reason for antisemitism is the unwillingness of Jewish scholars to present Judaism effectively: 'the long persistence of anti-Semitism may be due in part to the unwillingness of Jewish scholars and thinkers to deal with it'. Finkelstein seems to have believed along Enlightenment lines that if only the Jews could fully articulate their contributions to civilization, then the antisemites would realize the error of their ways. Today, of course, we know that the very opposite may be true: antisemitism of the Nazi variety battens onto *precisely* the idea that the Jews have contributed far too much to civilization.

Finkelstein argues that the history of Western culture is written with 'scant reference to such towering figures as Maimonides and Crescas, and none at all to the penetrating insights of the Talmud'. The centrality of the Talmud to Finkelstein's view of the Jewish contribution to civilization is captured in his quotation of something Louis Brandeis said to him: 'You may study the Talmud; I practice it.' Yet, oddly enough, with the exception of Judah Goldin's historical essay 'The Period of the Talmud', no chapter in the volumes discusses the Talmud itself. Although Saul Lieberman is listed as a member of the planning committee, Finkelstein was evidently unable to get his colleague down the hall to produce an essay on this subject. Perhaps he felt that the Talmud's contribution to civilization might be addressed by Jacob Rabinowitz's essay 'The Influence of Jewish Law on Common Law' or by Mordecai Kaplan's essay 'A Philosophy of Jewish Ethics'. But the first is far too specific and technical, while the latter—to which I shall return—is too general and idiosyncratic to fit the bill. That the Talmud is missing is particularly striking since the two volumes that cover 'the role of Judaism in civilization' contain chapters on Hellenistic Jewish literature, Judaeo-Arabic literature, Yiddish literature, medieval Hebrew poetry, the modern renaissance of Hebrew literature, and the mystical element in Judaism—in addition to more obvious entries on the Jewish contributions to music, art, medicine, and science, and the influence of the Bible on European literature.

In this arrangement, which would be altered in later editions, Finkelstein implicitly asserts that literary movements *internal* to Jewish culture ought to be considered integral parts of the role of Judaism in civilization.

Although the Jews' role in civilization is framed in broad cultural terms, it is really religion that Finkelstein sees as Judaism's primary contribution. He tells a series of anecdotes to explain why 'it is no extravagance to call Judaism the unknown religion of our time'. Many of these stories conclude with non-Jews—or even Jews—telling Finkelstein that Judaism is a '"tribal" religion, obsolete in the modern world' or that the laws of the sabbath are 'your ancient wilderness customs'. In one case, in a remark that speaks volumes about Jewish politics in the 1940s, a 'famous Jewish philanthropist' argued that the fact that Finkelstein observed *kashrut* meant that 'I was necessarily in favor of the terrorists who were then wreaking havoc in Palestine and could not be convinced that . . . *kashrut* is irreconcilable with violence.' The Revisionist underground Irgun (Etzel) and the Stern Gang (Lehi) would surely have been surprised to discover that their violent opposition to the British stemmed from the dietary laws!

Finkelstein also relates how the publisher invited him to speak to the sales representatives to talk up the book. At the time, the working title was *Judaism and the Jews*. The representatives were perplexed by the title since, as one of them said, 'Judaism has merely archaeological interest, having ceased to exist more than eighteen centuries ago, with the fall of Jerusalem . . . In contrast . . . the Jews are a contemporary phenomenon.' Hence the revision of the title to what we have today. But Finkelstein, like many authors, was not happy about the change made for marketing reasons. His very purpose, now intensified, was to assert more strongly than ever that Judaism is quintessentially a religion. To this end, he devotes considerable attention in the foreword—echoing Roth—to denouncing the idea that the Jews constitute a race. Basing himself on the anthropologist Melville Herskovitz's essay, he argues that the Jews of today bear little genetic resemblance to the Israelites who came out of Egypt. The Jewish people have both absorbed proselytes and lost members to assimilation: 'the Talmud maintains that the descendants of Sisera, Haman, and Titus included the foremost Jewish scholars of their time; Queen Victoria proudly regarded herself as a descendant of King David'.[12] Since he rather implausibly calculates that the number of Jews who descended from Abraham and Sarah would be 1,125,899,906,842,624—a number larger than all the people who have ever lived—the Jews, like everyone else, must have intermarried. In short: 'probably the whole world is kin'. Jews differ from others because of what they believe, not who their parents were.

[12] Finkelstein (ed.), *The Jews*, p. xxvii.

This refutation of a racial definition of Judaism was clearly a response to Nazi antisemitism, even if Finkelstein's explicit theory of antisemitism blames ignorance of the Jews' contribution to civilization. Here is indirect evidence of how the dark shadow of the Holocaust clouded Finkelstein's project, even though he refused to acknowledge it explicitly. But his attack on racism also leads directly—if surprisingly—to a celebration of intermarriage, since he argues, on the one hand, that great Jewish scholars have enemies of the Jews (Sisera, Haman, and Titus) in their genealogies and, on the other, that great rulers of the world (Queen Victoria) descend from great Jews (King David). This is a position that clearly contradicts a central tenet in the Jewish religion and one that would become anathema to spokespersons for American Jewry once the intermarriage rate accelerated in the 1960s. While this was certainly not Finkelstein's intent, it does illustrate that the issue of intermarriage was less pressing in the late 1940s than was the accusation of Jewish racial exclusivity. In fact, inter-marriage only came on the radar screen of American Jewry as a major issue in the 1960s.[13]

Finkelstein saw his work as a defence of Judaism as a religion and as an attempt to show that the modern Jew can only be understood as the product of biblical and talmudic Judaism. Judaism, he argues, is essentially *sui generis*. To be sure, 'many of the forms used by the Jews originated among peoples of earlier times', but all these studies, while interesting, shed no more light on Judaism than the study of the origin of the alphabet on the ideas of Shakespeare. Whatever the genesis of the rituals of Judaism, they have developed a unique significance that is usually unrelated to their accidental, extra-religious origins.[14]

So much for the embeddedness of Jewish culture in its surroundings. Even though Finkelstein pays some lip-service to the idea of mutual cultural interaction, his focus is resolutely on the way Jews have influenced Western civilization and not vice versa. While Christianity and Islam seem to think of Judaism as a relic of the past, the task of Jewish scholarship is to persuade them of a truth known for centuries by Jews: that the younger religions are 'fruits of its own planting; as part of man's endless future; as steps toward the realization of the prophetic vision of peace'.

[13] For some treatments of this issue, see Sidney Goldstein, 'American Jews 1970: A Demographic Profile', in Marshall Sklare (ed.), *The Jew in American Society* (New York, 1974), and A. Schwartz, 'Intermarriage in the United States', ibid. In his introduction to Schwartz's essay, Sklare notes that in the previous work Schwartz edited on American Jewish sociology (*The Jews: Social Patterns of an American Group* (Glencoe, Ill., 1958)), intermarriage merited only one paragraph out of over 650 pages! So the clear rise in intermarriage rates from below 10 per cent in the period before the Second World War (and even well after the war) to nearly 50 per cent today instigated a change in consciousness only in the 1960s. For a recent discussion of this issue in contemporary context, see Jonathan Sarna, *American Judaism* (New Haven, 2004), 360–4.

[14] Finkelstein (ed.), *The Jews*, p. xxviii.

In a peculiarly American burst of optimism, Finkelstein argues that the hostility between religions, especially antisemitism, cannot be resolved by secularism—what he calls 'a retreat from religion'—but by 'a world in which religion will have been vindicated'. Not paganism but monotheism is the key to a messianic future. He therefore takes great solace in what he describes as a religious renaissance in both American Christianity and Judaism, which he believes is based on a desire for mutual toleration. Whether this view of the American religious scene was really accurate in the late 1940s, a decade and a half before Vatican II began, seems to me debatable. It may rather reflect Finkelstein's own 'subject position' (to use a postmodernism), sitting on Morningside Heights. But it certainly captures the optimistic mood of American Jewish culture as reflected in the tercentenary five years later. And it is oddly prophetic of where America as a whole was to end up religiously by the end of the twentieth century, when evangelical Christianity combined with a renaissance of Orthodox Judaism to produce a characteristically American religious revival.

For Finkelstein, the task of explaining Judaism to America was an essential part of this Jewish religious renaissance. He concludes his foreword grandiloquently:

> Turning the pages of the historical essays in this volume—written with scientific objectivity—it is hard to escape the conviction that all this has a Meaning, and a Purpose; and that in this remarkable tale there is . . . a manifestation of God . . . Having read and re-read the various chapters I feel more than ever convinced that the writers, who so generously and painstakingly gave of themselves by sharing with us their knowledge and by helping us see through the detailed facts the greatness expressed in them, have performed an act of *kiddush ha-shem*, the sanctification of the Name of God.[15]

With this astonishing statement, the foreword ends. Even if traditional Jews often use the phrase *kidush hashem* to signify a particularly pious act, it seems hard to imagine that four years after the Holocaust one might resort for such a project to a term that also means martyrdom. Perhaps we have here another piece of evidence of how in the late 1940s the Holocaust remained an undigested experience for American Jews.

I do not propose to survey all of the essays on 'the role of Judaism in civilization'. As already indicated, the original four-volume work includes a series of chapters on various Jewish literatures side by side with essays that deal specifically with 'the Jewish contribution' to such and such a field. In the abridged, three-volume paperback edition, the single volume entitled *The Jews: Their Role in Civilization* contains only the second type of essay, the first having been segregated off to their own volume on Jewish religion and

[15] Finkelstein (ed.), *The Jews*, p. xxxiii.

culture. What had originally been a bold, if unarticulated, argument for including 'internalist' Jewish literatures in Western civilization now assumed a more traditional and limited character: civilization was what others created and Jews might or might not make contributions to it.

Some of the essays in this volume are straightforward studies, such as Jacob Rabinowitz's discussion of how various technical features of rabbinic and medieval Jewish property laws seem to have infiltrated into English common law.[16] Others have a more overtly apologetic cast, such as Milton Konvitz's often strained argument that Judaism not only does not contradict democracy, but is actually a source for it.[17] Konvitz strives mightily to explain that the doctrine of the chosen people is compatible with an egalitarian ethos, that Judaism values all human lives equally, and that the rabbinical elite was part of the common people. Whatever one might think about these propositions, it is clear that in the wake of the Second World War and the onset of the cold war, American Jews felt it imperative to demonstrate their adherence to what they saw as core American values. Konvitz recognizes that socialist Marxism, as well as the philosophies of John Dewey and Bertrand Russell, have doctrines of equality, but these are secular philosophies; religion can only arrive at such a doctrine via monotheism. The implicit argument, like Finkelstein's in his foreword, is that American democracy rests less on the secular Enlightenment and more on ethical monotheism.

I do, however, want to devote some specific attention to one other essay in this volume, that of Mordecai Kaplan, which is entitled 'The Contribution of Judaism to World Ethics'.[18] Judaism, says Kaplan, was the first civilization to recognize the primacy of ethics. He argues that Judaism's primary contribution to world ethics lies in the taming of the 'will-to-power' by subordinating power to moral law. Kaplan thus sides with Kant against Nietzsche, but he claims that only Judaism takes Kant's individual basis for ethics and turns it into a collective imperative. Kaplan offers a kind of thumbnail history of Western philosophy in which he lays heavy blame at the feet of the Greek Sophists, whom he calls the fathers of moral nihilism. Socrates and his disciples, of course, tried to counteract Sophistic nihilism and, in fact, the Stoics articulated principles so much like those of Judaism that Philo of Alexandria saw Stoicism and Judaism as virtually identical. But the fact that Stoicism did not prevent the moral degeneration of the Roman Empire demonstrates that it could never become the philosophy of a collective, as

[16] Jacob J. Rabinowitz, 'The Influence of Jewish Law on the Development of the Common Law', in Finkelstein (ed.), *The Jews*.

[17] Milton R. Konvitz, 'Judaism and the Democratic Idea', in Finkelstein (ed.), *The Jews*.

[18] Mordecai M. Kaplan, 'The Contribution of Judaism to World Ethics', in Finkelstein (ed.), *The Jews*.

had Judaism. It was Judaism—and, through it, Christianity and Islam—that saved the Mediterranean world from the nihilism of the late Roman Empire. Indeed, Kaplan does not hesitate to speak of 'the Judeo-Christian way of life', although, as we shall see, this expression was not, in fact, all that characteristic of his thought.

In the modern period, the same moral nihilism and worship of political power enjoyed a renaissance, starting with Machiavelli's *Prince* and, later, Nietzsche's philosophy. This nihilism culminated, according to Kaplan, in the 1930s with the rise of fascism (it is interesting that Kaplan, like Finkelstein, seems more fixated on the *rise* of Nazism than on its genocidal denouement in the Holocaust and the Second World War). Fascism goes further than any earlier nihilistic philosophy in that it turns individual nihilism into a collective project. In this respect, Judaism is the precise obverse of fascism since it is, for Kaplan, the purest instance of collective morality.

Kaplan's essay could easily have been written by Abraham Geiger or Moritz Lazarus in the nineteenth century, so redolent is it of the kind of ethical apologetics one encounters in that literature (indeed, Kaplan includes Lazarus's *Ethics of Judaism* in his bibliography).[19] He is so insistent on the ethical superiority of Judaism as to take great exception to James Breasted's argument in his book *The Dawn of Conscience*[20] that 'the Egyptians had possessed a standard of morals far superior to the Decalogue over a thousand years before the Decalogue was written'. To this, Kaplan acidly replies: 'he speaks not as a scientist but as a special pleader. If ever there was a case where comparisons are odious it certainly is this one.'[21] For Kaplan, it is just as odious to claim that Jewish civilization might be derivative as it is to claim that another was superior to it in morality.

Kaplan's essay in Finkelstein's collection both follows *and* deviates from positions that he took in 1934 in his *magnum opus*, *Judaism as a Civilization*, a work whose arguments he more or less recycled for the next half-century.[22] The clear implication of the essay is that the Jewish contribution to civilization is an ethical theory that challenges a lineage of thought from the Sophists to twentieth-century fascism. But if ethics is an 'essence' of Judaism, then conversion of Western civilization to this morality—a truly Judaeo-Christian morality—would efface some of the essential difference between the Jews and

[19] Moritz Lazarus, *The Ethics of Judaism in Four Parts*, trans. Henrietta Szold (Philadelphia, 1900–1).

[20] James Henry Breasted, *The Dawn of Conscience* (New York, 1933).

[21] Ibid., 682.

[22] Mordecai M. Kaplan, *Judaism as a Civilization: Toward a Reconstruction of American-Jewish Life*, enlarged edn (New York, 1957). For an excellent interpretative essay on Kaplan, see Arnold Eisen's introduction to a new edition of *Judaism as a Civilization* (Philadelphia, 1994).

their neighbours. And, this difference is exactly what drives *Judaism as a Civilization*. In that work, Kaplan anticipates postmodernism by arguing for the 'otherness' of Judaism. Indeed, this insistence on otherness was to make Kaplan one of the vociferous critics of the 1954 American Jewish tercentenary, which he accused of promoting Jewish assimilation.

Kaplan distinguishes between 'otherness' and 'unlikeness'. Unlikeness is a difference in quality, while otherness is difference in essence. Kaplan considers differences between religions to be in the category of unlikeness, which corresponds to his insistence that religion is a secondary or epiphenomenal characteristic of a civilization. He defines a civilization as 'that nexus of a history, literature, language, social organization, folk sanctions, standards of conduct, social and spiritual ideals, aesthetic values which in their totality form a civilization'.[23] Religion, which in Kaplan's vocabulary is limited to doctrinal issues or matters of belief, is therefore secondary to the 'folkways' of a civilization.

Now, if morality is a part of religion, then it is as unessential to Judaism as is the belief in a personal God, which, as is well known, was Kaplan's radical stand that got him declared a heretic in 1946 by a group of Orthodox rabbis who publicly burned his prayer book.[24] But—as the essay in Finkelstein's anthology demonstrates—Kaplan clearly regarded morality as much more essential to Jewish civilization than belief in what he calls the 'God-idea'. So, this 'contribution' of Jewish morality to Western civilization would undermine the very task that Kaplan set for modern Judaism, namely, 'to save the [essential] otherness of Jewish life'.

This tension—perhaps even contradiction—in Kaplan's thought can actually be found in *Judaism as a Civilization* itself. On the one hand, Kaplan argues that only by conceiving of Judaism as a civilization can the modern crisis of Judaism be solved by reinforcing a sense of otherness. He adamantly rejects the search for what he calls 'the Jewish contribution to universal values'. America, he says, may provide the most fertile soil for retaining Jewish otherness as a result of an analysis that sounds dated to our ears but reflects the realities of the inter-war period. America, he suggests, will never become the kind of monolithic nation-state envisioned by French revolutionary republicanism since American Catholicism incites a militant Protestant reaction. This rivalry between a Protestant majority and a Catholic minority will both keep America a Christian nation *and* prevent the full assimilation of the Jews. In other words, the cause of Jewish separatism is furthered by Catholic separatism: the Catholic Church is the unwitting

[23] Kaplan, *Judaism as a Civilization*, 178.

[24] For a recounting of this incident and an excellent evaluation of Kaplan's relationship to Orthodoxy, see Jeffrey Gurock, *A Modern Heretic and a Traditional Community: Mordecai Kaplan, Orthodoxy and American Judaism* (New York, 1997).

handmaiden of the Jews! Where others might decry the forces of anti-Catholicism, which were also typically antisemitic, Kaplan sees a virtue: 'perhaps America is destined to depart from the strict logic of democratic nationalism and to achieve a new cultural constellation in which historical civilizations, or churches, may be permitted to conserve the finest products of their experience and contribute them to the sum total of American culture and civilization'.[25] Although anti-Catholicism is now a thing of the past, Kaplan's vision is clearly prophetic in several ways: he imagined what we would today call multiculturalism—or what Horace Kallen in his time called cultural pluralism—*and* he envisioned the possibility that a Christian revivalism in America might ironically come to benefit the Jews.

Yet, the idea that American civilization could be shaped by the contributions of separate civilizations, such as that of the Jews, suggests that the Jewish contribution to non-Jewish civilization has value after all. In a series of radical statements, Kaplan argues for hyphenated identities in contemporary America. There should be no prohibition on adopting non-Jewish folkways, provided that this is a conscious and explicit process. Like Finkelstein, he even welcomes intermarriage, provided the homes are Jewish and the children are given a Jewish upbringing: 'It is only an openly avowed policy of this kind [that is, an acceptance of mixed marriage] that can make the position of the Jews tenable in America. For nothing is so contrary to the ideal of cultural and spiritual cooperation as the unqualified refusal of one element of the population to intermarry with any other.'[26] Kaplan's vision of the relationship of Judaism to America is nothing short of messianic:

> Torah should mean to the Jew nothing less than civilization which enables the individual to effect affirmative and creative adjustments in his living relationships with reality . . . But to the Jew in the diaspora, it must, in addition, spell the duty of beholding in the non-Jewish civilization by which he lives a potential instrument of salvation. He must help to render that civilization capable of enhancing human life as the Torah enhanced the life of Israel.[27]

How exactly one is to square non-Jewish civilization as an instrument for salvation with maintaining Jewish otherness remains an unresolved problem in Kaplan's *magnum opus*.

In the end, Kaplan also reinstates religion at the centre of his philosophy. The divorce between modern civilization and religion is, at best, a temporary phenomenon; in the future, religion will again become central to civilization, a view that, as we have seen, was central to Finkelstein's programme as well. To be sure, what Kaplan means by religion is idiosyncratic: it must be redefined to exclude the idea of a transcendent God. Instead, it

[25] Kaplan, *Judaism as a Civilization*, 79. [26] Ibid. 418–19. [27] Ibid. 414.

should signify what Kaplan calls the 'will-to-live' represented in the *sancta* of a religion. Redefined in this way, Judaism turns out to be the most 'religious' of all religions and therefore the one best suited to animate American civilization in the future.

Kaplan has rightly been criticized for the optimism and rationality of his philosophy. But it seems to me that just as problematic is the contradiction between Jewish civilization as 'Other' *and* as the model for contemporary America. Nevertheless, all of these difficult issues in Kaplan's thought—like those in Finkelstein's foreword to *The Jews*—may well reflect the transitional moment immediately before and after the Second World War, when the Jews felt themselves to be at once a threatened minority *and* a potentially equal partner in the American dream. Torn between these contradictory social forces, perhaps it is not surprising that the writings of certain Jewish intellectuals were equally rent by contradictions.

A half-century later, though, certain aspects of Kaplan's and Finkelstein's visions have certainly come to fruition. Religion continues to occupy a central place in American culture and politics, and, in fact, one might argue that it occupies a much more central place than it did in the 'golden decade'. But in much closer correspondence to Kaplan's view than Finkelstein's, Judaism has shed a narrowly religious definition in favour of a much broader cultural identity, what Kaplan would call a 'civilization'. In part, this is because multiculturalism has revived Horace Kallen's cultural pluralism of the immigrant period in a new form.[28] But multiculturalism does not require the defensive and often apologetic argument that a culture's virtue lies in its 'contribution to civilization'. In addition, one might argue that multiculturalism obviates the often sterile discussion of whether a culture is derivative or original. All cultures are, in fact, hybrid, a position that Kaplan seems to endorse for America. That is, all cultures evolve in constant interaction with their surroundings, absorbing some ideas and practices, resisting others, and, probably most commonly, translating what is foreign into their own idiom.

This is the approach that I have taken with my twenty-two collaborators in the recently published *Cultures of the Jews: A New History*.[29] Like

[28] See Horace Kallen, *Culture and Democracy in the United States* (New York, 1924). For a discussion of Kallen's views as against those of America as a 'melting pot', see my 'The Melting Pot and Beyond: Jews and the Politics of American Identity', in David Biale, Michael Galchinsky, and Susannah Heschel (eds), *Insider/Outsider: American Jews and Multiculturalism* (Berkeley, 1998). I argue that the Jews helped shape American multiculturalism, but a consequence of this contribution has been the exclusion of the Jews from paradigmatic minority status. Although in this work the contributors suggest various ways in which Jews have contributed to both America's self-definition and the Western canon, they also demonstrate ways in which they deviated from them. The Jews are at once insiders *and* outsiders, contributors to the majority *and* defenders of their own minority culture.

[29] David Biale (ed.), *Cultures of the Jews: A New History* (New York, 2002).

Finkelstein's *The Jews*, this work represents the work of a new generation of scholars of Jewish Studies, but, as opposed to Finkelstein's, half of the contributors are from Israel and half from abroad (all but one of these from the United States). Moreover, the Israelis include a large group born in America, and the Americans include some who have lived for considerable periods in Israel. There is now a growing sense of a common scholarly community in which old imagined categories like 'the Jerusalem School' or 'Diaspora Jewish Studies' are breaking down.

Indeed, one of the goals of this cultural history is to subject some of the treasured dichotomies of what might be called 'Judaism' to new criticism: exile versus sovereignty, Jewish versus non-Jewish culture, elite versus popular culture. Following historians such as Carlo Ginzburg and literary critics like Stephen Greenblatt, the goal of the work is to show the circulation of culture between Jews and non-Jews and between different groups within the Jewish world. The focus is on the differences between Jewish cultures in different places and ages, as well as their similarities: cultures in the plural rather than in the singular.

This cultural history very deliberately parts company with Finkelstein in its refusal to place Judaism—or religion—at the centre. It is therefore, one might say, more faithful to the title that the publisher forced on Finkelstein: *The Jews* rather than *Judaism and the Jews*. But it also realizes Kaplan's programme for seeing Judaism as civilization. If that programme was ahead of its time, it is perhaps more suited to—and therefore less racked by its own internal contradictions in—an America where Jews no longer need to pound on the doors of society and plead for admission based on their claims of contributions to civilization.

Indeed, if one adopts the admittedly dubious language of a 'clash of civilizations', it is striking that the Jews are now seen as very much a part of the 'West' rather than as a people of the Orient.[30] And, the West is, of course, the Christian West, in which even secularism is seen as a dialectical product of the history of Western Christianity. Now, if there was any civilization in premodern times to which the Jews made the greatest contribution, it was unquestionably the Islamic. But the Jews have now become an integral part of the Christian West, or, as in the case of the state of Israel, an outpost of Western civilization. No longer do Jewish scholars feel compelled to defend the Jewish contributions to the civilization in which they now feel themselves entirely at home. The challenge, however, may be the opposite: to find reasons, as did Kaplan, for why they should still be considered Other.

[30] See Ivan Kalmar and Derek Penslar (eds), *Orientalism and the Jews* (Waltham, Mass., 2004).

Contributors

DAVID BERGER is Professor of Jewish History at Yeshiva University.

DAVID BIALE is Emanuel Ringelblum Professor of Jewish History and Director of the Program in Jewish Studies at the University of California, Davis.

JEREMY COHEN holds the Abraham and Edita Spiegel Family Foundation Chair for European Jewish History at Tel Aviv University.

RICHARD I. COHEN holds the Paulette and Claude Kelman Chair in French Jewry Studies in the Department of Jewish History at the Hebrew University of Jerusalem.

MARK H. GELBER is Professor of Comparative Literature and German-Jewish Studies at Ben-Gurion University, Beer Sheva.

SUSANNAH HESCHEL is Eli Black Associate Professor of Jewish Studies at Dartmouth College, Hanover, New Hampshire.

ELLIOTT HOROWITZ is Associate Professor of Jewish History at Bar-Ilan University, and co-editor of the *Jewish Quarterly Review*.

DAVID N. MYERS is Professor of Jewish History and Director of the Center for Jewish Studies at the University of California, Los Angeles, and co-editor of the *Jewish Quarterly Review*.

MOSHE ROSMAN is Professor in the Department of Jewish History at Bar-Ilan University.

DANIEL SCHROETER holds the Teller Family Chair in Jewish History at the University of California, Irvine.

YAACOV SHAVIT is Professor in the Department of Jewish History at the University of Tel Aviv.

Bibliography

ABITBOL, MICHEL, 'The Encounter between French Jewry and the Jews of North Africa: Analysis of a Discourse (1830–1914)', in Frances Malino and Bernard Wasserstein (eds), *The Jews in Modern France* (Hanover, NH, 1985).

—— *Le Passé d'une discorde Juifs et Arabes du VIIe siècle à nos jours* (Paris, 2003).

ABRAHAMS, HAROLD M., 'The Jew and Athletics', in H. Newman (ed.), *The Real Jew: Some Aspects of the Jewish Contribution to Civilization* (London, 1925).

ABRAHAMS, ISRAEL, 'Professor Schürer on Life under the Jewish Law', *Jewish Quarterly Review*, OS 11 (1899), 626–42.

—— 'Sabbath (Jewish)', in James Hastings (ed.), *Encyclopaedia of Religion and Ethics* (Edinburgh, 1919).

ADLER, CYRUS, 'Sabbath Recovery in American in Jewish Life', *Jewish Forum*, 16/4 (Dec. 1933), 127–8.

—— ISIDORE SINGER, et al. (eds), *The Jewish Encyclopedia: A Descriptive Record of the History, Religion, Literature, and Customs of the Jewish People from the Earliest Times to the Present Day*, 12 vols (New York, 1901–6).

ADLER, MICHAEL (ed.), *British Jewry Book of Honour* (London, 1922).

ALCALAY, AMMIEL, *After Jews and Arabs: Remaking Levantine Culture* (Minneapolis, 1993).

—— 'Intellectual Life', in Reeva Spector Simon, Michael Menachem Laskier, and Sara Reguer (eds), *The Jews of the Middle East and North Africa in Modern Times* (New York, 2003).

ALEXANDER, EDWARD, 'Multiculturalism's Jewish Problem', [*American Jewish*] *Congress Monthly* (Nov.–Dec. 1991), 7–10.

ANDERSON, MARK M., 'German Intellectuals, Jewish Victims: A Politically Correct Solidarity', *Chronicle of Higher Education* (19 Oct. 2001), <http://chronicle.com/ free/v48/i08/08b00701.htm>.

APTOWITZER, VICTOR, *Kain und Abel in der Agada, den Apokryphen, der hellenistischen, christlichen und muhammedanischen Literatur* (Vienna, 1922).

ARAD, GULIE NE'EMAN, *America, its Jews and the Rise of Nazism* (Bloomington, Ind., 2000).

ARNOLD, B. T., and D. B. WEISBERG, 'A Centennial Review of Friedrich Delitzsch's "Babel und Bibel" Lectures', *Journal of Biblical Literature*, 121 (2002), 441–57.

ASCHHEIM, STEVEN E., 'The Jews Within: The Myth of "Judaization" in Germany', in Jehuda Reinharz and Walter Schatzberg (eds), *The Jewish Response to German Culture from the Enlightenment to the Second World War* (Hanover, NH, 1984).

—— 'The Publication of Moritz Goldstein's "The German-Jewish Parnassus" Sparks a Debate over Assimilation, German Culture and the Jewish Spirit', in Sander L. Gilman and Jack Zipes (eds), *Yale Companion to Jewish Writing and Thought in German Culture 1096–1996* (New Haven, 1997).

ASHTOR, ELIYAHU, *The Jews of Moslem Spain*, 3 vols (Philadelphia, 1973).

ASSIS, YOM TOV, 'The Judeo-Arabic Tradition in Christian Spain', in Daniel Frank (ed.), *The Jews of Medieval Islam: Community, Society, and Identity* (Leiden, 1995).

ASSMAN, JAN, *Moses the Egyptian: The Memory of Egypt in Western Monotheism* (Cambridge, Mass., 1997).

AVINERI, SHLOMO, *Varieties of Zionist Thought* [Hara'ayon hatsiyoni ligvanav: perakim betoledot hamaḥashavah hale'umit hayehudit] (Tel Aviv, 1980).

AYOUN, RICHARD, 'Les Juifs livournais en Afrique du Nord', *La Rassegna Mensile di Israel*, 50 (1984), 650–705.

—— and BERNARD COHEN, *Les Juifs d'Algérie: Deux mille ans d'histoire* (Paris, 1982).

BAECK, LEO, *Judaism and Christianity* (Philadelphia, 1960).

BAER, MARC DAVID, 'The 1660 Fire and the Islamization of Space in Istanbul', *International Journal of Middle East Studies*, 36 (2004), 162–3.

BAER, YITZHAK, *A History of the Jews in Christian Spain* (Philadelphia, 1961).

BAKKER, JOHAN DE, 'Slaves, Arms, and Holy War: Moroccan Policy vis-à-vis the Dutch Republic during the Establishment of the 'Alawi Dynasty', Ph.D. diss. (University of Amsterdam, 1991).

BAR-ITZHAK, HAYA, *Jewish Poland: Legends of Origins* (Detroit, 2001).

BAR-KOCHVA, BEZALEL, 'The Anti-Jewish Treatise of Apollonius Malon' (Heb.), *Tarbiz*, 69/1 (1999), 6–58.

BARNAI, JACOB, 'The Jews of Muslim Countries in Modern Times and the "Jerusalem School of History"' (Heb.), *Pe'amim*, 92 (2002), 83–115.

BARON, SALO W., 'The Jewish Factor in Medieval Civilization', *Proceedings of the American Academy for Jewish Research*, 12 (1942), 1–48.

—— *A Social and Religious History of the Jews*, 3 vols (New York, 1937).

—— 'Turkey's Golden Age', in Baron, *A Social and Religious History of the Jews*, xviii (New York, 1983).

BAT YE'OR, *The Dhimmi: Jews and Christians under Islam* (Rutherford, NJ, 1985).

BAUER, WALTER, 'Jesus der Galiläer', in *Festgabe für Adolf Jülicher* (Tübingen, 1927); repr. in Bauer, *Aufsätze und Kleine Schriften*, ed. Georg Strecker (Tübingen, 1967).

BECK, EVELYN TORTON, *Kafka and the Yiddish Theater* (Madison, Wis., 1973).

BELLING, VERONICA, '"Ahavat Yehonatan": A Poem by Judah Leo Landau', *Polin*, 15 (2002), 243–8.

BEN-AMOS, AVNER, 'An Impossible Pluralism? European Jews and Oriental Jews in the Israeli History Curriculum', *History of European Ideas*, 18 (1994), 48–9.

BENBASSA, ESTHER, and ARON RODRIGUE, *A History of the Judeo-Spanish Community, 14th–20th Centuries* (Berkeley, 2000).

BÉNÉTON, PHILIPPE, *Histoire de mots: Culture et civilisation* (Paris, 1975).

BENVENISTE, ÉMILE, *Problèmes de linguistique générale* (Paris, 1966).

BERGER, DAVID, 'Jacob Katz on Jews and Christians in the Middle Ages', in Jay M. Harris (ed.), *The Pride of Jacob: Essays on Jacob Katz and his Work* (Cambridge, Mass., 2002).

—— *The Jewish–Christian Debate in the High Middle Ages: A Critical Edition of the 'Nizzahon Vetus' with an Introduction, Translation, and Commentary* (Philadelphia, 1979).

—— 'Maccabees, Zealots, and Josephus: The Impact of Zionism on Joseph Klausner's *History of the Second Temple*', in Shaye J. D. Cohen and Joshua Schwartz (eds), *Studies in Josephus and the Varieties of Ancient Judaism: Louis H. Feldman Jubilee Volume* (Leiden, forthcoming).

—— 'On the Uses of History in Medieval Jewish Polemic against Christianity: The Search for the Historical Jesus', in Elisheva Carlebach, John M. Efron, and David N. Myers (eds), *Jewish History and Jewish Memory: Essays in Honor of Yosef Hayim Yerushalmi* (Hanover, NH, 1998).

—— 'Religion, Nationalism, and Historiography: Yehezkel Kaufmann's Account of Jesus and Early Christianity', in Leo Landman (ed.), *Scholars and Scholarship: The Interaction between Judaism and Other Cultures* (New York, 1990).

BERGHAHN, KLAUS L., *The German–Jewish Dialogue Reconsidered: A Symposium in Honor of George L. Mosse* (New York, 1996).

BEVAN, EDWIN R., and CHARLES J. SINGER (eds), *The Legacy of Israel* (Oxford, 1927).

BIALE, DAVID (ed.), *Cultures of the Jews: A New History* (New York, 2002).

—— GALCHINSKY, MICHAEL, and SUSANNAH HESCHEL, 'Introduction: The Dialectic of Jewish Enlightenment', in David Biale, Michael Galchinsky, and Susannah Heschel (eds), *Insider/Outsider: American Jews and Multiculturalism* (Berkeley, 1998).

BIALIK, H. N., *Devarim shebe'al peh*, 2 vols (Tel Aviv, 1935).

BIRKENTHAL, BER, *The Memoirs of Ber of Bolechow*, ed. Mark Vishnitzer (London, 1922; repr. New York, 1973).

BODIAN, MIRIAM, *Hebrews of the Portuguese Nation* (Bloomington, Ind., 1997).

BONFIL, ROBERT, 'The Historian's Perception of the Jews in the Italian Renaissance: Towards a Reappraisal', *Revue des Études Juives*, 143 (1984), 59–82.

BONUS, ARTUR, *Zur Germanisierung des Christentums* (Jena, 1911).

BOUSSET, WILHELM, *Der Antichrist in der Überlieferung des Judentums, des Neuen Testaments, und der alten Kirche* (Göttingen, 1895).

—— *Kyrios Christos. Geschichte des Christusglaubens von den Anfänge des Christentums bis Irenaeus* (Göttingen, 1913).

—— *Die Religion des Judentums im neutestamentalischen Zeitalter* (Berlin, 1903).

BOX, GEORGE H., 'How Judaism Fought Paganism', in H. Newman (ed.), *The Real Jew: Some Aspects of the Jewish Contribution to Civilization* (London, 1925).

BOYARIN, DANIEL, and JONATHAN BOYARIN, 'Diaspora: Generation and the Ground of Jewish Identity', *Critical Inquiry*, 19 (1993), 693–725.

BOYARIN, JONATHAN, 'The Other Within and the Other Without', in Laurence J. Silberstein and Robert L. Cohn (eds), *The Other in Jewish Thought and History: Constructions of Jewish Culture and Identity* (New York, 1994).

BRACHER, KARL DIETRICH, *Die deutsche Diktatur. Entstehung Struktur Folgen des Nationalsozialismus* (Frankfurt am Main, 1979).

BRAESE, STEPHAN, *Die andere Erinnerung. Jüdische Autoren in der Westdeutschen Nachkriegsliteratur* (Vienna, 2001).

BRAUDEL, FERNAND, *On History* (*Écrits sur l'histoire*), trans. Sarah Matthews (London: Weidenfeld & Nicolson, 1980).

BREASTED, JAMES HENRY, *The Dawn of Conscience* (New York, 1933).

BRENNER, MICHAEL, VICKI CARON, and URI R. KAUFMANN (eds), *Jewish Emancipation Reconsidered: The French and German Models* (Tübingen, 2003).

BREUER, MORDECHAI, *Modernity within Tradition: The Social History of Orthodox Jewry in Imperial Germany*, trans. Elizabeth Petuchowski (New York, 1992).

BRODER, HENRYK, and MICHEL P. LANG (eds), *Fremd im eigenen Land. Juden in der Bundesrepublik* (Frankfurt am Main, 1979).

BUBER, MARTIN, 'The Two Foci of the Jewish Soul', in Fritz A. Rothschild (ed.), *Jewish Perspectives on Christianity: Leo Baeck, Martin Buber, Franz Rosenzweig, Will Herberg, and Abraham J. Heschel* (New York, 1990).

—— *Two Types of Faith* (New York, 1951).

BUDDE, KARL, 'The Old Testament and the Excavations', *American Journal of Theology*, 6 (1902), 685–708.

—— 'The Sabbath and the Week', *Journal of Theological Studies*, 30 (1928), 1–15.

BULTMANN, RUDOLF, *Primitive Christianity in its Contemporary Setting*, trans. R. H. Fuller (London, 1956).

—— *Primitive Christianity* (New York, 1956).

BURKITT, FRANCIS C., 'The Debt of Christianity to Judaism', in Edwyn R. Bevan and Charles Singer (eds), *The Legacy of Israel* (Oxford, 1927).

BUTCHER, S. H., 'Greece and Israel', in Butcher, *Harvard Lectures on Greek Subjects* (London, 1904).

BUTLER, E. M., *The Tyranny of Greece over Germany: A Study of the Influence Exercised by Greek Art and Poetry over the Great German Writers of the Eighteenth, Nineteenth and Twentieth Centuries* (Cambridge, 1935).

CAHILL, THOMAS, *The Gifts of the Jews: How a Tribe of Desert Nomads Changed the Way Everyone Thinks and Feels* (New York, 1998).

CAPLAN, KIMMY, 'The Life and Sermons of Israel Herbert Levinthal (1882–1982)', *American Jewish History*, 87 (1999), 1–27.

CARDOSO, ISAAC, *Ma'alot ha'ivrim: perakim*, trans. Yosef Kaplan (Jerusalem, 1971).

CESARANI, DAVID, *The Jewish Chronicle and Anglo-Jewry, 1841–1991* (Cambridge, 1994).

CHAKRABARTY, DIPESH, *Provincializing Europe: Postcolonial Thought and Historical Difference* (Princeton, 2000).

CHAMBERLAIN, HOUSTON STEWART, *Die Grundlagen des neunzehnten Jahrhunderts* (Munich, 1899); trans. John Lees as *Foundations of the Nineteenth Century* (New York, 1910).

CHETRIT, JOSEPH, 'Discours et modernité dans les communautés juives d'Afrique du Nord à la fin du XIXe siècle', in Esther Benbassa (ed.), *Transmission et passages en monde juif* (Paris, 1997).

—— 'Jewish Theatre: A Chapter in Moroccan Jewry's Wrestle with Modernization' (Heb.), in Haim Saadoun (ed.), *Maroko* (Jerusalem, 2003).

—— 'Hebrew National Modernity against French Modernity: The Hebrew Haskalah in North Africa at the End of the Nineteenth Century' (Heb.), *Mikedem umiyam*, 3 (1990), 11–76.

CHEYETTE, BRYAN, and LAURA MARCUS (eds), *Modernity, Culture, and 'the Jew'* (Cambridge, 1998).

CHOURAQUI, ANDRÉ, *Marche vers l'Occident: Les Juifs d'Afrique du Nord* (Paris, 1952).

CLAY, A. T., *Amurru, the Home of the Northern Semites* (Philadelphia, 1909).

CLIFFORD, JAMES, *Routes: Travel and Translation in the Late Twentieth Century* (Cambridge, Mass., 1997).

COHEN, ABRAHAM, 'Great Jewish Thoughts', in H. Newman (ed.), *The Real Jew: Some Aspects of the Jewish Contribution to Civilization* (London, 1925).

COHEN, MARK R., 'Leone de Modena's Riti: A Seventeenth-Century Plea for Social Toleration of Jews', *Jewish Social Studies*, 34 (1972), 287–319.

—— 'Medieval Jewry in the World of Islam', in Martin Goodman (ed.), *The Oxford Handbook of Jewish Studies* (Oxford, 2002).

—— *Under Crescent and Cross* (Princeton, 1994).

COHEN, MITCHELL, 'In Defense of Shaatnez: A Politics for Jews in a Multicultural America', in David Biale, Michael Galchinsky, and Susannah Heschel (eds), *Insider/Outsider: American Jews and Multiculturalism* (Berkeley, 1998).

COHEN, RICHARD I., 'Jews and the State: The Historical Context', in Ezra Mendelsohn (ed.), *Jews and the State: Dangerous Alliances and the Perils of Privilege*, Studies in Contemporary Jewry, 19 (New York, 2003).

—— 'Urban Visibility and Biblical Visions: Jewish Culture in Western and Central Europe in the Modern Age', in David Biale (ed.), *Cultures of the Jews: A New History* (New York, 2002).

COHEN, ROBERT, 'Passage to a New World: The Sephardi Poor of Eighteenth Century Amsterdam', in Lea Dasberg and Jonathan N. Cohen (eds), *Neveh Ya'akov: Jubilee Volume Presented to Dr. Jaap Meijer on the Occasion of His Seventieth Birthday* (Assen, 1982).

COHEN, SHAYE J. D., and JOSHUA SCHWARTZ (eds), *Studies in Josephus and the Varieties of Ancient Judaism: Louis H. Feldman Jubilee Volume* (Leiden, 2006).

COHON, SAMUEL S., 'The Place of Jesus in the Religious Life of his Day', *Journal of Biblical Literature*, 48 (1929), 82–108.

CORCOS, DAVID, 'The Attitude of the Almohadic Rulers towards the Jews' (Heb.), *Zion*, 32 (1967), 137–60.

CUDDIHY, JOHN, *The Ordeal of Civility* (New York, 1974).

DAICHES, SALIS, 'Judaism as the Religion of the Law', in H. Newman (ed.), *The Real Jew: Some Aspects of the Jewish Contribution to Civilization* (London, 1925).

DALMAN, GUSTAV, *Worte Jesu*, i (Leipzig, 1898), 223.

DARLING, LINDA T., 'Rethinking Europe and the Islamic World in the Age of Exploration', *Journal of Early Modern History*, 2 (1998).

DAVIES, ALAN T., 'The Aryan Christ: A Motif in Christian Anti-Semitism', *Journal of Ecumenical Studies*, 12 (Fall, 1975), 569–79.

DAVIS, FLOYD JAMES, *Minority-Dominant Relations: A Sociological Analysis* (Arlington Heights, 1978).

—— (ed.), *Understanding Minority-Dominant Relations: Sociological Contributions* (Arlington Heights, 1979).

DE HAAS, JACOB (ed.), *The Encyclopedia of Jewish Knowledge* (New York, 1934).

DELEUZE, GILLES, and FÉLIX GUATTARI, *Kafka: Pour une littérature mineure* (Paris, 1975).

DELITZSCH, F., *Babel and Bible*, ed. C. H. W. Johns (New York, 1903).

DERRIDA, JACQUES, *Archive Fever: A Freudian Impression*, trans. Eric Prenowitz (Chicago, 1996).

Deutschchristentum auf rein-evangelischer Grundlage. 95 Leitsätze zum Reformationsfest 1917 by Hauptpastor Friedrich Andersen in Flensburg, Professor Adolf Bartels in Weimar, Kirchenrath D. Dr. Ernst Katzer in Oberloßnitz bei Dresden, and Hans Paul Freiherr von Wolzogen in Bayreuth (Leipzig, 1917).

Deutsche mit Gott. Ein deutsches Glaubensbuch (Weimar, 1941).

DINER, DAN, 'Geschichte der Juden—Paradigma einer europaïschen Geschichtsschreibung', *Gedachtniszeiten* (2003), 246–62.

D'ISRAELI, ISAAC, *The Genius of Judaism* (London, 1833).

DOWDEN, STEPHEN D., and MEIKE G. WERNER (eds), *German Literature, Jewish Critics: The Brandeis Symposium* (Rochester, NY, 2000).

DRACHMAN, BERNARD, *Looking at America* (New York, 1934).

—— *The Unfailing Light: Memoirs of an American Rabbi* (New York, 1948).

DRIVER, S. R., 'Edersheim, Alfred', in *Dictionary of National Biography*, xxii, suppl. 1 (London, 1901), 600–1.

—— 'Hebrew Authority', in D. G. Hogarth (ed.), *Authority and Archaeology, Sacred and Profane: Essays on the Relation of Monuments to Biblical and Classical Literature* (London, 1899).

—— 'Sabbath', in James Hastings (ed.), *Dictionary of the Bible*, 5 vols (New York, 1911–12), iv. 320–1.

DYER, RICHARD, *White* (London, 1997), 16.

EDERSHEIM, A., *The Life and Times of Jesus the Messiah*, American edn (repr. Grand Rapids, Mich., 1950), ii. 52, 777–87.

EFRON, JOHN M., 'From Mitteleuropa to the Middle East: Orientalism through a Jewish Lens', *Jewish Quarterly Review*, 94/3 (2004), 490–520.

—— 'Orientalism and the Jewish Historical Gaze', in Ivan Davidson Kalmar and Derek J. Penslar (eds), *Orientalism and the Jews* (Hanover, NH, 2004).

—— 'Scientific Racism and the Mystique of Sephardic Racial Superiority', *Leo Baeck Institute Year Book*, 38 (1993), 75–96.

EISEN, ARNOLD, Introduction to *Judaism as a Civilization*, new edn (Philadelphia, 1994).

—— 'Jews, Jewish Studies, and the American Humanities', *Tikkun*, 45 (1989), 23–9.

EISENBETH, M., 'Les Juifs en Algérie et en Tunisie à l'époque turque (1516–1830)', *Revue Africaine*, 96 (1952), 347–50.

ELIAS, NORBERT, *The Civilizing Process*, trans. Edmund Jephcott (New York, 1978); first pub. as *Über den Prozess der Zivilisation. Soziogenetische und psychogenetische Untersuchungen* (Basel, 1936).

—— *The Germans: Power Struggles and the Development of Habitus in the Nineteenth and Twentieth Centuries*, ed. Michael Schröter, trans. Eric Dunning and Stephen Mennell (New York, 1996).

ELON, A., *The Pity of It All: A History of Jews in Germany 1743–1933* (New York, 2002).

EMERTON, J. A., 'Samuel Rolles Driver', in C. E. Bosworth (ed.), *A Century of British Orientalists, 1902–2001* (Oxford, 2001), 122–38.

ENDELMAN, TODD M., *The Jews of Georgian England, 1714–1830* (Philadelphia, 1979).

—— *Radical Assimilation in English History* (Bloomington, Ind., 1990).

ESCHELBACHER, JOSEPH, *Das Judentum und das Wesen des Christentums* (Berlin, 1908).

ETKES, IMMANUEL, *The Gaon of Vilna: The Man and his Image*, trans. Jeffrey M. Green (Berkeley, 2002).

ETTINGER, SHMUEL, 'The Beginning of Change in the Attitude of European Society towards the Jews', *Scripta Hierosolymitana*, 7 (1961), 193–219.

—— *Modern Anti-Semitism: Studies and Essays* [Ha'antishemiut ba'et haḥadashah: pirkei meḥkar ve'iyun] (Tel Aviv, 1978).

—— 'The Position of the Deists on Judaism and its Influence on the Jews' (Heb.), in Ettinger, *Studies in Modern Jewish History*, i: *History and Historians* (Jerusalem, 1992), 215–24.

—— (ed.) *History of the Jews in the Islamic Countries* [Toledot hayehudim be'aretsot ha'islam], 3 vols (Jerusalem, 1986).

FEBVRE, LUCIEN, *Civilisation: Le Mot et l'idée* (Paris, 1930).

FELDMAN, ABRAHAM J., *Contributions of Judaism to Modern Society* (Cincinnati, 1930).

FELICE, RENZO DE, *Jews in an Arab Land: Libya, 1835–1970* (Austin, Tex., 1985).

FICHTE, J. G., *Addresses to the German Nation*, trans. R. F. Jones and G. H. Turnbull (Chicago, 1922).

—— *Werke*, ed. Fritz Medicus, iv (Leipzig, 1912).

FILIPPINI, JEAN-PIERRE, 'Les Juifs d'Afrique du Nord et la communauté de Livourne au XVIIIe siècle', in Jean-Louis Miège (ed.), *Les Relations intercommunautaires juives en Méditerranée occidentale, XIIIe–XXe siècles* (Paris, 1984).

—— 'Les Négociants juifs de Livourne au XVIIIe siècle', *Revue des Études Juives*, 132 (1973), 672–3.

—— 'Le Rôle des négociants et des banquiers juifs de Livourne dans le grand commerce international en Méditerranée au XVIIIe siècle', in Ariel Toaff and Simon Schwarzfuchs (eds), *The Mediterranean and the Jews: Banking, Finance and International Trade (XVI–XVIII Centuries)* (Ramat Gan, 1989).

FINKELSTEIN, LOUIS (ed.), *The Jews: Their History, Culture, and Religion* (Philadelphia, 1949; 4th edn, 3 vols, New York, 1970).

FLEISCHMANN, JACOB, *The Problem of Christianity in Modern Jewish Thought (1770–1929)* [Be'ayat hanatsrut bamaḥashavah hayehudit mimendelson ad rozentsveig] (Jerusalem, 1964).

FLEISCHMANN, LEA, *Dies ist nicht mein Land. Eine Jüdin verlässt die Bundesrepublik* (Hamburg, 1980).

FRANK, ANDRE GUNDER, *ReOrient: Global Economy in the Asian Age* (Berkeley, 1998).

FREUD, SIGMUND, *Civilization and its Discontents*, ed. and trans. James Strachey (New York, 1962; based on 1st edn, Vienna, 1930).

—— *The Future of an Illusion* (1927).

FRIEDLANDER, GERALD, *The Jewish Sources of the Sermon on the Mount* (New York, 1911).

GALCHINSKY, MICHAEL, 'Scattered Seeds: A Dialogue of Diasporas', in David Biale, Michael Galchinsky, and Susannah Heschel (eds), *Insider/Outsider: American Jews and Multiculturalism* (Berkeley, 1998).

GAMPEL, BENJAMIN R., 'A Letter to a Wayward Teacher: The Transformations of Sephardic Culture in Christian Iberia', in David Biale (ed.), *Cultures of the Jews* (New York, 2002).

GANS, EDUARD, 'Drei Reden im Kulturverien' (1821); repr. in *Der judische Wille*, 1/1–3 (1919); trans. into Heb. in Paul R. Mendes-Flohr (ed.), *Modern Jewish Studies: Historical and Philosophical Perspectives* [Ḥokhmat yisra'el: hebetim historiyim ufilosofiyim] (Jerusalem, 1979).

GARCÍA-ARENAL, MERCEDES, and GERARD WIEGERS, *A Man of Three Worlds: Samuel Pallache, a Moroccan Jew in Catholic and Protestant Europe* (Baltimore, 2003).

GARTNER, LLOYD P., *The Jewish Immigrant in England, 1870–1914* (Detroit, 1960).

—— 'The Midpassage of American Jewry', in Jonathan Sarna (ed)., *The American Jewish Experience*, 2nd edn (New York, 1997).

GATES, HENRY LOUIS, JR., *Wonders of the African World* (New York, 1999).

GEIGER, A., *Das Judenthum und seine Geschichte bis zum Ende des zwölften Jahrhunderts* (Breslau, 1865).

—— *Das Judenthum und seine Geschichte bis zur Zerströrung des zweiten Tempels* (Breslau, 1865).

—— *Selected Writing on Religious Reform*, ed. M. A. Meyer, trans. G. Eliashberg (Jerusalem, 1979).

—— *Über den Austritt aus dem Judenthume. Ein aufefundener Briefwechsel* (Leipzig, 1858).

GELBER, MARK H. (ed.), *Confrontations/Accommodations: German-Jewish Literary and Cultural History from Heine to Wassermann* (Tübingen, 2004).

GERBER, S., 'History of the Jews in the Middle East and North Africa from the Rise of Islam until 1700', in Reeva Spector Simon, Michael Menachem Laskier, and Sara Reguer (eds), *The Jews of the Middle East and North Africa in Modern Times* (New York, 2003).

GILMAN, SANDER L., *Jews in Today's German Culture* (Bloomington, 1995).

—— and KAREN REMMLER (eds), *Reemerging Jewish Culture in Germany: Life and Literature since 1989* (New York, 1994).

GILMAN, SANDER L., and JACK ZIPES (eds), *Yale Companion to Jewish Writing and Thought in German Culture, 1096–1996* (New Haven, 1997).

GOFFMAN, DANIEL, *The Ottoman Empire and Early Modern Europe* (Cambridge, 2002).

GOITEIN, S. D., *From the Land of Sheba: Tales of the Jews of Yemen* (New York, 1947; rev. edn, 1973).

—— *Jews and Arabs: Their Contacts through the Ages* (New York, 1955).

—— *A Mediterranean Society*, i: *Economic Foundations* (Berkeley, 1967).

GOLDBERG, DAVID T., 'Introduction: Multicultural Conditions', in Goldberg (ed.), *Multiculturalism: A Critical Reader* (Cambridge, Mass. 1994).

GOLDBERG, HARVEY E., *Jewish Life in Muslim Libya: Rivals and Relatives* (Chicago, 1990).

—— 'Religious Responses among North African Jews in the Nineteenth and Twentieth Centuries', in Jack Wertheimer (ed.), *The Uses of Tradition: Jewish Continuity in the Modern Era* (New York, 1992).

—— (ed.), *Sephardi and Middle Eastern Jewries: History and Culture in the Modern Era* (Bloomington, Ind., 1996).

GOLDSCHMIDT, J. [ISRAEL], *Das Wesen des Judentums* (Frankfurt am Main, 1907).

GOLDSTEIN, MORITZ, 'Deutsch-jüdischer Parnass', *Der Kunstwart*, 25 (1912), 281–94.

—— 'German Jewry's Dilemma: The Story of a Provocative Essay', *Leo Baeck Institute Yearbook*, 2 (1957), 236–54.

GOLDSTEIN, SIDNEY, 'American Jews 1970: A Demographic Profile', in Marshall Sklare (ed.), *The Jew in American Society* (New York, 1974).

GOLDZIHER, IGNAZ, *Tagebuch* (Leiden, 1978).

GOMBRICH, E. H., *In Search of Cultural History* (Oxford, 1969).

GORDON, JUDAH LEIB, *Letters* [Igerot] (Warsaw, 1893).

GORDON, MILTON M., *Assimilation in American Life* (New York, 1964).

GOREN, ARTHUR, 'A Golden Decade for American Jews: 1945–1955', in Jonathan Sarna (ed)., *The American Jewish Experience*, 2nd edn (New York, 1997).

GRAETZ, HEINRICH, 'Correspondence of an English Lady', in Graetz, *The Structure of Jewish History and Other Essays.*

—— *Essays, Memoirs, Letters* [Darkhei hahistoriyah hayehudit], ed. Shmuel Ettinger (Jerusalem, 1969).

—— *Geschichte der Juden* (Berlin, 2002).

—— 'Historical Parallels in Jewish History', in Graetz, *The Structure of Jewish History and Other Essays.*

—— *History of the Jews*, 6 vols (Philadelphia, 1956; first pub. in Eng., 1891).

—— 'The Significance of Judaism for the Present and the Future (1889–1900)', in Graetz, *The Structure of Jewish History and Other Essays.*

—— *The Structure of Jewish History and Other Essays*, ed. and trans. Ismar Schorsch (New York, 1975).

GRAETZ, MICHAEL, *The Jews in Nineteenth-Century France: From the French Revolution to the Alliance Israélite Universelle*, trans. Jane Marie Todd (Stanford, Calif., 1996).

GRAFTON, ANTHONY, 'Germany and the West 1830–1900', in K. J. Dover (ed.), *Perceptions of Ancient Greece* (Oxford, 1992).

GRAMLEY, HEDDA, *Propheten des deutschen Nationalismus. Theologen, Historiker und Nationalökonomen 1848–1880* (Frankfurt am Main, 2001).

GRAUE, PAUL, *Deutsch-evangelisch* (Stuttgart, 1894).

—— *Unabhängiges Christentum* (Berlin, 1904).

GRAUPE, HEINZ MOSCHE, *Die Entstehung des Modernen Judentums. Geistgeschichte der deutschen Juden 1650–1942*, ii: *Revidierte und erwietere Aufgabe* (Hamburg, 1977).

GREENBERG, CHERYL, 'Pluralism and its Discontents: The Case of Blacks and Jews', in David Biale, Michael Galchinsky, and Susannah Heschel (eds), *Insider/Outsider: American Jews and Multiculturalism* (Berkeley, 1998).

GRIMM, GUNTER E., and HANS-PETER BAYERDÖRFER (eds), *Im Zeichen Hiobs. Jüdische Schriftsteller und deutsche Literatur im 20. Jahrhundert* (Königstein, 1985).

GRIMME, HUBERT, Review of A. Geiger, *Was hat Muhammed*, *Orientalistische Literatur-Zeitung*, 7 Jahrgang, no. 6 (June 1904), 226–8.

GRUNDMANN, WALTER, 'Das Heil kommt von den Juden. Eine Schicksalsfrage an die Christen deutscher Nation', *Deutsche Frömmigkeit*, 6 (Sept. 1938), 1–8.

—— 'Das Messiasproblem', in Grundmann (ed.), *Germanentum, Christentum und Judentum*, Studien zur Erforschung ihres gegenseitigen Verhältnisses, Sitzungsberichte der zweiten Arbeitstagung des Instituts zur Erforschung des jüdischen Einflusses auf das deutsche kirchliche Leben vom 3. bis 5. März 1941 in Eisenach (Leipzig, 1942).

—— and KARL FRIEDRICH EULER, *Das religiöse Gesicht des Judentums. Entstehung und Art* (Leipzig, 1942).

GÜDEMANN, M., 'Spirit and Letter in Judaism and Christianity', *Jewish Quarterly Review*, OS 4 (1892), 345–56.

GUROCK, JEFFREY S., 'From Exception to Role Model: Bernard Drachman and the Evolution of Jewish Religious Life in America, 1880–1920', *American Jewish History*, 76 (1986–7), 456–84.

—— *A Modern Heretic and a Traditional Community: Mordecai Kaplan, Orthodoxy and American Judaism* (New York, 1997).

GUSTAV, WEIL, *Biblische Legenden der Muselmänner. Aus arabischen Quellen zusammengetragen und mit jüdischen Sagen verglichen* (Frankfurt am Main, 1845).

GUSTAV, WEIL, *Historisch-kritische Einleitung in den Koran* (Bielefeld, 1844).

HABSHUSH, HAYYIM, *Travels in Yemen: An Account of Joseph Halevy's Journey to Najran in the Year 1870*, ed. S. D. Goitein (1939; Jerusalem, 1941).

HACKER, JOSEPH R., 'Ottoman Policy towards the Jews and Jewish Attitudes toward the Ottomans during the Fifteenth Century', in Benjamin Braude and Bernard Lewis (eds), *Christians and Jews in the Ottoman Empire*, 2 vols (New York, 1982), i, 117–26.

HAGNER, DONALD A., *The Jewish Reclamation of Jesus* (Grand Rapids, Mich., 1984).

HAHN, HUGO, *Kämpfer Wider Willen. Erinnerungen aus dem Kirchenkampf 1933–1945*, ed. Georg Prater (Metzingen,1969).

HALBERTAL, MOSHE, *Between Torah and Wisdom: Rabbi Menachem Hameiri and the Maimonidean Halakhists in Provence* [Bein torah leḥokhmah: rabi menaḥem hame'iri uva'alei hahalakhah hamaimunim beprovens] (Jerusalem, 2000).

HALÉVY, JOSEPH, 'La Religion des anciens babyloniens et son plus récent historien M. Sayce', *Revue de l'Histoire des Religions*, 9/1 (1888), 169–218.

HARISON, PETER, *Religion and the Religions in the English Enlightenment* (New York, 1990).

HARNACK, ADOLF, *Das Wesen des Christentums* (Leipzig, 1900).

HARRIS, JAY M. (ed.), *The Pride of Jacob: Essays on Jacob Katz and his Work* (Cambridge, Mass., 2002).

HARRISON, BRIAN, 'The Sunday Trading Riots of 1855', *Historical Journal*, 8 (1965), 219–45.

HARTMAN, GEOFFREY H., 'Introduction: Darkness Visible', in Hartman (ed.), *Holocaust Remembrance: The Shapes of Memory* (Oxford, 1994).

—— (ed.), *Bitburg in Moral and Political Perspective* (Bloomington, Ind., 1986).

HATHAWAY, JANE, 'Problems of Periodization in Ottoman History: The Fifteenth through the Eighteenth Centuries', *Turkish Studies Association Bulletin*, 20/2 (Fall 1996), 25–31.

—— 'Rewriting Eighteenth-Century Ottoman History', *Mediterranean Historical Review*, 19/1 (June 2004), 29–52.

HAYIM OF VOLOZHIN, *The Soul of Life* [Nefesh haḥayim] (Vilna, 1874).

HEINE, HEINRICH, 'Shakespeares Mädchen und Frauen', in Heine, *Sämtliche Werke*, x (Munich, 1964).

HERBERG, WILL, *Protestant, Catholic, Jew: An Essay in American Religious Sociology* (Garden City, NY, 1955).

HERMAND, JOST, *Judentum und deutsche Kultur. Beispiele einer schmerzhaften Symbiose* (Cologne, 1996).

HERMSDORF, KLAUS, 'Deutsch-jüdische Schriftsteller?', *Zeitschrift für Germanistik*, 3 (1982), 278–92.

HERTZ, J. H., 'The Battle for the Sabbath at Geneva', *Transactions of the Jewish Historical Society of* England, 13 (1932–5), 189–246.

—— 'Calendar Reform', *Jewish Guardian*, 6 Mar. 1925.

—— *Sermons, Addresses, and Studies*, 3 vols (London, 1938), ii. 265–92.

HERTZBERG, ARTHUR, *The Zionist Idea: A Historical Analysis and Reader* (New York, 1959).

HERZL, THEODOR, *The Complete Diaries*, ed. Raphael Patai, trans. Harry Zohn, i (New York, 1960).

HESCHEL, SUSANNAH, *Abraham Geiger and the Jewish Jesus* (Chicago, 1998).

—— 'Anti-Judaism in Christian Feminist Theology', *Tikkun*, 5/3 (1990), 25–8, 95–7.

—— 'Configurations of Patriarchy, Judaism and Nazism in German Feminist Thought', in Tamar Rudavsky (ed.), *Gender and Judaism* (New York, 1995).

—— 'Jewish Studies as Counterhistory', in David Biale, Michael Galchinsky, and Susannah Heschel (eds), *Insider/Outsider: American Jews and Multiculturalism* (Berkeley, 1998).

—— 'The Theological Faculty at the University of Jena as a "Stronghold of National Socialism"', in Uwe Hoßfeld, Jürgen John, and Rüdiger Stutz (ed.), *Kämpferische Wissenschaft. Studien zur Universität Jena im Nationalsozialismus* (Cologne, 2003).

—— 'When Jesus Was an Aryan: The Protestant Church and Antisemitic Propaganda', in Robert Ericksen and Susannah Heschel (ed.), *Betrayal: The German Churches and the Holocaust* (Minneapolis, 1999).

HESS, JONATHAN M., 'Johann David Michaelis and the Colonial Imaginary: Orientalism and the Emergence of Racial Antisemitism in Eighteenth-Century Germany', *Jewish Social Studies*, 6 (2001), 56–101.

HIRSCHBERG, H. Z., *A History of the Jews in North Africa* [Toledot hayehudim be'afrikah hatsefonit: hatefutsah hayehudit be'aretsot hamagreb mimei kodem ve'ad zemanenu], 2 vols (Leiden, 1974–81).

—— *Inside Maghreb: The Jews in North Africa* [Me'erets mevo hashemesh: im yehudei afrikah hatsefonit be'aretsoteihem] (Jerusalem, 1957).

HIRSCHFELD, HARTWIG, *Beiträgen zur Erklärung des Koran* (Leipzig, 1886).

—— 'Essai sur l'histoire des Juifs de Médine', 2 pts., *Revue des Études Juives*, 7 (1883), 167–93; 10 (1885), 10–31.

—— *Jüdische Elemente im Koran. Ein Beitrag zur Koranforschung* (Berlin, 1878).

HODGE, DAVID L., 'Domination and the Will in Western Thought and Culture', in John L. Hodge, Donald K. Struckmann, and Lynn Dorland Trost (eds), *Cultural Bases of Racism and Group Oppression* (Berkeley, 1975).

HODGSON, MARSHALL, *The Venture of Islam: Conscience and History in a World Civilization*, 3 vols (Chicago, 1974).

HORCH, HANS OTTO, 'Bravoroese Wissenschaft?', <http://www.literaturkritik.de/public/rezension.php?rez_id=7135>.

—— *Deutsch-jüdische Literatur*, Studienbrief. FernUniversitaet Gesamthochschule in Hagen, pts I and II (Hagen, 1995, 1998).

—— 'Was heisst und zu welchem Ende studiert man deutsch-jüdische Literaturgeschichte? Prolegomena zu einem Forschungsprojekt', *German Life and Letters*, NS 49/2 (1996), 124–35.

—— and ITTA SCHEDLETZKY, 'Die deutsch-jüdische Literature und ihre Geschichte', in Julius H. Schoeps (ed.), *Neues Lexikon des Judentums* (Gütersloh, 1992).

HOROWITZ, ELLIOTT, '*Jewish Life in the Middle Ages* and the Jewish Life of Israel Abrahams', in D. N. Myers and D. B. Ruderman (eds), *The Jewish Past Revisited: Reflections on Modern Jewish Historians* (New Haven, 1998).

HOROWITZ, SARA R., 'The Paradox of Jewish Studies in the New Academy', in David Biale, Michael Galchinsky, and Susannah Heschel (eds), *Insider/Outsider: American Jews and Multiculturalism* (Berkeley, 1998).

HOURANI, ALBERT, *Islam in European Thought* (Cambridge, 1991).

HUFFMON, H. B., '*Babel und Bibel*: The Encounter between Babylon and the Bible', in M. P. O'Connor and D. N. Freedman (eds), *Backgrounds for the Bible* (Winona Lake, Ind., 1987).

HUNNICUTT, B. K., 'The Jewish Sabbath Movement in the Early Twentieth Century', *American Jewish Historical Quarterly*, 69 (1979–80), 196–225.

HUNTINGTON, SAMUEL P., *The Clash of Civilizations and the Remaking of World Order* (New York, 1996).

INALCIK, HALIL, 'Foundations of Ottoman–Jewish Cooperation', in Avigdor Levy (ed.), *Jews, Turks, Ottomans: As Shared History, Fifteenth through the Twentieth Century* (Syracuse, NY, 2002).

—— 'The Heyday and Decline of the Ottoman Empire', in P. M. Holt, Ann K. S. Lambton, and Bernard Lewis (eds), *The Cambridge History of Islam*, 2 vols, i: *The Central Islamic Lands* (Cambridge, 1970).

ISENBERG, NOAH, ' Developments in German Jewish Studies from 1980 to the Present', in Peter Uwe Hohendahl (ed.), *German Studies in the United States* (New York, 2003).

ISRAEL, JONATHAN I., *European Jewry in the Age of Mercantilism, 1550–1750* (Oxford, 1985).

JABOTINSKY, ZE'EV, 'The East' (Heb.), first pub. in Russian in *Razsvet*, 26 Sept. 1926.

—— 'An Exchange of Compliments', in Jabotinsky, *Nation and Society* [Umah veḥevrah] (Jerusalem, 1950).

—— 'Jews and Russian Literature', in Jabotinsky, *On Literature and Art* [Al sifrut ve'omanut] (Jerusalem, 1948), 61–8.

JACOB, WALTER, *Christianity through Jewish Eyes: The Quest for Common Ground* (Cincinnati, 1974).

JACOBS, JOSEPH, *Jewish Contributions to Civilization: An Estimate* (Philadelphia, 1919, 1920).

JASPER, WILLI, *Deutsch-jüdischer Parnass. Literaturgeschichte eines Mythos* (Berlin, 2004).

JASTROW, MARCUS, 'The Hebrew and Babylonian Accounts of Creation', *Jewish Quarterly Review*, OS 8 (1901), 620–54.

—— *Hebrew and Babylonian Traditions* (New York, 1914).

—— 'The Original Character of the Hebrew Sabbath', *American Journal of Theology*, 2 (1898), 312–52.

JOSEPH, M., *Judaism as Creed and Life*, 2nd edn (London, 1910).

KAFFANKE, EVA-MARIA, *Der deutsche Heiland. Christusdarstellungen um 1900 im Kontext der völkischen Bewegung* (Frankfurt am Main, 2001).

KALLEN, HORACE, *Culture and Democracy in the United States* (New York, 1924).

—— 'The Melting Pot and Beyond: Jews and the Politics of American Identity', in David Biale, Michael Galchinsky, and Susannah Heschel (eds), *Insider/Outsider: American Jews and Multiculturalism* (Berkeley, 1998).

KALMAR, IVAN, and DEREK PENSLAR (eds), *Orientalism and the Jews* (Waltham, Mass., 2004).

KAMEN, HENRY, 'The Decline of Spain: A Historical Myth?', *Past and Present*, 81 (Nov. 1978), 24–50.

—— *The Spanish Inquisition* (New Haven, 1997).

KAMINER, VLADIMIR, *Russendisko. Mein deutsches Dschungelbuch* (Munich, 2000).

KAPLAN, MORDECAI M., 'The Contribution of Judaism to World Ethics', in Louis Finkelstein (ed.), *The Jews: Their History, Culture, and Religion* (Philadelphia, 1949; 4th edn, 3 vols (New York, 1970).

—— *Judaism as a Civilization: Toward a Reconstruction of American-Jewish Life* (New York, 1934; enlarged edn (New York, 1957).

—— Preface to *Judaism as a Civilization: Toward a Reconstruction of American-Jewish Life* (Philadelphia, 1967; repr. 1981).

KAPLAN, YOSEF, *An Alternative Path to Modernity: The Sephardi Diaspora in Western Europe* (Leiden, 2000).

—— 'Bom Judesmo: The Western Sephardic Diaspora', in David Biale (ed.), *Cultures of the Jews: A New History* (New York, 2002).

—— 'Political Concepts in the World of the Portuguese Jews of Amsterdam during the Seventeenth Century: The Problem of Exclusion and the Boundaries of Self-Identity', in Yosef Kaplan, Henry Méchoulan, and Richard Popkin (eds), *Menasseh ben Israel and his World* (Leiden, 1989).

KAPLAN, YOSEF, 'The Self-Definition of the Sephardic Jews of Western Europe and their Relation to the Alien and the Stranger', in Benjamin R. Gampel (ed.), *Crisis and Creativity in the Sephardic World, 1391–1648* (New York, 1997).

KATZ, DAVID S., *Philo-Semitism and the Readmission of the Jews to England, 1603–1655* (Oxford, 1982).

—— *Sabbath and Sectarianism in Seventeenth-Century England* (Oxford, 1988).

KATZ, JACOB, *Exclusiveness and Tolerance: Jewish–Gentile Relations in Medieval and Modern Times* (Oxford, 1961).

—— 'German Culture and the Jews', in Jehuda Reinharz and Walter Schatzberg (eds), *The Jewish Response to German Culture: From the Enlightenment to the Second World War* (Hanover, NH, 1985).

—— 'Traditional Jewish Society and Modern Society', in Shlomo Deshen and Walter P. Zenner (eds), *Jews among Muslims: Communities in the Precolonial Middle East* (Houndmills, 1996).

—— *Tradition and Crisis: Jewish Society at the End of the Middle Ages*, trans. and with afterword by Bernard D. Cooperman (New York, 1993; first pub. as *Masoret umashber: Haḥevrah hayehudit bemotsa'ei yemei habeinayim*, Jerusalem, 1958).

—— *With My Own Eyes: The Autobiography of a Historian*, trans. Ann Brenner and Zipora Brody (Hanover, NH, 1995).

KAUFMANN, YEHEZKEL, *Exile and Alien Lands* [Golah venekhar] (Tel Aviv, 1929).

KAZAL, RUSSELL A., 'Revisiting Assimilation: The Rise, Fall, and Reappraisal of a Concept in American Ethnic History', *American Historical Review*, 100 (Apr. 1995), 437–71.

KAZENELSON, SIEGMUND, *Juden im deutschen Kulturbereich*, 2nd edn (Berlin, 1959).

KENT, C. F., *Israel's Laws and Legal Precedents: From the Days of Moses to the Closing of the Legal Canon* (New York, 1907).

KILCHER, ANDREAS B., 'Einleitung', in Kilcher (ed.), *Metzler Lexikon der deutsch-jüdischen Literatur* (Stuttgart, 2000).

—— 'Was ist deutsch-jüdische Literatur? Eine historische Diskursanalyse', *Weimarer Beiträge*, 45 (1999), 485–517.

—— and OTFRIED FRAISSE (eds), *Metzler Lexikon jüdischer Philosophen* (Stuttgart, 2003).

KING, KAREN, *What Is Gnosticism?* (Cambridge, Mass., 2003).

KIRSCHSTEIN, ARTHUR J., *The Jew: His Contribution to Modern Civilization* (Denver, 1930).

KLAUSNER, JOSEPH, *History of the Second Temple* [Historiyah shel habayit hasheni], 2nd edn, 5 vols (Jerusalem, 1951).

—— *From Jesus to Paul* [Miyeshu ad polus] (Tel Aviv, 1940).

KOHLER, K., 'Assyriology and the Bible', *Yearbook of the Central Conference of American Rabbis*, 13 (1903), 110–11.

KONVITZ, MILTON R., 'Judaism and the Democratic Idea', in Louis Finkelstein (ed.), *The Jews: Their History, Culture and Religion* (New York, 1949), 1092–1113.

KRAUSS, SAMUEL, 'The Jews in the Works of the Church Fathers', *Jewish Quarterly Review*, os 5 (1892), 122–57; 6 (1894), 82–99, 225–61.

KREMER, S. LILLIAN, Introduction to Kremer (ed.), *Holocaust Literature*, i (New York, 2003).

KROJANKER, GUSTAV (ed.), *Juden in der deutschen Literatur* (Berlin, 1922).

KUPER, ADAM, *Culture: The Anthropologists' Account* (Cambridge, Mass., 1999).

KUROKAWA, MINAKO (ed.), *Minority Responses* (New York, 1970).

KWIET, KONRAD, GUNTER E. GRIMM, and HANS-PETER BAYERDÖRFER, 'Einleitung', in Grimm and Bayerdörfer (eds), *Im Zeichen Hiobs. Jüdische Schriftsteller und deutsche Literatur im 20. Jahrhundert* (Königstein, 1985).

LAMPING, DIETER, *Von Kafka bis Celan. Jüdischer Diskurs in der deutschen Literatur des 20. Jahrhunderts* (Göttingen, 1998).

LANDAU, J. L., *Judaism in Life and Literature* (London, 1936).

—— 'The Sabbath', in H. Newman (ed.), *The Real Jew: Some Aspects of the Jewish Contribution to Civilization* (London, 1925); repr. in Landau, *Judaism in Life and Literature* (London, 1936).

LANGDON, STEPHEN, 'Archibald Henry Sayce as Assyriologist', *Journal of the Royal Asiatic Society of Great Britain and Ireland for 1933* (1933), 499–503.

LARSEN, M. T., 'The "Babel/Bibel" Controversy and its Aftermath', in Jack Sasson (ed.), *Civilizations of the Ancient Near East*, i (New York, 1995).

LASKI, NEVILLE, *The Jewish Contribution to Civilization* (Cardiff, 1937).

LASKIER, MICHAEL M., *The Alliance Israélite Universelle and the Jewish Communities of Morocco, 1862–1962* (Albany, NY, 1983).

LAUTERBACH, J. Z., *Rabbinic Essays* (Cincinnati, 1951).

LAVENDAR, ABRAHAM D., 'Arabic-Islamic and Spanish Mediterranean Influences on "the Jewish Mind": A Comparison to European-Christian Influence', *Journal of Ethnic Studies*, 8/4 (1981), 25–35.

LAZARUS, MORITZ, *Die Ethik des Judentums* (Frankfurt am Main, 1898, 1911); trans. Henrietta Szold as *The Ethics of Judaism in Four Parts* (Philadelphia, 1900–1).

LECKY, W. E. H., *Democracy and Liberty*, 2 vols (New York, 1896).

LEFFLER, SIEGFRIED, *Christus im Dritten Reich der Deutschen. Wesen, Weg und Zielsetzung der Kirchenbewegung Deutsche Christen* (Weimar, 1935).

LERNER, DANIEL, *The Passing of Traditional Society* (New York, 1958).

LEROY-BEAULIEU, ANATOLE, *Israel among the Nations: A Study of Jews and Antisemitism*, trans. Frances Hellmann (New York, 1895).

LEUTHEUSER, JULIUS, *Die deutsche Christusgemeinde* (Weimar, 1935).

LEVINE, ROBERT A., and DONALD T. CAMPBELL, *Ethnocentrism: Theories of Conflict, Ethnic Attitudes, and Group Behavior* (New York, 1972).

LEVINSOHN, I. B., *The Book of Ahiyah Hashiloni the Visionary* [Sefer aḥiyah hashiloni heḥozeh] (Leipzig, 1839).

LEVY, AVIGDOR, *The Sephardim in the Ottoman Empire* (Princeton, 1992).

LEWIS, BERNARD, *The Crisis of Islam: Holy War and Unholy Terror* (New York, 2003).

—— *The Jews of Islam* (Princeton, 1984).

—— 'The Pro-Islamic Jews', *Judaism*, 17 (1968), 391–404.

—— *What Went Wrong? Western Impact and Middle Eastern Response* (New York, 2002).

LIBERLES, ROBERT, *Salo Wittmayer Baron: Architect of Jewish History* (New York, 1995).

LINDESKOG, GOSTA, *Die Jesusfrage im neuzeitlichen Judentum. Ein Beitrag zur Geschichte der Leben-Jesu-Forschung* (Uppsala, 1938).

LIPMAN, V. D., *Social History of the Jews in England, 1850–1950* (London, 1954)

LIPTZIN, SOL, *Germany's Stepchildren* (Philadelphia, 1944; repr. 1961).

LOW, ALFRED D., *Jews in the Eyes of the Germans: From the Enlightenment to Imperial Germany* (Philadelphia, 1979).

LOWENSTEIN, STEVEN M., 'Jewish Participation in German Culture', in Michael A. Meyer (ed.), *German-Jewish History in Modern Times*, iii: *Integration in Dispute 1871–1918* (New York, 1996–8).

LUZZATTO, SIMONE, *Discorso circa il stato de gl'hebrei: Et in particolar dimoranti nell'inclita città di Venetia* (Venice, 1638).

LYOTARD, JEAN-FRANÇOIS, *Heidegger and 'the Jews'*, trans. A. Michel and M. S. Roberts (Minneapolis, 1990).

MALINOVICH, NADIA, 'Orientalism and the Construction of Jewish Identity in France, 1900–1932', *Jewish Culture and History*, 2/1 (1999), 1–25.

MANASSEH B. ISRAEL, *Menasseh ben Israel's Mission to Oliver Cromwell: Being a reprint of the pamphlets published by Menasseh ben Israel to promote the re-admission of the Jews to England, 1649–1656*, ed. Lucien Wolf [London, 1901].

MANN, VIVIAN B., THOMAS F. GLICK, and JERRILYNN D. DODDS (eds), *Convivencia: Jews, Muslims, and Christians in Medieval Spain* (New York, 1992).

MARCHAND, SUZANNE, 'Philhellenism and the *Furor Orientalis*', *Modern Intellectual History*, 1 (Nov. 2004), 331–58.

MARCUS, IVAN G., 'Beyond the Sephardic Mystique', *Orim*, 1 (1985), 35–8.

MARTI, K., *The Religion of the Old Testament*, trans. G. A. Bienemann (London, 1907).

MAYBAUM, IGNAZ, *Synagogue and Society: Jewish Christian Collaboration in Defence of Western Civilisation* (London, 1944).

MAYER, HANS, *Aussenseiter* (Frankfurt am Main, 1975).

MEEK, T. J., 'The Sabbath in the Old Testament', *Journal of Biblical Literature*, 33 (1914), 201–12.

MEINHOLD, JOHANNES, *Sabbat und Woche im Alten Testament* (Göttingen, 1905).

MENDES-FLOHR, PAUL R., 'Fin de Siècle Orientalism, the Ostjuden, and the Aesthetics of Jewish Self Affirmation', in Mendes-Flohr, *Divided Passions: Jewish Intellectuals and the Experience of Modernity* (Detroit, 1991).

—— *German Jews: A Dual Identity* (New Haven, 1999).

—— and JEHUDA REINHARZ (eds), *The Jew in the Modern World: A Documentary History* (Oxford and New York, 1980; repr. 1995).

MENOCAL, MARIA ROSA, *The Ornament of the World: How Muslims, Jews, and Christians Created a Culture of Tolerance in Medieval Spain* (Boston, 2002).

MEYER, MICHAEL A., *The Origins of the Modern Jew: Jewish Identity and European Culture in Germany* (Detroit, 1967).

—— *Response of Modernity: A History of the Reform Movement in Judaism* (New York, 1988).

MEYERSON, MARK D., *A Jewish Renaissance in Fifteenth-Century Spain* (Princeton, 2004).

MICHAEL, REUVEN, *Heinrich Graetz: The Historian of the Jewish People* [Heinrikh grets: hahistoriyon shel ha'am hayehudi] (Jerusalem, 2003).

MICHMAN, DAN, 'A Third Partner of World Jewry? The Role of Memory of the Shoah in the Search for a New Present-Day European Jewish Identity', in Konrad Kwiet and Jurgen Matthaus (eds), *Contemporary Responses to the Holocaust* (Westport, Conn., 2004).

MODENA, LEON, *Historia degli riti hebraici* (Paris, 1637).

MONTEFIORE, C. G., *The Bible for Home Reading*, 2 vols (London, 1909).

—— 'Notes on the Religious Value of the Fourth Gospel', *Jewish Quarterly Review*, OS 7 (1895), 24–74.

—— *The Synoptic Gospels* (first pub. 1927; New York, 1968).

MOORE, DEBORAH DASH, *At Home in America: Second Generation New York Jews* (New York, 1981).

—— *To the Golden Cities: Pursuing the American Dream in Miami and L.A.* (New York, 1994).

MOORE, G. F., *Judaism in the First Centuries of the Christian Era*, 3 vols (Cambridge, Mass., 1927–30).

—— 'Solomon Schechter: Scholar and Humanist', *Menorah Journal*, 2 (1916), 1–6.

MORRIS, LESLIE, and KAREN REMMLER (eds), *Contemporary Jewish Writing in Germany: An Anthology* (Lincoln, Nebr., 2002).

MOSES, STÉPHANE, and ALBRECHT SCHÖNE (eds), *Juden in der deutschen Literatur*, proceedings of a symposium, Zur deutsch-jüdischen Literaturgeschichte, the Hebrew University, Jerusalem, 1983 (Frankfurt am Main, 1986).

MOSSE, GEORGE L., *The Crisis of German Ideology: The Intellectual Origins of the Third Reich* (New York, 1964).

—— *German Jews beyond Judaism* (Bloomington, Ind., 1985).

—— *Die völkische Revolution. Über die geistigen Wurzeln des Nationalsozialismus* (Frankfurt am Main, 1991).

MYERS, DAVID N., *Reinventing the Jewish Past* (New York, 1995).

NEUSNER, JACOB, '"Judaism" after Moore: A Programmatic Statement', *Journal of Jewish Studies*, 31 (1980), 141–56.

New German Critique, 90, special issue: *Taboo, Trauma, Holocaust* (2003).

New German Critique, 91, special issue: *Paul Celan* (2004).

NEWMAN, AMY, 'The Idea of Judaism in Feminism and Afrocentrism', in David Biale, Michael Galchinsky, and Susannah Heschel (eds), *Insider/Outsider: American Jews and Multiculturalism* (Berkeley, 1998).

NEWMAN, H. (ed.), *The Real Jew: Some Aspects of the Jewish Contribution to Civilization* (London, 1925).

NIETZSCHE, FRIEDRICH, *Beyond Good and Evil*, ed. Walter Kaufman (New York, 1989).

—— *The Dawn of Days*, trans. J. M. Kennedy (New York, 1964).

NIPPERDEY, THOMAS, *Religion im Umbruch. Deutschland 1870–1918* (Munich, 1988).

NIRENBERG, DAVID, *Communities of Violence: Persecution of Minorities in the Middle Ages* (Princeton, 1996).

NOLDEN, THOMAS, *Junge jüdische Literatur* (Würzburg, 1995).

OBELKEVICH, JAMES, 'Religion', in F. M. L. Thompson (ed.), *The Cambridge Social History of Britain, 1750–1950*, 3 vols (Cambridge, 1990), iii.

O'DOCHARTAIGH, POL (ed.), *Jews in German Literature since 1945: German-Jewish Literature?* (Amsterdam, 2000).

OLENDER, MAURICE, *The Languages of Paradise: Race, Religion and Philology in the Nineteenth Century*, trans. Arthur Goldhammer (Cambridge, Mass., 1992).

OWEN, ROGER, review of *The Cambridge History of Islam*, *Journal of Interdisciplinary History*, 4 (1973), 287–98.

PAMUK, SEVKET, 'The Ottoman Empire in the Eighteenth Century', *Itinerario*, 24/3–4 (2000), 104–15.

PARET, RUDI, *The Study of Arabic and Islam at German Universities: German Orientalists since Theodor Nöldeke* (Wiesbaden, 1968).

PASTO, JAMES, 'Islam's "Strange Secret Sharer": Orientalism, Judaism, and the Jewish Question', *Comparative Studies in Society and History*, 40 (1998), 437–74.

PATAI, RAPHAEL, *Ignaz Goldziher and his Oriental Diary* (Detroit, 1987).

PELIKAN, JAROSLAV, 'Judaism and the Humanities', in Shaye J. D. Cohen and Edward L. Greenstein (eds), *The State of Jewish Studies* (Detroit, 1990).

PERLES, FELIX, *Boussets 'Religion des Judentums im neutestamentalischen Zeitalter kritisch untersucht'* (Berlin, 1903).

PETERS, MADISON C., *Justice to the Jew: The Story of What He Has Done for the World* (New York, 1921).

PFLEIDERER, OTTO, *Das deutsche Nationalbewußtsein in Vergangenheit und Gegenwart. Rede zur Feier des Geburtstages Seiner Majestät des Kaisers und Königs am 27. Januar 1893* (Berlin, 1895).

PINTO, DIANA, 'The Jewish Challenges in the New Europe', in Daniel Levy and Yfaat Weiss (eds), *Challenging Ethnic Citizenship: German and Israeli Perspectives on Immigration* (New York, 2002).

—— *A New Identity for Post-1989 Europe*, JPR/Policy Paper 1 (London, 1996).

—— 'The New Jewish Europe: Challenges and Responsibilities', *European Judaism*, 31/2 (1998), 1–15.

PITERBERG, GABRIEL, 'Domestic Orientalism: The Representation of "Oriental" Jews in Zionist/Israeli Historiography', *British Journal of Middle Eastern Studies*, 23 (1996), 125–45.

PUSCHNER, UWE, *Handbuch zur völkischen Bewegung, 1871–1918*, ed. Uwe Puschner, Walter Schmitz, and Justus H. Ulbright (Munich, 1996).

—— *Die völkische Bewegung im wilhelminischen Kaiserreich. Sprache—Rasse—Religion* (Darmstadt, 2001).

RABINBACH, ANSON G., and JACK ZIPES, 'Lessons of the Holocaust', *New German Critique*, 19 (1980), 3–7.

RABINOWITZ, JACOB J., 'The Influence of Jewish Law on the Development of the Common Law', in Louis Finkelstein (ed.), *The Jews: Their History, Culture, and Religion* (Philadelphia, 1949; 4th edn, 3 vols (New York, 1970).

RAJAK, TESSA, 'Jews and Greeks: The Invention and Exploitation of Polarities in the Nineteenth Century', in Rajak, *The Jewish Dialogue with Greece and Rome: Studies in Cultural and Social Interaction* (Leiden, 2001).

RAPHÄEL, FREDDY, *Judaïsme et capitalisme: Essai sur la controverse entre Max Weber et Werner Sombart* (Paris, 1982).

RAVID, BENJAMIN C. I., *Economics and Toleration in Seventeenth Century Venice: The Background and Context of the 'Discorso' of Simone Luzzatto* (Jerusalem, 1978).

—— '"How profitable the nation of the Jewes are": The *Humble Addresses* of Menasseh ben Israel and the *Discorso* of Simone Luzzatto', in Jehuda

Reinharz and Daniel Swetchinski (eds), *Mystics, Philosophers, and Politicians: Essays in Jewish Intellectual History in Honor of Alexander Altmann* (Durham, NC, 1982).

REARDON, BERNARD, *Liberalism and Tradition: Aspects of Catholic Thought in Nineteenth-Century France* (Cambridge, 1975).

REICH-RANICKI, MARCEL, *Über Ruhestörer. Juden in der deutschen Literatur* (Munich, 1973).

REID, D. A., 'Playing and Praying', in M. Daunton (ed.), *The Cambridge Urban History of Britain*, iii (Cambridge, 2000).

REINHARZ, JEHUDA, 'The Response of the Zionistische Vereinigung für Deutschland and the Centralverein deutscher Staatsbürger jüdischen Glaubens to Antisemitism during the Weimar Republic' (Heb.), in Abraham Margaliot and Yehoyakim Cohavi (eds), *History of the Holocaust: Germany* (Jerusalem, 1998).

—— and SCHATZBERG, WALTER (eds), *The Jewish Response to German Culture*, proceedings of an international conference held at Clark University, 1983 (Hanover, NH, 1985).

REMMLER, KAREN, 'The "Third Generation" of Jewish-German Writers after the Shoah Emerges in Germany and Austria', in Sander Gilman and Jack Zipes (eds), *Yale Companion to Jewish Writing and Thought in German Culture, 1096–1996* (New Haven, 1997).

RENAN, ERNEST, *Histoire générale et système comparé des langues sémitiques*, 5th edn (Paris, 1893).

—— *Œuvres complètes*, ed. Henriette Psichari, 10 vols (Paris, 1947–61).

RICHTER, I. A. L., 'Worin lag die vorzügliche Kultur der Greichen?', *Sulamith*, 1 (1806), 125–47.

RIDLEY, JANE, *The Young Disraeli* (London, 1995).

ROBACK, ABRAHAM A., *Jewish Influence in Modern Thought* (Cambridge, Mass., 1929).

ROBERTSON, RITCHIE, *The 'Jewish Question' in German Literature 1749–1939* (Oxford, 1999).

RODINSON, MAXIME, *Europe and the Mystique of Islam* (Seattle, 1987).

—— 'The Western Image and Western Studies of Islam', in Joseph Schacht and C. E. Bosworth (eds), *The Legacy of Islam* (Oxford, 1974).

RODRIGUE, ARON, *French Jews, Turkish Jews: The Alliance Israélite Universelle and the Politics of Jewish Schooling in Turkey, 1860–1925* (Bloomington, Ind., 1990).

ROSENZWEIG, FRANZ, 'Atheistic Theology: From the Old to the New Way of Thinking', trans. Robert G. Goldy and H. Frederick Holch, *Canadian Journal of Theology*, 14/2 (1968), 79–88.

ROSMAN, MOSHE, 'Defining the Post-Modern Period in Jewish History', in Eli Lederhendler and Jack Wertheimer (eds), *Text and Context: Essays in*

Modern Jewish History and Historiography in Honor of Ismar Schorsch (New York, 2005).

—— 'Hybrid with What? The Variable Contexts of Polish Jewish Culture: Their Implications for Jewish Cultural History and Jewish Studies', in Yaron Eliav and Anita Norich (eds), *Jewish Cultures and Literatures* (Providence, RI, 2007).

ROTH, CECIL, *Benjamin Disraeli: Earl of Beaconsfield* (New York, 1952).

—— *The Jewish Contribution to Civilization* (Eng. edn, first pub. London, 1938; New York, 1940; 2nd edn, Oxford, 1943).

—— *The Jews in the Renaissance* (Philadelphia, 1959).

ROTH, LEON, *Jewish Thought as a Factor in Civilization* (Paris, 1954).

ROTH, NORMAN, *Conversos, Inquisition and the Expulsion of the Jews from Spain* (Madison, 1995).

—— 'The Jews in Spain in the Time of Maimonides', in Eric L. Ormsby (ed.), *Moses Maimonides and his Time* (Washington, DC, 1989).

ROUBEY, LESTER W., 'Simeone Luzzatto's *Discorso* (1638): An Early Contribution to Apologetic Literature', *Journal of Reform Judaism*, 28 (1981), 57–63.

ROZEN, MINNA, 'The Leghorn Merchants in Tunis and their Trade with Marseilles at the End of the Seventeenth Century', in Jean-Louis Miège (ed.), *Les Relations intercommunautaires juives en Méditerranée occidentale, XIIIe–XXe siècles* (Paris, 1984).

RUDERMAN, DAVID B., 'Cecil Roth, Historian of Italian Jewry: A Reassessment', in David N. Myers and David B. Ruderman (eds), *The Jewish Past Revisited: Reflections on Modern Jewish Historians* (New Haven, 1998).

RUNES, DAGOBERT D., *The Hebrew Impact on Western Civilization*, abr. edn (New York, 1951).

SAID, EDWARD W., *Orientalism* (New York, 1978).

SANDERS, E. P., *Paul and Palestinian Judaism: A Comparison of Patterns of Religion* (Philadelphia, 1977).

SARNA, JONATHAN, *American Judaism* (New Haven, 2004).

SAYCE, A. H., *Assyria: Its Princes, Priests, and Peoples*, 2nd edn (London, 1926).

—— *Babylonians and Assyrians: Life and Customs* (London, 1899).

—— *Lectures on the Origin and Growth of Religion as Illustrated by the Religion of the Ancient Babylonians* (London, 1887).

—— *The Religion of Egypt and Babylonia* (Edinburgh, 1902).

—— *Reminiscences* (London, 1923).

—— *Social Life among the Assyrians and Babylonians* (London, 1893).

SCHAPIRO, ISRAEL, *Die haggadischen Elemente im erzählenden Teil des Korans*, i (Leipzig, 1907).

SCHAUSS, HAYYIM, *The Jewish Festivals: From their Beginnings to our Own Day*, trans. Samuel Jaffe (New York, 1938).

SCHECHTER, RONALD, *Obstinate Hebrews: Representations of Jews in France, 1715–1815* (Berkeley, 2003).

SCHECHTER, SOLOMON, 'Higher Criticism—Higher Anti-Semitism', in Schechter, *Seminary Addresses and Other Papers*, ed. Louis Finkelstein (New York, 1959).

—— 'The Law and Recent Criticism', *Jewish Quarterly Review*, OS 3 (1891), 754–66; repr. slightly rev. in Schechter, *Studies in Judaism*, i (Philadelphia, 1896).

SCHNEIDER, GEORG, *Der Heiland Deutsch. Eine gegenwartsnahe Darleitung der Botschaft Jesu* (Stuttgart, 1935).

SCHOLEM, GERSHOM, *On Jews and Judaism in Crisis: Selected Essays*, ed. Werner J. Dannhauser (New York, 1976).

SCHORSCH, ISMAR, 'From Messianism to Realpolitik: Menasseh ben Israel and the Readmission of the Jews to England', *Proceedings of the American Academy for Jewish Research*, 45 (1978), 187–209.

—— *Jewish Reactions to German Anti-Semitism, 1870–1914* (New York, 1972).

—— 'The Myth of Sephardic Superiority', *Leo Baeck Institute Year Book*, 34 (1989), 47–66.

—— 'The Place of Jewish Studies in Contemporary Scholarship', in Shaye J. D. Cohen and Edward L. Greenstein (eds), *The State of Jewish Studies* (Detroit, 1990).

SCHRADER, EBERHARD, *Die Keilinschriften und das Alte Testament*, ed. H. Zimmern and H. Winckler, 3rd edn (Berlin, 1903).

SCHROETER, DANIEL J., 'A Different Road to Modernity: Jewish Identity in the Arab World', in Howard Wettstein (ed.), *Diasporas and Exiles: Varieties of Jewish Identity* (Berkeley, 2002).

—— 'Orientalism and the Jews of the Mediterranean', *Journal of Mediterranean Studies*, 4/2 (1994), 183–96.

—— 'Royal Power and the Economy in Precolonial Morocco: Jews and the Legitimation of Foreign Trade', in Rahma Bourqia and Susan Gilson Miller (eds), *In the Shadow of the Sultan: Culture, Power, and Politics in Morocco* (Cambridge, Mass., 1999).

—— *The Sultan's Jew: Morocco and the Sephardi World* (Stanford, 2002).

SCHULMAN, KALMAN, *History of the World* [Divrei yemei olam], iv (Vilna, 1867).

SCHÜTZ, HANS, *Juden in der deutschen Literatur. Eine deutsch-jüdische Literaturgeschichte im Überblick* (Munich, 1992).

SCHWARTZ, A., 'Intermarriage in the United States' in Marshall Sklare (ed.), *The Jew in American Society* (New York, 1974), 307–31.

—— *The Jews: Social Patterns of an American Group* (Glencoe, Ill., 1958).

SCHWARZ, EGON, 'Der "Beitrag" der Juden zur deutschen Literatur', *Literatur und Kritik*, 229–30 (1988), 385–401.

SEBAG, PAUL, *Histoire des Juifs de Tunisie: Des origines à nos jours* (Paris, 1991).

SHAVIT, YAACOV, *Athens in Jerusalem: Classical Antiquity and Hellenism in the Making of the Modern Secular Jew*, trans. Chaya Naor and Niki Werner (London, 1997).

—— 'Have Jews Imagination? Jews and the Creative Arts', in Shavit, *Athens in Jerusalem: Classical Antiquity and Hellenism in the Making of the Modern Secular Jew* (London, 1999).

—— *History in Black: African-Americans in Search of an Ancient Past* (London, 2001).

—— and MORDECAI ERAN, *The War of the Tablets: The Defence of the Bible in the 19th Century and the Babel–Bibel Controversy* [Milḥemet haluḥot: hahaganah al hamikra bame'ah hatesha esreh upolmos bavel vehatanakh] (Tel Aviv, 2003).

SHAW, STANFORD J., *The Jews of the Ottoman Empire and the Turkish Republic* (New York, 1991).

SHOHAT, ELLA, 'Rupture and Return: Zionist Discourse and the Study of Arab Jews', *Social Text* 75, 21/2 (Summer 2003), 49–74.

SHWARTZ, SHULY RUBIN, *The Emergence of Jewish Scholarship in America: The Publication of the Jewish Encyclopedia* (Cincinnati, 1991).

SILBER, MICHAEL K., 'The Emergence of Ultra-Orthodoxy: The Invention of a Tradition', in Jack Wertheimer (ed.), *The Uses of Tradition: Jewish Continuity in the Modern Era* (New York, 1992).

SILBERSTEIN, LAURENCE J., 'Benign Transmission versus Conflicted Discourse: Jewish Studies and the Crisis of the Humanities', *Soundings*, 74 (1991), 485–507.

—— 'Mapping, Not Tracing: Opening Reflection', in Silberstein (ed.), *Mapping Jewish Identities* (New York, 2000).

—— 'Others Within and Others Without: Rethinking Jewish Identity and Culture', in Laurence J. Silberstein and Robert L. Cohn (eds), *The Other in Jewish Thought and History: Constructions of Jewish Culture and Identity* (New York, 1994).

SIMON, ROBERT, *Ignac Goldziher: His Life and Scholarship as Reflected in his Works and Correspondence* (Leiden, 1986).

SINGER, CHARLES and DOROTHEA, 'The Jewish Factor in Medieval Thought', in Edwyn R. Bevan and Charles Singer (eds), *The Legacy of Israel* (Oxford, 1927).

SMITH, G., *Assyrian Discoveries: An Account of the Explorations and Discoveries on the Site of Nineveh*, 2nd edn (London, 1875).

SMITH, W. ROBERTSON, and S. A. COOK, 'Sabbath', in *Encyclopaedia Britannica*, 11th edn, xxiii (Cambridge, 1911).

SOMBART, WERNER, *Die Juden und das Wirtschaftsleben* (Leipzig, 1911).

SORIN, GERALD, *The Prophetic Minority: American Jewish Immigrant Radicals, 1880–1920* (Bloomington, Ind., 1985).

SORKIN, DAVID, *The Transformation of German Jewry, 1780–1840* (New York, 1987).

SPENGLER, OSWALD, *The Decline of the West*, trans. Charles Francis Atkinson (New York, 1926).

STARR, D. B., 'The Importance of Being Frank: Solomon Schechter's Departure from Cambridge', *Jewish Quarterly Review*, 94 (2004), 12–18.

STEIN, SARAH ABREVAYA, *Making Jews Modern: Yiddish and Ladino Newspapers of the Russian and Ottoman Empire* (Bloomington, Ind., 2003).

—— 'Sephardi and Middle Eastern Jewries since 1492', in Martin Goodman (ed.), *The Oxford Handbook of Jewish Studies* (Oxford, 2002), 327–62.

STERN, DAVID, 'The Anthological Imagination in Jewish Literature', *Prooftexts*, 17/1 (1997), 1–7.

STERN, FRANK, *Dann bin ich um den Schlaf gebracht. Ein Jahrtausend jüdisch-deutsche Kulturgeschichte* (Berlin, 2003).

STERN, FRITZ, *The Politics of Cultural Despair: A Study in the Rise of the Germanic Ideology* (New York, 1961).

STILLMAN, NORMAN A., *The Jews of Arab Lands: A History and Source Book* (Philadelphia, 1979).

—— *The Jews of Arab Lands in Modern Times* (Philadelphia, 1991).

—— 'From Oriental Studies and Wissenschaft des Judentums to Interdisciplinarity' (Heb.), *Pe'amim*, 92 (2002), 63–82.

—— *Sephardi Religious Responses to Modernity* (Luxembourg, 1995).

STOLER, ANN, 'Racial Histories and their Regimes of Truth', *Political Power and Social Theory*, 11 (1997), 183–206.

STONEHILL, CHARLES ARCHIBALD (ed.), *The Jewish Contribution to Civilization* (Birmingham, 1940).

STRAUSS, HERBERT A., and CHRISTHARD HOFFMANN, *Juden und Judentum in der Literatur* (Munich, 1985).

STÜBEN, JENS, and WINFRIED WÖSLER (eds), in cooperation with ERNST LÖWY, *'Wir tragen den Zettelkasten mit den Steckbriefen unserer Freunde'. Beiträge jüdischer Autoren zur deutschen Literatur seit 1945* (Darmstadt, 1993).

SUTCLIFFE, ADAM, 'Enlightenment and Exclusion: Judaism and Toleration in Spinoza, Locke and Bayle', *Jewish Culture and History*, 2/1 (1999), 26–43.

TAL, URIEL, *Christians and Jews in Germany: Religion, Politics and Ideology in the Second Reich, 1870–1914* (Ithaca, NY, 1975).

THOMAS, ANN, *Barbary and Enlightenment: European Attitudes towards the Maghreb in the Nineteenth Century* (Leiden, 1987).

TILGNER, WOLFGANG, 'Volk, Nation und Vaterland im protestantischen Denken zwischen Kaiserreich und Nationalsozialismus (ca. 1870–1933)', in Horst Zilleßen (ed.), *Volk—Nation—Vaterland. Der deutsche Protestantismus und der Nationalismus* (Gütersloh, 1970).

TOAFF, RENZO, 'La nazione ebrea de Livorno dal 1591 al 1715 nascita e sviluppo di una comunità di mercanti', in Ariel Toaff and Simon Schwarzfuchs (eds), *Mediterranean and the Jews: Banking, Finance and International Trade (XVI–XVIII Centuries)* (Ramat Gan, 1989).

[TOLAND, JOHN], *Reasons for Naturalizing the Jews in Great Britain and Ireland: On the Same Foot with All Other Nations* (London, 1714).

TOURY, JACOB, 'Emancipation and Assimilation: Concepts and Conditions' (Heb.), *Yalkut moreshet*, 2 (1964), 167–82.

TSUR, YARON, *The Evolution of a Culture: The Jews of Tunisia and Other Islamic Countries* [Sipur tarbut: yehudei tunisyah ve'aratsot muslimiyot aḥerot] (Jerusalem, 2003).

—— 'Israeli Historiography and the Ethnic Problem' (Heb.), *Pe'amim*, 94–5 (2003), 26–33.

—— 'The Tunisian Jewry at the End of the Pre-Colonial Period' (Heb.), *Mikedem umiyam*, 3 (1990), 77–113.

TUCHMAN, G., and H. G. LEVINE, '"Safe Treyf": New York Jews and Chinese Food', *Contemporary Ethnography*, 22 (1992), 382–407; repr. in B. C. Shortridge and J. R. Shortridge (eds), *The Taste of American Place* (Lanham, Md., 1997).

TURNER, BRYAN S., *Weber and Islam* (London, 1974).

VALENSI, LUCETTE, 'Multicultural Visions: The Cultural Tapestry of the Jews of North Africa', in David Biale (ed.), *Cultures of the Jews: A New History* (New York, 2002).

VEBLEN, THORSTEIN, 'The Intellectual Pre-eminence of Jews in Modern Europe', *Political Science Quarterly*, 34 (1919), 33–42; repr. in M. Lerner (ed.), *The Portable Veblen* (New York, 1959).

VERTLIB, VLADIMIR, *Zwischenstationen* (Munich, 1999).

VOLKMAR, GUSTAV, *Die Religion Jesu und ihre erste Entwicklung nach dem gegenwärtigen Stande der Wissenschaft* (Leipzig, 1857).

VOLKOV, SHULAMIT, 'A Stunning Success: The Example of the Jews in Science' (Heb.), in Volkov, *The Magic Circle: Jews, Antisemites, and Other Germans* [Bema'agal hamekhushaf: yehudim, antishemiyim vegermanim aḥerim] (Tel Aviv, 2002).

VON DOHM, CHRISTIAN WILHELM, *Über die bürgerliche Verbesserung der Juden* (Berlin, 1781).

VON GRUNEBAUM, G. E., *Classical Islam: A History, 600–1258* (London, 1970).

Von Stöcker zu Naumann. Ein Wort z. Germanisierung des Christentums (1896).

WALDSTREICHER, DAVID, 'Radicalism, Religion, Jewishness: The Case of Emma Goldman', *American Jewish History*, 80 (1990), 74–92.

WALZER, MICHAEL, 'Multiculturalism and the Politics of Interest', in David Biale, Michael Galchinsky, and Susannah Heschel (eds), *Insider/Outsider: American Jews and Multiculturalism* (Berkeley, 1998).

WASSERSTROM, STEVEN M., *Between Muslim and Jew: The Problem of Symbiosis under Early Islam* (Princeton, 1995).

WEBER, FERDINAND WILHELM, *System der altsynagogalen Palästinischen Theologie. Aus Targum, Midrasch, und Talmud* (Leipzig, 1880).

WEBSTER, HUTTON, *Rest Days: A Study in Early Law and Morality* (New York, 1916).

WEIL, GUSTAV, *Mohammed der Prophet. Sein Leben und Seine Lehre. Aus handschriftlichen Quellen und dem Koran geschöpft und dargestellt* (Stuttgart, 1843)

WEISSBERG, LILIANE, 'Reflecting on the Past, Envisioning the Future: Perspectives for German-Jewish Studies', *German Historical Institute Bulletin*, no. 35 (Fall, 2004), 11–32; <http://www.ghi-dc.org/bulletinF04/35.11.pdf>, accessed 17 Sept. 2006.

WESSELY, NAPHTALI HERZ, *Words of Peace and Truth* [Divrei shalom ve'emet] (Berlin, 1782).

WHITFIELD, STEPHEN, 'Multiculturalism and American Jews', *Congress Monthly* (Sept.–Oct. 1995), 7–10.

WIESE, CHRISTIAN, *Wissenschaft des Judentums und protestantische Theologie in wilhelminischen Deutschland* (Tübingen, 1999).

WILSON, WILLIAM RAE, *Travels in the Holy Land: Egypt*, 2 vols, 3rd edn (London, 1831).

WOLF, IMMANUEL, 'Über den Begriff einer Wissenschaft des Judentums', *Zeitschrift für die Wissenschaft des Judentums*, 1 (1822), 1–24.

WOLFF, J., 'Eine Jahrhundert-Betrachtung', *Der Israelit*, 108 (28 Dec. 1899), 3027–9.

WRIGHT, TERENCE R., 'The Letter and the Spirit: Deconstructing Renan's *Life of Jesus* and the Assumptions of Modernity', *Religion and Literature*, 26/2 (Summer 1994), 55–71.

YERUSHALMI, YOSEF HAYIM, *From Spanish Court to Italian Ghetto. Isaac Cardoso: A Study in Seventeenth-Century Marranism and Jewish Apologetics* (New York, 1971).

YINGER, J. MILTON, 'Contraculture and Subculture', *American Sociological Review*, 25 (1960), 625–35.

—— *Countercultures: The Promise and Peril of a World Turned Upside Down* (New York, 1982).

ZAFRANI, HAÏM, *Études et recherches sur la vie intellectuelle juive au Maroc de la fin du 15e au début du 20e siècle*, 3 vols (Paris, 1972–80).

—— *Mille ans de vie juive au Maroc* (Paris, 1983).

ZANTOP, SUSANNE, *Colonial Fantasies: Conquest, Family, and Nation in Precolonial Germany* (Durham, NC, 1997).

ZENNER, WALTER P., and DESHEN, SHLOMO, 'Jews among Muslims in Precolonial Times: An Introductory Survey', in Shlomo Deshen and Walter P.

Zenner (eds), *Jews among Muslims: Communities in the Precolonial Middle East* (Houndmills, 1996).

ZIPPERSTEIN, S. J., *Elusive Prophet: Ahad Ha'am and the Origins of Zionism* (Berkeley, 1993).

ZOHAR, TSEVI, *Luminous Face of the East: Studies in the Legal and Religious Thought of Sephardic Rabbis of the Middle East* [He'iru penei hamizraḥ: halakhah ve-hagut etsel ḥakhmei yisra'el bamizraḥ hatikhon] (Tel Aviv, 2001).

—— *Tradition and Change: Rabbis in Egypt and Syria Confront the Challenge of Modernization, 1880–1920* [Masoret utemurah: hitmodedut ḥakhmei yisra'el bemitsrayim uvesuryah im etgerei hamodernizatsyah 1880–1920] (Jerusalem, 1993).

ZUNZ, LEOPOLD, 'Beleuchtung der *Théorie du judaïsme* des Abbé Chiarini', in Zunz, *Gesammelte Schriften* (Berlin, 1919).

—— 'Etwas über die rabbinische Literatur', in Zunz, *Gesammelte Schriften* (Berlin, 1919).

ZWEIG, STEFAN, Preface to Charles Archibald Stonehill, *The Jewish Contribution to Civilization* (Birmingham, 1940).

Index

Italicized page numbers indicate contributions to this volume.

Printed and bound by CPI Group (UK) Ltd, Croydon, CR0 4YY

09/06/2025

14685820-0002